Passage works

Manchester University Press

Passage works

Ruth Beckermann's art

Patricia Allmer and John Sears

MANCHESTER UNIVERSITY PRESS

Published by Manchester University Press
Oxford Road, Manchester, M13 9PL

www.manchesteruniversitypress.co.uk

British Library Cataloguing-in-Publication Data
A catalogue record for this book is available from the British
Library

ISBN 978 1 5261 7250 1 hardback

First published 2025

The publisher has no responsibility for the persistence or
accuracy of URLs for any external or third-party internet
websites referred to in this book, and does not guarantee
that any content on such websites is, or will remain, accurate
or appropriate.

EU authorised representative for GPSR:
Easy Access System Europe, Mustamäe tee 50, 10621
Tallinn, Estonia
gpsr.requests@easproject.com

Typeset by Newgen Publishing UK

For Zoë

Contents

Figures

Some of the images in this book are screen grabs which are reproduced here under the fair dealing guidelines relating to criticism and review as suggested by the Intellectual Property Office (published 12 June 2014).

Acknowledgements

We are very grateful to Ruth Beckermann, who provided valuable comments and guidance on an early draft of the manuscript.

An early version of part of Chapter 8 was presented at the international conference *IT HURTS! Violence against Women in Art and Society*, held at the Sigmund Freud Museum in Vienna in March, 2023. The authors would like to thank the conference organisers Elena Shapira and Daniela Finzi and the Museum Director Monika Pressler. The anonymous peer reviewers offered comments that in every case improved on the original manuscript, and we're grateful for their careful attention. We would also like to thank Emma Brennan, Paul Clarke, Matthew Frost, Michelle Houston and the exceptional team at Manchester University Press for their commitment to and support for this book.

Introduction: "One possible way to start"

The narrative is a passage—the *Passagenwerk* for Benjamin, the uncanny working through of an analytical journey for Freud—a passage that commences without the promise of a conclusion. [...] Here history is not the 'neutral' site of a science or universal truth; it is, rather, the place of remembering and a composing of fragments that reside in an interpretation that identifies the limits of representation and the threshold of silence. Here, incompleteness and dissonance hint at what is but is neither seen nor heard. (Iain Chambers)[1]

It is hard, in the wake of the Holocaust, to get beyond the sense of diffuse danger, of a darkness that cannot be encompassed or given finite shape. (Eva Hoffman)[2]

Das ist eben eine Möglichkeit zu beginnen. [That is after all one possible way to start]. (Ruth Beckermann)[3]

We're looking out of the carriage window onto the late evening city as the train pulls out of a central Vienna station, passing away from the inner city, while a man's voice relates, in articulate Viennese German, detailed information about family connections, lines of descent, journeys, destinations. As he speaks, the view scrolls always left, halting intermittently as the train stops at junctions and local stations before moving on, slow, then faster, gathering speed. Lights pass by, windows, lamps, glimpses of domestic interiors or shopfronts, snatches of the horizon, then blackness as we pass a tall, indeterminate edifice that blocks any view, then more fading views of bits of skyline, outlines of buildings, occasional lights spilling from windows, the skeletal branches of leafless trees silhouetted against the sky. The landscape gradually changes from urban to suburban, the outskirts of the city settling to a quiet, darkening evening, outlined hills visible in the distance, encroaching on the ever-greying sky. The train crosses the Danube, steeped in deepening gloom, a string of streetlights blurred like slow-moving tracer bullets indicating another bridge further along the banks. A sudden cluster of orange lamps as the train reaches the right bank and proceeds slowly away from the city, passing on into the darkening countryside beyond. All the while, as the train moves on, the man's voice lists names, places, relations, trades, mothers and fathers and brothers and sisters and uncles and aunts, cousins, boys and girls, his long, detailed narrative punctuated by repeated words – deported, disappeared, murdered, somewhere, somewhere, somewhere in Poland, disappeared, dead. We listen to the voice, as the view drifts on into a darkness now only briefly interrupted by the occasional signs of civilisation outside, momentary gleams and blurs. "All three of them deported, killed in Poland." The father's brother, a little better off than the rest of the family, able to lend money once in a while, two or three shillings, "the uncle himself and the aunt, deported, dead". Places – "the ghetto centre, Łódź – Litzmannstadt, it was called, then". "From there she was deported, she disappeared, was killed somewhere in the Polish Nazi holocaust." By now the screen is virtually dark, only occasional groups of dim illuminations, a single line of square lights moving right to left across the centre, like the foxholes at the edges of a roll of film, the frames overexposed to blackness just as the narrating voice exposes us to the history it recounts, a history, it states, that "many […] do not want to know". As the voice ceases, a melancholy saxophone can be heard, the view from the window – no longer the city or its suburbs, but the dark emptiness of rural Austria at night – now a featureless gloom, like Eva Hoffmann's "darkness that cannot be encompassed or given finite shape", only glimmers, passing street lights that betray the constant passage of the train. And there, nowhere, at the obscure beginning of what may be a long journey into night, the film we are watching ends.

The closing ten-minute segment of Ruth Beckermann's *Wien retour* (*Return to Vienna*, 1983),[4] effectively an appendix or coda to the film, depicts this passage by train from city to country, evening to night, ignorance to knowledge, memory to history. Embodying what John Akomfrah calls "the idea of memory as counter-cartography",[5] *Return to Vienna* (discussed in detail in Chapter 2) examines through narrative and archived visual resources a dimension of inter-war Austrian (and specifically Viennese) history largely omitted from the official, touristic narratives of the country, which tend to elide Habsburg glory and post-war rebirth into a nostalgic continuum uninterrupted by reality (but haunted, inevitably, by the events it avoids). The passage from the evening city to the darkness of the countryside is also the passage from the partially known and recollected (the fragments of information presented by the closing monologue) to the unknowable, unimaginable, unusable but disturbingly insistent past of traumatic memory. This closing sequence offers a dramatic and emotionally shocking reversal of the earlier, optimistic and utopian political agenda of *Return to Vienna*, its narrative offering a potential contemporary reconstruction from surviving shards (dispersed memories, secreted photographs, salvaged documents) of a destroyed community. The ending tells, instead, of the violent dissolution of that community, its forced dispersal and destruction by agents whose historical assumption of power is one of the film's subjects. This history constitutes a passage into darkness that demands constant, urgent reconfigurations of knowledge, history and ethics, and one that, manifest or implicit in a diverse range of forms and themes, traverses Beckermann's entire oeuvre.

Born in Vienna in 1952 to Jewish parents who had survived the Holocaust, Beckermann has since the late 1970s produced a substantial oeuvre of films, artworks, exhibitions, and books and essays. She studied art history and journalism at the University of Vienna, in Tel Aviv, and in New York, before taking classes in film and photography at the New York School of Visual Arts. She completed a doctorate in philosophy in Vienna in 1977, and that year joined the newly founded independent group of Austrian film-makers Syndikat der Filmschaffenden (known since 1989 as the Verband Filmregie Österreich [Austrian Director's Guild]). In the late 1970s and early 1980s she collaborated on her first film projects with other film-makers including director and producer Joseph Aichholzer and Franz Grafl (with both of whom she co-founded the independent film distribution company Filmladen [Film Shop] in 1978), and Michael Stejskal. She directed *Return to Vienna*, her first full-length feature, in collaboration with Aichholzer in 1983. While not her first work, this film initiated Beckermann's extended project of historical and cultural analysis and recuperation. Essaying

across multiple media and produced across nearly five decades, this
project interrogates identity and geography as constantly shifting
formations of the intersections between past, present, and future.
The oeuvre offers a complex and careful analysis of the constructedness of historical narratives, and their roles in generating and
sustaining, as well as challenging and subverting, myths of identity and difference. Taking as her central interlinked themes Austria
and its history and politics, her own identity as a post-Holocaust
European Jewish woman, and historical and contemporary experiences of migration and displacement, Beckermann develops wider
meditations on the persistence of European memory, and the meanings of Europe itself; on the geopolitics of borders, migrations, and
identities; on memories and traumas, and their place in the analysis
of social rituals; and, insistently, on the image as politicised marker
of presence and absence, repository of the traces of historical violence but also site (sight) of intervention, analysis, and protest.

Beckermann's cinematic production alone explores an extraordinary breadth of topics through a variety of forms. Her early,
shorter documentary films (discussed in Chapter 1 below) focus on
Viennese and Austrian class politics, tracing the emergent impacts
of globalisation on provincial and metropolitan Austria through
attention to how localised social and industrial disputes relate to
broader national and international tensions. Subsequent works
employ a variety of autobiographical, historical, performative, and
other narrative registers to address varied but interlinked topics like
the collapse of socialist-run Vienna and the rise of Austro-fascism
in the early 1930s (*Return to Vienna*, 1983, and the book *Die
Mazzesinsel: Juden in der Wiener Leopoldstadt 1918–1938*, 1984);
the impact on various communities in contemporary America of
the election in 2008 of Barack Obama and the coincident global
economic crash (*American Passages*, 2011); life in 1980s Israel
(*Nach Jerusalem / Towards Jerusalem*, 1990); the contemporary
residues of Austrian imperial history (*Ein flüchtiger Zug nach dem
Orient / A Fleeting Passage to the Orient*, 1999); contemporary
Austrian politics and culture (a controversial photography exhibition in *Jenseits des Krieges / East of War*, 1996; the 1986 election as Austrian Chancellor of the former Nazi Kurt Waldheim in
Waldheims Waltzer / The Waldheim Waltz, 2018); experimental
'performances' of historical Austrian literary texts (letters between

Paul Celan and Ingeborg Bachmann in *Die Geträumten* / *The Dreamed Ones*, 2017, and the pornographic novel *Mutzenbacher* in her 2022 film of the same name); and Beckermann's own Jewish family history (its European diasporic roots in *Die papierene Brücke* / *Paper Bridge*, 1987, the first film narrated by Beckermann, and the local dynamics of the communities inhabiting her residential street in Vienna in *homemad(e)*, 2001).[6]

Beckermann's writings (many yet to be translated into English) flesh out and interweave theoretical positions and historical arguments addressing modern Austrian and Jewish experience, and explore various facets of Jewish and Austrian history that frame a wider enquiry into ethical relations within contemporary cosmopolitanism. They draw on personal experiences and cultural histories refracted through critical engagements with a diversity of writers, from Jean Améry to Stefan Zweig, Walter Benjamin to Hannah Arendt – the latter "an important intellectual authority for me", Beckermann stated in 2019.[7] Her curatorial and installation works, closely affiliated to her films and writings, explore how images can record narratives (*Leben!*, 2008) or mask their cultural and historical repression (*The Missing Image*, 2012), and how those narratives construct alternative, overlapping versions of historical experience (*europaMemoria*, 2003–6, its accompanying book co-edited with film critic Stefan Grissemann [b. 1964]). Beckermann's works exist in complex and dynamic relations with post-war Austrian political and social history as well as with the nation's extensive traditions of feminist and avant-garde art, and her film work engages with Austrian cinematic history and with ongoing debates on the forms and functions of documentary and the essay film in relation to European and wider traditions and influences – for example, adapting interview and filmic/pictorial methods deriving from Chris Marker, Claude Lanzmann, Jean Rouch, Chantal Akerman, Agnès Varda, and other major documentary precursors.

Austria after 1945

As this brief overview suggests, the importance of post-war Austrian political and cultural history, with all its embedded tensions and contradictions and, above all, the constant if barely repressed pressure of the recent Nazi past – the major historical context for Beckermann's work – cannot be understated (she explores the Jewish experience of this history in her 1989 essay *Unzugehörig* (*Unbelonging*), the arguments of which underpin the following discussions). Her career began during the reformist social democratic government of 1970–83, under the Chancellorship of the Jewish leader of the SPÖ (Austrian Socialist Party), Bruno Kreisky (1911–90), who led a minority government from 1970 until winning a parliamentary majority in October 1971. In 1972, Austria became an informal member of the European Economic Community (eventually joining the EU fully in 1995), confirming the assimilation into Western European identities and economic policies that characterised the "Kreisky Era". This period was characterised by enduring economic stability and prosperity despite the global pressures of the oil crisis, but also marked by persistent if muted anti-Semitic attacks on Kreisky co-ordinated by the opposition right-wing ÖVP (Austrian People's Party), symptoms of Austria's "pervasive" postwar Judeophobia[8] and of the historical legacies of Nazism which Austrian culture was, in the 1970s, yet to confront fully. Kreisky himself intermittently downplayed his own Jewishness (partly in order to assert his assimilationist and anti-Zionist credentials – he once called Israel a "police state" run by men with a "fascist mentality").[9] He accommodated former Nazis in his cabinets, publicly expressed disdain for Jewish people, and engaged in an extended and acrimonious conflict with the internationally renowned Nazi-hunter Simon Wiesenthal.[10]

In 1945, the newly liberated Austria, initially occupied by the Allies but allowed to self-govern, began leveraging its new internationally sanctioned freedom to define its national identity *against* that of Nazi Germany, with which it had since the Anschluß of March 1938 been (arguably enthusiastically) unified, but which now was repositioned as a former aggressor and "occupying nation". Constructing the narrative that the Austria occupied by the Nazis between 1938 and 1945 was during that period no longer Austria, but part of a larger Germany, and thus could not be held responsible for the actions of an occupying nation, the country thus opportunistically constructed itself, and was recognised by the Allies, as a victim, rather than an active perpetrator, of Nazism. This crucial political sleight-of-hand would dominate narratives and myths of Austrian history in subsequent decades. In 1955, the four occupied zones of post-war Austria, under American, French, British and Russian control, were reunited as the Second Republic was formally restored, and the newly independent nation joined the United Nations as a politically neutral zone, a border state buffering the newly oppositional blocs of the emergent Cold War (but a covert deal between the two main political parties excluded communist influence from government, orienting the country firmly towards the west). This neutrality lent Austria strategic and political weight, reinforcing efforts to redefine the nation as Austrian (rather than German); but it also facilitated its temporary function as a transit zone for refugees (especially Jewish migrants) from Eastern Europe and the USSR. Elizabeth Anthony has recently documented some of the ways the post-war Austrian governments exploited the country's ambiguous status to impose, despite all that had passed, brutally anti-Semitic policies (for example, withholding financial support and tax relief for Jewish Austrian victims of Nazism until 1949 – "For the second time within a decade", Anthony writes, "the Austrian government robbed the Jews")[11] while under pressure from Allied occupation forces to implement de-Nazification strategies.

Such processes continued half-heartedly through the 1950s, while Cold War pressures increasingly distracted attention from recent history, which most Austrians were anyway only too happy to forget.[12] As Steven Beller notes, "Most Austrians came to see the former Nazis as having been victimised [...] [and] *coerced* into enjoying the advantages of party membership just as Austria itself had been *forced* to enjoy the material benefits of the Third Reich".[13] Austrian relations with returning Jewish survivors were problematised by the prevailing public perception that former Nazis were being victimised by Allied courts while returning Jewish citizens were compensated; thus, by the 1970 election, the ÖVP candidate Josef Klaus could define himself as "Ein echter Österreicher" (an authentic Austrian) in opposition to Kreisky's implicitly non-Austrian Jewishness,[14] a politically motivated assertion of ethnic purity of crucial significance in the post-war construction of the Austrian nation-state. These perceptions of Austrian cultural and ethnic identity and difference persist through the post-war period. The far-right anti-immigration and anti-Semitic FPÖ (Freedom Party of Austria), founded in 1956 by former Nazi minister and

SS officer Anton Reinthaller (1895–1958), won over a quarter of the vote in elections in 1999 and 2017, both times forming short-lived coalition governments with the ÖVP.[15]

The political climate of the 1970s defined much of Austria's subsequent development, establishing core ideological values, economic policies, and international relations that positioned the country politically and strategically, particularly in relation to the developing European Economic Community in the west, and the Soviet Union and post-Soviet Russia in the east. During this time, prevailing myths of pre-war Vienna and Habsburg nostalgia – both conveniently prior to and, in their eastward-stretching and aristocratic imperial grandeur, semiotically and geographically distinct from, the 1933–45 Third Reich – were established as key elements of the nation's tourist imaginary, itself a fundamental dimension of the post-war Austrian self-image and a significant driver of its economic success. The country was also, however, rocked by major, historically resonant political scandals of the 1980s – notably the Reder affair of January, 1985, when the FPÖ coalition defence minister Friedhelm Frischenschlager publicly welcomed Walter Reder, Austria's last imprisoned Nazi war criminal, on his release and return from Italy, on the eve of the meeting of the World Jewish Congress in Vienna; and the Waldheim affair of 1986, an event of global impact that wholly reconfigured Austrian and international relations to the Nazi past, explored by Beckermann in *The Waldheim Waltz*, discussed in Chapter 4. This ambivalence – defining a nation both prosperous and forward-facing, but, from the mid-1980s, increasingly mired in navigating the persistent, burdensome and internationally shameful legacies of its mid-century history – defines what Egon Schwarz has called Austria's "deviant consciousness",[16] in which the history it shares with Germany is constructed as distinct, separate, of no relevance to the modern nation, while simultaneously directly and palpably influencing significant aspects of that nation's identity and development. As Schwarz puts it, the two nations share "the uncomfortable past",

> in which all norms of civilized behaviour were broken, all cultural accomplishments denied, massive crimes committed by an inordinate number of individuals and organizations, while the non-involved acted as if they saw nothing. This disturbing fact overshadows the intellectual life and impairs the international perception of both

countries. This is true to an even higher degree in Austria, where a political party that refuses to break unequivocally with a discredited past has been [in 1999] elected to be part of the government.[17]

Radikal anders: narrative and difference

Beckermann's analyses of different facets of this complex Austrian history repeatedly deterritorialise the modern nation and its peoples and histories, unearthing and exploring narratives that expose the traumatic repressions and conflicts returning from this "uncomfortable" past to undermine or fracture its apparent ideological integrity. Her works develop a poetics of representation that engages with, and seeks responses to, what Iain Chambers (in the epigraph to this chapter) calls the "incompleteness and dissonance" of history as "a place of remembering and composing of fragments" – a national history constantly revised and processually reconfigured from different perspectives. The narrating voice of *Return to Vienna*, recounting its fragmented version of a history of atrocity, violent displacement, and murder while the camera shows a country sliding into darkness, provides one powerful example of this cinematic deterritorialisation. Image and spoken narrative combine with music to produce a deeply affective sequence in which personal remembrance and historical allegory interweave via a series of formal tensions that embody those between repressive and utopian narratives of Austrian history. The relentless detail of the film's documentation of names, places, and destinies counters the increasingly fuzzy obscurity of the view from the train window. Memory contradicts perception; accurate recollection becomes a matter of narrative force, a shift from descriptive recollection to persuasive declaration.

Beckermann's aesthetic engagements with these competing narratives of post-war Austrian history construct a discursive field in which national identity becomes pluralised, and questions of difference emerge as defining and productively destabilising elements. The resulting differences of perspective, and in particular their shifting, destabilising effects on national self-perception, are major preoccupations of Beckermann's oeuvre. In an interview in 2003 with Stefan Grissemann discussing the installation *europaMemoria* (exhibited in Graz, Austria in 2003, the Museum Moderner Kunst in Vienna in 2004–5, and the Maison des arts Créteil in Paris in 2006), Beckermann stressed the emphasis on narrative and the differences that emerge from the processes of its construction:

> Every narrative is a construction, even without a camera or without being recorded. The presence of the camera and the detail of the frame, in which the faces move in such astonishingly different ways, reinforce the constructed aspect still more: then, in montage, once again only one piece of this construction is selected. Artificiality is therefore a fact. And memory changes, it depends a lot on the moment in which it is reproduced. Today, one tells a story about one's childhood differently from [*anders als*] the way one would have done so, say, ten years ago, or will do ten years hence, because it is seen from a different perspective [*weil man andere Blicke darauf wirft*].[18]

One of the interviewees in *europaMemoria*, Senegalese Maimouna Sy-Dogondke, expresses a similar argument slightly differently: "I have four different [*verschiedene*] personalities, that I'm changing according to the situation and according to the place where I am right now."[19] Beckermann's emphasis is on how perspectives shift through time; Sy-Dogondke emphasises how she transforms her sense of self according to her spatial situation. If every narrative is a construction, or what Chambers calls a passage or "working through" of an "analytical journey", so too is every identity; both are malleable, fluctuating forms, constantly open processes of temporal and spatial transformation. Difference and transformation are the core, productively disruptive and destabilising, concerns of *europaMemoria* in its exploration – via 25 eight-minute filmed interviews, screened simultaneously in 25 booths, with people resident in Europe but originating elsewhere – of the constitution of contemporary Austrian and, more widely, European identities as contingent amalgams of disparate, globally sourced memories and experiences, its presenting of different, emergent (but equally constructed, equally artificial) narratives of displacement and becoming which work to disrupt the prevailing, nationalistic ones of establishment and belonging. The Europe of the early twenty-first century, Beckermann's installation emphasises, is (like the Austria explored in her other works) constituted by plural and multiple identities and their diverse histories, a product of migration and its endless conjunctions with historical trauma – as Karen Remmler argues in relation to Beckermann's films, "a migration that takes place along the fissures of man-made atrocity, the Shoah, failed Communism, colonialism, and fascism".[20] The inexorable "fact" of the "artificiality" of narrative, combined with the perspectival shifting consequent on movement through time and resultant shifts of historical context, provides a provisional set of co-ordinates for mapping Beckermann's work and its careful exploration of worlds and histories "seen from a different perspective". In various interviews and essays, she articulates elements of an aesthetic theory to account for the effects of these complementary mobilities. Her 1987 essay "Erdbeeren in Czernowitz" ("Strawberries in Czernowitz") explores the Bukovinan city, the 'absent centre' of *Paper Bridge* in which she was forbidden to film by the Soviet authorities. Czernowitz exists, Beckermann suggests, somewhere between popular and personal memory, official history and present-day reality, perceived by its contemporary residents as "a city that resembled their memory from afar, through the windows of a moving car".[21] In a 1991 interview with Christa Blümlinger discussing *Towards Jerusalem* (a film explored in Chapter 3), she addresses the intersections of different modalities of distance of time/place/present/ past embedded in the ambiguity of the German word *Nach*, which means both 'towards' and 'after', thus playing on temporal and spatial connotations, a pun with significant implications for the political dimensions of Beckermann's project:

> The word 'after' has both local as well as temporal importance – one can be on the way to a certain place, but in consciousness already be 'after'. I chose the title because it was clear to me that, as a European Jew, I had one on the one hand consciousness shaped by the Shoah, but also on the other hand a positive diaspora identity, so could not arrive in a real, depicted [*abgebildeten*] Jerusalem.[22]

Jerusalem (like Czernowitz) exists in Beckermann's film only as an imaginary or utopian place, an object of longing or desire. Such places exist in Beckermann's filming of them as double entities – sites of longing constructed by the cinematic imaginary, and real but inaccessible places outside the frames of their imaginary constructions. Jerusalem's status in particular is for Beckermann explicitly utopian, epitomising in her film the utopic drive of the Israeli dream: "All of Israel", she argues, "is the unique – fascinating and terrifying – realisation of a utopia".[23]

Difference(s)

The *differences* at stake in this shifting, mobile cinematic and wider aesthetic positionality – this utopian blurring of spacing and temporisation – will constitute one dimension of the discussions of Beckermann's films and artworks that comprise this book. Beckermann's awareness both of the fact of difference and of its importance for understanding her work, palpable throughout her interview with Grissemann, plays across the language she deploys in articulating her conception of the function of art to conceive the possibility of new identities and positions – indeed, in conceptualising such an ambitious utopian space as a "New Europe", one of the express aims of *europaMemoria* – without evading or repressing the histories that determine the conditions through which these novel perspectives become possible:

> It is a matter of changing [*Veränderung*] the perspective: so that one begins to also see the point of view of the respective others – whether they are Jews in Austria, Algerians in France, or people from the former Belgian Congo. One has to take into account the history of the victims. [...] If we want to achieve a new Europe, then colonialism will once more become an influential subject, but now in Western Europe, where the children of the former colonised countries will once again remind us of history. And at some time perhaps, even the history of the monarchy in Austria will have to be told in a radically different [*radikal anders*] way.[24]

Art is one way of effecting the change of perspective necessary to accommodate the viewpoint of the other; in doing so, Beckermann suggests, the repressed of history returns, emerging in representations of a newly possible utopian vision of a decolonial Europe, and a newly configured, truly *post*-Nazi Austria, whose histories (beginning, for Beckermann, with that of the nineteenth-century Austrian monarchy and its imperial legacies) may be "told in a radically different way". Or, to phrase it differently, seeing/filming things from "a different perspective" (or from the perspective of difference) opens the space for a comprehension of art as political allegory, in which the given text assumes its significance from how it introduces, into the historical context by which it is defined, the potential for the emergence of "radical difference". This is the perspective of the other, opposing and challenging the very concept of the "echter Österreicher", an other conceived here by Beckermann in decolonial terms through a conception of identities differentiated by and imbricated within complex, multiple, shifting imbrications within the networks of power and history partly mapped in her works. Difference thus operates at a multitude of levels across the oeuvre; in Beckermann's own sense of Jewish and left-wing political difference (against the deeply traumatic backdrop of Austrian history and its persistent influence in the present); in her engagement with the Austrian sense of its own difference from the rest of Europe (in relation to all the internal differentiations implied by the very concept of 'Europeanness'); and, in Austria's own historically burdensome, slippery self-mythologies, the nation's evident but repressed difference from itself.

Difference, for Beckermann, is also intrinsic to the production of art. It plays across the *europaMemoria* interview like an insistent motif: "Europe as space, today, where very different [*verschiedene*] people with very different [*verschiedene*] memories live";[25] "In Austria", Beckermann continues, "schoolchildren, a good many of whom are Bosnian, Serbian or Turkish, are taught Austrian history, yet that was experienced in a very different [*ganz anders*] way elsewhere, from another perspective".[26] In such statements about the experiences of people 'other' than European and Austrian, it's hard not to hear another voice, not to read a hidden script of autobiographical narrative encoding in an expressed sensitivity to the experience of the other a different, alternative narrative of the speaker's self, with its own experience of histories 'other' than those taught in schools. As this book will argue, this experience of difference embeds itself deeply in Beckermann's works, threading into the textual tapestries of her films, books, and installation works a multitude of figures – references and allusions, structuring motifs, recurrent images, prevailing tropes and metaphors – whose contours reveal endlessly shifting perspectives across the expanded field of cultural enquiry constituting the oeuvre. In its utilisation of movement or passage between different spaces (urban/suburban/rural), times (evening/night, past/present), discursive modalities (memory/history) and representational codes (film/spoken narrative/music), the closing sequence of *Return to Vienna* indicates one key dimension of Beckermann's works – their preoccupation with the spaces *between* sites, identities, and histories, and with the passage of the viewing subject across this in-between space. This 'inbetweenness' or interstitiality, a state of border-consciousness and dislocatedness, and its passage or transition, manifest themselves in the generic and formal choices Beckermann has made.

Interstitiality

Critics have noted the significance in Beckermann's works of interstitiality and its traversing, the position of being continually (dis-)located and mobile, in-between histories, genres, identities, and operating at their margins or borders, in the liminal spaces where one edges alongside the other. Christina Guenther argues that Beckermann's cinematic aesthetic, which she situates "at the margins of documentary film",[27] produces "filmic" or "ethnographic travelogues"[28] in which *process* is integral: "central to her films is the process of investigation and experimentation with forms of representation."[29] Nick Pinkerton echoes this perception, noting how Beckermann's films "give us the impression of a life lived in transit",[30] presenting worlds seen from marginal positions through screens or windows. Katya Krylova focusses on how Beckermann attends to the experience of "marginalised groups" like women, African Americans, asylum seekers, or Jewish minorities in Eastern Europe.[31] Krylova locates another interstitial dimension of the film *homemad(e)* (2001), Beckermann's personal re-visioning of Agnès Varda's *Daguerreotypes* (1976), in the transitional economic and cultural, as well as historical, status of the film's location: "Beckermann's micro-journey around her own street allows her to show a community in flux, poised between the street's traditional image as a bustling Jewish textile quarter and a twenty-first century leisure economy."[32] Extending this insight, Karen Remmler's Benjaminian reading of memory and history in Beckermann's works emphasises the disjunctive effects of differences between perception and representation:

> intangible sites of memory draw attention to discrepancies in the way the past is perceived and represented in the nexus between subjective recollection and historical documentation. [...] This perspective allows sites to emerge in Beckermann's films, for example, through the unadulterated spoken word and through disjunctures between what we hear and what we see.[33]

This poetics of "discrepancy", "double perspectives", and "disjuncture" describes the space between perception and representation, which Remmler calls "the intangible space of memory", which emerges (in an installation like *europaMemoria*) as "the 'in-between space' between the frontal shots of faces and the invisible (inter)viewer".[34]

These critical insights describe some (but by no means all) of the interstitialities and mobile positionalities that structure Beckermann's oeuvre. They reinforce the sense that Beckermann's films and installations work, as she asserts, "in between the images", locating the force of her cinema, in particular, in its aesthetic proximity to "the tradition of written culture"[35] – as seen, for example, in the 2019 Salzburg Festival installation *Joyful Joyce*, which offered a multi-media celebration of Joyce's 1928 visit to Salzburg, juxtaposing his fear of thunderstorms alongside the ten "thunderwords" that punctuate the cyclical mythic-historical patterns of his 1939 novel *Finnegans Wake*. This use of Joyce suggests a deeply modernist literary focus; speaking of her early films, Beckermann states: "The Vienna that I created for myself existed in literature – Schnitzler, Roth, the Austro-Hungarian Empire. [...] In high school I belonged to a group of girls who read Camus and Sartre – so, in a way, existentialism and Habsburg history were both the tutors of my youth."[36] This emphasis on principally twentieth-century and modernist literary and philosophical sources for her cinematic themes, or rather on her imaginary, subjective version of the modern literary thought-world these texts constructed and disseminated, is crucial and will inform much of the discussion in this book. It implies complex intergeneric and transmedial dimensions to the processes of filmic and artistic production that dynamise Beckermann's works, investing them with deep contextual significances along a multitude of axes.

Essaying

A key element of Beckermann's interstitiality is thus intergeneric and intermedial, and is expressed formally in the hybrid essay-documentary films for which she is internationally renowned. In these works, intergeneric situations emphasise the constructedness of narratives through a process of historical and (auto-)biographical imagining or mything. Interstitiality defines the loose, inclusive narrative and thematic indeterminacies associated with the essay film's generic hybridity. As Laura Rascaroli notes (echoing Remmler's emphasis on disjunction and discrepancy), "the essay film, as thinking cinema, thinks interstitially – [...] to understand how the essay film works, we must look at how it forges gaps, how it creates disjunction".[37] Rascaroli defines the essay film as "a dialectical form that thinks not exclusively through verbal commentary, but also via an audiovisual and narrative disjunctive practice that creates textual gaps in which new meanings are allowed to emerge".[38]

From *Return to Vienna* onwards, Beckermann's texts characteristically use the open, fragmentary, inconclusive, or incomplete forms of the essay and essay film to examine and deconstruct historical narratives, not least those constituting the national myths of Austria, exposing the gaps and disjunctions in their ostensibly totalising or homogenising versions of the past. The choice of form articulates Beckermann's position in relation to her themes in a variety of ways. The essay allows, for example, a flexible space for meditation in terms both poetic and polemic. As John D'Agata and Deborah Tall argue of the lyric essay, it "partakes of the poem in its density and shapeliness, its distillation of ideas and musicality of language. It partakes of the essay in its weight, in its overt desire to engage with fact, melding its allegiance to the actual with its passion for imaginative form."[39] Writing of Chris Marker's film *Le Tombeau d'Alexandre* (*The Last Bolshevik*, 1992), David Foster extends this poetic dimension of the essay to argue for its reorganisation of narrative form: "The metaphoricity of poetic discourse replaces narrative organization with strategies of correlation and re-imagination."[40]

The formal openness of the essay resulting from such strategies and their (re-) arrangement of subjective positions defocusses theme and topic, a counter-narrative 'dislocation' that, Ursula Biemann argues, corresponds symbolically with the movements and diasporas of transnational experience:

Not unlike transnationalism, the essay practices dislocation; it sets across national boundaries and continents and ties together disparate places through a particular logic. In the essay, it is the voice-over narration that ties the pieces together in a string of reflections that follow a subjective logic. The narration in the essay, the authorial voice, is clearly situated in that it acknowledges a very personal view, a female migrant position, a white workers' position, a gay black position, etc.—and this distinguishes it from a documentarian voice or a scientific voice. The narration is situated in terms of identification, but it isn't located in a geographic sense. It's the translocal voice of a mobile, travelling subject that doesn't belong to the place it describes but knows enough about it to unravel its layers of meaning. [...] [T]he essayist approach is not about documenting realities but about organizing complexities.[41]

The essay film's "subjective logic" resists the conventional authority of the impersonal ("scientific") documentary narrative voice and the associated certainties of locatedness and positioning. Dislocated rather than situated, concerned with subjective logic and the resulting provisionality of statements, reflective on rather than of, exploring fields of connections, organising complexities, and product of the ruminations of "a mobile, travelling subject" – these features of the essay and essay film indicate the genre's usefulness for the countering of those narratives of totalisation and closure, myths of origin and destiny, and ideologies of hierarchy and value with which Beckermann's works grapple.

Home and *Unzugehörig/*'unbelonging'

The interstitiality of the essay film offers an unfixed position from which to exercise a cinematic gaze – a position relative to but distinct from the subject matter, embodying also an experience of disconnection or dislocation, a blurring of the Real, a disorientation that the looseness of the genre exploits in its efforts to "organise complexities" and reflect "about" its topics. The dislocation may be temporal as well as spatial – Beckermann notes in her essay "In Praise of Detours" that " 'elsewhere' and 'what once was' are closer to each other than one thinks".[42] Unfixedness and dislocation are recurrent conditions in Beckermann's works, providing ways of thinking about one of her central themes, that of home or *Heimat*. The German word conveys a deeper sense than the English of a conceptual and emotional complex of meanings to do with homeland, home territory, rootedness and being settled and embedded, and a sense of belonging within the traditions definitive of a historically resonant locale and social context. For Beckermann, this network of meanings is deeply problematic; her experience of living in post-war Austria is (she asserts in various texts) precisely the opposite – one of unsettled, uprooted, excluded non-belonging, of alienated, unhomely distance from the social and cultural world she nevertheless in some way inhabits.

Her theoretical term for this experience, elaborated in her 1989 book-length essay of the same title, is *Unzugehörig* or 'unbelonging', a term analogous to the German writer Hans Mayer's description of his post-Shoah status as "A Revokable German" (*Ein Deutscher auf Wiederruf*),[43] or Jean Améry's characterisation of his native Austria, after 1938, as "the hostile homeland".[44] Less a concept and more a descriptor for a condition of being, 'unbelonging' denotes a disorienting sense of displacement and ambivalent unsituatedness that simultaneously alienates both the subject experiencing it and the place (city, country, world) in relation to which it is experienced. In his biography of Sigmund Freud, Peter Gay emphasises Freud's early sense that, as a Jew, he was expected by gentile Austrians to feel "*nicht volkszugehörig*" – "a stranger to the Austrian people".[45] The connection between Beckermann's argument and the experience of alienation of the founder of psychoanalysis is significant, and the experience of 'unbelonging' is figured, in many of Beckermann's works, as a non-ghostly version of the disturbing out-of-placeness associated with the Freudian uncanny or *unheimlich*, the unhomely. "Unbelonging" furthermore relates closely to the contradictory psychological and political effect encapsulated in Jacques Derrida's neologism "hostipitality", in which the hostile and the hospitable are merged (via the shared but conflicting etymology of 'host' and 'enemy' in the root *hostis*) into a permanent and irresolvable conflict.[46] It also encapsulates a series of dystopian connotations that rest in tension with the utopian drive that organises Beckermann's oeuvre, from the ideal political communities of her early documentaries to the utopian social desires behind the imagined nations explored in films like *Towards Jerusalem* and *American Passages*. As a descriptor of the conflicted condition of being Jewish in post-war Austria, amid the nation's extended cultural and political state of denial about its complicity in the Holocaust, the word *Unzugehörig* works like Derrida's neologism, like a dream image or rebus, compressing a multitude of connotations into a single word. From its literal 'un-to-belong' (*Gehörig* means 'deserved' or 'proper' but also 'belonging', 'being a part of') we might derive *hörig sein*, meaning 'to be enslaved', and *zugehör*, equipment. The Old High German etymological root *gihōren* generates *hören* ('to hear'), *an-, er-* and *zuhören* ('to listen') and *gehorchen* ('to obey'); while the negative *ungehörig* means 'disobedient', 'improper', 'rude'. The word *Zug*, an accidental product of German compounding inside the word, means 'railway train', a mode of transport obviously (as in *Wien Retour*) of deep historical significance in relation to Beckermann's abiding themes.

As this cluster of meanings suggests, the 'Unzugehörig' condition connotes a "feeling" Beckermann associates with the immediate post-war decades (and much of *Unbelonging* explores her childhood experiences in post-war Vienna, offering a version of the national history filtered through a specifically Jewish lens) but which, she suggests in the 'Preface' (added to the 2005 edition of the book), resurfaces powerfully in the early twenty-first century in relation to the Austrian celebrations of two anniversaries, the 60th of the end of World War II and the 50th of the declaration of the Second Republic: "Leafing through the commemorative books, the speeches of the conservative Federal Chancellor and the socialist Federal President, the exhibitions and events, I felt the feeling of not belonging, which had weakened in the 1990s, reappear."[47]

In 2005, 'unbelonging' relates to residual, contested histories and their ideological resolution into a persuasive but exclusionary grand narrative by the performative symbolism of state power. In 1989, it was experienced, Beckermann argues, by the post-war children of Jewish parents in Austria, as a moment of retrospective realisation or recognition, a flash of understanding that recalibrated memory and recontoured, for those who remembered, the configurations of difference marking the country's history: "No matter how painful their childhood experiences were, looking back, they realized that the feeling of 'unbelonging' eventually opened their eyes to the world."[48]

Egon Schwarz cites the well-known lines from Strauss's *Die Fledermaus*, "Glücklich ist, wer vergißt, was nicht mehr zu ändern ist" ["Happy is he who forgets what cannot be changed anymore"], to describe the post-war Austrian relation to history.[49] The experience of 'unbelonging' forcefully counters this romantic complacency, disrupting any possibility of happy forgetfulness and its implicit erasure of discomfiting historical realities. It is closely connected to the Freudian understanding of the *Nachträglichkeit* ('belatedness', or 'afterwardsness') of trauma, "a mechanism" (Bistoen, Vanheule and Craps argue) "that literally alters the subjective interpretation of the past, in such a way that this altered memory causes new and unexpected effects in the present".[50] 'Unbelonging' is experienced as an uncanny and insistent disruption of the present by the past, a consequence (in this context) of breaching the post-war Austrian taboo on 'looking back', and in doing so seeing the past and its events clearly. It reveals, among other things, the artificiality of received narratives of national identity, exposing their constructedness as it opens spaces for alternative narratives of becoming. Spatially, it is partly a product of the "cartographies of intersectionality" that, Avtar Brah argues (in relation to Black and Asian experiences in Britain, and echoed in Akomfrah's "memory as counter-cartography" noted earlier), are integral to the construction of difference and its disruptive centrality "to discourses of nation, nationalism, racism, and ethnicity".[51] In relation to Austrian and European histories, these cartographies assume key significance in Beckermann's works.

The condition of 'unbelonging' constitutes a deterritorialised border state of physical and political being that, Beckermann suggests, is integral to – even definitive of – the historically palimpsestic and composite identity of the Austrian Jew inhabiting the post-war nation. Cathy S. Gelbin and Sander L. Gilman argue of mid-century exiled Jewish authors like Joseph Roth, Stefan Zweig and Lion Feuchtwanger that they "link the deterritorialized figure of the Jew, whom they position in the palimpsest of the cosmopolitan, to peripheral and liminal subjectivities from the pre-modern fringes of the Austro-Hungarian Empire rather than its centres". Such writers (Gelbin and Gilman suggest) "propose a cosmopolitan prototype in the Jew's mobile and liminal subjectivity, which effects a transient belonging through contingent and shifting regional affiliations".[52] Beckermann's post-Holocaust conception of 'unbelonging' defines, perhaps unavoidably, a more sceptical position, dynamised in part by her critical response (for example, in the 2015 installation *The Missing Image*, addressed in Chapter 8 below) to deeply problematic Viennese efforts to commemorate the Holocaust in monuments, like Alfred Hrdlicka's disastrous *Mahnmal gegen Krieg und Faschismus* (*Monument against War and Fascism*, 1988–90), which depicts Orpheus entering Hades but leaves unstated the problematic political implications for postwar Austria of the mythic prohibition on his looking back. *The Missing Image* exemplifies how Vienna itself becomes, in several of Beckermann's works, the space most associated with the condition of 'unbelonging'. Débora Kantor argues that

> To Beckermann, Vienna is *Heimat* and yet *unheimlich*; a platform for the self and a place of estrangement; the territory of a youthful (contemporary) Jewish life [...] and the site of ominous repetition of the past [...]: Vienna is at the heart (better yet, it is the heart) of Beckermann's films. Still, this is in no way a cinema of rooted homeland.[53]

Interviewed by Julia K. Baker and Imelda Rohrbacher in 2009, Beckermann discussed the complex psychotopography of her versions of Vienna:

> Vienna from the outside does not really feature in my films [...]. It is very difficult to shoot Vienna because I know it so well. Looking at something anew is always different. The state of being inside while simultaneously being outside is very important because if you are only on the inside, you do not see anything. The state of being outside and to know what is going on despite of it is of course an excellent position.[54]

This "inside-outside" condition (another variety of in-betweenness, a neither-nor situation, which lends the title to a major 1994 collection of essays, including three by Beckermann, on Jewish and Gentile culture in Austria and Germany)[55] expresses well the type of double-consciousness inculcated by the experience of 'unbelonging'. It also suggests Beckermann's grasping of the potential advantages the condition offers for assuming a position from which to perform her cultural critiques.

Linked with Austria's own post-war geopolitical border situation and the baleful influence of a long period of Austro-fascism and Nazism retrospectively positioned as interstitial, "in-between", and thus ostensibly marginal to and distinct from democratic republican manifestations of the nation (but relentlessly revealed in Beckermann's works, as in Austrian history itself, to be central, integral to, and definitive of the ideological trajectories taken by both democratic versions of the nation), 'unbelonging' takes on a series of significances. It implies an interstitial state of being, an uncertain and unstable yet potentially productive, critically poised existence between histories and geographies, peripheral to (and yet definitive of) those identities and historical narratives that have assumed ideological centrality in the construction of the nation. 'Unbelonging' informs Beckermann's analysis of the Habsburg empire via an enquiry into the voyages of Empress Elisabeth and her disappearance from late nineteenth-century Austrian public life in *A Fleeting Passage to the Orient*; and in her revisiting of modernism's mythological allegories in the analysis of globalisation and migrancy in *Those Who Go Those Who Stay*. Experiences of dislocation from history and geography are addressed in the different but analogous travelogues of *Paper Bridge* and *Towards Jerusalem*, explored in Chapter 3. A different kind of 'unbelonging' – that experienced by the artist-figure at large in the post-war world – is scrutinised in the 'dramatisation' in *The Dreamed Ones* of the romantic exchange of letters between Paul Celan and Ingeborg Bachmann, both writers unanchored and itinerant in the post-war world. Most recently, Beckermann explores the alienating effects of male sexual power in *MUTZENBACHER*.

Several of these works explore 'missing images' – absences, repressions or omissions from the pictorial record whose temporary restoration to view in film and art (or otherwise – the Wehrmacht photographs which are the subject of agitated arguments in *East of War* are conspicuously *not* shown in the film, and the Empress Elisabeth's refusal of the image leaves only indirect traces of her passage through history for the film-maker to pursue) momentarily shifts the parameters of perception and comprehension, and thus recalibrates public and critical awareness of that which is elided or suppressed by official narratives and histories. Beckermann develops a variety of aesthetic strategies to address what Rascaroli calls "the difficulty of making a film [or, indeed, an artwork in any medium] about something missing".[56] Beckermann echoes this statement in a 2013 interview with Karin Schiefer when she remarks, "Maybe it would be a good idea to make a film about everything that you can't film."[57] This recurrent preoccupation, clearly motivated by the immense history of loss and absence to which the devastating darkness at the end of *Return to Vienna* gestures, expresses a concern with "The missing images, the voids in the archive [which] come to represent the unavoidable incompleteness of knowledge, the holes in historical memory, the intangibility of truth, and the limitations of thought."[58]

Passages

Out of these diverse contexts and frames of reference, Beckermann creates artworks that insistently probe tensions and passages between a variety of polarised positions – local/global, rooted/rootless, static/mobile, historical/contemporary, memory/repression, ocular/auditory, visual/verbal, documentary/drama – and across ethnic, gender, national, racial, linguistic and generational borders and continua, haunted always by the post-Holocaust and postmemorial condition of being Jewish in the aftermath of trauma. A key trope that insists across these works is that of the *passage* itself, marking a persistent transhistorical and transnational experience of movement between places, times, contexts, and conditions – a condition embodied in the saying (cited several times by Beckermann) "Trees have roots. Jews have legs." Rootlessness, originating in the diasporic condition of migrant Jewish communities, figures the experience of being permanently *en passant*, in passage from one place, time, situation, to the next.

The passage (from the Latin *passus*, step) works as a mobile and malleable concept affording a variety of approaches to Beckermann's oeuvre, embodying in the multiple ambiguities inherent in the word's semantics a plethora of potential significances for the critical interpretation of her art. Mary Ann Caws reads the term 'passage' in relation to surrealist poetry's concern with "the corridor between moments, situations, states, at once spatial, temporal, psychological, sociological, and anthropological [...] the place of ritual and psychological transformation, the moment of shift and displacement of sentiment, the consciousness of a textual turn".[59] Passages evoke the liminal, the proximal, the nearby and the distant, borders and edges and thresholds and the act of transitioning across or between or among them, a movement (the simplest meaning of 'passage') which may be voluntary or enforced: 'passage' is thus distinct from, but linked to, the notion of 'travel'.[60] These are central concerns of works like *Paper Bridge*, *Towards Jerusalem*, *A Fleeting Passage to the Orient*, *American Passages* and *Those Who Go Those Who Stay*. A passage leads from and to, suggesting further deictics of location, collocation, and dislocation; 'passage' describes both movement and the spaces passed along, through and between. Passage can be temporal as well as spatial; it expresses the passing of time and the movement from one historical period or decade or situation to another, or (as in *Return to Vienna*) the transition from (personal) memory to (public) history. At metaphorical levels passage furthermore connotes rites and rituals of movement between stages of individual and social development (like the rites of passage examined in *Zorro's Bar Mitzvah*), as well as the potential of disguise and reconstituted identity in the notion of 'passing': in both contexts the passage implies the potential for change and transformation, for development and renewal. A passage is additionally a length of text or a sequence of film or music (a bridge passage, for example, inaugurates a new musical theme by effecting transition from one part of a composition to the next), passed over by the eyes of the reader/viewer, cited (sighted) by the critic and analyst; and the passing of letters between correspondents (explored in the epistolary form of *The Dreamed Ones*).

Conceptions of the passage preoccupy recent criticism of Jewish and other cultural production, evident in titles like Sidra DeKoven Ezrahi's *Booking Passage: Exile and Homecoming in the Modern Jewish Imagination* (2000),[61] or the edited collections *Passages of Belonging* (2019) and *Passages: Moving Beyond Liminality in the Study of Literature and Culture* (2022).[62] For the editors of *Passages of Belonging* the passage constitutes a kind of chronotope, an exemplar of the inseparability of time and space in narrative configurations of events, movements, tropes: passages are (they argue) "highly complex situations, experiences, and forces".[63] This Bakhtinian conception of spatio-temporality resonates with the essayistic complexities of Beckermann's works. When Marine Aubry-Morici defines 'essayism' (a word coined by Viennese novelist Robert Musil) as "an idea captured as it unfolds in time under the guise of a path",[64] the connection between the meandering indeterminacy of the essay form and the process of passage through an argument or description, or through the linking together of disparate elements in a narrative, is clear. The notion of the passage also suggests key works of criticism that resonate in relation to Beckermann's oeuvre, notably Walter Benjamin's *Arcades Project* (or, in German, *Passagenwerk*) and writings on Benjamin, like Pierre Missac's *Walter Benjamin's Passages*.[65] In two interviews with Karin Schiefer, Beckermann emphasises the importance of Benjamin's thought for her own work. In 2013 she states

> passages are themselves a theme [of my works], and not only with reference to places: *Zorro's Bar Mitzvah* deals with a 'rite de passage'. *Those who Go Those who Stay* takes as its theme the moving onwards and passing through, also in open, fragmentary form, which Benjamin chose to write about.[66]

And in an earlier (2011) interview on *American Passages* she asserts: "In Walter Benjamin's *Passagenwerk* the term 'passage' not only pertains to the geographical dimension but also takes on a temporal and psychological meaning. It describes various passages."[67]

These "various passages" inform our analysis of Beckermann's œuvre, an analysis which itself follows multiple expanded passages of enquiry as it moves roughly chronologically (with some thematic deviations from strict sequence) through a range of works which represent recurrent themes and concerns. The passage, perhaps above all, condenses in its transitory and "fragmentary" incompleteness and its multiple connotations the conditions and experiences of essayistic interstitiality, in-betweenness, and 'unbelonging' which deeply structure Beckermann's aesthetics, and therefore constitute some of the organising principles of the readings which follow.

Notes

1 Iain Chambers, *Mediterranean Crossings: The Politics of an Interrupted Modernity* (Durham, NC: Duke University Press, 2008), pp. 27–8.

2 Eva Hoffman, *After Such Knowledge: A Meditation on the Aftermath of the Holocaust* (London: Vintage, 2005), p. 127.

3 Ruth Beckermann and Stefan Grissemann, "We All Direct Our Own Memories: Interview", in Ruth Beckermann and Stefan Grissemann (eds), *europaMemoria* (Vienna: Czernin Verlag, 2003), pp. 20–2.

4 Beckermann's films will be introduced by their German and English titles. All subsequent references will use English titles.

5 John Akomfrah, "Memory and the Morphologies of Difference", in Marco Scotini and Elisabetta Galasso (eds), *Politics of Memory: Documentary and Archive* (Berlin: Archive Books, 2014), p. 35.

6 Subsequent references to Beckermann's works will use English titles, except where the German title is the specific object of discussion.

7 Flavia Dima, "Present Histories: An Interview with Ruth Beckermann", *Kinoscope*, 12 April 2019, at https://read.kinoscope.org/2019/04/12/present-histories-an-interview-with-ruth-beckermann/ (accessed 18 July 2023).

8 Robert S. Wistrich, *From Ambivalence to Betrayal: The Left, the Jews, and Israel* (Lincoln: University of Nebraska Press, 2012), p. 501.

9 Cited in Wistrich, *From Ambivalence to Betrayal*, p. 502.

10 Wistrich comments that "Wiesenthal's battle against Austrian historical forgetfulness and his very public defence of the Jewish memory of the Holocaust remained anathema to Kreisky" (p. 502). See also Pierre Secher, "The 'Jewish' Kreisky: Perception or Reality?", *History of European Ideas* Vol. 20 Nos. 4–6 (1995), 865–70.

11 Elizabeth Anthony, *The Compromise of Return: Viennese Jews after the Holocaust* (Princeton: Princeton University Press, 2021), pp. 43–84; p. 65.

12 See Anthony, *The Compromise of Return*, pp. 214–15.

13 Steven Beller, *A Concise History of Austria* (Cambridge: Cambridge University Press, 2006), p. 259.

14 Beller, *A Concise History of Austria*, p. 273 (italics original).

15 Under a more moderate, liberal-democratic leadership, the FPÖ had formed a coalition with the SPÖ in 1983.

16 Egon Schwarz, "Austria, Quite a Normal Nation", *New German Critique* No. 93 (Autumn 2004), 175–91; 177.

17 Schwarz, "Austria, Quite a Normal Nation", 183.

18 Beckermann and Grissemann, "We All Direct Our Own Memories", pp. 24–6.

19 Maimouna Sy-Dogondke, in Beckermann and Grissemann, *europaMemoria*, p. 68.

20 Karen Remmler, "Geographies of Memory: Ruth Beckermann's Film Aesthetics", *Studies in 20th and 21st Century Literature* Vol. 31 No. 1 (Winter 2007), 206–35: 228.

21 "Sie würden eine Stadt finden, die nur von ferne, durch die Scheiben eines fahrenden Autos ihrer Erinnerung gleicht." Beckermann, "Erdbeeren in Czernowitz", in Christoph Ransmayr (ed.), *Im blinden*

Winkel: Nachrichten aus Mitteleuropa (Frankfurt am Main: Fischer, 1987), p. 109.

22 "Das Wort 'nach' hat sowohl örtliche wie zeitliche Bedeutung – man kann sich auf dem Weg zu einem bestimmten Ort befinden, in seinem Bewußtsein jedoch schon 'danach' sein. Ich habe deswegen den Titel gewählt, weil mir klar war, dass ich als europäische Jüdin mit einem einerseits durch die Schoah geprägten Bewußtsein, andererseits aber auch mit einer positiven Diaspora-Identität, nicht in einem realen, abgebildeten Jerusalem ankommen kann." Beckermann, interview with Christa Blümlinger, 11 January 1991, *Internationales Forum des jungen Films Berlin 1991* (41st Berlin International Film Festival), flier 26.

23 "Ganz Israel ist die einmalige – faszinierende und erschreck-ende – Verwirklichung einer Utopie." Beckermann, interview with Blümlinger, 11 January 1991, Promotional flier, 21 *Internationales Forum des jungen Films 26 / 41 Internationale Filmfestspiele Berlin* (Berlin, 1991), n.p.

24 Beckermann and Grissemann, "We All Direct Our Own Memories", pp. 14–16.

25 Beckermann and Grissemann, "We All Direct Our Own Memories", p. 12.

26 Beckermann and Grissemann, "We All Direct Our Own Memories", p. 14.

27 Christina Guenther, "Cartographies of Identity: Memory and History in Ruth Beckermann's Documentary Films", in Robert von Dassanowsky, and Oliver C. Speck (eds), *New Austrian Film* (Oxford: Berghahn, 2011), p. 64.

28 Guenther, "Cartographies of Identity", p. 65.

29 Guenther, "Cartographies of Identity", p. 67.

30 Nick Pinkerton, "The Present Absence", in Eszter Kondor and Michael Loebenstein (eds), *Ruth Beckermann* (Vienna: Synema, 2019), p. 2.

31 Katya Krylova, "Melancholy Journeys in the Films of Ruth Beckermann", *Leo Baeck Institute Yearbook* Vol. 59 (2014), 249–66: 255.

32 Krylova, "Melancholy Journeys in the Films of Ruth Beckermann", 263.

33 Remmler, "Geographies of Memory", 210.

34 Remmler, "Geographies of Memory", 227.

35 Alexander Horwath and Michael Omasta, "'Cinema Should also Be about the Before, the After, and Everything in Between': A Conversation with Ruth Beckermann", in Eszter Kondor and Michael Loebenstein (eds), *Ruth Beckermann* (Vienna: Synema, 2019), p. 15.

Hereafter cited as Horwath and Omasta, "A Conversation with Ruth Beckermann".

36 Horwath and Omasta, "A Conversation with Ruth Beckermann", p. 20.

37 Laura Rascaroli, *How the Essay Film Thinks* (Oxford: Oxford University Press, 2017), p. 11.

38 Rascaroli, *How the Essay Film Thinks*, p. 23.

39 John D'Agata and Deborah Tall, "New Terrain: The Lyric Essay", *Seneca Review* 27 (1997), 7–8: 7.

40 David Foster, "'Thought-Images' and Critical-Lyricisms: The Denkbild and Chris Marker's *Le Tombeau d'Alexandre*." *Image and Narrative* Vol. 10 No. 3 (2009), 3–14: 8.

41 Ursula Biemann, "Performing Borders: Transnational Video", in Nora M. Alter and Timothy Corrigan (eds), *Essays on the Essay Film* (New York: Columbia University Press, 2017), p. 262.

42 Ruth Beckermann, "In Praise of Detours", in Therese Henningsen and Juliet Joffé (eds), *Strangers Within: Documentary as Encounter* (London: Prototype, 2022), p. 41.

43 See Jack Zipes, "The Critical Embracement of Germany: Hans Mayer and Marcel Reich-Ranicki", in Zipes and Leslie Morris (eds), *Unlikely History: The Changing German-Jewish Symbiosis, 1945–2000* (Basingstoke: Palgrave Macmillan 2002), p. 185.

44 Jean Améry, "How Much Home Does a Person Need?", in *At the Mind's Limits* (trans. Sidney Rosenfeld and Stella P. Rosenfeld) (London: Granta, 1999), p. 52. Beckermann's essay on Améry discusses how by 1930 he "had already experienced the decisive rupture, the ejection from his inner home, from the WE". Beckermann, "Jean Améry and Austria" (trans. Dagmar C. G. Lorenz), in Lorenz and Gabriele Weinberger, *Insiders and Outsiders: Jewish and Gentile Culture in Germany and Austria* (Detroit: Wayne State University Press, 1994), p. 83.

45 Peter Gay, *Freud: A Life for Our Time* (Basingstoke: Macmillan, 1988), p. 27.

46 See Jacques Derrida, "Hostipitality" (trans. Barry Stocker with Forbes Morlock), *Angelaki* Vol. 5 No. 3 (December 2000), 3–18; and Anne Dufourmantelle and Jacques Derrida, *Of Hospitality* (trans. Rachel Bowlby) (Stanford: Stanford University Press, 2000).

47 "Beim Durchblättern der Gedenkbücher, bei den Reden des konservativen Bundeskanzlers wie des sozialistischen Bundespräsidenten, in den Ausstellungen und Veranstaltungen, spürte ich das Lebensgefühl der Unzugehörigkeit, welches in den 90er-Jahren schwächer geworden war, wieder auftauchen." Ruth Beckermann, 'Einleitung', *Unzugehörig: Österreicher und Juden nach 1945* (Vienna: Löcker, 2005) (n.p.).

48 "Wie schmerzhaft ihre Kindheitserlebnisse auch waren, rückblickend erkennen sie, daß ihnen das Gefühl der Unzugehörigkeit schließlich die Augen und die Welt geöffnet hat". Beckermann, *Unzugehörig*, p. 11.

49 Schwarz, "Austria, Quite a Normal Nation", 176.

50 Gregory Bistoen, Stijn Vanheule, and Stef Craps, "Nachträglichkeit: A Freudian Perspective on Delayed Traumatic Reactions", *Theory and Psychology* Vol. 24 No. 5 (2014), 668–87: 674.

51 Avtar Brah, *Cartographies of Diaspora: Contesting Identities* (London: Routledge, 1996), p. 14.

52 Cathy S. Gelbin and Sander L. Gilman, *Cosmopolitanisms and the Jews* (Ann Arbor, MI: University of Michigan Press, 2017), pp. 117, 116.

53 Débora G. Kantor, "Ruth Beckermann: Documentarian of the Present", *Jewish Film and New Media* Vol. 8 No. 2, Fall 2020, 226–38: 226–7. Capitalisation amended.

54 Julia K. Baker and Imelda Rohrbacher, " 'E/motion Pictures': Conversations with Austrian Documentary Filmmakers Mirjam Unger and Ruth Beckermann", *Women in German Yearbook* Vol. 25 (2009), 234–51: 246.

55 Lorenz and Weinberger (eds), *Insiders and Outsiders: Jewish and Gentile Culture in Germany and Austria*.

56 Rascaroli, *How the Essay Film Thinks*, p. 99.

57 Karen Schiefer, "Ruth Beckermann on Her Essay on Escape and Volatility, *Those Who Go Those Who Stay*" (interview), *Austrian Films* (October 2013), at www.austrianfilms.com/news/en/filmmaking_itself_is_one_theme_of_the_film_ruth_beckermann_talks_about_those_who_go_those_who_stay (accessed 12 January 2023).

58 Rascaroli, *How the Essay Film Thinks*, p. 172.

59 Mary Ann Caws, *A Metapoetics of the Passage: Architextures in Surrealism and After* (Hanover, NH: University Press of New England, 1981), p. 11.

60 See Johan Fornäs, "Passages across Thresholds: Into the Borderlands of Mediation", *Convergence* Vol. 8 No. 4 (2002), 89–106, esp. the discussion and definition of "passage", pp. 90–1.

61 Berkeley, CA: University of California Press.

62 Carola Hilfrich, Natasha Gordinsky, and Susanne Zepp (eds), *Passages of Belonging: Interpreting Jewish Literatures* (Berlin: de Gruyter, 2019); Elizabeth Kovach, Jens Kugele, and Ansgar Nünning (eds), *Passages; Moving Beyond Liminality in the Study of Literature and Culture* (London: UCL Press, 2022).

63 "Introduction", Hilfrich et al. (eds), *Passages of Belonging*, p. 1.

64 Marine Aubry-Morici, "The Essayistic Narrativisation of Forms in the 20th Century: A Comparative Study", in Massimo Fusillo, Gianluigi

Simonetti and Lorenzo Marchese (eds), *Thinking Narratively: Between Novel-Essay and Narrative Essay* (Berlin: de Gruyter, 2022), p. 104.

65 Pierre Missac, *Walter Benjamin's Passages* (trans. Sherry Weber Nicholson) (Cambridge, MA: MIT Press, 1995).

66 Schiefer, "Ruth Beckermann on Her Essay on Escape and Volatility, *Those Who Go Those Who Stay*".

67 Karin Schiefer, "American Passages: Interview with Ruth Beckermann", 24 February 2011, at www.ruthbeckermann.com/en/publications/texts/american-passages/ (accessed 12 January 2023).

1

Politics and history – early films

If performativity has often been associated with individual performance, it may prove important to reconsider those forms of performativity that only operate through forms of coordinated action, whose
condition and aim is the reconstitution of plural forms of agency and
social practices of resistances. (Judith Butler)[1]

Revolution is closed, but insurgency is open ... And, the map is
closed, but the autonomous zone is open. (Hakim Bey)[2]

Beckermann's earliest film projects, interlinked historically and
thematically, were collaborative explorations of Austrian political
events of the late 1970s and early 1980s, in each case documenting and exploring protest as a form of politicised social expression
within (and specifically against) the capitalist-bureaucratic structures of the Austrian state. She has referred to *Arena besetzt (Arena
Squatted*, 1977), *Auf amol a Streik (Suddenly a Strike*, 1978), and
*Der Hammer steht aut der Wies'n da draussen (The Steel Hammer
out There on the Grass*, 1981) as *Flugblattfilme* (pamphlet films),
thus foregrounding their political dimensions while distinguish-
ing them in terms of scale and duration from her longer, more
essayistic later films. The films document (respectively) the occupation of a Viennese former slaughterhouse scheduled for demolition to provide space for new headquarters for the textile company
Schöps; a strike at a tyre factory in Traiskirchen, Lower Austria;
and protests against the closure of a steelworks in the Styrian
city of Judenburg. Austrian industrial and class relations, and the
agency and organisation of public protest and demonstration, thus
constitute the principal frames of reference of this series of films.
They map a version of 1970s and 1980s Austria divided by class
and generation-gap differences, and explore the emergence within

and despite these differences of momentary possibilities for new utopian forms of community, early affirmations of Beckermann's interest in utopic desire.

Austrian cinema of the 1970s occupied, and responded to, a unique and complex historical and cultural context. The 2020 Viennale retrospective of the decade emphasised its transitional status, between the restrictively conservative management of film funding and other production difficulties in the 1960s and the establishment in 1980 of state funding for the industry, and noted the "aesthetic rigour, social commitment and [...] extraordinary formal inventiveness" of Austrian directors at the time:

> The 1970s were a moment apart in the history of Austrian cinema, a time of transition between its post-World War II past, dominated by largely commercial productions made for easy export to Germany, and what we could define as its current era, distinguished by an art-house cinema conscious of its specific national traits and recognised the world over.[3]

The creativity of this period is analogous to the historically coincident flowering of aesthetic experiment and productivity by Austrian women artists evident in collections like the Sammlung Verbund's *Feministische Avantgarde* (*The Feminist Avant-Garde*), producing artworks in which aesthetics and politics productively combine. Beckermann notes (in her 2007 interview with Bert Rebhandl, included on the DVD box set of her films) that her first films were initially conceived as parts of "a political project" which was never intended to be cinematic but was, instead, overtly interventionist: "Our concern wasn't to present ourselves as filmmakers."[4] These works were made against the international backdrop of a burgeoning feminist film practice, manifest elsewhere in Austrian cinema during the 1970s and 1980s in films by Maria Lassnig, Linda Christanell, Christiane Adrian-Engländer (aka Moucle Blackout), Lisl Ponger, Angela Hans Schierl, Mara Mattuschka and Ursula Pürrer. The more immediate, wider cultural arena of Austrian avant-garde experimentation of the 1970s (including the avant-garde films of, among others, Kurt Kren, VALIE EXPORT and Peter Kubelka), and its close connections to the revolutionary political groups operating in 1970s Vienna, provides a further important context for Beckermann's films, which utilise

long-established avant-garde techniques of montage and juxtaposition to convey their political messages. Viennese Aktionism had,
in the 1960s, announced Austria's radical post-war avant-gardism,
and through the next decade a diverse range of artists expanded
the conventional boundaries of their practice in photography, film,
video and performance art, gradually distancing their production
from the deliberately provocative (and highly masculinist) extremes
of Aktionist interventionism. The Austrian performance artist and
film-maker VALIE EXPORT, interviewed by Gary Indiana in 1982,
noted the importance of the 1970s Viennese cultural scene and its
move away from Aktionist concerns:

> I was very influenced, not so much by Aktionism itself, but by the
> whole movement in the city. It was a really great movement. We had
> big scandals, sometimes against the *politique*; it helped me to bring
> out my ideas. The content of Viennese Aktionism was not so impor-
> tant. I did my actions in another way, with video. The Aktionism
> artists never worked with media. They made films, yes, but to docu-
> ment their work.[5]

A pivotal moment came in 1975 with the organised withdrawal of
46 women artists from a scheduled exhibition titled *Österreichische
Künstlerinnen der Gegenwart* (*Contemporary Austrian Women
Artists*) at the Volkskundemuseum Wien/Austrian Museum of Folk
Life and Folk Art, in protest at the appointment of an all-male
selection committee. This led to the creation of the Internationale
Aktionsgemeinschaft Bildender Künstlerinnen (International
Women Artists Action Committee, or IntAkt), launched in 1977
and holding a women's art festival, *Focus: Art by Women*, at
Vienna's Secession in 1984.[6]

The combination of creativity and protest extended to Austrian
art film of the period. Despite the absence of an Austrian equivalent
to the German *Oberhausener Manifest* of February 1962 (which set
the avant-garde tone of 1960s German film by rejecting 'conventional' cinematic style and calling for "a new film language")[7] there
were, in the 1960s and 1970s (Robert von Dassanowsky writes),
"several schools of experimentation and avant-garde filmmaking"[8]
in the country. These originated in responses to Italian neo-realism
but owed more "to fringe forces like Andy Warhol and Yoko Ono
than to any mainstreamed European New Wave narrative styles".[9]

Peter Kubelka's films, in particular, offer useful insights into the ways Austrian cinematic and artistic avant-gardes intermeshed. His *Arnulf Rainer* (1960), seven stroboscopic minutes of apparently randomly alternating black and white screens with accompanying static bursts, offers a powerful contrast to the sumptuous nostalgia-industry *Heimat-films* that then dominated the Austrian theatres (discussed in Chapter 5 below). Described by Stefan Grissemann as "One of the pillars of modernist cinema",[10] Kubelka's film premiered in Vienna in May 1960; most of the audience left the theatre before its end.

Austria's engagement with its more recent past, in controversial dramatic films like Franz Novotny's *Staatsoperette* (*State Operetta*, 1977), a brutal satire of pre-Anschluß (1927–38) social and political history, and Franz Antel's *Der Bockerer* (1981), one of the first films to confront and explore the nation's involvement in the Third Reich, constituted another element of the political-cinematic context from which Beckermann's early films emerge. Interviewed in 2016 she recalled the cultural milieu she inhabited around this time:

> In the post-Arena [i.e. late-1970s] days, everyone from the scene was constantly meeting up at demonstrations, or at the Hermi – a bistro-pub in the Kumpfgasse, and later at the Phönixhof. At night, you could run into everyone there, from Maoists and Trotskyists to Young Socialists, and naturally filmmakers too – Bernd Neuberger, Lukas Stepanik and Margareta Heinrich, who later went on to found the film company Extrafilm. But I associated with the Trotskyists more, even though I never became a member.[11]

Clearly influenced politically by this leftist Viennese political and cultural dynamism, Beckermann's early films document the impact on social and political relations in Austria of emergent globally inflected neoliberal economic and management policies. Together the films constitute a mapping of some of the major tension points in what is effectively an extended class struggle over the gradual ideological process of replacing all previous measures of social performance with economic ones, alongside the restructuring of modes of production or their relocation away from traditional local/national contexts into global networks of exchange and distribution. Implicit in the attention these films pay to the specific historical contexts of the disputes they represent is the shadowy presence of another, larger, historical perspective, one in which the immediate contexts of modern Austrian capitalist and industrial relations have been shaped by wartime and post-war networks of influence, the residues of which persist to contaminate contemporary situations. More subtly, the films suggest connections between these processes – the direct influence of mid-century 'innovations' in management and industrial strategy on 1970s–80s transformations.

Critical writing on Beckermann rarely engages at any length with these early works (although several accounts, on which we'll draw below, exist of the events and their contexts). This lacuna suggests their tangential relation to what has been established as the central, critically validated corpus which, consensus suggests, begins in 1983 with *Return to Vienna*. Nick Pinkerton, for example, merely mentions this "trio of early works engaged with the Austrian labour movement" in order to situate *Return to Vienna*,[12] and Renata S. Posthofen similarly notes "Beckermann's first two [sic] films" before turning her attention to later works.[13] Armin Thurnher's essay "Andere Zeiten: Zu vier Filmen Ruth Beckermanns" summarises the largely pessimistic political context of 1970s neoliberal globalisation in relation to these films,[14] emphasising Beckermann's political prescience in focussing on the impacts of this economic paradigm shift, and arguing that her early work "takes up decisive motifs early on; in this [i.e. historical] sense too it is an early work".[15] As Anton Pelinka and others have argued, twentieth-century Austrian history presents a nation deeply structured in complex and mutable ways by the effects of internationalism and cosmopolitanism *avant la lettre*.[16] Beckermann's early films, in this reading, constitute documents of events already belated, recording protests against transformations already underway or even accomplished, and rooted in the nation's problematic history. They also explore very local expressions of political resistance against an economic paradigm shift that was global in scale. In doing so, they make a series of points about Austrian history and social relations that resonates forwards into her later works. One contention of our discussion of these films is that, in largely ignoring them, criticism makes the same mistake as Austria itself, in its repression of the history that both determines the trajectory of, and undermines all efforts to reposition, the contemporary nation.

This chapter proposes readings of these films that briefly contextualise their production before expanding this set of frames historically, and focus on the significance of the events they document in relation to the processes of historical revision undertaken in the 1970s and 1980s by Austrian artists, writers and film-makers concerned with redressing the (largely wilful) amnesia that had characterised post-war Austria's relation to its past. These early films, we suggest, engage closely with specific contemporary events which, when situated in relation to this repressed Austrian history, reveal nascent versions of recurrent themes and concerns to which Beckermann will return. They are thus more closely connected to her later works than criticism has hitherto suggested, and explore in documentary style a provisional set of thematic territories in which we can detect a variety of threads that eventually lead to different elements of some of the later works.

Discussing *Suddenly a Strike* (Figure 1.1) and *The Steel Hammer out There on the Grass* in his 2007 essay "Work in Motion", Siegfried Mattl follows Thurnher in emphasising their response to the "almost complete imprinting of the social construction of reality through the conditions of industrial production".[17] Mattl calls these films "*agitatorisch*" (agitational) and connects them to a long tradition of films depicting factory workers at the gates, the beginning of which coincides with the origins of cinema, in the Lumière brothers' filming of (mainly) women emerging from a factory in *La sortie des ouvriers de l'usine Lumière à Lyon* (*Workers Leaving the Lumière Factory in Lyon*, 1895; the third version of this film was screened on 28 December 1895) (Figure 1.2). Mattl focusses on the insistent motif of the factory gate as a threshold at which "everything is set in motion", especially the dynamic relation between mass and individual,[18] suggesting a wider reading positioning these films as originary points, sites of cinematic departure and "threshold [*Schwelle*, or swell, wave] experiences" of passage in the sense implied by Walter Benjamin.[19] Developing through works by Dziga Vertov and Sergei Eisenstein, this tradition was specifically reinvigorated in the late 1960s by the French Groupes Medvedkine, which took their name from the (then) largely forgotten Soviet director of satirical films, Alexander Medvedkin (1900–89), whom Emma Widdis calls "a figure at once profoundly experimental, and profoundly pragmatic".[20] Initially established by the factory workers in response to criticisms[21] of Chris Marker and Mario Marret's *À bientôt espère* (*Be Seeing You*, 1967–8), a documentary about the Rhodiacéta textile workers' strike and factory occupations in Besançon (a strike which continued until 1971), the Groupes Medvedkine's "untimely resuscitation of the legacy of Soviet factography"[22] focussed on making collective films oriented against bourgeois individualism and involving non-professionals directly in film production. Documenting industrial action and social protest in France through offering "the simple description of events [...] as protest",[23] key Groupe Medvedkine works include *Puisqu'on vous dit que c'est possible* (*We Maintain It Is Possible*, 1973), a collective film (directed by Marker, a member of the group) about the workers' strike at and temporary occupation of the LIP clock and watch factory also in Besançon;[24] and Bruno Muel's *Avec le sang des autres* (*With the Blood of Others*, 1974), which explored the daily lives of the workers during the 1973–4 Peugeot strike in Souchaux, and opens with shots of workers exiting the factory gates while being serenaded by a brass band and chanteuses. While Beckermann has stated that the first Marker film she saw was

Figure 1.1 Ruth Beckermann (dir.), *Suddenly, a Strike*, 1978. © Ruth Beckermann Filmproduktion.

Figure 1.2 Lumière brothers (dir.), *Workers Leaving the Lumière Factory in Lyon*, 1895.

Sans Soleil in Florence in 1984,[25] elements of Groupe Medvedkine style and form are clearly evident in her early films, suggesting the force of this French documentary movement in constructing an available and usable visual and formal rhetoric for her examination of social and industrial relations in 1970s and 1980s Austria.

Arena Squatted

The collaborative film *Arena Squatted* (i.e. 'occupied') is the first and (at 77 minutes) longest of Beckermann's early documentaries, exploring what will later become some of her central filmic concerns – the documenting of her own cultural and historical experience alongside or within an analysis of an event, situation, or context; the camera's encounter with the speaking voice, the dialogic engagement or what Beckermann calls "interaction" with represented and speaking subjects; and the exploration of the ideology of the documentary gaze and its relations to power.

Made with Josef Aichholzer and Franz Grafl, the film is an edited compilation of video footage made during the events it represents, and is thus deeply coded by the haphazard, destructured and constantly improvised, emergent and unstable social reality it records. As Beckermann notes in her 2007 interview with Rebhandl, "the aesthetics of the film fit the aesthetics of the Arena movement".[26] It is also a significant manifestation of the avant-garde ideology expressed in late-1970s Vienna, and a major counter-cultural document in its own right. The *Close Up* festival in London in 2017 (the first British retrospective of Beckermann's films) described *Arena Squatted* as "a documentation of a utopia and its end, but also an attempt to make cinema politically useful".[27] The utopian–utilitarian conception also organises the editorial process, and lends the film a didactic air which works in tension with its amateurish aesthetics; its concern with a short-lived political utopia furthermore foreshadows Beckermann's later interest in larger-scale social 'utopias' like Israel (in *Towards Jerusalem*) and the USA (in *American Passages*).

The Arena occupation was an important event in the context of 1970s Viennese urban activism, and consequently *Arena Squatted* is significant in relation to other film and wider cultural engagements with comparable forms of protest across Europe. Susan Ingram's chapter on the Arena occupation notes, for example, significant earlier protests and squats in Amsterdam in 1965, Zürich in 1968, West Berlin in 1971, and Frankfurt and Hamburg in 1972–3.[28] In late June 1976, a cultural centre in the St Marx area of the Landstraße district of Vienna – what would become the Arena, then located in a disused slaughterhouse, but at that time the site from 1975 of the annual city-funded Arena Vienna Festival, a major alternative arts venue that had been established in 1951 when the city was under allied occupation – was threatened by the city council with closure and demolition. The council intended to sell the land to the textile company Schöps, whose owner Leopold Böhm planned to invest in real estate by building the company's new headquarters there. Organised by Viennese autonomist groups who called themselves *Die Arenauten* ("the Arenauts"), the Viennese (counter-) cultural community rallied in protest, occupying the buildings for nearly three months until their forced closure on 1 October, and establishing within them a series of events and 'happenings' (theatrical, musical and cinematic, alongside cafés and children's education and entertainment provision). What ensued constituted an extended carnivalesque form of protest within a temporary site in which forms of protest and resistance were developed and explored via impromptu-organised political, cultural and aesthetic debate and expression. The occupation established an alternative social order within which those elements of 1970s Austrian culture largely undervalued or simply ignored by society – specifically forms of avant-garde aesthetic practice, and some elements of the utopian forms of social re-organisation they espoused – came into momentary or potential existence in what (following Hakim Bey) might be understood as a "Temporary Autonomous Zone" (TAZ),[29] an actually existing situation or "festival of eccentricity"[30] in which collectivist ideologies were briefly allowed to operate. The first speaker in the film emphasises this collectivist dimension: "It was always collective decisions, and collective events [*Veranstaltungen*]." And later, another speaker asserts: "According to existing legislation, some laws were transgressed, but we are a community, we feel responsible for what happens here."

While the events and practices defining this temporary zone of social resistance were constructed by the Viennese and wider Austrian media as mere left-wing agitation, some public responses were more sympathetic:

> Individual media described the action as a left-wing uprising, but overall the response was surprisingly positive. It was very clear that several diverse groups of young people had come together, above all artists from many disciplines. The boundaries between artists and audience were abolished. Beatrix Neundlinger and others organized the 'Café Schweinestall'. Video groups moved in, as did motorbike rockers. Social workers [...] looked after young people who had fled from reform schools.[31]

Over the summer, major international high- and pop-cultural figures visited and performed in the occupied space, including the English musician John McLaughlin and the Canadian poet and singer Leonard Cohen, along with Austrians including writer Elfriede Jelinek, playwright Peter Turrini, actor and comedian Lukas Resetarits, and the ensemble of the Kärntnertortheater (with a production of Bertolt Brecht's *St Joan of the Stockyards*), alongside numerous well-known Viennese artists and performers, such as the musicians Wolfgang Ambros and Georg Danzer. Vienna's principal cultural newspaper, *Der Falter*, was founded amid the Arena occupation. The events in the Arena were freely attended by thousands of visitors, until pressure from the city council forced the end of the occupation by cutting the site's power and telephone lines. Most of the surrounding buildings were later demolished, leaving the Arena building itself which still stands as Austria's largest alternative cultural centre.[32]

The Arena occupation exemplified a specific and highly symbolic moment in the stratified post-war cultural life of Vienna, exposing several tensions behind the superficial façade of the city's cultural image – a countercultural/pop-cultural phenomenon existing publicly within a city famed for its official high cultural events and traditions (and particularly its classical music and the touristic pull it exercised – Mozart's grave lies in the Sankt Marx cemetery, only twenty minutes' walk from the Arena); a firmly established and popular annual social event suddenly threatened with closure as a consequence of an individual business investment decision; an arts venue momentarily transformed into a site of public political engagement and protest. Simultaneously it drew inspiration from both the contemporary Western vogue for cultural 'happenings' and the long (but severely interrupted by the Anschluß and the war) tradition of Viennese avant-gardism and aesthetic radicalism, from the *fin-de-siècle* Secession artists (formed in 1897) and the Wiener Werkstätte (1903), through the post-war Wiener Gruppe (1952) of language artists, to the 1960s Aktionists, with their emphasis on "painting's inevitable expansion into public space, theatrical if not social".[33] Günter Brus's notorious "Uni-Ferkelei" ("Uni-obscenity") performance during *Kunst und Revolution* at the University of Vienna on 7 June 1968, which involved him singing the Austrian national anthem while masturbating and smeared with faeces, and led to criminal charges against him and other leading Aktionists, constituted one extreme pole of the developing intersections in Austria between public art and political protest from the late 1960s onward.

The Arena occupation can be understood as an 'event' within this tradition. Indeed, Robert Foltin has argued that it is seen as "the closest Austria has come to the global events of 1968",[34] while

Gerald Raunig (citing Rolf Schwendter) invokes a strange historical belatedness in asserting that the Arena movement demonstrated
how "1968 did not take place in Austria until 1976".[35] Further
dimensions of influence can be found in the Fluxus movement, with
its "bridging and frequently merging [of] all forms of art – temporal, spatial, and literary – with music in a dominant position";[36]
and (as noted earlier) in work by the loose grouping of Austrian
women artists of the 1960s and 1970s now known as the Feminist
Avant-Garde. Politically, the Arena occupation emulated elements
of the squatter movements of the 1960s and 1970s, particularly
in relation to the potential political and gendered radicalism of
the squatted space – as Christine Wall has argued in relation to
London's squatter movements, "Squats delineated a spatial framework for the women's liberation movement in the 1970s, providing
for women's centres, refuges from domestic violence, workplaces,
and nurseries as well as homes".[37] This aspect of the Arena occupation is only tangentially addressed in *Arena Squatted*, in its attention to the quotidian and domestic arrangements in certain areas of
the squat.[38]

Nevertheless, productive intersections of traditions of aesthetic
and political action thus formed the ground of the Arena occupation, which was articulated in terms drawing on 1960s anti-Vietnam
war protests and 1970s feminist politics (reacting in particular against the perceived excessive patriarchalism of Aktionism,
a reaction which, as is evident in the work of VALIE EXPORT,
Birgit Jürgenssen and others, was deeply informed by the works of
women surrealist artists).[39] A further significance lay in the occupation's clear derivation from and importing of specifically American
models of protest as performance, leading to an event textured by
the overlapping of Austrian- and English-language performances,
musical forms and visual aesthetics, many of which are documented
in *Arena Squatted*. The Arena occupation as represented in the film
can thus be understood as an extended aesthetic 'happening', a
complex multimedial collaborative art-political project occupying
a passage of time as well as a geographical space – the Arena literally becoming an *arena* in which were performed elements of a
spectacle diverging radically from that promoted by postmodern
capitalist organisation. The coinciding of the arena of subversive
spectacular performance with the Arena of occupation testifies to

the dynamically hybridical forces at work in Austrian avant-garde culture of the 1970s.

Several performances were recorded and numerous participants interviewed by the occupiers, using video, Super 8 and 16 mm film. This material was compiled alongside many still photographs and ten hours of sound tapes. This raw material – all found footage and documents – provided the basis for the collaborative film project which became *Arena Squatted*. The footage was processed on video and transferred onto 16 mm film, as there were few video players in Austria in 1977.[40] The film's ostensible focus was on social relations as facilitators of protest, and on the mechanisms of power at work in suppressing them. "We did not document the Arena as a unique event in history, but rather showed how the mechanism of political oppression operates," stated the production team.[41]

Arena Squatted presents, then, a documentary narrative of the Arena occupation that (as noted earlier), in its combination of still photography and moving images with participant commentary and narrated voice-over, stylistically resembles Marker and Marret's *À bientôt, j'espère*, a film that effectively performs an archaeology of the developing political awareness that will erupt a year later in Les evenements of May 1968. The evident influence of revived Russian style also reacts pointedly against the prevailing styles and themes of 1970s Austrian documentary. Conventional biographical and historically themed films like Hans Conrad Fischer's *Ludwig van Beethoven* (1970) and *Das Leben Anton Bruckners* (*The Life of Anton Bruckner*, 1974) exploited a rich and visually sumptuous vein of nostalgic public sentiment (which Beckermann will later subtly critique with her own film about the Empress Elisabeth), while historical montage-films like Alfred Kaiser's *Kaiserschnitt – Eine Operette* (*Caesarian – An Operetta*, 1978) and Ernst Schmitt Jr.'s *Wienfilm 1896–1976* (*Vienna Film 1896–1976*, 1977) offered more critical but still largely formally conventional explorations of Austrian history. The influence of contemporary generic fads like the West German sex film stimulated hybrid pseudo-documentaries like Fritz Frons' parodic-misogynist *Hurenreport – Sexvariation blutjunger Mädchen* (*Report on Prostitution*, 1972), and Austrian versions of nascent post-colonial consciousness were evident in films like Götz Hagmüller's *Die denkwürdige Wallfahrt des Kaisers Kanga Mussa von Mali nach Mekka* (*The Memorable Journey of*

Emperor Kanga Mussa from Mali to Mecca, 1977), which re-enacts a pre-colonial fourteenth-century West African pilgrimage.[42] Such films exemplify a popular and commercially funded documentary movement that sought to expand audience attention to spaces outside contemporary Austria, to historical or biographical perspectives removed from daily life. Beckermann's early films invert this focus, zooming in on the micropolitics of local labour and social relations as expressions of key tensions, rather than ideological continuities, in contemporary Austrian society.

While thematically distinct from this generic context, *Arena Squatted* nevertheless uses many conventional documentary devices like interviews, establishment shots, recordings of musical performances and narrated expository voice-over, alongside a montage of textual inter-titles, cartoons and still images, all lent conventional realist authenticity by their monochrome presentation. We see images of crowds enjoying musical performances, children creating art, women working in the café kitchens, groups of people discussing strategy and arguing politics. These camera-eye views of scenes contribute to the representation of the occupation as a carnivalesque event, a festival in which conventional social practices are momentarily suspended. The film's use of musical performances, which connects it most explicitly to cinematically documented counter-cultural moments like the Woodstock festival of 1968, offers one level of symbolic expression operating beyond the documentary conventions of narrative and narration. Indeed, the soundtrack provides a striking insight into the intensity and dynamism of the events. A sequence early in the film records a performance of a version of Country Joe McDonald's *I-Feel-Like-I'm-Fixin'-to-Die Rag*, famous from Michael Wadleigh's *Woodstock* (1970) and huge popular with the Austrian youth of the 1970s, here adapted with German lyrics protesting the events leading to the occupation. This co-option into German language and musical forms of American protest rock and folk typified the music of the Arena. Predating the general connection of Viennese squatter culture with punk that Foltin discusses in his history of Austrian squats,[43] musical performances in the Arena, as documented in the film, were largely folk or rock, with a few more avant-garde elements such as one involving flute and voice by English musician Bob Downes.

Several aspects of *Arena Squatted* indicate its importance for Beckermann's subsequent film oeuvre. Its emphasis on Austrian socialist activism prefigures later films like *Return to Vienna* and provides an early manifestation of Beckermann's extended enquiry into the potentials of utopian thought in Austrian and specifically Viennese contexts; while its striking and probably unintentional attention to specifically Jewish dimensions of the Arena occupation largely unnoticed or underplayed in contemporary media and subsequent historical accounts of the occupation, and representative of dimensions of Viennese life largely absent from other cinematic genres of the time. These elements limn an alternative narrative on which we will briefly focus, a shadow-history haunting the film's official documentation of aesthetic protest.

In a key sequence early in the film, before the audience in the Arena main hall, Leonard Cohen performs *Un as der Rebbe zingt*, a traditional Yiddish folksong he had played a few weeks earlier during his 14 June concert at the Wiener Konzerthaus (part of his 1976 European tour) (Figure 1.3).[44] This sequence cements via the

Figure 1.3 Leonard Cohen in Ruth Beckermann (dir.), *Arena Squatted*, 1977. © Ruth Beckermann Filmproduktion.

auratic significance of Cohen's presence a series of tropes – folk solidarity and pop popularity, the marginalised (Jewish/Yiddish, connected by extension to the Viennese working class) voice, the functions of song and performance in social communication – that resonate with the film's wider intention of documenting marginal social formations. Cohen clearly constitutes an important cultural marker for Beckermann (a quote from his 1987 song "First We Take Manhattan" provides the epigraph for *Unbelonging*), and his attendance at the Arena occupation affirms its significance for international cosmopolitan and Jewish audiences as well as the localised Viennese groups that comprise it.

The film also documents a performance by the Viennese folk-rock band Die Schmetterlinge. The band, who provided Austria's entry to the 1977 Eurovision song contest, play their version of *Das Lied von der Erde*, a song connected tangentially to the Yiddish song performed by Cohen. It was written by the Ukrainian songwriter Jura Soyfer (1912–39) as part of his 1936 play *Der Weltuntergang* (*The End of the World*).[45] In 1920, Soyfer's rich Jewish family fled the Communists to Istanbul and then Vienna, where he began writing anti-fascist texts for cabaret performances. He became a Socialist and wrote for *Arbeiter-Zeitung* and *Schulkampf*, idolising in particular Bertolt Brecht, whose combination in his theatre-works of folk art and music with cabaret songs and agit-prop practices was influential on Soyfer's own writing, evident, for example, in the posthumously published *Dreigroschenoper angewandt* (*Threepenny Opera Applied*). In 1934, Soyfer protested against the rise of Austro-Fascism and campaigned for the Austrian communists (KPÖ), a political position and context Beckermann later explores in her first full feature film, *Return to Vienna* (discussed in the next chapter). Working in Vienna as a journalist, he relayed information about the situation in Austria to England via the English poet John Lehmann. In 1937 Soyfer was accidentally arrested and imprisoned for three months; released in 1938, he tried to flee the Nazis by posing as a tourist travelling to Switzerland but was re-arrested on 13 March 1938, and deported to Dachau, where he met the composer Herbert Zipper and authored the famous *Dachaulied*, and then to Buchenwald, where he enjoyed brief notoriety as a composer of anti-Nazi songs and performances. He died of typhus on 16 February 1939.[46] Like Cohen's performance of the Yiddish

folk song, the performance of Soyfer's song at the Arena thus resonates with a particular dimension of Austrian history – the overlap
between communist utopian thought and Jewishness – that will
become a central theme in Beckermann's later work, while being
of implicit and largely missed critical significance at the time of the
Arena occupation.

Another detail of the historical context behind *Arena Squatted*
concerns the municipal–political context of the occupation, centring on the role of Schöps and its owner Leopold Böhm in the city
council decision to bulldoze the site (except for the largest building,
which remains standing). Born into a bourgeois Jewish family in
1922, Böhm fled the Nazis in 1938 and joined the British army in
1940 (his parents died in the Holocaust). After the war he worked
in Haifa for an oil extraction company, returning to Vienna in 1952
to search for his parents.[47] Joining his uncle's textile business, Böhm
eventually oversaw its expansion into a nationwide trading empire
and, in the 1970s, purchased the Arena site with Israeli–Austrian
businessman Ariel Muzicant, a significant Jewish cultural figure in
Vienna and later an executive member of the Vienna Wiesenthal
Institute for Holocaust Studies. The involvement of Schöps in the
city's closing down of the Arena and its occupation frames the complex historical imbrication, not addressed in the film, of business
and municipal interests in the background of *Arena Squatted*.

Suddenly, a Strike

Suddenly, a Strike was filmed by Filmladen Wien at the Semperit
rubber tyre works in Traiskirchen. The film's title (a Lower-Austrian
dialect version of "Auf einmal", "suddenly") combines two allusions to Sergei Eisenstein – first, his *Strike!* of 1924, and second,
the intertitle immediately preceding the 'Odessa Steps' sequence
of *Battleship Potemkin* (1925), which comprises the single word
"Suddenly …". It locates and dates its action in the opening subtitle
"Semperit Traiskirchen 17.4 – 11.5.1978", shown over a still shot
of men sitting round a bar table smoking and drinking. A sequence
follows in which men discuss earnings (apart from Beckermann's
narration and her occasionally audible questioning of participants,
women are virtually absent from the entire film). A sense of tectonic

political shifts is immediately foregrounded as the camera focusses on one man saying "Six years ago they were top earners ...". The subsequent discussion centres on what the men used to do, what they were previously paid, and what has been taken away from them; the next speaker narrates the origins of the dispute, one year ago, in summer 1977 (much of the discussion contests dates and sequences of events). The film then cuts to a sequence of still shots of machines and workers on the factory floor, while the female narrator outlines the background of the strike and describes the mechanical and manual processes of tyre production.

This binary structure, oscillating between sequences depicting groups in dialogic debate and individuals expressing opinions, and narrative voiceover providing contextual detail against montage sequences of stills or moving images, organises much of the film. Beckermann comments (in the 2007 interview with Rebhandl) that the film's aesthetics derive very clearly from her own background in journalism. She emphasises the origins of its use of photomontage and photocollage in Agitprop art and the works of John Heartfield. A specific industrial semiotic (shots of factory chimneys, company logos, maps of distribution) prevails, giving the film the air of a public information television broadcast. There are also echoes of Austrian television programmes like Peter Turrini and Wilhelm Pevny's *Die Alpensaga* (1976–80), a chronicle-drama which mapped Austrian twentieth-century history by focussing on one family's experiences, and which featured (in the fourth episode, *Die feindlichen Brüder*) family and village discussions about unionisation and the modernisation and rationalisation of traditional Austrian agricultural practices.

At one point in *Suddenly, a Strike* the narrator tells us of the Semperit "tradition of enforcing demands" ("bei Semperit gibt es eine gewisse Tradition Vorderungen durchzusetzen"), and of Semperit's struggles and mergers due to "overproduction in the world market and the resulting increased competition". The brief summary of the company's industrial history is a synecdoche of a longer narrative that remains implicit but reveals something of why, beyond its contemporary significance, Beckermann and her team may have considered the strike worthy of filming. Founded in 1896 as the Miskolczy and Co. OHG rubber goods factory, Semperit (from the Latin *Semper it*, 'It always works') was a major tire and solid rubber manufacturers for the Austrian and German market. Established in 1906, the brand was incorporated fully in 1985 into the German company Continental, which had taken a stake in the company after the Anschluß in 1938. According to Markus Schmitzberger, "The lettering 'Semperit' or the production code 'nto' can still be found on many vehicles and tracked vehicles of the Second World War (e.g. Panzerkampfwagen IV or V)."[48] Before 1938 (writes Gerald D. Feldman),

> The company's chief products were tires and tubes for every type of motor vehicle and bicycle along with rubber footwear and other rubber goods. It was also active in coal mining. In addition to being the most important rubber producer in Austria, it also had branches in Cracow, Budapest, Bucharest, and Yugoslavia. Some of the shares were held through a holding company in Switzerland.[49]

During the war, Semperit manufactured tyres and tank tracks (the narrator of *Suddenly, a Strike* informs us that Director Meier was known as "Panzer Meier", a nickname describing his aggressive negotiating style but also echoing this aspect of the company's history), and exploited forced labour imported by the Nazis from Poland. The company was also connected by the covert actions of its General Director Franz Messner to Viennese resistance to Nazi occupation. Messner was found out by the Nazis and (Feldman writes)

> was beheaded on January 9, 1945. He had made considerable contributions to the German war effort in his work as Semperit general director, but he was also a member of a small Catholic resistance group and, under the code name "Oysters", had provided the Office of Strategic Services with information on industry and production.[50]

The company's website offers a historical timeline which elides the period between 1936 and 1956, and also omits any mention of the strike Beckermann films in 1978.[51]

In 1978, Semperit was majority-owned by the state-owned Austrian bank Creditanstalt (which held 31 per cent of the company at the Anschluß, increasing to majority ownership of nearly 55 per cent soon after) and closely linked to a subsidiary of the French Michelin company. Management strategies of profit maximisation were thus connected to ideological developments international business and finance capital, while the legacy ownership and financing of these policies derived partly from mergers and share-dealing during the Nazi years. The link to Creditanstalt (noted by the narration of *Suddenly, a Strike*) developed during the 1930s and through the war, when Semperit (in a move to internationalism under the territorially expansionist auspices of the Third Reich that foreshadowed the post-war move towards globalisation consequent on the rise of neoliberalism) expanded its activities into several German-occupied nations that offered new kinds of resource. As Feldman notes, for example,

> progress was also made in Slovakia, where Semperit was expanding its sales organization [...]. Although the Slovak government was eager for the country to have a rubber industry of its own, Semperit was striving to undertake a modest amount of production in addition to selling its products. This included buying up a Jewish property that was being auctioned off for its raincoat production.[52]

In the early 1940s, the company also explored buying up Jewish-owned shares in a Romanian company, and (Feldman comments) struggled to comply with Nazi racial policies in relation to its numerous half-Jewish employees in the various territories in which it was then operating.[53]

These aspects of Semperit's wartime history, unlikely to have been wide public knowledge in Austria in 1978, nevertheless shadow the company's implementing in the late 1970s of the US-driven neoliberal agenda in pressuring its workforce to accept a pay cut for a change in working practices which, the union argued, actually increased their workload.[54] *Suddenly, a Strike* emphasises the significance of the Austrian Social Partnership (the voluntary system of general co-operation on economic questions, developed since the 1950s between labour, business, and government)[55] and its conventions of democratic negotiation and compromise, which are presented as qualities under threat from the new neoliberal management strategies. The film explores the micropolitics of localised union protest – arguments, negotiations, compromises – against this backdrop of globalisation, understood implicitly as a historical echo or repetition of darker events. A pivotal moment in the negotiations mapped by the film is the factory management's introduction of a "9 Punkte Rationalisierungsprogramm", initially rejected by the negotiating committee, forcing the intervention of the Austrian Chancellor, Bruno Kreisky, in the dispute – a dance of positions satirised by the film's use of Manfred Deix's cartoons of Kreisky banging union and management heads together to the accompaniment of a jazz version of the Blue Danube waltz.[56] The resolution of the strike is accompanied by an agreement to pay rises from August 1978, and rejection of the 9-point programme (but agreement to co-operate on a different process of rationalisation; the Creditanstalt director reassured shareholders that salary costs would be covered by increased productivity). The film presents another satirical sequence of portraits of the negotiators with speech bubbles stating various positions, accompanied by music and followed by footage of workers leaving the factory. It concludes pessimistically with the management planning extensive changes that will also affect working conditions, including the closure of Semperit's Viennese headquarters and the sacking of 600 workers there, and subsequent relocation to cheaper provincial sites.

The dispute's international resonances (echoing the company's international expansion during the Third Reich) are foregrounded in the film's mention of the Swiss Firestone Scandal, also in 1978, in which a tyre factory in Canton Baselland was closed by its USA-based owners, a decision described at the time as "brutal", "shocking" and "arrogant".[57] Sabine Pitteloud analyses the Firestone closure in relation to the "implications of US multinationals' activities in Europe after 1945",[58] exploring how competing narratives about the reasons for the factory closure mobilised "the different stakeholders – labour unions, trade associations, and governmental representatives – [to develop] divergent narratives related to 'nationality' in order to legitimate the strategies to be adopted."[59] This level of internationalist standardisation of working practices and output targets remains implicit in Beckermann's representation of the Semperit strike, but is nevertheless present at the film's end, in the residual potential for more drastic or severe managerial transformations, and the labour redundancies consequent on increased workforce efficiency.

Suddenly, a Strike thus represents the dispute's immediate impacts on workers and the community of industrial action, while also contextualising its causes and consequences in relation to a wider historical narrative of rationalisation which echoes managerial strategies developed during the crucial period of Austrian history largely repressed by the nation at the time of the strike. It seeks ways of capturing and comprehending the tensions between the complex, morally shaded micropolitics of the local dispute (which nevertheless draws in as arbiters key figures from the Austrian government and the union movement) and the indeterminate, nebulous but materially impactful influence of global economic and ideological forces. In August 2007, Beckermann returned to Traiskirchen with editor Dieter Pichler (with whom she would later also work on *American Passages* and *The Dreamed Ones*). They made a short film (composed mainly of still photographs with her narrative voice-over), which makes two important points about the impact of neoliberal policies: the factory workforce now comprises 400, rather than the 5000 of 1978; and the town is thriving as a site of consuming rather than production. A similar set of macro-concerns is evident in Beckermann's next film, which explores the impact of the global 1970s steel crisis on an Austrian town.

The Steel Hammer out There on the Grass

The Steel Hammer out There on the Grass (1981),[60] directed by Beckermann in collaboration with Aichholzer and Michael Stejskal, documents the impacts of neoliberal rationalisation in the state-owned Austrian steel industry. Focussing on a steelworks in Judenburg, Styria (coincidentally the birthplace of film-maker Elfi Mikesch [b.1940], whose *Zechmeister* was made in the same year), it charts the resistance of the workers and the public to the imposition of new work rotas, quotas, and practices, and records accounts of the impact of the changes on individual lives. Writing of the Austrian steel industry a year before the film was made, Oskar Grünwald, the director of the Österreichische Industrieverwaltung, noted "the factories at Judenburg, with an electric steelworks and a bar steel rolling mill, both of which are due to be closed down in the not-too-distant future" and, later, that "[t]he Siemens-Martin steel works in Kapfenberg, Judenburg, Liezen, Ternitz and Donawitz were shut down. Closure of the remaining steel production in Judenburg is scheduled to take place in 1981. Ingot steel production will then be concentrated in Linz, Kapfenberg and Ternitz."[61]

The Judenburg steelworks had been founded as Steirische Gußstahlwerke in 1906 by entrepreneurs Sebastian Danner and

Konrad (Kurt) Wittgenstein (older brother of the philosopher Ludwig) with money loaned from Kurt's father Karl, a mining and steel magnate and one of the richest European men of his generation (and a board member of Creditanstalt, majority owners in 1978, as we've seen, of Semperit), who owned a scythe factory in the town.[62] The works were incorporated after the Anschluß into the Austrian steel conglomerate 'Alpine Montan AG Hermann Göring, Linz', the largest steel manufacturers in the Reich, and benefited from Nazi investment (under the 'Ostwerk' commitment to support the Reich's 'newly acquired' Eastern regions) in 1942–3, as well as from imported foreign slave labour. Their entire stock and equipment were plundered by the Red Army after the liberation in 1945. The Marshall Plan funded the installation of new machines, and subsequently the Judenburg steelworks became part of VOESTalpine, a conglomerate that incorporated the former Steirische Gußstahlwerke AG along with other subsidiaries into Vereinigte Edelstahlwerke AG (VEW), the largest element of the VOESTalpine group. These mergers coincided with the oil and steel crises of the mid-1970s which accelerated a series of industry transformations, the social and political impacts of which (as with *Suddenly, a Strike*) are the subject of *Steel Hammer*. The film captures a pivotal moment in a developing industrial and economic crisis that will eventually (in 1985) culminate in the bankruptcy of the conglomerate, the redundancy of nearly half the 80,000 workforce, and the resignation of its management board. This was the "VOEST-debacle", described by current (as of 2023) CEO Wolfgang Eder as "this deep 'valley of tears'".[63] The collapse of VOEST triggered a national industrial crisis which led to the privatisation of the Austrian steel industry and the reconfiguration through the 1990s of industrial relations across the entire nation.[64]

Steel Hammer opens with Captain Beefheart's *Hard Working Man* ("Work my hammer for the factory / foreman always wanna fight") playing over a black screen, which then cuts to a street view of marching protesters, their banners bearing slogans like "Wahrheit: wer sagt sie uns?" (Truth: who will tell us?) and "Wir marschieren für Judenburg" (We march for Judenburg). A church bell tolls, as the female narrating voice situates the action in Judenburg, May 1981. Establishment shots draw attention to the diversity of industrial, urban, and rural spaces characterising the area, while interviews are conducted indoors and outside, at the factory gates. Through cutting and montage, the film effectively maps out its view of a labour community living within the opposition between the diverse exteriors and the febrile social and political atmosphere it documents. Filmed mostly in colour with some monochrome sequences, the montage and sound editing of this film are noticeably more accomplished than in Beckermann's earlier films, creating a sense of detailed intensity and urgency to the narrative while also emphasising the constructed, cinematic element of the final product.

Steel Hammer registers a key moment in the decline of the Austrian steel industry, nationalised in 1946 but by 1981 (the narration informs us) "a cheap supplier of raw material for private sector industry", along with "the impact of the international crisis" which began in 1975. As with the Semperit strike, the narrative is ostensibly located firmly in the contemporary, and involves the familiar 1970s neoliberal trajectory of industrial restructuring and rationalisation, increased internal competition, relocation of production or its replacement by cheaper imported materials, and consequent shrinkage of workforce and increase of productivity, along with a nostalgic sense of the contemporary lack of worker solidarity. These processes resulted, in this case, the effective closure of the Judenburg plant. Underpinning the extensive political debates represented in the film is the cultural memory of mass unemployment in the 1930s, a memory that frames the film's exploration of the management position and its effects on the workers. An important figure in the negotiations, works council member (Betriebsrat, sozialistische Fraktion) Horst Skvarca, sums up his despairing attitude to the management strategy: "I can only characterize this as inhuman",[65] a description he repeats this in his later speech to the workforce.

The debates about union power, trust, and class relations are part of the wider historical process of redefining the compromises involved in the post-war Austrian Social Partnership, which, as the manager and Works Council Chairman (Betriebsratsobmann) Franz Güttersberger clearly states, has become, in his understanding of the case of the Judenburg steelworks, outmoded and "a problem". One consequence of this, discussed at length in the film, is the declining influence and even questionable utility of the unions as representatives of labour interests. Another is the sense of unanchored disorientation experienced by the workers themselves as they struggle to comprehend and adapt to the new demands. As one interviewee puts it in the film, "People feel they are losing ground, and that they have no perspective to hold onto" – an early expression of the alienated precarity characteristic of neoliberal economic conditions. One interviewee in the film insists that worker solidarity has declined "since the 1930s" and the days of "the old socialists", a constitution of community in nostalgia that pointedly evades (or represses) the politics of the period remembered.[66]

This question of contemporary community and its effectiveness, or even viability, in the face of neoliberalism recurs in each of Beckermann's early films. In charting utopian forms of social organisation as expressions of resistance to capitalist rationalisation, these films provide ideological groundwork for her later examinations of Austrian politics, particularly in relation to the Waldheim affair of 1986 (discussed in Chapter 4). Andrea Reiter has considered how Jewish-Austrian artists and writers of the postwar generation (including Beckermann) differed from the generation of Holocaust survivors in their willingness to engage in forms of social protest, "repeat[ing] 'acts' prefigured in the alternative culture of the avant-garde and protest culture"[67] of the 1960s and 1970s. Drawing on Judith Butler's theorisations of protest and play, Reiter argues that this different set of influences enabled these artists to transfer "the emerging counter discourse into literary and filmic texts that expressed their Jewish perspective, which they discovered and developed in their opposition to"[68] events like those Beckermann explores in her early documentaries.

The connection between global shifts of policy and the deperspectivised or disoriented experience of the workforce constitutes the central dramatic tension in *Steel Hammer*, but the real crisis explored in the film is (as in *Suddenly, a Strike*) that of the function and declining effectiveness of unions in the face of government-sponsored neoliberalisation, just as *Arena Squatted* explores the possibility of counter-cultural social formations in the face of the overriding capitalist prioritisation of property and investment. More broadly, these films are linked by their considerations of the impact of neoliberal policies on notions of collectivity and community, particularly in the wake of the 1968-generation protests – echoes of which permeate all three films – and how these immediate histories are grounded in wider historical perspectives that exist only tangentially or fractionally in relation to contemporary events. Each film thus invites viewers to enquire into the specifically *Austrian* and twentieth-century history behind the events examined. *Steel Hammer* implicitly connects this specific historical context to those wider events gestured to in the history behind the Judenburg steelworks, and, as seen above, by comments made by various contributors. Like the contemporary performance in *Arena besetzt* of a song written by anti-fascist protestor Jura Soyfer, this question establishes a ground of documentary enquiry which Beckermann's next film, *Return to Vienna*, elaborates in distinct but related directions.

Notes

1 Judith Butler, *Notes Towards a Performative Theory of Assembly* (Cambridge, MA: Harvard University Press, 2018), p. 9.

2 Hakim Bey, *TAZ – Temporary Autonomous Zone, Ontological Anarchy, Poetic Terrorism* (New York: Autonomedia, 1991), p. 103.

3 Maria Giovanna Vagenas, "Rediscovering the Forgotten Gems of a Decade: Austrian Auteurs of the 1970s at the Viennale", *Senses of Cinema* (May 2021), at www.sensesofcinema.com/2021/festival-reports/rediscovering-the-forgotten-gems-of-a-decade-austrian-auteurs-of-the-1970s-at-the-viennale/ (accessed 25 February 2023). Among the films shown at this festival were Antonis Lepeniotis' *Stadtbahn* (1966), *Der Tod des Dr. Antonio durch die Renaissance der geistigen Gesellschaft* (1968), *Ho Anthropos* (1970), and *Das Manifest* (1974), Herbert Holba's *Flipper* (1968) and *Genesis* (1969), *Ein wenig sterben* (Mansur Madavi, 1981), and *Weht die Angst, so weht der Wind* (Manfred Kaufmann, 1982).

4 "Es ging uns nicht darum uns als Filmemacher darzustellen." Beckermann, "Interview with Bert Rebhandl", 9 August 2007, DVD box set. All subsequent reference to this interview, which is spread across all the DVDs comprising the box set, will be cited as "Interview with Rebhandl", 2007.

5 Gary Indiana, "Valie Export by Gary Indiana", *BOMB* magazine (1 April 1982), at https://bombmagazine.org/articles/valie-export (accessed 22 January 2023).

6 Elke Krasny, "'For Us, Art Is Work': IntAkt – International Action Community of Women Artists", in Agata Jakubowska and Katy

Deepwell (eds), *All-women Art Spaces in Europe in the Long 1970s* (Liverpool: Liverpool University Press, 2018), p. 100. See also Gabriele Schor (ed.), *Feminist Avant-Garde – Art of the 1970s* (Munich: Prestel, 2016), p. 28. For wider discussions of Austrian avant-garde cinema, see Peter Tscherkassky (ed.), *Film Unframed: A History of Austrian Avant-Garde Cinema* (Vienna: Synema, 2012).

7 Scott MacKenzie (ed.), *Film Manifestos and Global Cinema Cultures: A Critical Anthology* (Berkeley, CA: University of California Press, 2014), pp. 152–3; p. 153.

8 Robert von Dassanowsky, *Austrian Cinema: A History* (Jefferson, NC: Macfarland, 2005), p. 195.

9 obert von Dassanowsky, *Austrian Cinema: A History* (Jefferson, NC: Macfarland, 2005), p. 196.

10 Stefan Grissemann, "Frame by Frame: Peter Kubelka", *Film Comment* (September–October 2012), at www.filmcomment.com/article/peter-kubelka-frame-by-frame-antiphon-adebar-arnulf-rainer/ (accessed 23 February 2023).

11 Horwath and Omasta, "A Conversation with Ruth Beckermann", p. 21.

12 Nick Pinkerton, "The Present Absence", in Kondor and Loebenstein (eds), *Ruth Beckermann*, p. 6.

13 Renata S. Posthofen, "Ruth Beckermann: Re-activating Memory – In Search of Time Lost", in Margarete Lamb-Faffelberger (ed.), *Out from the Shadows: Essays on Contemporary Austrian Women Writers and Filmmakers* (Riverside: Ariadne Press, 1997), p. 264.

14 "Sieht man die Filme über die Semperit-Arbeiter oder die Stahlarbeiter in der Steiermark, wird einem klar, dass die Sozialdemokratie politisch widerstrebend nur nachvollzog, was wirtschaftlich global vor sich ging. Margaret Thatcher wurde 1975 Vorsitzende der englischen Konservativen und 1979 Premierministerin, aber schon vor ihr hatte ihr Vorgänger, der Sozialdemokrat Jim Callahan dem Keynesianismus abgeschworen. Ronald Reagan wurde 1981 Präsident der USA, aber der Neoliberalismus hatte seine ideologische Offensive schon Anfang der 1970er-Jahre mit massiver Unterstützung der US-amerikanischen Industrie gestartet." Armin Thurnher, "Andere Zeiten: Zu vier frühen Filmen Ruth Beckermanns", in Horwath and Omasta (eds), *Ruth Beckermann*, p. 44.

15 Thurnher, "Andere Zeiten", p. 45.

16 See, for example, Günter Bischoff, Anton Pelinka, Fritz Plasser and Alexander Smith (eds), *Global Austria – Austria's Place in Europe and the World* (Contemporary Austrian Studies Vol. 20) (New Brunswick: Transaction Publishers, 2011).

17 Siegfried Mattl, "Work in Motion" (2007) (trans. Samia Geldner), in Monica Lendl (ed.), *Ruth Beckermann Film Collection: Texte/Texts/ Textes* (Vienna: Ruth Beckermann Film Production, 2007), p. 83 (translation modified).

18 Mattl, "Work in Motion", p. 82.

19 "The threshold must be carefully distinguished from the boundary. A *Schwelle* [threshold] is a zone. Transformation, passage, wave action are in the word *schwellen,* swell, and etymology ought not to overlook these senses." Walter Benjamin, *The Arcades Project* Konvolut O2a, 1 (trans. Howard Eiland and Kevin McLaughlin) (Cambridge, MA: Belknap Press of Harvard University Press, 2002), p. 494.

20 Emma Widdis, *Alexander Medvedkin* (London: IB Tauris, 2005), p. 21. See also Anne Philipe, "Medvedkine, tu connais? Interview avec Slon et Chris Marker", *Le Monde* (2 December 1971), 17. Reprinted in Alter, *Chris Marker*, pp. 139–44.

21 Trevor Stark notes that "the film was met with a largely hostile reception, even among those who had actively participated in its production. The union leaders either refused to attend the screening or vehemently aired their protests. In response, Marker held a discussion after the projection, recorded by the soundman Bonfanti. One worker states, 'I think that the director is incompetent. ... And I also think, and I say it bluntly, that the workers of Rhodia have simply been exploited.' Another criticizes Marker for the fact that women in the film appear exclusively as wives rather than as workers and militants in their own right." (Trevor Stark, "'Cinema in the Hands of the People': Chris Marker, the Medvedkin Group, and the Potential of Militant Film", *October* 139 (Winter 2012), 117–50: 126).

22 Stark, "'Cinema in the Hands of the People'", 119.

23 Nicole Brenez, "For It Is the Critical Faculty That Invents Fresh Forms", in Michael Temple and Michael Witt (eds), *The French Cinema Book* (London: Palgrave/BFI, 2007), p. 233.

24 The LIP dispute is the subject of another film, *Les LIP – l'imagination au pouvoir* (2007) by Christian Rouaud. See review by Serge Halimi, *Le Monde diplomatique*, 20 March 2007, at www.monde-diplomatique. fr/carnet/2007–03–20-LIP (accessed 23 February 2023).

25 Horwath and Omasta, "A Conversation with Ruth Beckermann", p. 24.

26 "Interview with Rebhandl", 2007.

27 *Close Up* film festival, London (3–24 September 2017), at www. closeupfilmcentre.com/film_programmes/2017/close-up-on-ruth-beckermann/ (accessed 21 November 2023).

28 Susan Ingram, *Siting Futurity* (London: Punctum Books, 2021), p. 43.

29 See Hakim Bey, *TAZ / Temporary Autonomous Zone, Ontological Anarchy, Poetic Terrorism* (Los Angeles: Autonomedia, 1991).

30 Hakim Bey, "Permanent TAZs", *Talklingmail 5* (Winter 1994), at http://dreamtimevillage.org/articles/permanent_taz.html (accessed 26 January 2023).

31 "Einzelne Medien beschrieben die Aktion als linksradikalen Aufstand, doch insgesamt war das Echo erstaunlich positiv. Zu offensichtlich war es, dass da die unterschiedlichsten Gruppen junger Menschen zusammengefunden hatten, voran Künstler vieler Sparten. Die Grenzen zwischen Künstlern und Publikum wurden aufgehoben. Beatrix Neundlinger organisierte mit anderen das "Café Schweinestall". Videogruppen zogen ebenso ein wie Motorrad-Rocker. Um aus Erziehungsheimen geflüchtete Jugendliche kümmerten sich Sozialarbeiter [...]". Erhard Stackl, "Als einen Sommer lang Freiheit war" (22 August 1976), at www.derstandard.at/story/2492068/als-einen-sommer-lang-freiheit-war (accessed 14 October 2023).

32 For a full contemporary account of the Arena occupation, see Ernst, Gustav (ed.), *Wespennest – Zeitschrift für brauchbare Texte und Bilder* 23: *Arenadokumentation* (12 July 1976).

33 "Viennese Actionism", in Hal Foster et al. (eds), *Art Since 1900* (London: Thames and Hudson, 2004), p. 464.

34 Robert Foltin, "Squatting and Autonomous Action in Vienna 1967–2012", in Bart van der Steen, Ask Katzeff and Leendert van Hoogenhuijze (eds), *The City Is Ours* (Oakland, CA: PM Press, 2014), p. 256.

35 Gerald Raunig, *Art and Revolution* (trans. Aileen Derieg) (New York: Semiotext(e), 2007), p. 188. See Rolf Schwendter, "Das Jahr 1968. War es eine kulturelle Zäsur?", in Reinhard Sieder, Heinz Steinert and Emmerich Tálos (eds), *Österreich 1945–1995* (Vienna: Verlag für Gesellschaftskritik, 1995), pp. 166–75.

36 Roswitha Mueller, *VALIE EXPORT: Fragments of the Imagination* (Bloomington, IN: Indiana University Press, 1994), p. xv.

37 Christine Wall, "Sisterhood and Squatting in the 1970s: Feminism, Housing and Urban Change in Hackney", *History Workshop Journal* 83 (2017), p. 83.

38 Beckermann's film does not address contemporary critiques of the gender politics of the ARENA occupation. See, for example, Felicitas, "Frauenhaus = Freudenhaus?" and eva-maria-angela, "ARENA bist du großer Söhne – und wo sind deine Töchter?", *AUF – Eine Frauenzeitschrift*, II:8 (September 1976), 20–2; 23–5.

39 For a discussion of post-war Germanophone women artists' uses of Surrealism, see Patricia Allmer, *The Traumatic Surreal: Germanophone*

Women Artists and Surrealism after the Second World War (Manchester: Manchester University Press, 2022).

40 *Ruth Beckermann Film Collection: Arena besetzt / Auf amol a Streik / Der Hammer steht auf der Wies'n da draussen* DVD booklet, p. 5.

41 *Ruth Beckermann Film Collection: Arena besetzt / Auf amol a Streik / Der Hammer steht auf der Wies'n da draussen* DVD booklet, p. 5.

42 For an account of 1970s Austrian documentary, see von Dassanowsky, *Austrian Cinema*, pp. 203–6.

43 Foltin, "Squatting and Autonomous Action in Vienna", pp. 257–8.

44 See www.setlist.fm/setlist/leonard-cohen/1976/wiener-konzerthaus-vienna-austria-3c53587.html The song had been popularised by West German folk singer Peter Rohland in a 1963 program of Yiddish music described by Phil Alexander as "index[ing] the unadorned clarity of protest song rather than anything recognisably or idiomatically 'Yiddish'". Phil Alexander, *Sounding Jewish in Berlin: Klezmer Music and the Contemporary City* (Oxford: Oxford University Press, 2021), p. 39.

45 The song had been released on the band's *Lieder fürs Leben* album in 1975.

46 See Donald G. Daviau (ed.), *Jura Soyfer and His Time* (Riverside: Ariadne Press, 1995); and Stephan Stompor, *Jüdisches Musik- und Theaterleben unter dem NS-Staat* (ed. Andor Iszak) (Hanover: Europäisches Zentrum für jüdische Musik, 2001).

47 "Leopold Böhm ist tot", *Kurier*, 4 April 2007, at https://web.archive.org/web/20070410014244/http://kurier.at/nachrichten/wirtschaft/68363.php (accessed 24 November 2023).

48 "Nach dem Anschluß 1938 beteiligte sich die deutsche Firma Continental an Semperit-Traiskirchen. Das Werk gehörte zu den wichtigsten deutschen Reifen- und Vollgummiherstellern, der nach dem Wegfall der südamerikanischen Kautschuk-Vorkommen von den Buna-Werken des IG Farben-Konzerns beliefert wurde. Auf vielen Fahrzeugen und Kettenfahrzeugen des Zweiten Weltkrieges lassen sich noch heute der Schriftzug "Semperit" oder das Fertigungskennzeichen "nto" finden (z.B. Panzerkampfwagen IV oder V)." Markus Schmitzberger, "Semperitwerk – Traiskirchen", at www.geheimprojekte.at/firma_semperit_traiskirchen.html (accessed 18 January 2023).

49 Gerald D. Feldman, *Austrian Banks in the Period of National Socialism* (Cambridge: Cambridge University Press, 2015), p. 305.

50 Feldman, *Austrian Banks in the Period of National Socialism*, p. 310.

51 See www.semperit.com/car/about-us (accessed 18 January 2023).

52 Feldman, *Austrian Banks in the Period of National Socialism*, p. 308.

53 Feldman, *Austrian Banks in the Period of National Socialism*, p. 309.

54 For a detailed summary of the strike and its background, see "Semperit Traiskirchen 1978", Organisation Arbeiterinnenkampf (ARKA), at www.arbeiter-innen-kampf.org/publikationen/marxismus-buecher/streiks-der-2-republik/semperit-traiskirchen-1978/ (accessed 18 January 2023).

55 See for a detailed discussion of the Social Partnership, Ewald Novotny, "The Austrian Social Partnership and Democracy", *Working Paper 93–1* (University of Vienna), at https://conservancy.umn.edu/bitstream/handle/11299/56472/WP931.pdf?sequence=1 (accessed 19 January 2023).

56 In her interview with Rebhandl, Beckermann discusses the process of filming these animations, and notes that these sequences were "handmade".

57 Sabine Pitteloud, "'American Management' vs 'Swiss Labour Peace'. The closure of the Swiss Firestone Factory in 1978", *Business History* Vol. 64 No. 9 (2020), 1648–65: 1648.

58 Pitteloud, "'American Management' vs 'Swiss Labour Peace'", 1648.

59 Pitteloud, "'American Management' vs 'Swiss Labour Peace'", 1649.

60 The title is taken from an interview with one of the factory workers, who states that the "The steel hammers were immediately demolished, today the hammers are out there, on the grass" ("die stehen jetzt dort draussen auf der Wiesn").

61 Oskar Grünwald, "Steel and the State in Austria", *Annals of Public and Cooperative Economics* Vol. 51 No. 4 (December 1980), 477–91: 479, 481.

62 See Alexander Waugh, *The House of Wittgenstein: A Family at War* (London: Bloomsbury, 2008), p. 42.

63 Interview with Hans Bürger, *20 Years on the Stock Exchange*, VoestAlpine Press Release, October 2015, p. 8, at www.ws-akademie.at/group/static/sites/group/.downloads/en/press/2015-voestalpine-ipo-1995-publication-en.pdf (accessed 20 January 2023).

64 See John Tagliabue, "Voest-Alpine Plight Affects All Austria", *New York Times*, 20 January 1986, Section D, p. 6.

65 "Ich kann das nur als unmenschlich bezeichnen".

66 This notion of community is discussed by Jean-Luc Nancy in *The Inoperative Community* (trans. Peter Connor et al.) (Minneapolis, MN: University of Minnesota Press, 1991), p. 10. See also Robert Bernasconi, "On Deconstructing Nostalgia for Community within the West: The Debate between Nancy and Blanchot", *Research in Phenomenology* Vol. 23 (1993), 3–21.

67 Andrea Reiter, *Contemporary Jewish Writing: Austria after Waldheim* (London: Routledge, 2013), p. 41.

68 Reiter, *Contemporary Jewish Writing*, p. 42.

2

From memory to history – *Return to Vienna* and *Die Mazzesinsel*

There was no stone that marked their passage. (Helen Epstein)[1]

This was not my special fate. My Jewish friends and colleagues, many hundreds of thousands of them, can tell similar things – it's a long time ago, much time has passed – not much is known about it anymore and there are many who don't want to know anything about it anymore, therefore it's good to talk about it now and then, to remember [*erinnert*] what kind of times these were in which one lived.[2]

The final, elegiac words of *Return to Vienna – Franz Weintraub 1924–1934* (1983) are spoken by the film's narrator Franz West (1909–84, formerly Franz Weintraub, his name changed to conceal his underground Communist Party activities and later retained due to its non-Jewish connotations). Historian, writer, communist and Jew, Franz recounts his memories of the Jewish and working-class political and cultural life of Vienna of the inter-war years. He summarises in these final words the individual and collective fate of his Jewish Viennese community, recounting his version of what Ruth Kluger calls "the remnant of the *mishpokke*".[3] Marking this community's dispersal, he recites names, family relations, trades and jobs, places, fates – a list leading into the darkness in which each light seen from the train window seems to correspond to a name, a family member, the last-mentioned being Franz's mother, who disappeared, he tells us, in the Łódź ghetto in Poland, sometime in 1941. Throughout the film, we hear his narrative, its events linked together like the carriages of the train we're travelling on at the end, or like the railway network itself, a resonant symbol linking the dispersed fates of which Franz speaks with the whole of European geography and history, and a figure of his own train of thought, selecting individual events, facts and narrative elements for combination and organisation. The resulting detailed account leads inexorably out of Franz's individual memory and into history. Franz's concluding remarks emphasise the temporal distance between historical events and his telling of them ("Much time has passed"), alongside the importance of "remembering" and "reminding" (the verb *erinnert* carries both possible meanings) as a counterweight to the culture of wilful "forgetting" ("there are many who don't want to know anything about it") that has, up to the 1980s, characterised post-war and post-Holocaust Austria. Beckermann is concerned in this film, and in her book *Die Mazzesinsel* (1984),[4] to which we'll turn at the end of this chapter, with excavating and exploring Austria's historically repressed collective memory, focussing initially on its working-class dimensions but shifting attention through the process of reconstruction to the Jewish elements. The result is a pair of texts actively engaging in reconstituting and recompiling and documenting versions of a violently dismembered past, finding a passage through a history partially erased but suddenly, in the present of 1980s Austria and Europe, returning. What *Return to Vienna* and *Die Mazzesinsel* expose, in their exploration of memories, documents, and other traces of the nation's suppressed histories, is the existence of an alternative set of narratives, a shadow-version of events returning to public consciousness through the acts of telling and showing.

Returning to Vienna

Made several years before the establishment of the concept of post-memorial studies by texts like Marianne Hirsch's *Family Frames* (1997), *Return to Vienna* constructs through Franz's narrative a corrective history of Austria's inter-war years. It offers an account of Viennese–Jewish experience which is simultaneously first-hand, for its narrator, and postmemorial, for its audience, which includes the film-makers Beckermann and Josef Aichholzer, born after the narrated events, who sit for much of its duration listening to Franz speak, providing only occasional prompts or questions. Loosely structured into a sequence of roughly ten-minute narrative segments or episodes separated by short montage sequences, with a musical soundtrack comprising popular and folk songs and film music alongside avant-garde classical work for solo saxophone and orchestra by French composer Max Dubois (1930–95), the narrative traces Franz's experience of living through the First Austrian Republic from the early 1920s to the disastrous general strike and armed rebellion (the Austrian Civil War) of February 1934, represented in the film through official documentary footage depicting Vienna's police marching in the streets, and artillery fire targeting municipal housing complexes.[5]

This extended archaeology of a period of Viennese (and wider Austrian) history reveals events that, in the early 1980s, were still severely repressed from the national consciousness. In 1983, Austria's official culture clung resolutely to the *"erste Opfer"* / "first victim" myths rapidly embedded in the national consciousness after 1945 (but established earlier, in the Moscow Declaration of 1 November 1943, which called Austria "the first free country to fall a victim to Hitlerite aggression").[6] Heidemarie Uhl points out (in 2006) that despite the broadcasting in Austria in 1979 of the television series *Holocaust*, publicly influential versions of the "victim theory" were still being promoted in 1982 in another popular televised history of the Second Republic, *Austria II*, which used highly selective documentary images to present the Anschluß "as a military occupation".[7] This myth of national victimhood worked over several decades to exonerate Austria and Austrians substantially, if not entirely, from any culpability in the Nazi atrocities. Only in the 1980s, as a result of a series of political scandals (some of which will be explored later in this book) and of the cultural impacts of works like *Return to Vienna*, did the ideological climate shift, and the possibility begin to develop of addressing historical reality and its traumatic effects on Austrian cultural and political identity. As late as 1989, Beckermann could write (in *Unzugehörig*) that "In this country after 1945, neither the entanglement of the Austrians with Nazism, nor the problem of Jews and non-Jews living together after Auschwitz, was discussed [...]. One does not speak about the relationship between Austrians and Jews."[8]

The country's amnesia, clearly not shared by Franz West, has troubled literary and cinematic engagements with Viennese and Austrian histories, and many writers have commented on its effects. Literary critic Marjorie Perloff, for example, in her 2004 memoir

The Vienna Paradox, ascribes Austria's apparently limited awareness of its modernist Jewish cultural history – specifically of the life and work of Arnold Schoenberg – partly to the "amnesia of the Nazi years and their aftermath".[9] Any act or work of Austrian postmemory thus requires an additional conscious volition, a wilful forcing of memory or anamnesia to expose hitherto repressed resources. Beckermann's film, at the vanguard of this shift, seeks by active remembering ("returning"), via Franz's narrative and archival images and footage, to redress this historical repression. Appearing in the immediate wake of ground-breaking Austrian films like Antel's *Der Bockerer* (which, Joseph W. Moser argues, "ruptured the post-war myth of Austrians as pure victims of Nazi aggression"),[10] *Return to Vienna* also influenced subsequent Austrian cinematic explorations of the country's Nazi past like Marc Adrian's *Nachfilm* (1995) and Lukas Stepanik and Robert Schindel's *Gebürtig* (2002).

Return to Vienna pulls the central post-war narrative of Austrian history away from its ideologically inflected insistence on uninterrupted continuity with stylised and selective memories of the Habsburg era, an age that persists in the film only in the visible traces of Viennese monuments like the Tegetthoff Statue (commemorating Baron Wilhelm von Tegetthoff's victory in the Battle of Lissa in 1866) that largely predate the events of the film's narrative. Franz's recollections, a wealth of personal and historical details, interrupt this prevailing cultural narrative with a radically different account of events that destabilises and redirects Austrian history. His personal memory (to use Jean-Pierre Vernant's terms) counters and reconfigures Austria's social memory, recalibrating and refocussing it from a different, renovating perspective.[11] Franz remarks several times on the clarity of his memories. The detail of his recall should, however, be tempered by Beckermann's cautionary note about her own childhood memories in her 1994 essay "Beyond the Bridges": "These memories do not capture the truth, although they do describe a perception of the truth."[12] Nevertheless, the tension between the level of remembered detail of (Franz's) individual memory and the obscuring will-to-forget or refusal of knowledge of (Austrian) cultural memory sits at the heart of *Return to Vienna*'s analysis of the political urgency of remembering and recollecting as correctives to Austria's "deviant consciousness".[13]

For much of the film, Franz narrates long passages recalling his historical experiences while sitting in his study in modern-day Vienna, surrounded by the tools of his scholarly work. He sits before a bookcase, on which one book's title is clearly visible – the *Arbeitsjournal* (1973; *Journals 1934–55*, 1993) of Bertolt Brecht[14] (Figure 2.1). This conspicuous book offers a densely resonant image pointing the viewer in several directions simultaneously, while layering into the film-text a variety of connotative potentials. Its prominence firmly locates Franz's Brechtian political and aesthetic stances within the film's contexts. It implies, for example, the performative dimension of Franz's narrative and its filmic presentation, which bears parallels with the Brechtian notion of epic theatre – the self-conscious presentation of dramatic action as an *act* of story-telling rather than an imitation of reality (the "portrayal of situations" rather than the "development of plots").[15] In her interview with Rebhandl in 2007, Beckermann describes Franz as "ein meisterhafter Erzähler" (a masterly narrator),[16] an epithet recalling Jorge Semprun's assertion at the beginning of his camp memoir *L'écriture ou la vie? (Literature? Or Life?)* that "Only the artifice of a masterly narrative will prove capable of conveying some of the truth of such testimony",[17] and also echoed in Fredric Jameson's discussion of Brechtian epic theatre and the "estranging potentials" of narrative: "[O]ne of the features of narrative in general, particularly in the practice of master-storyteller, is that it can expand or contract, be spun out in great or savoury detail over hours, or concentrated into the most pithy anecdote."[18] Franz's narrative conforms closely to this description, in its encompassing (as Brecht does in his *Arbeitsjournal*) of both highly detailed recall of specific events and a wider (but acute) political consciousness, perhaps retrospectively magnified, of the underlying social and economic forces shaping the historical period he describes. The conspicuous book thus constitutes a site of complexity in the film's contexture, expressing this polysemy while the film's narrative traces one thread through a turbulent and, for many, fatal period of Austrian and European history. Through this layered intersection of multifaceted imagery with the double narrative drive of subjective biography and historical narrative, *Return to Vienna* deals explicitly with what Marianne Hirsch calls "those violent historical forces that have rewritten family plots in the twentieth

Figure 2.1 Ruth Beckermann (dir.), *Return to Vienna*, 1983.
© Ruth Beckermann Filmproduktion.

century"[19] – forces of displacement and exile, social unrest and revolution, and, eventually, genocide.

The film deploys several strategies of representation in constructing its variant of what Annette Insdorf calls "documentaries of return",[20] a sub-genre of Holocaust documentary in which survivors or exiles return to their hometowns to assess continuity and change. 'Returning' in memory to the Vienna of 50 years earlier, Franz (himself an exile who returned to the city) narrates directly to the camera for most of the film, occasionally providing a voice-over accompanying constellations of mainly monochrome still and moving images which (again reminiscent of Brechtian strategies of defamiliarisation) constitute different illustrative assemblages of documented history, revivifying the history of inter-war Austria. These Markeresque passages of the film, offering a visual archive comprising evocative period metonymies of a life-world systematically destroyed by the Austro-fascism whose development Franz traces, present alternative codes for the viewer's interpretation. Both defiant and nostalgic, they testify to the uncanny endurance (despite the force of cultural repression) of images, their remarkable historical afterlives as documents and traces. Alongside punctuating moments of Brechtian self-referentiality that insistently expose Beckermann's filming process and her presence as interviewer (a recurrent strategy in her works), the foregrounding of the 'epic', 'master-storyteller' dimension of Franz's narrative markedly shifts from (but sustains the relation between film-making and action of) the interventionist documentary style of earlier films like *Arena Squatted*. *Return to Vienna* deploys a form of narrative-and-montage film-making (centring in this case on a male narrator, with all the questions about patriarchal authority and power that this focus brings) that inserts the viewer critically and self-consciously into the history it relates, while emphasising the constructedness and performed delivery of that history.

As Christina Guenther argues, the archival elements of the film work "to underscore the authenticity of [Franz's] narrative description of the period",[21] but they also, at times, subtly undercut it, offering carefully angled alternative perspectives on his narration. For example, the principal structures of cultural difference addressed in *Return to Vienna* are those of class and Jewishness, and Beckermann deploys subtle forms of juxtaposition to insert into Franz's narrative her own commentary on them. As Franz recounts his university life, we see Catholic election posters featuring blatantly anti-Semitic slogans and iconography, while he narrates: "Then later at university ... maybe that was one of the bad things, that you were always hurting inside, but you learned to live with anti-Semitism as a normal phenomenon."[22] The film cuts to archive footage from a promotional advertisement celebrating the relations of the Viennese to animals: "*Wiens Tierfreundlichkeit ist weltberühmt*" (Vienna's love for animals is world famous). Montage thus ironically underlines Franz's experience of, and insistence on, the 'normality' of Viennese anti-Semitism in contrast with the city's ostensibly remarkable 'care' for its pets, carefully underlining the implications of his recollections of normalised anti-Semitism. In another segment Franz recalls the petit-bourgeois and Jewish emphasis on the importance of education of sons. Glancing briefly at his interviewer, he smiles and, eventually, adds "and daughters". The film cuts for several seconds to a still photograph of the Vienna city council, a room full of dark-suited men, an imposingly paradigmatic image of patriarchal authority. Ironic montage thus highlight's Franz's self-correction and challenges his repeating of the social-democratic rhetoric of 'equality' by emphasising the absence of women from the city's political power-structures.

Return to Vienna and Austrian history

Discussing *Return to Vienna* in interviews, Beckermann emphasises the key terms 'discovery' and 'difference'. Her archival research for the film led, she says, to her "discovery" of the working-class history (which she calls a "different tradition")[23] of inter-war Vienna, and, in particular, the intersection of this class history with that of the Jewish community of the city. Interviewed in 2020 by Débora Kantor, Beckermann comments:

> [*Return to Vienna*] was supposed to be a film about the working-class people in the second district of Vienna, where Jews lived at the time. During the research I found out that it had been mainly a Jewish district before the war, so I found some of the working-class people who were Jews, and there was one that was such a good narrator that I decided, after doing interviews with many people, to make a film just about him. This was the beginning of this search for Jewish roots in Vienna.[24]

"I wanted to film the history of the workers' movement during the period between the two world wars", Beckermann told Rebhandl in 2007, "and by doing many, many recorded interviews with many former Communists or still-active Communists, Partisans, Socialists, I found Franz West".[25] During these interviews, she notes elsewhere, she "stumbled onto this Jewish history" which "presented me with a different Vienna and a different tradition, about which I had known nothing before".[26] This geographical and historical difference is connected to her sense of the "novelty" of the material unearthed by her research:

> The film is full of photos and old film footage, which at the time, however, was brand new [to me]. Some of the photos had already become familiar through exhibitions coming up at that time about Red Vienna. But we really searched for and discovered the film footage, partly in the various district offices of the Socialist Party [...].[27]

This "different" Vienna becomes also, Beckermann suggests elsewhere, the discovery of a crucial difference *within* the city's identity. In "Beyond the Bridges" (which reworks some parts of her introductory essay to *Die Mazzesinsel*) she considers the distinctness of Leopoldstadt in relation to the rest of the city: "The Leopoldstadt of the pre-war era must have been unique, very different from the rest of Vienna, and at the same it was so much part of the city that it did not seem exotic." "Difference" coupled with an integral familiarity thus characterises the district, which (she argues) "was a phenomenon only for someone who was passing through".[28]

What began, then, as a cinematic inquiry into the history of Vienna's working class (and thus an extension of the thematic concerns of Beckermann and Aichholzer's earlier documentaries) became (like the Vienna it revealed) something different from itself, shifting during the period of preparation and research and via attention to the complex political sectarianism of the time towards a documentation of the city's Jewish history, of which Beckermann became more fully aware during this period. Alongside its revisiting Viennese and Austrian history, *Return to Vienna* presents a history of this difference. It inaugurates Beckermann's extended deconstruction of Austrian identity and its insistent construction of her own unbelonging, exposing the Jewish/working-class nexus of ethnic and economic differences residing within, but repressed by and in constant tension with, Austria's 'official' historical narratives, especially those concerning national identity. Franz's first-hand account of moments of class and anti-Semitic conflict in interwar Vienna delineates multiple sites of this tension, revealing fracture-lines in the official narratives, exposing the repressed differences within identities and ideologies.

"Discovery" is another recurrent trope in Beckermann's comments on the film ("I found Franz West") and the process of researching it. "I had been very engaged in Austrian literature of the 19th century", Beckermann comments, "and for the first time, I had found a connecting link, though with a completely different political perspective, to Schnitzler, Joseph Roth, etc. In short, an articulate Viennese way of speaking ... so for me it was a completely new world that I had discovered."[29] Writing in 2000, journalist Hella Pick makes a similar point about her own research and its impact on her personal relation to Austria: "This has been a voyage foremost of rediscovery, but also of discovery, of coming to a closer understanding of my roots and learning aspects of Austria's past and present which I had previously ignored."[30] This trope of "discovery" echoes the emphasis on discovery characterising Freudian psychoanalysis (a profoundly Viennese phenomenon wholly contemporary with the events recollected in *Return to Vienna*). From his early work with Breuer on hysteria onwards, Freud frequently presented his theories as "discoveries" (for example, "the discovery that different sexual factors, in the most general sense, produce different pictures of neurotic disorders").[31] Beckermann's emphasis on "discovering" the history explored in the film echoes the Freudian emphasis on psychoanalytic subjects' (self-) "discovery" of their own past through the act of speaking to an analyst. In a telling metaphor, perhaps echoing the "Sprachlose Lieder" ("speechless songs") of Paul Celan, a central figure in her later works,[32] she characterises Austria's silence about its history in the early 1980s as "speechlessness": "In this very speechless (*sprachlosen*) Austria of those years, speechless even in the cultural scene, where the language tended to be gross and harsh, I wanted to show somebody who can articulate [as Franz West does]."[33]

Franz West's narrative account of inter-war Austria fills the inarticulate vacancy of this national "speechlessness", "articulating" (in the double sense of "speaking of" and "joining together") that which contemporary Austria is unable to, or refuses to, express. His narrative provisionally restores to language that which had hitherto been unutterable, exposing to analysis a crucial dimension of the nation's political unconscious and radically redefining the contours of Austria's archival imaginary. Christina Guenther calls *Return to Vienna* "Beckermann's project of historical restoration, an artistic reconstruction".[34] Through its implicit echoing of the practices of psychoanalysis (Franz's narrative exposing the buried 'unconscious' of the contemporary nation), Beckermann's film appears as a diagnostic or excavatory text, concerned with both "restoring" a lost (destroyed) past and pursuing through the technique of the "talking cure" a psychoanalytic investigation of a nation characterised by repression and unacknowledged residual historical traumas.

Returning, remembering

Return to Vienna alludes in its title to (and thus remembers) a long literary and cinematic tradition of "returns to Vienna", from Stefan Zweig's 1914 *feuilleton* "Heimfahrt nach Österreich" (relating his journey home from Ostend to Austria on the eve of World War I) and his later "Going Home to Austria" (a chapter in *The World of Yesterday: Memoirs of a European*, published posthumously after Zweig's suicide in 1942), to journalist and essayist Hilde Spiel's memoir *Rückkehr nach Wien*, translated as *Return to Vienna: A Journal* (which recounts her return to Austria from England in 1946).[35] Hillary Hope Herzog, defining this "slim genre of *Rückkehrliteratur* (the literature of return)", calls it "a special variant of exile literature",[36] an epithet that captures some of the complexities of Franz's narrative. The genre extends to film: Anne Ziegler and Webster Booth performed the duet "You Will Return to Vienna" in' *Waltz Time* (1945), a British film (and an early extra-territorial prototype of the cloying nostalgia of the post-war Austrian 'Heimatfilm', discussed in Chapter 5) made by Vienna-born German Paul L. Stein, who emigrated to Britain in 1931 to escape Nazism after working in Berlin and the US. The dramatic film trilogy *Wohin und zurück* (*Where to and Back*) by Axel Corti, the first part of which was made in 1982 (thus predating *Return to Vienna*), deals specifically with the Jewish–Austrian experience of exile and return.[37] Beckermann's film adds to this tradition, stepping back inside what Ingeborg Bachmann calls the city's "monstrous past"[38] in a variety of ways – historically and geographically (opening and closing with the view from the window of a moving train, arriving into Vienna at the start, departing the city at the end, so that the body of the movie offers a passage through the city and through a particular sequence of events during a particular moment in history); but also thematically, symbolically and ideologically, in the sense that the film (re-) constructs a version of historical, inter-war Vienna as a chronotope, employing a variety of narrative and visual/auditory cues to convey the dense, contextual particularity of the time and place represented.

The film's framing narrative voice (that of actor Paula Loew) stages two distinct and actual "returns" to the city. Eight minutes in, the opening narration relates Franz Weintraub's family background and origins, recording that he was born in Magdeburg, Germany in 1909 and that the family "returned to Vienna" in 1924 when he was aged 14; at historical and biographical moment of "return" Franz's narrative begins. The framing narrator summarises his personal history after 1934 – his being arrested and imprisoned (we see three police mugshots of a young Franz, dated 6.10.1934); his later becoming a leading member of the now illegal Communist Party; and, after the Anschluß in 1938, his being hunted by the Gestapo, and escape via Prague and Paris to England. He then worked on an Austrian refugee committee in London and took the name West "which he kept on his return to Austria (zurück nach Österreich) in October 1945". Now (in 1983), we're told, he lives in Vienna working (like Beckermann) on a history of the Austrian labour movement. Two "returns" to the city thus frame the events of Franz's narrative; the rhythm of departure-return brackets the unsettling, destabilised historical period and the eventual horrors of non-returning departure that he recounts.

Despite his ostensible focus on working-class political life, Franz foregrounds from early on his Jewishness, reframing conventional myths of Viennese culture from this perspective, which is initiated in the film's opening segment, depicting a contemporary analogue of the arrival by train in Vienna of the travelling Jewish citizen of the Habsburg empire and its chaotic aftermath. This sequence is followed by contemporary footage of the city, and particularly images of the Prater, the city's vast amusement park with its signature Ferris wheel, the Riesenrad, a deeply resonant location in Viennese film history[39] (Figure 2.2). As the train arrives into Vienna at the beginning of the film, the framing narrative begins at the moment the Ferris wheel comes into view from the left, and the first words spoken are "Das Riesenrad ...", as the framing narration begins:

> The Ferris wheel was the first impression of Vienna for many thousands of Jews arriving in the residential city from all parts of the monarchy via the northern rail line. Most found a place to stay in Leopoldstadt, near the Prater and the North Railway Station. The apartments were cheaper here than in the other districts, and a decisive factor was the presence of other Jews, relatives, people from the same town, people who could help, who were already living here. Here the climate of the old homeland could still be felt everywhere.[40]

Figure 2.2 Ruth Beckermann (dir.), *Return to Vienna*, 1983.
© Ruth Beckermann Filmproduktion.

The symbolic, 'centrifugal' pull of the wheel is thus established. The narrator relates broad historical details about the comfort and assurance offered by the city's second district, the Leopoldstadt, to arriving Jewish migrants – a sense of community, of shared culture and history, and often of family ties, centring on the image of the Ferris wheel.

This opening situates *Return to Vienna* in relation to a long tradition of Austrian cinematic uses of the Prater coinciding with the history of the nation's film industry – as Michael Burri states, "The first booths to show films in 1896 helped stake the park's claim as Vienna's birthplace of the cinema theatre. It has remained a place for the projection of dreams and desires."[41] From Willy-Schmidt Gentner's romance *Prater* (1936), starring Magda Schneider (mother of Romy Schneider), to its role in Max Ophüls' Hollywood noir *Letter from an Unknown Woman* (1948) and Ernst Schmidt Jr's examination of the park's audiences in his experimental film *P.R.A.T.E.R.* (1963–6), the park constitutes a complex cinematic *topos*, elements of which *Return to Vienna* uses in developing its own narrative base, 'returning' to cinematic tradition just as it returns to the literary tradition of returning to Vienna.[42] The rotating Ferris wheel, in particular, became an international cinema icon thanks to its prominence in Carol Reed's *The Third Man* (1949), and made regular appearances in Austrian '*Heimatfilme*' of the 1950s, a tradition to which *Return to Vienna* ironically alludes.[43]

A resonant introductory motif for a film about remembering, the Prater's Riesenrad also works, within the film's retrospective relation to history, as a powerful symbol of foreboding. It was opened in 1897, to mark the 50th anniversary of the rule of Emperor Franz Joseph, by Gabor Steiner (1858–1944), a Jewish theatre director and entrepreneur who had also, in 1895, bought a cinématographe from the Lumière brothers and opened Vienna's first cinema (a sadly unsuccessful enterprise). Another of Steiner's projects was *Venedig in Wien*, a huge reconstruction in the Prater of a mechanical simulated Venice, and (in its early days) "by far the most important entertainment venue in all of Vienna", regularly attended by (among others) the city's anti-Semitic mayor Karl Lueger.[44] The wheel quickly became an important part of the cityscape and cultural life for some Viennese communities ("it became a tradition in Vienna", notes Norman D. Anderson in his history of Ferris wheels, "that [Catholic] children, for a treat after their first Communion, should be taken on [a] carriage ride in the Prater, and then as a grand climax, for a ride on the Giant Wheel").[45] The Riesenrad was "Aryanised" (i.e. stolen) by the Nazis after the Anschluß in 1938 and its Jewish owner, a Prague-born merchant called Eduard Steiner (unrelated to Gabor), was killed in Auschwitz in 1944.[46]

Like Brecht's *Arbeitsjournal*, the Riesenrad is a potent and complex image, embedding a series of conflicting connotations which will overshadow much of the film's subsequent content. It condenses the major motifs of Franz's narrative and of *Return to Vienna* – the circularity of return alongside the intersecting significances accruing to history and memory, leisure and politics, image and narrative, social and private spaces. The initial sense of Vienna's (implicitly) ambivalent hospitality to incoming Jewish citizens is immediately undermined further by Franz's narrative. His first words accompany a series of aerial shots of the Pater from the Ferris wheel, and immediately puncture the preconceptions implied by the opening narration about being Jewish in interwar Vienna:

Since the whole of the second district was from the viewpoint of Nazi provocation automatically considered a Jewish district and one could always expect Jews in the main avenue, we often experienced, and were told even more often, that Nazi groups, groups of Nazi youths, who left the Wurstelprater [the funfair], came up the main avenue often with megaphones, and shouted "Jews out", stormed out and shouted "Heil Hitler". And that repeatedly led to some panic.[47]

Franz quickly recalibrates the conventional construction of the Prater as a place of leisurely or homely safety and relaxation by emphasising its vulnerable openness and its obvious concentration of the city's Jewish population, making it a prime and easy target for marauding Nazi gangs.[48] He notes in addition that the nearby Zur weißen Rose (To the White Rose) restaurant was a regular meeting place for the Nazis; he recalls their chants of "jagt die falschen Wiener in die Bukovina" ["chase the false Viennese back to Bukovina"], and their frequent physical attacks on young socialists. These assertions quickly establish the specifics of personal experience rather than general perceptions. Franz's voice offers detailed recollection that perceives Austria's Nazi past not as a history to be erased or repressed, but as the remembered experience of a condition of constant and gradually increasing threat to himself and his community. This corrective rhetorical manoeuvre characterises the history related in *Return to Vienna*, emphasising the transformation of Vienna (and Austria) from a place of welcoming, cosmopolitan hospitality to one of dangerous, nationalistic hostility and of Jewish "unbelonging".

Franz's opening speech is followed by a montage of still images and archive footage of old Leopoldstadt (many reproduced in Beckermann's book *Die Mazzesinsel*) – the railway station, tramlines, the Riesenrad, the Tegetthoff Statue on the Praterstern, shots of the bustling and crowded urban cityscape, a street violinist, the entrance to a synagogue, scrolling right to left just as the camera had recorded the train's arrival in Vienna – accompanied by the melancholy descending single piano notes of Erich Meixner's *Stummfilmmusik* (Meixner was a member of Die Schmetterlinge, who performed in the Arena occupation in 1976). We see a brief moment of Franz working at his desk, before his narrative proper begins with an establishment shot of him sitting, Beckermann and Aichholzer facing him, in his office. Beckermann asks: "Wie waren so ihre ersten Eindrücke nach eurer Ankunft in Wien?" ("What were your first impressions on arriving in Vienna?"). Emphasising his family's largely assimilationist sense of Jewish identity, Franz quickly foregrounds his ethnic Jewishness as the basis of his experience of difference, expressed as a complex awareness of change and estrangement rapidly transforming into community identification:

> Coming to Vienna was of course a complete change from my life in Magdeburg. At first we were complete strangers, which made me realize quite quickly that the situation had changed and that this related to my Jewishness. After two or three days walking up and down in the building where I lived, seeing the people there, seeing name tags, that's the first time I became aware – in contrast with my apartment in the Tränsberg district of Magdeburg, where Weintraub was the only Jew far and wide – that there were a lot of Jewish families, Jewish children. Then I came to school, completely alien from the children, the boys who I didn't know. But even there – the second, third day showed that ... it was almost like I had to look around to find a Christian, because of course with this strong Jewish peer group, those who crowded around me were Jews. That was indeed completely different.[49]

In Germany, Franz's Jewishness needed to be concealed, hidden. In the Leopoldstadt, by contrast, nearly everyone was Jewish so there was no longer any need for such secrecy:

> We didn't try to disappear. [...] I remember the time in Magdeburg, where for as long as possible you didn't draw attention to your Jewishness. So perhaps one hid oneself as such. There was no need to do that [in Leopoldstadt], and it was hardly possible anyway.[50]

This "difference" defines the atmosphere of belonging experienced by his family in Vienna, a climate also evident in the sounds in the streets of different German accents from various origins, which he calls "einen neuen Klang der Sprache" ("A new sound in the language").[51]

The cosmopolitan "difference" of Vienna (its distinction from the near-mono-ethnic Magdeburg) was also, of course, the "difference", accrued by the wealthy (or, at least, wealthier) capital city that distinguished it from the rest of Austria, a distinction over which Beckermann's film, with its more-or-less exclusive focus on life in the capital, largely elides. Vienna, persisting as a disproportionately large imperial capital of a country dramatically truncated in the wake of the Habsburg collapse (Beckermann calls the Vienna of 1919 "the oversized capital of a starving republic"),[52] existed in a problematic residual relation to Austria's provinces. Hilde Spiel notes that the "ethnic diversity" of the city made it "an exact microcosm of the lost Habsburg empire".[53] But ethnic and ideological tensions largely imperceptible in (although by no means absent from) the city were rife elsewhere in the country, manifest in ways that would later come to define key elements of Austria's post-1945 fantasy of its own history, as Lisa Silverman argues:

> From the viewpoint of the provinces, interwar Vienna loomed large as a dangerous 'Jewish' metropolis – superficial, ugly, crass, corrupt, depraved, socialist, capitalist, materialist, decadent, modern, and immoral, depending on the demands of political or cultural expediency. In turn, the provinces functioned as the site of all that was pure, good, beautiful, respectable, and moral – values that many sought to include in a new 'Austrian' sensibility. [...] Vienna's Jews were to Vienna as Vienna was to Austria: a critical symbol as 'Other' necessary for self-definition. Vienna had already been coded internally as 'Christian', thanks to *fin-de-siècle* mayor Karl Lueger, whose well-known political antisemitism furthered the divide between 'Jew' and 'non-Jew.'[54]

Part of *Return to Vienna's* critique centres on the destructive permeation of Vienna's progressive cosmopolitanism by the provincial ideological values of the rest of Austria. In Franz's recollections, the spaces of the city – streets, cafés, the university, the tram – become potential sites of violent, hostile encounter, transformed by the constant seepage of conservative provincial attitudes into the ostensibly liberal metropolitan space. Asked by Beckermann whether he encountered anti-Semitism, he replies "Ununterbrochen" ["Constantly"]; he narrates a specific incident in which he was attacked by a mob of Nazis outside the university. Such events, in which the experience of (ethnic, class) difference transforms into that of actual and violent conflict, are interconnected symbolically in Franz's memory as exemplars of the ways in which Vienna and its Jewish districts were rapidly transforming from places of safety and community into places of unbelonging and threat.

'Red Vienna' and anti-Semitism

The Viennese world to which Franz and his family return in 1924 from Magdeburg in Germany was one notable (again) for its *difference*, particularly in relation to his experience of being Jewish, but also for its political distinction. *Return to Vienna* returns historically (as the film's subtitle tells us) to the period between 1924 and 1934, during Austria's First Republic, but not to the golden-age high-cultural Vienna of art, literature, and psychoanalysis. Rather, the film returns to a city that was, as Gareth Dale notes, "the only European metropolis to be run by a labour party",[55] a city whose vibrant political and cultural life was deeply structured by its large Jewish community.

The utopian "experiment to create a working-class culture in the socialist enclave of Vienna",[56] known as 'Red Vienna' (an epithet enthusiastically reiterated by the Christian Democrats and other right-wing parties), emerged from the social and economic crises resulting from the demise of the Habsburg empire at the end of World War I. The Social Democratic Party (SPÖ) won a majority in the first post-war municipal council elections on 4 May 1919, which were also the first Austrian elections held under universal male and female suffrage. This historical moment constituted a hinge-point in Austrian history, "a crisis" (Alexandra Seibel argues) "generated by Viennese modernity [and] characterized by the asynchronicity of a monarchy that is dying out and a rapidly forming mass society".[57] Responding via social and economic policies to this sense of historical crisis, 'Red Vienna' lasted until February 1934, when a planned protest in the form of a general strike failed to materialise, and Austria collapsed into sixteen days of civil war, resulting in the dissolution of the First Republic and the imposition in May that year by the dictatorship of the Christian-Social Party's Engelbert Dollfuß (1892–1934) of a new, Catholic and (in imitation of Italy, with whom the Austrian government hoped to cosy up to resist the advances of Nazi Germany) corporatist–fascist Constitution. Dollfuß had already outlawed the Austrian Social Democratic, Communist and Nazi parties, and would be assassinated in an attempted Nazi coup on 25 July 1934. The rise of Nazism thus killed off the experiment of 'Red Vienna', leading to the establishment of Austro-fascism and then Nazism.

Responding to the dire economic conditions in the wake of World War I, the socialist Viennese leaders taxed luxury goods and services to fund a variety of progressive socialist economic and cultural policies. Writing in 1927, Hungarian politician and journalist Zsigmond Kunfi described this as "forcing the rich to dip into their surpluses and contribute to a generous welfare and culture policy".[58] These taxes included the "Breitner tax" Franz mentions in Beckermann's film, named after Vienna's finance councillor Hugo Breitner, which raised revenues to support carefully and transparently costed improvements in public health, women's rights, and education (with the encouragement of worker participation in sports, cinema, and high-cultural activities like theatre and the arts); and the funding and development of new municipal social housing projects like the Karl-Marx-Hof (1927–30) and Karl-Seitz-Hof (1926–33), the modern architectural forms of which (Helmut Gruber argues) "contributed to a sense of political power among the workers, encouraged by the socialist leaders, that was more apparent than real".[59] Gruber emphasises that 'Red Vienna' was a social-democratic project, based on "the principle of proletarian democracy, which allowed the socialists to bind the communists and other radical groups to decisions by majority rule".[60] Consequently (Gruber contends) the Communist party (KPÖ) (with which Franz West is most closely aligned during the period of which he narrates, and which he later joins) "remained a sect throughout the period".[61]

A complicating factor in the 'Red Vienna' narrative was the persistence in the city of dangerously reactionary forces, particularly those of anti-Semitism, which (as Franz West details) worked constantly to expose and exploit differences within the metropolitan community. As early as September 1919, a decree aimed mainly at Jewish war refugees demanded the expulsion from Austria of former imperial citizens lacking Austrian residency rights,[62] and in 1923 the University of Vienna closed temporarily "due to anti-Semitic unrest",[63] a moment Bruce F. Pauley considers "the climax of the early post-war period in Austria so far as anti-Semitism was concerned".[64] More widely, as Steven Beller argues, "The culture clash between the Jewish modern culture of 1900 Vienna and the conservative culture of the rest of Austrian society had only been exacerbated by war and the ensuing crisis."[65]

Pervasive anti-Semitism was thus one consequence of Austria's 'imperial trauma' resulting from the collapse of the Habsburg regime. Jewish people lived in 'Red Vienna' in a condition of permanent threat, as the editors of the *Red Vienna Sourcebook* point out:

> While the Red Vienna era was tumultuous for all Viennese citizens, Vienna's Jewish inhabitants experienced the years of the First Republic in a state of perpetual crisis. World War I unleashed a violent anti-Semitic tempest against the Jewish populations of wide swaths of Eastern Europe, including Jewish citizens of former crown lands such as Galicia and Bukovina.[66]

In his history of café culture and Jewish life, Sachar M. Pinsker comments that, around the *fin-de-siècle*,

> Jewish migration and acculturation occurred in the context of conflicting ideologies and political movements that merged in the cafés of Vienna. At the same time, cafés became identified as 'Jewish spaces', as well as breeding grounds for literary and artistic modernism.[67]

Lisa Silverman summarises the extensive contribution of this immigrating Jewish population to the political and cultural machinery of Red Vienna:

> Modern dance, music, and literature continued to thrive, and the city became a site of unprecedented initiatives in housing, education, culture, and public works programs—of which Jews were often at the forefront. The overwhelming majority of Viennese Jews voted for the Social Democratic Party in both municipal and national elections. Jews also comprised nearly 80 percent of the movement's intellectual leadership as well as the majority of socialist student organizations and editors of socialist publications.[68]

Furthermore, Beller emphasises the extensive Jewish contribution to Austrian popular mass culture" and a significant but largely "unarticulated" contribution to Viennese operetta.[69] Writing of Vienna's Jews in the interwar period, Beckermann comments that "they contributed to the unique ambiance of 'Red Vienna' as the most enthusiastic adherents of the intellectual and messianic Austro-Marxist movement, which (like psychoanalysis and Zionism) had evolved at the time of a specifically Viennese Jewish identity crisis of the *fin de siècle*".[70]

The social and political experiment in working-class culture was, then, heavily influenced by, and deeply enmeshed with, the Viennese Jewish community, leading in turn to that community's "crisis of identity", a crisis Franz's narrative articulates through recounting tensions between his progressive political identification with social-democratic and socialist ideas, and the traditionalist pull of residual religious and other traditions that still organised aspects of his family's lives, alongside his ethnic identity which, in the end, was definitive. One effect of Beckermann's film is to recalibrate the utopian history of 'Red Vienna' through Franz's developing awareness of the significance of his Jewish-Austrian, alongside his working-class socialist, identity and experience, so that Jewish experience of the period arguably emerges, by the film's end, as the principal and (with hindsight) most historically significant one.

After a long passage detailing his family's experiences of Jewish life in Germany and Vienna, Franz makes little mention of this extensive cultural enmeshment between Jewish and non-Jewish communities at the level of cultural production and seems largely to underplay the significance of his family's Jewishness. His principal interests, he stresses, were politics and football (he was a fan of the "Violets', who became "Austria", the club identified most with the city's coffee house culture and its intelligentsia), and his deep, active involvement in the politics of this period provides much of the ideological texture of *Return to Vienna*. His investment in the cultural excitement of 'Red Vienna', and his complex awareness of the multitude of potentials of the time, establish a subtle tension throughout his narrative between the forward-looking, future-oriented utopianism of Viennese democratic socialism in the interwar years, and the retrospective act of remembering, of looking back from the early 1980s from the perspective of an elderly Jewish survivor. This tension modulates, as events in the intervening period between remembered and remembering gradually take shape, while the film progresses towards the related but distinct performance of *remembrance* as a commemoration of lost futures. Echoing and sustaining this critical ambivalence, Gruber's history of the socialist experiment of 'Red Vienna' pointedly begins with a chapter titled "Obituary for Austrian Socialism".

15 July 1927

The central episode of Franz's recollections, and arguably of the film, is his account of the events of 15 July 1927, a pivotal and deeply traumatic moment in inter-war Austrian history, arguably the beginning of the end of 'Red Vienna', and an event in which he recalls participating directly. Known as the "Julirevolte" (July revolt) or "Wiener Justizpalastbrand" (the burning of the Palace of Justice), the events on this day illustrate the fragmented and confused complexities of Austrian politics of the time, being triggered by a sequence of incidents outside the capital, thus exemplifying in microcosm the process by which the city's progressive metropolitanism and cosmopolitanism were by the late 1920s being contaminated and corroded by elements deriving from reactionary Austrian provincialism.

On 30 January 1927, in the Social-Democratic stronghold of Schattendorf in Burgenland (in eastern Austria), a demonstration by the left-wing Republikanischer Schutzbünd (Republican Protection League) was confronted by members of the right-wing Frontkämpfervereinigung Deutsch-Österreichs (the German-Austrian Frontline Soldier's Union) who opened fire, killing a disabled Croatian veteran and an 8-year-old child.[71] Three men of the Soldier's Union were tried for murder but, on 14 July, were acquitted by a Viennese court. Viennese workers rapidly organised protests and, on 15 July, a mass demonstration in the city resulted in the burning of the Palace of Justice during "the most violent urban riots Austria had experienced since March 1848".[72] Police chief Johann Schober responded by deploying armed officers who were ordered to shoot at the crowd, resulting in 89 dead (including several city officials) and 120 seriously injured. During these events, Vienna's Palace of Justice was burned down by arsonists.

Franz's narrative account of the events of 15 July, dynamised by complementary montages of still and moving images, details his involvement in the demonstrations on this day, which, he recalls, began as a normal summer's day. He recollects in remarkable detail what he wore, and that he was on his way to visit friends in Glockengasse or Czerningasse (two streets just west of the Prater, connected by Rotensterngasse [Red Star Street]) when he encountered a group of people he recognised as workers by their clothes, from whom he learned of the acquittal of the murderers. This part of his narrative is accompanied by still shots and archive footage of the burning Palace of Justice, and of the crowd suddenly scattering in front of Café Raimund on Volksgartenstraße, opposite the Volkstheatre and minutes from the Parliament and Rathaus. The film shows photographs of police shooting at the fleeing crowd. Franz recalls his fear and his disbelief that such events could happen in Vienna and realised quickly that the 15 July riot heralded a fundamental change in Austrian politics. At this point the film cuts to archive footage of lines of helmeted Heimwehr troops marching with batons, intercut with shots of protesters holding banners and posters. No music or narrative voice accompanies this montage; silence marks the moment of historical rupture in *Return to Vienna* as a climactic opposition between different configurations of social power. Franz's narrative of these events is organised by tensions between individual and social experience, and between immediate, rational perception, and emotional confusion; his carefully ordered recollections are of fear and confusion, precisely those elements of perception that resist easy narrative sequentialisation.

Two major (and deeply contrasting) texts of the early 1930s by major Vienna-based writers – Sigmund Freud's *Civilisation and Its Discontents* (1930) and Elias Canetti's *Die Blendung* (translated as *Auto da Fé*; 1935, written 1931) – respond with varying degrees of directness to the 15 July events.[73] Franz's narrative bears comparison in particular with Canetti's, himself also caught up in the protesting crowds that day. Canetti, like Franz West, had arrived in Vienna from Germany in 1924 (beginning his university studies there), and (again, like Franz) recalls the 15 July events over 50 years later, in his written memoir *Die Fackel im Ohr* (*The Torch in my Ear*), published a few years before *Return to Vienna* in 1980. He differs markedly from Franz, however, in showing little interest in the politics behind the event. Instead, his attention is focussed on a theoretical analysis of his life-changing experience of the *crowd* on that day, which profoundly influenced his major work *Masse und Macht* (*Crowds and Power*, 1960). Despite their shared secular Jewishness, Viennese residency, and being highly cultured and skilful narrators, Canetti and Franz West occupy radically different class positions. Canetti's high-bourgeois lifestyle contrasts with Franz's working-class precarity, while the latter's political convictions distance him from the mainly aesthetic and cultural themes that preoccupy Canetti. Their shared proximity amid the masses that gathered on 15 July, however, and above all their emotional responses to the experience, imply an affective commonality transcending these differences; Franz's feeling "terribly afraid" is echoed in Canetti's "I was dreadfully frightened, especially" of the corpses of those shot by the police.[74]

Die Mazzesinsel

Return to Vienna closes (as we've seen) with Franz's recounting the fates of various members of his extended family, an indirect recollection of the experience of the Holocaust which he himself escaped. The segment starts with Franz inserting a cassette tape into a player, having recorded this section of his reminiscences the evening before. Lorenz considers this closing monologue a kind of "Kaddish", the Jewish prayer in praise of God while mourning for the dead.[75] "Leaving behind the city", writes Christina Guenther of this sequence, "enshrouded in darkness, and the memory of the Leopoldstadt of the 1920s and 30s, we are reminded of the transitoriness and destruction of that geo-culture and time."[76]

Echoing a sequence in Chantal Akerman's *News from Home* (1976) depicting the view from a moving New York subway train, the overwhelming message of the closing passage of *Return to Vienna* concerns history's movement into moral and political darkness. The decline into night of the cinematic image of the city reinforces the sense of the failure of the image itself, its absence at this moment of historical crisis. While narrative persists, the image of the past, *Return to Vienna* suggests, has been lost, erased. The challenge of this suggestion is taken up in Beckermann's book *Die Mazzesinsel* published in 1984, a year after *Return to Vienna*, which features many of the still images included in the film (Figure 2.3), and is explicitly concerned with recuperating fragments of a shattered history as a repository of cultural memory.[77]

Formally distinct from *Return to Vienna* by presenting a collage of textual and image fragments rather than a sequential narrative, *Die Mazzesinsel* (a descriptive nickname for Vienna's Leopoldstadt district, located between the Danube and the Danube Canal) nevertheless shares the film's concern with archive retrieval and

Figure 2.3 Ruth Beckermann (dir.), *Return to Vienna*, 1983.
© Ruth Beckermann Filmproduktion; Ruth Beckermann (ed.),
'*Läden in der Tandelmarktgasse 8. 1903*', *Die Mazzesinsel*, p. 52.

recuperation. The book documents Jewish life in the Leopoldstadt
during 'Red Vienna', from 1918 to 1938 (expanding the historical range of Franz West's narrative), through photographs, extracts
from literary texts, and images of cultural ephemera – newspaper
clippings, drawings and sketches, propaganda leaflets, and advertising (Figure 2.4). Excerpts offering diverse descriptions and accounts
are presented from texts by numerous writers active during the
interwar years, including Canetti, Joseph Roth, Franz Marek,
Martha Hofmann and Rosel Bardin, alongside extracts from some
of those interviewed by Beckermann while researching *Return to
Vienna* (like Joshua Blumenfeld and Josef Toch). The photographs
depict street scenes, landmarks and monuments (like the Tegetthoff
monument mentioned earlier),[78] buildings and shop fronts, alleys
and urban gardens, cramped and poverty-stricken domestic interiors; or family groups and school classes, people celebrating the
Sabbath, busy fruit and vegetable markets, street musicians, men
playing football, and portraits of individuals like the actor Heinrich
Eisenbach (1870–1923) (alongside Felix Salten's appreciation of

him).[79] Many of these images are undated or ascribed a rough historical provenance. This changes in the final thirteen pages, which present mostly dated photographs of the Nazi terror beginning in March 1938 – images of men painting anti-Semitic slogans on shopfronts, of Jewish men forced by Nazi thugs to scrub the streets clean while crowds of smiling Austrians look on, of synagogues and schools destroyed by acts of arson, and the book's final image, of the Café Rembrandt daubed with the Star of David and the word "Jud" scrawled on its wall. "Buckets and toothbrushes and smiling faces", writes Beckermann, "ended the local history of the Mazzesinsel once and for all."[80]

This essay (also titled "Die Mazzesinsel") establishes the photographic image as the basis of Beckermann's attempt to reconstruct from surviving fragments a version of this historical community and its lifestyle which were, she writes (using a word repeated in her interview with Rebhandl), "destroyed".[81] She focusses on family photographs as records of loss, images working not as vehicles of remembrance but as evidence of destruction. In doing so, Beckermann completes the shift from addressing (in her earlier documentaries) class politics and working-class history, to

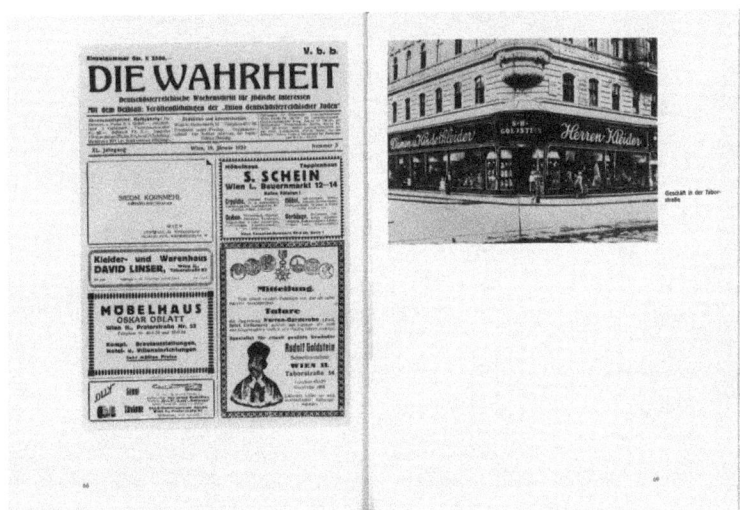

Figure 2.4 Ruth Beckermann (ed.), *Die Mazzesinsel*, pp. 68–9.

exploring the intersectionalities of Jewish cultural history – a shift also from the impersonality of the class-political to a more subjectively oriented (auto-)biographical exploration of the political-as-personal. The essay starts with a description of a family portrait which is reproduced (but uncaptioned) on the first page of the essay (Figure 2.5). Occupying the top half of the page, the picture shows an anonymous family group of nine people, three men, five women and a child, arranged (as Beckermann notes) with "the men protectively on the edge, the most beautiful woman as an eye-catcher in the middle, the youngest between the old".[82] It is the (dis)location of this image from its intended or "natural" ["natür-lichen"] social and historical function (by extension, the condition it shares with the other images in the book) that concerns Beckermann. A family document handed down the generations, a source of alienated or "distanced curiosity" for children and grandchildren marvelling at the old-fashioned styles of dress,[83] the photograph has become also a memento of a destroyed way of life, a token of a "story not told" – both Marianne Hirsch's

Figure 2.5 Anonymous, Family portrait, Ruth Beckermann (ed.), *Die Mazzesinsel*, p. 8.

photograph as "chronicle" of "family rituals"[84] and a document (Beckermann argues) of their violent displacement and destruction: "Family albums went around the world, and to the concentration camps. In a cupboard in Jerusalem one may find sumptuous silk and velvet albums and faded little booklets with tiny, jagged-edged photographs from [*aus*] Dachau. Nobody knows who they belonged to."[85]

The physical and geographical displacement of such documents generates a corresponding generic displacement from family portrait to what Walter Benjamin famously described (referring to Eugène Atget's photographs) as a record of "a crime scene".[86] Beckermann's essay documents this 'crime' by focusing on that which is recorded in the images and prose passages but absent from the present – prominent elements of life in the cafés and synagogues of the Leopoldstadt, presented with a hindsight that allows the perception of material absences, or "gaps", standing symbolically for moments of violent historical erasure:

> On summer evenings, the singsong of the prayers drifts from the open windows. Sometimes one looks down at a large, wildly overgrown vacant lot [*Baulücke*] – the place where once stood a synagogue, the Schiffschul, now a memorial to the eradication. Here, on Kristallnacht, the Nazi fury raged, on windows and chandeliers, before it turned on the people. The gap [*Die Lücke*], the story of which is not told on the red-white flagged boards which normally narrate historical monuments, is ephemeral [*vergänglich*, transitory, transient] like our memory of the victims. Grass has already grown over it. Soon a new house will stand in its place.
>
> Here and there a trace [*Spur*], which leads nowhere.[87]

This rhetoric of gaps, vacancies and absences, untold experience and fragmentary traces, powerfully focusses the post-memorial sense of loss that both frames and permeates *Return to Vienna* and *Die Mazzesinsel*, becoming in subsequent works a foundational trope of Beckermann's developing art as it seeks multiple routes of passage through erased, repressed, or elided histories in an extended effort of retrieval.

Exhibited as an annex to, but separate from, a key Viennese cultural event of 1984, the Künstlerhaus photographic exhibition and catalogue *Versunkene Welt* (*Sunken World*) comprising

Figure 2.6 The seventh year of Chajes-Gymnasium, 1931, as reproduced in Ruth Beckermann (ed.), *Die Mazzesinsel*, pp. 116–17.

"close to 400 pictures of Austrian and East European Jews" curated by Joachim Riedl, and accompanied by a film festival and an academic conference,[88] *Die Mazzesinsel* bequeathed a significant intertextual legacy. French artist Christian Boltanski used an image from the book (of the 1931 seventh year of Chajes Gymnasium [grammar school])[89] as the source of the enlarged portraits in his installation *Autel de lycée Chases* (1987) (Figure 2.6). Beckermann's text thus influences the inauguration of an extended process of Austrian and wider cultural anamnesia and retrieval. Like *Return to Vienna*, its 'returning' to Vienna's history is both nostalgic and insistently forward-looking, inserting into Austrian cultural memory the suppressed, ostensibly "missing images" of a counter-history that, until the early 1980s, had remained largely unrecalled, unspoken in post-war Austrian culture, and, in the process, transforming that culture. In her next film, Beckermann expands on her own family narratives and their proximity to this recuperated history.

Notes

1 Helen Epstein, *Children of the Holocaust: Conversations with Sons and Daughters of Survivors* (New York: Penguin/Putnam, 1979), p. 11.

2 "Das war nicht mein Sonderschicksal. Meine jüdischen Freunde und Kollegen, viele hunderte tausende, können Ähnliches erzählen – schon lang her, viel Zeit ist vergangen – man weiß nicht mehr viel davon und es gibt viele, die nichts mehr davon wissen wollen. Deshalb ist es doch gut, wenn man ab und zu davon spricht, daran erinnert, was das für eine Zeit war in der man damals gelebt hat."

3 Ruth Kluger, *Landscapes of Memory: A Holocaust Girlhood Remembered* (London: Bloomsbury, 2003), p. 7. *Mishpokke* is Yiddish for 'family'.

4 The title has been translated by scholars as *Matzo Island*, but the term refers to a district in Vienna, so we have decided to stay with Beckermann's original title.

5 West published a short written account of his experiences online. See Franz West "Man war in etwas drinnen, das eine neue Welt schaffen sollte", *Dokumentationsarchiv des österreichischen Widerstandes*, at www.doew.at/erinnern/biographien/erzaehlte-geschichte/erste-republik/franz-west-man-war-in-etwas-drinnen-das-eine-neue-welt-schaffen-sollte (accessed 22 November 2023).

6 For an extended discussion of this myth and its effects, see Hella Pick, *Guilty Victim: Austria from the Holocaust to Haider* (London: I. B. Tauris, 2000).

7 Heidemarie Uhl, "From Victim Myth to Co-Responsibility Thesis: Nazi Rule, World War II, and the Holocaust in Austrian Memory", in Richard New Lebow, Wulf Kansteiner and Claudio Fogu (eds), *The Politics of Memory in Postwar Europe* (Durham, NC: Duke University Press, 2006), pp. 40–78; p. 60.

8 "In diesem Land wurde nach 1945 weder die Verstrickung der Österreicher in den Nationalsozialismus noch die Problematik eines Zusammenlebens von Juden und Nichtjuden nach Auschwitz öffentlich diskutiert. [...] Von der Beziehung zwischen Österreichern und Juden spricht man nicht." Beckermann, *Unzugehörig*, p. 18.

9 Marjorie Perloff, *The Vienna Paradox: A Memoir* (New York: New Directions, 2004), p. 7.

10 Joseph W. Moser, "*Bockerer / Der Bockerer*", in Robert von Dassanowsky (ed.), *World Film Locations: Vienna* (London: Intellect, 2012), p. 80.

11 See Susan Rubin Suleiman, *Crises of Memory and the Second World War* (Cambridge, MA: Harvard University Press, 2006), pp. 43–4.

12 Ruth Beckermann, "Beyond the Bridges" (trans. Dagmar C. G. Lorenz), in Lorenz and Gabriele Weinberger (eds), *Insiders and Outsiders: Jewish and Gentile Culture in Germany and Austria* (Detroit: Wayne State University Press, 1994), p. 301.

13 Egon Schwarz, "Austria, Quite a Normal Nation", *New German Critique* No. 93 (Autumn, 2004), 177.

14 Bertolt Brecht, *Arbeitsjournal 1938–1955* (ed. Werner Hecht) (Berlin: Suhrkamp, 1973); *Journals 1934–1955* (trans. Hugh Rorrison, ed. John Willett) (London: Methuen, 1993).

15 See Fredric Jameson, *Brecht and Method* (London: Verso, 1988), p. 43.

16 "Interview with Rebhandl", 2007.

17 Jorge Semprun, *Literature or Life* (trans. Linda Coverdale) (New York: Viking, 1997), p. 13.

18 Jameson, *Brecht and Method*, p. 43.

19 Marianne Hirsch, *Family Frames: Photography, Narrative, and Postmemory* (Cambridge, MA: Harvard University Press, 1997), p. 33.

20 Annette Insdorf, *Indelible Shadows: Film and the Holocaust* (Cambridge: Cambridge University Press, 2010), pp. 300 ff.

21 Christina Guenther, "The Politics of Location in Ruth Beckermann's 'Vienna Films'", *Modern Austrian Literature* Vol. 37 No. 3/4 (2004), 33–46: 35.

22 "Später dann auf der Universität … vielleicht ist das einer der bösen Dinge gewesen, daß man so innerlich immer wieder verletzt war, aber gelernt hat mit dem Antisemitismus als normale Erscheinungsform zu leben."

23 "Interview with Rebhandl", 2007.

24 Débora G. Kantor and Ruth Beckermann, "Ruth Beckermann: Documentarian of the Present", *Jewish Film and New Media: An International Journal* Vol. 8 No. 2 (2020), 226–38; 229. Beckermann discusses her use of "archival footage" in this interview with explicit reference to *The Waldheim Waltz*, in which she uses material from her own archive (pp. 233–4).

25 "Interview with Rebhandl", 2007.

26 "Interview with Rebhandl", 2007.

27 "Interview with Rebhandl", 2007. Beckerman is referring to exhibitions like *Mit uns zieht die neue Zeit: Arbeiterkultur in Österreich 1918–1934*, held at the Österreichische Gesellschaft für Kulturpolitik and the Meidlinger Kulturkreis in der Straßenbahn-Remises, Vienna, 23 January–3 May 1981.

28 Beckermann, "Beyond the Bridges", p. 304. See also "Die Mazzesinsel", *Die Mazzesinsel*, p. 12.

29 Beckermann, "Interview with Rebhandl", 2007.

30 Pick, *Guilty Victim*, p. 222.

31 Sigmund Freud, "The Psychotherapy of Hysteria", in Freud and Joseph Breuer, *Studies on Hysteria, The Pelican Freud Library Vol. 3* (ed. Angela Richards, trans. James and Alix Strachey) (Harmondsworth: Penguin, 1983), pp. 337–93; p. 340.

32 "In Ästen / staut sich schwarz / die Schwüle sprachloser Lieder." ("In branches / the swelter of speechless songs / chokes black"). Paul Celan, "Finsternis" ("Darkness"), in John Felstiner (ed. and trans.), *Selected Poems and Prose of Paul Celan* (New York: W. W. Norton, 2001), pp. 12–13.

33 "Interview with Rebhandl", 2007.

34 Guenther, "The Politics of Location in Ruth Beckermann's 'Vienna Films'", p. 37.

35 Stefan Zweig, "Heimfahrt nach Österreich", *Neue Freie Presse,* 1 August 1914, p. 1; *The World of Yesterday: Memoirs of a European* (trans. Anthea Bell) (London: Pushkin Press, 2009), pp. 305–27; Hilde Spiel, *Rückkehr nach Wien: Ein Tagebuch* (Vienna: Milena, 2009); *Return to Vienna – A Journal* (trans. Christine Shuttleworth) (London: Ariadne Press, 2011). In 1997 businessman Otto Binder (1910–2005) published his account of growing up in Red Vienna, his subsequent imprisonment by the Austro-fascist government, and incarceration in 1938 in Buchenwald and Dachau by the Nazis, under the title *Wien – Retour: Bericht an die Nachkommen Salzburg Buchenwald Stockholm* (Köln: Bohlau, 1997).

36 Hillary Hope Herzog, *Vienna Is Different: Jewish Writers in Austria from the Fin-de-siècle to the Present* (New York: Berghahn, 2011), p. 208.

37 Axel Corti, *Wohin und zurück – Teil 1: An uns glaubt Gott nicht mehr – Ferry oder Wie es war* (1982); *Wohin und zurück – Teil 2: Santa Fé* (1986); *Wohin und zurück – Teil 3: Welcome in Vienna* (1986).

38 "I am from Austria, from a small country that, to say it euphemistically, has tried to step outside history but has an overpowering, monstrous past." Ingeborg Bachmann, Interview with Joseph-Hermann Sauter, 15 September 1965, in *Wir müssen wahre Sätze finden: Gespräche und Interviews* (Munich: Piper, 1991), pp. 63–4. Translation by Marjorie Perloff.

39 See Todd Herzog, "Wonder Wheel: The Cinematic Prater", in von Dassanowsky (ed.), *World Film Locations: Vienna*, pp. 88–9. Herzog argues that the Prater, "Like cinema, [...] is a dream-machine, a desire-machine, a memory-machine, and a time-machine" (p. 89). See also Alexandra Seibel, *Visions of Vienna: Narrating the City in 1920s*

and 1930s Cinema (Amsterdam: Amsterdam University Press, 2017), pp. 28–35.

40 "Das Riesenrad war für viele tausende Juden der erste Eindruck von Wien, wenn sie mit der Nordbahn aus allen Teilen der Monarchie in die Residenzstadt kamen. Die meisten fanden in der Leopoldstadt eine erste Bleibe, in der Nähe des Praters und des Nordbahnhofs. Hier waren die Wohnungen billiger als in den anderen Bezirken und was das Entscheidende war – hier lebten schon andere Juden, Verwandte, Menschen aus dem gleichen Shtetl, Menschen die in der Fremde weiterhelfen konnten. Hier war das Klima der alten Heimat noch überall zu spüren."

41 Michael Burri, "*Prater* (1936)", in von Dassanowsky (ed.), *World Film Locations: Vienna*, p. 26.

42 See also *Praterbuben* (*Prater Boys*, Paul Martin, 1946), one of the first post-war Austrian films. See von Dassanowsky, *Austrian Cinema: A History*, p. 120. Arthur Schnitzler's *Der Weg ins Freie* (1908) is just one of many literary representations of the Prater amusement park, constructing it as "a democratic playground for all classes" (Eva Kuttenberg, "A Postmodern Viennese Narrative: Lilian Faschinger's *Wiener Passion*", *Monatshefte* Vol. 1 No. 1 (2009), 73–87: 74.

43 For an extended discussion of the Prater in Viennese cinema, see Christian Dewalt and Werner Michael Schwarz (eds), *Prater Kino Welt: Der Wiener Prater und die Geschichte des Kinos* (Vienna: Filmarchiv Austria, 2005).

44 Klaus Hödl, *Entangled Entertainers: Jews and Popular Culture in Fin-de-Siècle Vienna* (trans. Corey Twitchell) (New York: Berghahn, 2019), pp. 66–8.

45 Norman D. Anderson, *Ferris Wheels: An Illustrated History* (Bowling Green, OH: Bowling Green State University Press, 1992), p. 104.

46 Beller, *A Concise History of Austria*, p. 251.

47 "Automatisch so wie der ganze 2. Bezirk als Judenbezirk gegolten hat war immer zu erwarten vom Standtpunkt der Naziprovokation her, daß genügend Juden in der Hauptallee waren und wir haben also oft erlebt und öfter noch erzählt bekommen, daß also Nazigruppen, Gruppen von Nazi Jugendlichen, so vom Wurstelprater rausgingen, die Hauptallee raufgekommen sind mit Megaphonen oder auch nur so und gschrien haben 'Juden raus', rausgestürmt sind, 'Heil Hitler' gerufen haben und das hat immer wieder zu Formen von leichter Panik geführt."

48 Dagmar C. G. Lorenz emphasises this point in her brief discussion of the film in her essay "The Jewish Topography of Filmic Vienna", in von Dassanowsky (ed.), *World Film Locations: Vienna*, pp. 48–9; p. 49.

49 "Das Wienkommen war natürlich eine völlige Veränderung gegenüber meinem Leben in Magdeburg. Zuerst war man völlig fremd, das was mir so eigentlich recht schnell zum Bewußtsein gekommen ist, daß eine veränderte Situation da ist, die sich auf meine Zugehörigkeit zum Judentum bezogen hat. Wie ich zwei, drei Tage in dem Haus in dem ich gewohnt hab bisserl auf und ab gegangen bin, die Leute dort gesehen habe, Namensschilder gesehen habe, ist mir eigenlich erst so zum Bewußtsein gekommen – gegenüber meiner Wohnung am Tränsberg in Magdeburg wo Weintraub der einzige Jud weit und breit war – hat's eine Menge jüdische Familien, jüdische Kinder gegeben. Dann bin ich in die Schule gekommen, völlig fremd von Kindern, Jungen [...] die ich nicht kannte. Aber auch da – zweiter, dritter Tag hat gezeigt, daß...das war schon fast so, daß ich mich umschauen musste um einen Christen zu finden, weil alles natürlich bei dieser starken jüdischen Mitschülerschaft, diejenigen die sich um mich gedrängt haben, Juden waren. Das war doch völlig anders."

50 "Wir haben also nicht versucht zu verschwinden. [...] ich erinnere mich an die Magdeburger Zeit, man hat [...] so lang man konnte nicht [...] an die große Glocke gehängt, daß man Jude ist. Man hat sich vielleicht also versteckt als solcher. Dazu war keine Notwendigkeit, und es war auch kaum möglich."

51 See also Lisa Silverman, *Becoming Austrians: Jews and Culture Between the Wars* (Oxford: Oxford University Press, 2012), p. 121.

52 Beckermann, "Beyond the Bridges", p. 305. See also "Die Mazzesinsel", in *Die Mazzesinsel*, p. 16; "Aus der kosmopolitischen Hauptstadt eines Vielvölkerreiches war Wien nach dem ersten Weltkrieg zum Wasserkopf einer hungernden Republik geworden".

53 Hilde Spiel, *Vienna's Golden Autumn – 1866–1938* (London: Weidenfeld and Nicolson, 1987), p. 227.

54 Silverman, *Becoming Austrians*, pp. 22–3.

55 Gareth Dale, *Karl Polanyi* (New York: Columbia University Press, 2016), p. 98.

56 Helmut Gruber, *Red Vienna: Experiment in Working-Class Culture 1919–1934* (Oxford: Oxford University Press, 1991), p. 5.

57 Seibel, *Visions of Vienna*, p. 32.

58 Zsigmond Kunfi, "Lessons of July 15" ("Der 15. Juli und seine Lehren", *Der Kampf* Vol. 20 No. 8 [1927]: 345–52) (trans. Peter Woods), in Rob McFarland et al. (eds), *The Red Vienna Sourcebook* (Rochester, NY: Camden House, 2020), pp. 713–7; p. 716.

59 Gruber, *Red Vienna*, p. 65.

60 Gruber, *Red Vienna*, p. 181.

61 Gruber, *Red Vienna*, p. 181.

62 McFarland et al. (eds), *The Red Vienna Sourcebook*, p. 725.

63 McFarland et al. (eds), *The Red Vienna Sourcebook*, p. 727. See also Beckermann, "Beyond the Bridges", pp. 306–7.

64 Bruce F. Pauley, *From Prejudice to Persecution: A History of Austrian Anti-Semitism* (Chapel Hill: University of North Carolina Press, 1992), p. 100.

65 Beller, *A Concise History of Austria*, p. 212.

66 Rob McFarland, Nicole G. Burgoyne, and Gabriel Trop, "Jewish Life and Culture", in McFarland et al. (eds), *The Red Vienna Sourcebook*, p. 192.

67 Sachar M. Pinsker, *A Rich Brew: How Cafés created Modern Jewish Culture* (New York: New York University Press, 2018), p. 111.

68 Silverman, *Becoming Austrians*, p. 16.

69 Beller, *A Concise History of Austria*, pp. 214–15.

70 Beckermann, "Beyond the Bridges", p. 306.

71 Confusion surrounded the early media coverage of the events. The *Kronen Zeitung* of 31 January 1927, for example, called the event "Ein blutiger Sonntag im Burgenland – Frontkämpfer gegen Schutzbündler", and reported three deaths and 18 wounded, noting that "ein zweites Kind soll kurz nachher seiner Verletzungen erlegen sein", and naming the victims as "der Kriegsinvalide Mathias Smaric aus Klingenbach", "der achtjährige Knabe Josef Grössing aus Schattendorf", and "noch ein dreizehnjähriger Knabe, der sich gleichfalls unter den Verletzten befand". Other sources described two deaths, one of a six-year-old boy; *Der Standard* notes a seven-year-old boy.

72 John W. Boyer, *Austria 1867–1955* (Oxford: Oxford University Press, 2022), p. 684.

73 See Gerald Stieg, "Canetti und die Psychoanalyse: Das Unbehagen in der Kultur und *Die Blendung*", in Adrian Stevens and Fred Wagner (eds), *Elias Canetti: Londoner Symposium* (Stuttgart: Verlag Hans-Dieter Heinz/Akademischer Verlag Stuttgart, 1991), pp. 59–73.

74 Elias Canetti, *The Torch in My Ear* (trans. Joachim Neugroschel) (London: Andre Deutsch, 1989), p. 247. See also Manès Sperber's recollections of this day in *All Our Yesterdays Vol. 2 – The Unheeded Warning: 1918–1933* (trans. Harry Zohn) (New York: Holmes and Meier, 1991), pp. 94ff.

75 Dagmar C. G. Lorenz, "Post-Shoah Positions of Displacement in the Films of Ruth Beckermann", *Austrian Studies* Vol. 11, 'Hitler's First Victim'? Memory and Representation in Post-War Austria (2003), pp. 154–170: 163–4.

76 Christina Guenther, "The Politics of Location in Ruth Beckermann's 'Vienna Films'", 37.

77 Ruth Beckermann (ed.), *Die Mazzesinsel: Juden in der Wiener Leopoldstadt 1918–1938* (Vienna and Munich: Löcker, 1984).

78 Beckermann, *Die Mazzesinsel*, p. 99.

79 Beckermann, *Die Mazzesinsel*, pp. 90–1.

80 "Kübel und Zahnbürste und lachende Gesichter beendeten die Lokalgeschichte der Mazzesinsel ein für allemal." Beckermann, "Die Mazzesinsel", p. 20.

81 Beckermann, "Die Mazzesinsel", p. 9.

82 "… die Männer beschützend an den Rand, die schönste Frau als Blickfang in die Mitte, das Jüngste zwischen die Alten". Beckermann, "Die Mazzesinsel", p. 9.

83 "Befremdet betrachtet". Beckermann, "Die Mazzesinsel", p. 9.

84 Marianne Hirsch, *Family Frames: Photography, Narrative and Postmemory* (Cambridge, MA: Harvard University Press, 1997), p. 7.

85 "Familienalben wanderten um die Welt und in die Konzentrationslager. In einem Schrank in Jerusalem kann man prächtige seidene und samtene Alben und vergilbte Büchlein mit winzigen, gezackt umrandeten Photos aus Dachau finden. Keiner weiß, wem sie gehörten." Beckermann, "Die Mazzesinsel", p. 9.

86 Walter Benjamin, "Little History of Photography" (1931), in *Selected Writings* Volume 2 Part 2 (ed. Michael W. Jennings, Howard Eiland, and Gary Smith; trans. Rodney Livingstone and others) (Cambridge, MA: Belknap Press of Harvard University Press, 1999), p. 527.

87 "An Sommerabenden dringt aus den offenen Fenstern der Singsang der Betenden. Manchmal schaut einer hinunter in eine große, wild überwachsene Baulücke – die Stelle, wo einst eine Synagoge, die Schiffschul, stand, ist noch ein Denkmal der Ausrottung. Hier drosch in der Kristallnacht die Naziwut an Scheiben und Lustern los, bevor sie sich an die Menschen machte. Die Lücke, deren Geschichte keine der rot-weiß beflaggten Tafeln erzählt, die sonst historische Sehenswürdigkeiten erläutern, ist vergänglich wie die Erinnerung an die Opfer. Gras is schon über sie gewachsen. Bald wird ein neues Haus an ihrem Platz stehen. Da und dort eine Spur, die nicht weiterführt." Beckermann, "Die Mazzesinsel", p. 10.

88 Aviva Cantor, "Behind the Headlines – Refusing to Forget the Past", *Jewish Telegraph Agency (New York) Daily News Bulletin* 220 (28 November 1984), p. 4; see Joachim Riedl (ed.), *Versunkene Welt* (Vienna: Jewish Welcome Service, 1984).

89 Reproduced in *Die Mazzesinsel*, pp. 116–17. Boltanski's use of this photograph is discussed in Marianne Hirsch and Leo Spitzer, "School Photos and their Afterlives", in Elizabeth H. Brown and Thy Phu (eds), *Feeling Photography* (Durham, NC: Duke University Press, 2014), pp. 252–72; and in Hirsch's *Family Frames*, pp. 259–60.

3

Diaspora or nation – *Paper Bridge* and *Towards Jerusalem*

These are not the names of present or former homes; they are more like the piers of bridges that were blown up, only we can't be quite sure of what these bridges connected. Perhaps nothing with nothing. But if so, we have our work cut out for us, as we look out from the old piers. Because if we don't find the bridges, we'll either have to invent them or content ourselves with living in the no-man's land between past and present. (Ruth Kluger)[1]

The 'place where people and books lived' has today 'succumbed to the lack of history', said Paul Celan, who, like other old Czernowitz residents, left and never returned to the city of his youth. They would only find a city that resembled their memory from afar, through the windows of a moving car. (Ruth Beckermann)[2]

This chapter explores two films made in the late 1980s, in which Beckermann develops her distinctive cinematic aesthetics of drift and encounter in order to explore different potential conjurations of post-war Jewish identity and their relations to the politics of memory and desire. *Paper Bridge* (1987) and *Towards Jerusalem* (1990) offer analogous but distinct engagements with Jewishness and the residual problematics of memory, history, and trauma in relation to conceptions of family and community. The earlier film explores irretrievable origins, situating its versions of post-war Jewish identity as a series of potentials located in spaces other than those provided by the geographical locales (nations, regions, cities) of *Return to Vienna* and *Die Mazzesinsel* and in opposition to the nostalgically charged imaginary homelands of interwar central Europe; the later one considers indeterminate destinies, scrutinising the projected establishment in Israel of a conception of Jewish identity grounded in the model of the nation-state and of Israel as a utopia or "Promised Land". Each film develops provisional and critical responses to the question asked, near the start of *Nach Jerusalem*, of Israel's Jewish settlers: "What did you dream of? In Tarnopol, Czernowitz, Berlin and Vienna?" Each film explores a different trajectory of the notion (its temporal potentials already mapped in *Return to Vienna*) of return – to sites of family ancestry as departed origins in *Paper Bridge*, and in *Towards Jerusalem* to a nation whose very identity and historical narrative is predicated on the 'return' of its diasporically displaced people.

These films explore theoretical terrain examined a few years later by Daniel and Jonathan Boyarin in their 1993 essay "Diaspora: Generation and the Ground of Jewish Diaspora" – the different potentials for Jewish identities offered by (on the one hand) the *territorialism* of the new nation state of Israel, with all the material and ideological machineries required to define, sustain and defend a territory within which a particular kind of Jewish identity, controlled and regulated by state apparatuses, can take root in the regulated practice of cultural sameness; and the transnational diasporic sense of community, or *genealogy*, existing outside the borders of the Jewish nation and grounded in the perpetuation of Jewish difference via cultural and religious traditions across generations. The Boyarins express a clear political preference for *genealogy* over *territorialism*, emphasising its offering of a "diasporist consciousness" which is, they argue, "devoid of exclusivist and dominating power".[3]

Beckermann's position is more ambivalent. Her reading in *Paper Bridge* of the effects of diaspora on the communities left behind, for example, attends closely to the nostalgia-effect it produces, and its influence on contemporary central-European versions of Jewish identity, which the film presents as simultaneously forward-facing and deeply (de-)structured by historical loss. In their 2003 book on Jewishness and diaspora, the Boyarins note in diasporic Jewishness a similar condition, "the paradoxic power of *nakhnuma*, survival and presence through absence and loss".[4] Discussing *Towards Jerusalem* with Christa Blümlinger in 1991, Beckermann emphasises how she "followed the logic of the journey, [of] the associations that arise from the images and the stories that appear in the film".[5] The "associative journey" (a phrase later used to describe *American Passages*) suggests a psychoanalytic trajectory reinforced by the concern of *Paper Bridge* with language and storytelling as ways of filling in the gaps resulting from "absence and loss", and with various signifying systems which simultaneously enable and frustrate communication (sometimes allowing personal narratives to be recounted, sometimes embodying the contested 'borderlands' between and among languages, policed by political power). The "associative" dimension suggests, furthermore, that the formal "logic" of movement is also the logic of metonymic displacement towards (but never reaching) the object of desire or "missing image", which, in each film, is a specific named but, in the end, unattained, place – the Bukovinan city of Czernowitz in *Paper Bridge* and the city of Jerusalem in *Towards Jerusalem*.

Paper Bridge: Figuring Jewish identity

> That paper bridge of mine, I built it when
> Not only the sky but also my eyes turned blue,
> And the sun was a golden wheel on its own path
> That led to my feet straight and true. (Kadya Molodowsky)[6]

Return to Vienna's effort to reconstruct a historically (and ideologically) distant moment of utopian social and political optimism and *Die Mazzesinsel*'s mapping of the lost Jewish community of 1920s Vienna mark Beckermann's shift of thematic focus from working class to Jewish versions of Austrian history, and her interest in their intersections. *Paper Bridge*, made a few years before the sudden collapse of the Soviet regimes that dominated Cold War Eastern Europe, cements this passage in its exploration of the dynamics and effects of European Jewish diasporas. The film orbits another absence, that of the pre-Holocaust Bukovinan capital Czernowitz (formerly Romanian Cernauti, now Ukrainian Chernivtsi). This location exists in contemporary, post-Holocaust Jewish memory, and in Beckermann's film, as a decentred site of remembered communal and familial histories, the constantly reified originary location of a subsequently dispersed, shattered Jewish community. Czernowitz was the birthplace of many important writers, not least the Israeli novelist Aharon Appelfeld (1932–2018), who survived the Transnistrian labour camps before immigrating in 1946 to Palestine, and the poets Rose Ausländer (1901–88) and Paul Celan

(1920–70) (the latter's relationship with Ingeborg Bachmann is the theme of Beckermann's later *The Dreamed Ones*).[7] Beckermann's father Salo, a Vienna-based textile merchant and a key interviewee in *Paper Bridge*, was also born there. Beckermann's parents signify one strand of the film's central metaphorical thread, which interweaves family and community histories, as the film's fundamental enquiry reaches back into their pasts, which are also, post-memorially, Beckermann's own.

This specifically personal dimension (Katya Krylova calls the film "an autobiographical documentary")[8] frames the film's contribution to the wider enquiry into what Beckermann describes as the four fundamental elements ("Die Elemente") of her identity – the Jewish traditions of Eastern Europe, the memory of the Holocaust, the specific national context of Austria and its history, and Zionism.[9] *Paper Bridge* addresses the necessary intertwining of all these elements; its journey traces the passages through various central European territories of Jewish communities displaced by the historical effects of war, Holocaust, migration, and exile. Instead of the mainly fixed locations of *Return to Vienna* (Franz's study, the Prater and Leopoldstadt, and Vienna itself) and the corresponding reliance on interior shot sequences, face-to-camera interviews, and archive material, *Paper Bridge* is structured by movement and displacement between and across scenes and narratives, the drifting imagery of Tel Aviv-born French camerawoman Nurith Aviv (b. 1945) (in the first of her several collaborations with Beckermann) seeking passage between different positions from which to attempt to apprehend traces of an elusive past.

The film thus structurally imitates its argument that diaspora is the condition both productive of and definitive of contemporary Jewish identity. In her discussion of Beckermann's films, Christina Guenther calls this process "charting identity"; it means (she argues) "a never-ending nomadic enterprise, a continuous routing or pathfinding without a specific destination. Through narration juxtaposed with images of actual geographical sites, cinema itself provides passage to re-experience".[10] "Re-experience" suggests a combination of physical revisiting (of spaces, places, territories and, metaphorically, historical periods and events) and intellectual and emotional reconsideration, a process of (re-) assessment in which (Beckermann stated in early 1987) "[t]he union of image and language should be established on another, deep rooted and multi-faceted level".[11] A long segment was filmed in Osijek an der Drau, then in the former Yugoslavia but now part of Croatia, at a filming location where acting extras pass time between performing scenes reconstructing life in the Nazi show camp at Theresienstadt for an American television dramatisation of Hermann Wouk's historical epic *War and Remembrance* (1978).[12] Referring to the discussions recorded in this sequence (but implicitly including herself within this frame), Beckermann has described *Paper Bridge* as "some kind of analysis or auto-analysis"[13] due to the "freshness" with which people (like the extras she films arguing about Jewish history) were able to speak of, and perhaps "re-experience" in doing so, their memories and their (in)comprehension of the past.

This passage towards the "union of image and language" takes place through the interweaving of a variety of locations and memories, languages, and cultures, tracing an elusive "figure in the carpet" (what Tzvetan Todorov, discussing Henry James's 1896 story of that title, calls "an absolute and absent cause")[14] that (the film implies) might link the multiple histories Beckermann uncovers. In recording the dim visual outlines and narrative descriptions of experiences and memories that may help constitute this figure, the camera drifts across central European landscapes, passing through diverse environments, recording encounters in which the primary mode of communication is the explanatory, often autobiographical, narrative, while Beckermann's voice-over offers a lyrical meditation (which, Christa Blümlinger suggests, takes "the form of a soliloquy")[15] stimulated by, and critically responding to, the images and narratives presented. Dagmar Lorenz argues that the film is structured like a road movie "with fast-changing locales and scenarios".[16] The experience of watching it suggests more a destructured, non-directional meandering, its constant disjunction and displacement between the episodic, unconnected, or not-obviously linked encounters and experiences evocative more of dream logic than sequential progression, and at times (as Krylova has commented) distinctly uncanny.[17]

The Eastern European sections of the film in particular construct a prevailing sense of uncanny anachronism, evident both in the extended shots of rural poverty and the depiction of social structures and rituals, along with tales which seem, to Beckermann's metropolitan, late-twentieth-century perspective, "as distant as the Middle Ages", a simile echoed by one of the Bukovinans interviewed in Florence Heymann's oral history of the region, when she describes her relationship with her mother: "Un seul génération nous séparait, mais elle faisait partie du Moyen Âge et moi du XXᵉ siècle."[18] Guenther notes the film's particular attention to socially symbolic spaces markedly differentiated by gender, a hierarchical structure that historically and culturally distances from modern, Western viewers the communities Beckermann encounters: "The foreignness of Romanian space is most clearly perceived through the archaic existence of the community who live in a pre-industrial world defined by an outdated, codified hierarchy of gender."[19] These features have the combined effect of rendering these extra-Austrian territories not homely but *unheimlich*, both familiar and strange, full of disturbing memories and the nostalgic lure of potential rootedness yet void of the certainties of actual geographic or territorial belonging. Each encounter in the film gestures towards a more complete but absent narrative, offering instead a partial, fragmentary account of history as somehow both proximal to and dependent upon subjective experience, while sustaining throughout the impression of a distanced, dislocated passage through history and geography.

Remembering Czernowitz

The implicit "deep rooted, multifaceted level" of significance towards which every element of the film is oriented finds surface expression in contemporary Czernovitsi, which is wholly absent from the film's cinematic locations because Beckermann was refused permission from the Soviet authorities to film there. The city nevertheless exists in the interstices of the film's segments, an absent centre gestured to by road signs and frequently cited in discussions, a place constructed in memory and narrative and exercising a strong centrifugal pull, a contested imaginary site just as the Bukovina has for long periods of its history been a contested historical territory.[20] Many recent books address the history of Czernowitz and its locale. Marianne Hirsch and Leo Spitzer's documenting of their own tracing of family and community links in Czernowitz, for example, discovers two decades after *Paper Bridge* a similar territory to that explored by Beckermann. "For me and my contemporaries", writes Hirsch, "children of exiled Czernowitzers, Czernowitz has always been a primordial site of origin".[21] Drawing on the accounts related in Heymann's history of the city and the wider Bukovina province, Hirsch and Spitzer emphasise the importance of cosmopolitanism in the retrospective imagining by subsequent generations of the two locales:

> In highlighting the assimilationist journey of Jews in the Bukovina and, especially, in Czernowitz during Franz Joseph's long imperial reign, the move 'from the *shtetl* to the *Stadt*," as Florence Heymann so aptly characterizes it – it is essential to stress one important, but perhaps easily overlooked, contextual fact. The Austro-Hungarian Habsburg empire, of which the Bukovina was an outlying Eastern European province, was not a nation-state, like its contemporary, the Bismarckian German Reich, but a multiethnic dynastic-state in which Austrians and Austrianized German-speakers were only a privileged minority of the population. In 1910, less than a quarter of the monarchy's inhabitants used German as their principal language. Austro-identified German-speaking Jews in the Habsburg realm at large were thus a minority within a minority, in the most idealised sense – 'an anomalous religious community within a privileged nationality,' as Fred Sommer has observed.[22]

For Beckermann, as for Hirsch and Spitzer and Heymann, Czernowitz exists partly as a multi-layered post-memorial site associated with the transmitted memories of the previous generation. In *Paper Bridge* the city is also the evasive, ever-displaced object of a cinematic quest. Either way, it figures in the film as a source of the nostalgia that qualifies the "diasporist consciousness" of post-war Jewish communities. Access to it, denied by contemporary geopolitics, is available (the film discovers) through the cultural imaginary – stories, texts, images, manifestations of what Rose Ausländer calls "the uprooted word".[23]

The "paper bridge" that Beckermann's film constructs is thus a means of short-circuiting the city's "ever more distant mythic aura",[24] a fabrication constituted in and by textual fragments, an assemblage of cultural threads and patches providing fragile means of passing across the voids of history and geography, of moving (as Hélène Cixous puts it in her discussion of the film) from "the visible to the spectral, from the present to the past".[25] For people like Beckermann's father, Salo (embodying the parental generation in the film), Czernowitz exists as a site of intense and deeply authenticating personal memory traversed by conflicting discourses of imperial trauma. The city registers the persistent shock of the sudden collapse of the Habsburg empire in 1918 as a form of imperial nostalgia, evident, for example, in the persistent belief, which Salo echoes, in the absence of anti-Semitism during, and even after, the period of Austrian Habsburg rule over the Bukovina: 'his' Czernowitz was, Salo tells Beckermann, "a place where there was almost no anti-Semitism". Nostalgia for the Habsburg-era Bukovina is a powerful and persistent cultural trope – Helga Mitterbauer and Carrie Smith-Prei note that "some people in the countries of the former Austro-Hungarian Monarchy have expressed the sentiment that the shared past before the First World War was preferable to the political systems that followed".[26] For Salo Beckermann, Czernowitz persists in the present day, reincarnated as Vienna: "In a sense, I never left Czernowitz. That's what Vienna is for me now," he states, echoing Heymann's description of the latter city as "Petite Vienne".[27] The connection between Czernowitz and Vienna suggests a deeper relation of repetition between the two cities, and implies perhaps that Beckermann's ostensible journey towards Czernowitz in *Paper Bridge* subtly repeats another enquiry, that of *Return to Vienna* into her own city and *its* Jewish histories, an implication reinforced by the imitation of the earlier film's structure in the formal circularity of *Paper Bridge*, its opening in and return at the end to contemporary Vienna.[28]

Uncanny repetition

Structured as a loose, essayistic travelogue, the film's dominant register is speculative, its circular structure strangely repetitive, its visual semiotic distinctly and unsettlingly dream-like, from the early shot of the horse-and-cart driving into the fog (repeating the carriage crossing the street, seen earlier through gauze blinds in the opening window views over Vienna's Hoher Markt), to the tracking shots of desolate, wintry central European landscapes, counterpointed at one moment by almost-surreal interjected footage of a sun-drenched Israeli beach. The soundscape contributes fully to this uncannily oneiric quality. The film opens with a series of unidentified knockings and scrapings over a black screen, continuing as the camera explores an empty attic space, its windows revealing the sunlit late-1980s Vienna. Doors slam inside, and horse hooves echo on the cobblestones outside. The layering of auditory and visual signs introduces a palimpsestic series of textual and narrative references, as Beckermann's voice-over begins with a question: "Die Geschichte von Hagazussa – kennst du sie?" ("The story Hagazussa – do you know it?"). Hillary Hope Herzog paraphrases the folktale of Hagazussa (a possible root for the German word *Hexe*, 'witch')[29] as

> the story of an outsider who has little contact with the villagers among whom she lived. Gradually, Hagazussa became nearly invisible and was able to move unseen through the attics and cellars of the homes in the village. Thus moving freely, Hagazussa learned many stories, such as the tale of the paper bridge that gives the film its title.[30]

As Reiter notes, the "paper bridge" of the film's title also derives from a parable recounted in *Die Wasserträger Gottes* (*God's Water Carriers*) (1974), the first volume of Austrian-French author and psychologist Manès Sperber's autobiography *All das Vergangene* (*All our Yesterdays*).[31] "The iron bridge", writes Sperber (1905–84),

> was the pride of the shtetl, yet everyone knew what would happen after the coming of the Messiah. There would suddenly be a second bridge, not iron, not stone, not even wood. No, it would be made of paper, yes indeed, cigarette paper. And the sceptics, the sinners, the blasphemers would naturally laugh at the paper bridge and choose the iron one. Yes, that was what they would do, and they would plunge into the water with the iron bridge and drown. But the pious, the people of faith, would not hesitate or be afraid, they would sing as they crossed the paper bridge into the happiness of everlasting life.[32]

Beckermann adapts the "paper bridge" – another embodiment of the potential passage towards a utopia, and an indicator that the film is driven not by nostalgia but by Beckermann's insistent interest in utopian concepts – from a symbol of faith into a symbolic medium of connection across generations, a marker of the ways narratives (spoken, written, cinematic) construct and transmit net-works of significance within which identities can be established, passed on, and inhabited.

The use of Sperber and the Hagazussa tale situate the film's examination of post-war Jewishness in an intertextual space in which definitive meaning (or fixed identity) is elusive, deferred from folktale to parable to autobiography (or from folk memory to personal, subjective memory). *Paper Bridge* similarly opens in an indeterminate location, directly questioning the viewer's cultural knowledge, establishing the interrogative tropes of uncertainty and enquiry. While the Hagazussa folktale is told, the view cuts to another image figuring indeterminacy and obscurity: a rear-view of a moving horse-drawn cart, bearing two riders, moving slowly for-wards along a country road into thick fog, trees looming alongside the route, cars carefully navigating past while, barely audible but rising to a crescendo as the tale ends and the carriage vanishes into the fog, we hear the Bulgarian State Television Female Choir singing the eerie folk song "Pilentze Pee" (A Bird Is Singing)[33] (Figure 3.1).

Figure 3.1 Ruth Beckermann (dir.), *Paper Bridge*, 1987.
© Ruth Beckermann Filmproduktion.

This sequence (the device is repeated later when Arvo Pärt's *Fratres* plays over a long tracking shot of another almost empty, fog-obscured road)[34] ends when the film cuts back to the attic windows, establishing a basic circular rhythm in the alternation between interior views out into open spaces and enclosed, claustrophobic exteriors: "Schaute in die Stadt hinein, schaute aus der Stadt hinaus" ("I looked into the city, I looked out of the city") says Beckermann a short while later. The next segment presents views of Vienna's Parliament building and its locale from a tram moving round the circular Ringstraße towards the stop at Dr Karl Renner Ring,[35] while the narrating voice begins the process of recollection, remembering another scarcely credible ("unglaublich", Beckermann calls it)[36] but historically real narrative, that of Beckermann's grandmother Rosa, who refused to wear the yellow star in Nazi-occupied Vienna, and escaped deportation to Theresienstadt by sleeping rough in the city's parks and gardens, pretending to be dumb ("Sie stellte sich stumm") to disguise her Yiddish-accented German. Her enforced historical silence balances the many contemporary voices (and specifically that of Beckermann) we will hear in the film, while the recollection of her experiences establishes another thread of transgenerational memory.

This opening interplay of voice, music, ambient sound and silence establishes the film's concerns with telling and hearing stories, mapping the contours of historically silenced communities whose traces nevertheless persist in inherited narratives. Its insistently circular visual sequencing (the inner ring tramline, the return to the Viennese attic and its window views, to which, at the film's end, we return again, underlining the repetitions resulting from such circularity) furthermore implies the consistency of *turning* and *returning* as its key cinematic tropes: the Orphic device of turning to look back (connecting it with the retrospective analytic gaze of *Return to Vienna*), the physical journey of returning to territories and histories long since vacated, in search of traces of what has been, in the disastrous interim, almost entirely erased. Each encounter throughout the film elaborates in some way this circularity and its symbolic expression, as the film seeks a passage through memory and history. These encounters, in turn, map different dimensions of the immense absence resulting from the Shoah, another (historical) absence around which *Paper Bridge* circulates, connected by close association to Czernowitz. Over coffee in Yugoslavia, two of the film extras (selected "representatives of the Jewish fate", the narration comments) argue over the possibility of Jewish resistance to Nazi violence: their debate is circular, their respective positions amicable but irreconcilable, their argument an extended metaphor for, or enactment of, the film's underlying and irresolvable question (and quest), just as their very presence in Yugoslavia is part of a media enactment, a repetition-as-representation of historical reality.

Within this formal circularity, Beckermann weaves symbolic threads that periodically reaffirm the film's thematic coherence. For example, the film's journey begins with a short sequence filmed in fog, at a border crossing somewhere in Eastern Europe, the red lights of its barrier flashing, as a radio scrolls through stations in multiple European languages. This scene is echoed later as the film cuts from a cold synagogue in Romania to a beach in Israel, and a sign saying BATHING AREA BORDER in Hebrew, English and Arabic. The fogged image recurs in another Romanian sequence filmed through a steamed-up window into a public sauna, formerly a Mikve or steamed bath for Jewish women, inhabited now by a group of naked peasant women, a central European image that evokes, but subtly subverts, Orientalist and exoticising visions like Ingres' *Le Bain turc* (1862) (Figures 3.2 and 3.3).

Figure 3.2 Ruth Beckermann (dir.), *Paper Bridge*, 1987.
© Ruth Beckermann Filmproduktion.

Figure 3.3 Jean Auguste Dominique Ingres, *Le Bain turc*, 1862.

The early sequence showing men sawing down a tree, a potent symbol of forced rootlessness, while the narration meditates on travel, placenames, and the lure of "going away", returns later as a symbolic motif adorning a gravestone in the cemetery at Sereth, explained to Beckermann by Herbert Gropper (whom the film crew met in Suceava the previous evening ("am Abend zuvor"), another folding back in the film's temporality) as "a matter of symbolism".[37] "In a year, when you come back, the whole cemetery will be fenced in, to resist the passage of time", explains Gropper, emphasising the connection between the circularity of return and that of enclosure or containment. Later still, the symbolism of the chopped-down tree returns again in a barge laden with piles of logs being towed along a river.

Such symbolic repetitions constitute crucial threads in the film's diverse tapestry of images of post-war Jewish identity. Its uses of parable (the tale of Hagazussa, the legends of "the wonders worked

by the Rabbi of Sadigura", the parable of the Jew lost in the forest)
sit in tension with other forms of narrative that work to erase or
supplant historical experience and substitute in place of diversity
versions of exclusive, monologic power – Russian efforts to erase
the past of the Bukovina (by removing road signs), or Ceausescu's
censorious manipulation of Romanian television news. The para-
bles are balanced and supported in other ways by the autobiographical tales and histories recounted by various interviewees.
Herbert Gropper's often comical interaction with Beckermann in
the Romanian cemetery; the teacher of Hebrew, Frau Rosenheck
of Botoshan, who also speaks Romanian and German, and represents a surviving trace of the legendary cosmopolitanism of
Czernowitz, where she was taught all these languages; the Diaspora
Museum in Tel Aviv, its displays asserting contemporary notions of
'authentic' Jewish identity, of which Beckermann expresses a meas-
ured scepticism (that will return later in *Towards Jerusalem*); Salo
Beckermann's accounts of his life in post-war Vienna and of the rise
of anti-Semitism in pre-war Czernowitz, and Bety Beckermann's
memories of living in Palestine, where she fled from Vienna, and of
the establishment of the state of Israel in 1948; the various life stories briefly recounted by the extras during their filming break – all
these tales ("die Geschichten", Beckermann's narration comments
wistfully) combine through a variety of thematic and tonal intersections, producing a multifaceted version of historically perspectivised multi-national Jewishness, a dialogic pluralism markedly
expanding and diversifying the largely monologic Vienna-centred
narrative of *Return to Vienna*.

Intertextuality and Jewish tradition

The film's extensive transmedial intertextuality reinforces this pluralism. In its exploration of how different narrative forms encode
and memorialise experience, *Paper Bridge* constructs alongside its
use of folktales and autobiographical narratives an extensive tissue of quotes and allusions, many noted by its numerous critics,
which connect it to a variety of authenticating literary and other
texts, specifically those of Jewish fiction and poetry, that function
as symbolic expressions of the transgenerational Jewish identity

it constructs. For example, along with the paraphrase of Manès Sperber quoted earlier, Beckermann may also have had in mind in titling the film Kadya Molodowsky's poem "Mayn papirene Brik" (My Paper Bridge), written in Yiddish and published in her collection *Dzshike Gas* in 1933 (and quoted in the epigraph cited earlier). Molodowsky's poem is (Kathryn Hellerstein suggests) "itself a kind of paper bridge".[38]

This intertextual network leads in many directions. Katya Krylova connects Beckermann's attention to place-names, a "submerged topography" of the Austro-Hungarian empire, with Ingeborg Bachmann's meditation on the "aura" of place names "and their status as topographical markers in her fourth Frankfurt lecture, 'Der Umgang mit Namen' ('The Treatment of Names')".[39] And Austrian novelist Robert Schindel's (b. 1944) appearance among the extras re-enacting Theresienstadt in contemporary Yugoslavia prompts a thread of textual connections demonstrating the influence of Beckermann's film. Schindel's novel *Gebürtig*, a key work of post-war Jewish literature described by Matti Bunzl as "the most critically and commercially successful product of the Jewish literary renaissance and arguably its definitive text",[40] was published three years after *Paper Bridge* and includes a dramatisation of the Theresienstadt re-enactment Beckermann films, complete with a fictional version of Beckermann herself (renamed Esther Lichtblau).[41] *Gebürtig* was, in turn, filmed by Schindel and Lukas Stepanik in 2009,[42] extending an intertextual line of descent echoing the trans-generational, genealogical, and cultural ones traced in *Paper Bridge*.

Beckermann's father is filmed unpacking clothes in his shop in Vienna. As he ponders the ease with which Nazism and anti-Semitism was 'sold' to the inhabitants of 1930s Czernowitz, the camera cuts to a tracking shot along a desolate, run-down Romanian street, drifting back from contemporary Vienna to the east European scenes Beckermann herself now cinematically recollects. Beckermann narrates: "'It's snowing history', I read in a novel. The less history, the easier it is to slip past events, or go through them."[43] Renate Posthofen points out that the last part of this passage (which reminds us of Hagazussa) quotes from the Russian fiction writer Ilya Ehrenberg;[44] the phrase "It's snowing history" also echoes a line in Bernard Malamud's 1966 novel *The Fixer*, which depicts the disastrous consequences of violent anti-Semitic scapegoating in pre-Soviet Russian Kiev for one man, the village 'fixer' Yakov Bok. *The Fixer* is loosely based on, and structured by, historical anti-Semitic miscarriages of justice including the notorious Dreyfus affair in France. "Rooted [argues Philip Davis] in such paradoxical structures [as] the religious-in-the-unreligious, [and] belief and unbelief struggling together",[45] the novel blends themes and motifs echoing Kafka, Solzhenitsyn and Koestler's *Darkness at Noon* (1940) with Yakov's reading (and increasingly comprehension of) a book on Spinozan ethics. Elements of this destructuring and disorienting paradoxicality (like restaging Theresienstadt in contemporary Osijek, or passing into Paradise over a bridge made of paper, or being prohibited from filming in the place on which your film is centred) permeate Beckermann's film in its efforts to discern significant patterns and features through the obscuring "snow" of history. The phrase in *Paper Bridge* echoes a passage linking Yakov's fate to his rapidly burgeoning grasp of forces beyond his control:

> Once you leave you're out in the open; it rains and snows. It snows history, which means what happens to somebody starts in a web of events outside the personal. It starts of course before he gets there. We're all in history, that's sure, but some are more than others, Jews more than some. [...] In history, thicker at times than at others, too much happens. [...] So the 'open,' he thought, was anywhere. In or out, it was history that counted – the world's bad memory.[46]

Echoing Jean Améry's bald statement of the fate of the intellectual in the concentration camps – "In the camp he became an unskilled labourer, who had to do his job in the open"[47] – "the open", perhaps offering a potential way out of the relentless returning circularity discussed above, nevertheless remains implicit in Beckermann's film, which returns at its end to the Viennese attic interior in which it opened.

Diasporic consciousness

Paper Bridge explores post-war Jewish identities as complex, pluralised products of conflicting pressures and desires, persistences and transformations, endlessly negotiated experiences and repeatedly retold narratives, seemingly simultaneously forward-looking and backward-facing, subject-positions and bodies of experience constantly (as in the arguments among the Theresienstadt-performing extras) contested and disputed. Together these tales and images offer fragments of a semi-mythical Jewish community, some "preparing to emigrate", others set on remaining, all traversed by transgenerational forces centring on the absent Czernowitz as ambivalent symbol of the centripetal push of history, the centrifugal pull of memory. The film explores the possibility that productive and progressive versions of Jewish identity exist in the aftermath of the Holocaust as potentialities constituted trans-generationally and diasporically rather than nationally or by other situations of locale. In contrast with Salo Beckermann's nostalgia for his sense of rootedness in the (now lost) locatedness and hospitality of Czernovitz, the film offers his narrative and its telling as a ground of identity, using them to produce a new thread of diasporic consciousness to contribute (along with many others) to the weaving of contemporary Jewishness.

Reinforcing this sense that geographical location fails to provide the longed-for rootedness, the last section of the film returns (again) to contemporary Vienna, its late-twentieth-century urbane cosmopolitanism now marked by a shift of emphasis tonally and thematically: not the uncanny difference of the (exotic, distant) past of Bukovina, but a city (Beckermann's birthplace) whose familiarity is tainted by the sinister resurgence in the late-1980s (another notable repetition) of performances of overt nationalist and anti-Semitic sympathy on its streets, in scenes disturbingly echoing those described in *Return to Vienna*. The contemporary home city becomes an *unheimlich* space, a territory again permeated by threat rather than a sense of belonging. Beckermann records footage of demonstrations and counter-protests in Stefansplatz around the election in 1986 of Kurt Waldheim, including an anti-Semitic diatribe directed at her own father – footage she later re-uses in *The Waldheim Waltz* (in another version of the trope of circularity and return). This brief passage is the only monochrome sequence in *Paper Bridge*, a self-conscious "change in style"[48] which gestures to the veritism of documentary by (Beckermann states) "forcing you out of the partly elegiac, inward-looking, very reflexive story into the present".[49] The prevailing uncanny element of the film is evident in another short passage, now in colour, starting with the entrance to the "Sigmund Freud" room in the exhibition *Traum und Wirklichkeit: Wien 1870–1930* (*Dream and Reality*, 1985), staged in the city's Künstlerhaus, which, as Krylova notes, once hosted the Nazis' notorious Decadent Art Exhibition).[50] Beckermann comments ironically that *Traum und Wirklichkeit* was one of the first public recognitions of the contribution of Jews to the city's cultural history – an event which the film offers (Dagmar Lorenz argues) as "an example of Vienna's cult of dead Jews"[51] in contrast with Beckermann's intended focus on the testimony and memories of the *living*, those inhabiting the potentialities of diasporic and transgenerational Jewishness rather than nostalgically mourning the dead and their lost territories.

The closing sequences return to this emphasis on living memories by documenting the autobiographical narratives of Salo and Bety Beckermann, respectively detailing his arrival in post-war Vienna from the East where he had fought in the Red Army, and her arrival there with her brothers from the newly formed Jewish state of Israel, having fled to Palestine from Austria with her mother and sisters after the Anschluß. Each maps a different geographical and historical passage from a traumatic past to present-day Austria; each is grounded in different ways in the optimism of post-war, post-Holocaust Jewish and Austrian regeneration. Beckermann counterpoints this remembered optimism with footage further evidencing the apparent contemporary decline of the city's Jewish population, in particular the diminished textile quarter of the city (including the street where she lives, which will receive closer attention in *homemad(e)*).

For all its evident concern (which receives much critical attention) with "journeying into melancholy", *Paper Bridge* presents (despite the constraints of formal and thematic circularity) an intellectually optimistic vision, each section of the film working prospectively to prefigure Beckermann's future range of concerns. The end of the film suggests neither the fraying of narrative threads, nor the wearing out of the carpet's elusive figure, but the figure of return itself as a kind of potential renewal. Near the film's end, in a final uncanny repetition, we return to the attic where it began, the director's home in Vienna, with its opening views through the window into the open spaces of the sunlit city. The cat looks out of the window again, but now the room is occupied by workmen painting window frames for installation, suggesting the possibility of new viewpoints and new perspectives, a revisioning of the world. Here, in the film's closing shots, we see a selection of Beckermann's family photographs, spread out on a blanket on the floor (a literalisation of the "figure in the carpet" metaphor, perhaps); her mother and father at their wedding, other family members, and, finally, Beckermann herself, as a young child. Closing on and affirming what Marianne Hirsch calls "the familiality of the gaze",[52] the film asserts at its end family photographs as a key medium of remembrance. One of Florence Heymann's Bukovinan interlocutors recalls seeing a performance of a Yiddish play, *Papieren Kindern*, in which young emigrants seek their fortunes in America, leaving behind only their photographs – the "paper children" – as mementoes for their parents.[53] The final shots of *Paper Bridge* emphasise the personal resonances of family photographs as 'papieren Kindern' offering enigmatic versions of the "paper bridge" that makes momentarily, symbolically accessible the (family and community) histories and diasporic consciousness sought throughout the film.

Towards Jerusalem

For as long as I live, I shall be thrilled by all those who came to the Promised Land to turn it either into a pastoral paradise of egalitarian Tolstoyan communes, or into a well-educated, middle-class Central European enclave, a replica of Austria and Bavaria. Or those who wanted to raise a Marxist paradise, who built kibbutzim on biblical sites and secretly yearned for Stalin himself to come one day to admit that 'Bloody Jews, you have done it better than we did'. (Amos Oz)[54]

I have established quite calmly that I do not belong here. (Arnold Zweig to Sigmund Freud, on his migration to Palestine)[55]

Paper Bridge ends with the silent eloquence of the photographic image. The film's traversing of multiple linguistic borders, its movement between passages of contemplation and recollection in search of a usable past, is momentarily muted by the weight of history contained in Beckermann's family photographs. A key moment in her next film, *Towards Jerusalem*, captures another kind of silence amid a society which, the film emphasises, is characterised by the insistent auditory and visual clamour of postmodernity.

In a modern city square, a group of Ethiopian women sit in the evening sun (Figure 3.4). A middle-aged Israeli woman tries, good humouredly, to engage one of them in conversation: "Do you speak English? French? Spanish, Italian, Arabic?" she asks. "Do you speak Arabic?" The reply is negative. "Ethiopian?" "Yes." "Speak Ethiopian", comes the reply. The Israeli woman comments: "She doesn't speak anything but Ethiopian. Too bad." Briefly embracing the Ethiopian woman, she turns to her friend. "These people are poor", she says, before turning away and exclaiming: "What a mess. They speak no language, not Hebrew, not English, not Arabic, no Italian, no French, no Spanish." She walks away, laughing. The camera cuts to show another elderly Ethiopian woman, her hand over her mouth, an extralinguistic but universal gesture signifying muteness, and perhaps outrage. The refusal to recognise Ethiopian as a legitimate language ("They speak no language ...") reveals much, of course, about the racial politics of the Israeli woman. This scene counterpoints a short passage set in a school, children of various ages and races talking to the camera, complaining of the

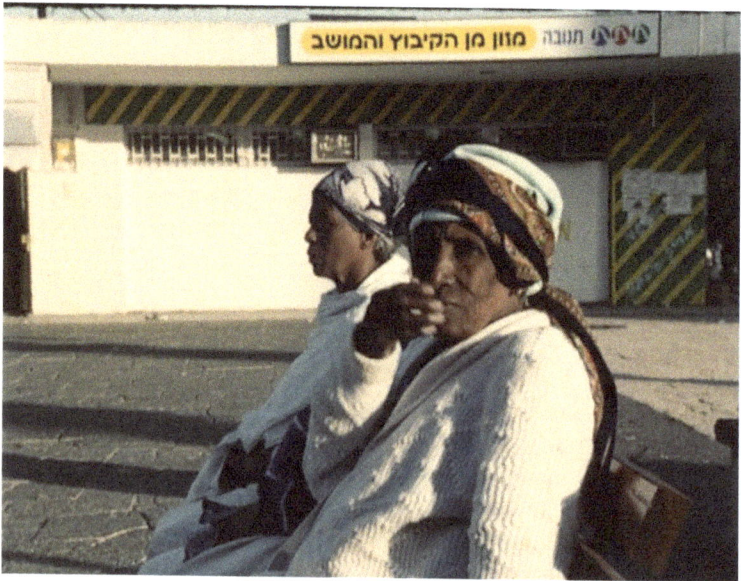

Figure 3.4 Ruth Beckermann (dir.), *Towards Jerusalem*, 1991.
© Ruth Beckermann Filmproduktion.

presence of Russians in their school. "I'd like to say something!" one of them insists. In the background, the radio ("The Voice of Israel") announces with a fanfare "the daily program in beginners' Hebrew". In the next sequence, a young woman code-switches fluently between Hebrew, Yiddish, and Russian as she tries to speak, with her Yiddish and Russian-speaking mother beside her, of their lives in Israel.

These multilinguistic social realities are a recurrent theme of *Towards Jerusalem*. Signs and languages become markers of territorial contestation, vying for attention as the film seeks to accommodate their diversity while navigating an ideological route through them via a carefully constructed and highly constrained episodic montage (Beckermann pointed out in a 1991 interview that the film's 23 distinct narratives are presented in only 121 individual shots).[56] From the opening frames, the viewer is immersed in a culture of excessive, bewildering semiosis. The title appears on a black screen sequentially in Hebrew, Arabic, Latin and German; the rush of fast-passing traffic gives way to a hum of voices speaking multiple languages, and we see people entering a cinema with its poster- and photo-adorned noticeboard, their way in through a claustrophobically enclosed passage through the security searches which are enforced in Israeli cinemas. As the camera pans inside the building, we glimpse through an open doorway and partly obscured by the dark shapes of viewers the screen, on which we see projected the American film actor Martin Landau in Woody Allen's *Crimes and Misdemeanours* (1989), his English words subtitled on the screen in Hebrew and French: "I remember my father telling me, the eyes of God are on us always." The collocation of the security guards with the cinematic evocation of the panopticism of divine omniscience establishes the critical relationship of *Towards Jerusalem* to the social world it records. Beckermann's film embodies in such moments what Hamid Naficy calls "border consciousness", which (he argues)

> emerges from being situated at the border, where multiple determinants of race, class, gender, and membership in divergent, even antagonistic, historical and national identities intersect. As a result, border consciousness, like exilic liminality, is theoretically against binarism and duality and for a third optique, which is multiperspectival and tolerant of ambiguity, ambivalence, and chaos.[57]

The film maps these intersecting identity-determinants by document-ing their multilingual and polysemic expression in Israeli society, while critiquing that society's ideological efforts to erase or sup-press precisely the "ambiguity, ambivalence, and chaos" resulting from the insistent presence of multiple distinct forms of Jewishness alongside other, non-Jewish, identities and histories within the field of languages, images and narratives the camera records.

One relentless impression of the noise and dynamism of the film's opening passages (which contrast markedly with the prevailing poverty and muted emptiness of the streets of northern Romania in *Paper Bridge*) is of Israel as palimpsest, a densely interwoven multi-layered fabric of contrasting and often conflicting signs, visual and auditory signifiers of a vibrant transnational collage of languages, histories, and cuisines inhabited and consumed by people originat-ing from all over the world, an embodiment of the endless mutabil-ity of difference rather than any fixity of identity.[58] If *Paper Bridge* maps diasporic spread and the resulting vacancies remaining in for-mer Jewish homelands, *Towards Jerusalem* traces the inverse pro-cess of return to a new, crowded homeland of a globalised diversity of Jewish identities. Dagmar Lorenz biographises this semiotic pol-ysemy, reading the film's "disjointed images and sounds" as a reg-ister of Beckermann's own sense of dislocation and unbelonging in the urban environments of Israel: "the Central European filmmaker feels as alien on the road to Jerusalem as she did among the rallying Austrians in the heart of Vienna."[59] The long travelling shots of the (comparatively) empty desert landscape which occur increasingly frequently towards the film's end suggest, however, further, non-autobiographical significances – for example, the recognition in the formal progression of *Towards Jerusalem* of the historical develop-ment of Israeli conceptions of land and habitat, noted by critics like Hana Morgenstern in her analysis of modernist experimentation in Hebrew poetry and its mapping of "the shift from *homeland as text* to *homeland as territory*".[60] As Morgenstern elaborates (and Beckermann's film implies), the collagistic poetics of modernist experimentation establish clear tensions with the linear teleologies characteristic of nationalist ideology and narratives.[61]

The film quickly establishes its dense significatory field. An early sequence emphasises the "kaleidoscopic" dialectical image pre-sented by the experience of urban Israel postmodernity, and, by metonymic extension, the country in its entirety.[62] Tracking shots along night-time streets of Tel Aviv display western advertising logos (notably the ubiquitous Coke sign) alongside a huge diversity of international cuisine, Chinatown Express next to Pizzeria Ristorante Rimini alongside the Bronx Café, accompanied by an urban soundtrack of snatches of Western music and advertising jingles punctuated by voices, English and Italian signs alongside Hebrew and Arabic ones.[63] In passages shot in sunlit streets, uniformed soldiers on leave mingle with the crowds, their weapons, markers of a militarised society, hugely conspicuous as they cross traffic junctions or loiter to light cigarettes in stationers' stalls. In the Café Kassit, people party, dancing, smoking, drinking, speaking German and Hebrew and English as they drunkenly recount the bar's history, which is also, they suggest, that of the culture of Tel Aviv. More walls of black-and-white photographs illustrate this history – portraits of former owners, famous clients, the city's and the nation's poets and actors and musicians: "You can see everything in these pictures", we're told (all the poets and actors named are, of course, Jewish; the "everything" we can see excludes the Palestinian community and *its* cultural figures). In another sequence, men haggle over buying dill, an advertising sign for Marlboro cigarettes conspicuous behind them. Mercedes and Volkswagen cars drive past. The radio – tuned to "The Voice of Israel from Jerusalem", establishing the city as the source of the "voice" of political power – speaks in Hebrew of Aeroflot suspending flights bringing Jewish people from Budapest (later we hear another station, "The Voice of Peace", broadcasting from "Somewhere in the Mediterranean" – actually from a former Dutch cargo ship – in English and French).

The camera pans along a shelf of porn magazines, as a woman digs in her bag for change to buy a newspaper from the vendor, who wears a US army bomber jacket. Reprising the disturbingly uncanny earlier shot of a silent, grinning woman sat in the corner of the partying Café, a mime artist stares directly at the camera, his enigmatic silence a momentary interruption of the film's prominent soundscape. Young people in leather jackets and t-shirts dance to rhythmic percussive music at an outdoor disco, while young men hawk portrait prints of the Rabbi of Lubavitch to the gathering crowd. A man, pitching like a 'Speaker's Corner' performer, displays an array of Jewish National Fund boxes, symbols of the long economic effort behind Israel's contemporary existence,[64] distributed to Jewish families to raise money for the settlement of Israel, one "supposedly from the beginning of the century" which bears the legend "Made in Palestine – Eretz Israel" (Figure 3.5). At this moment we first hear the violin notes of Tchaikovsky's *Serenade mélancolique*, marking the emotional significance of these boxes in the matrix of cultural memory being traced. Beckermann has commented on her memories of these charity boxes, one of which she owned as a child, into which she deposited her savings, thus literally investing in Israel's future.[65] Laden with conflicting personal, cultural, historical, and economic values, the charity boxes express the complex intersection of intimate individual memory with the global economic network of exchange. They embody the potential ambiguity of individual signs within the networks of signifiers that constitute modern Israel.

Throughout this complex montage of scenes and images the trope of the photocollage insists as a visual counterpoint to the

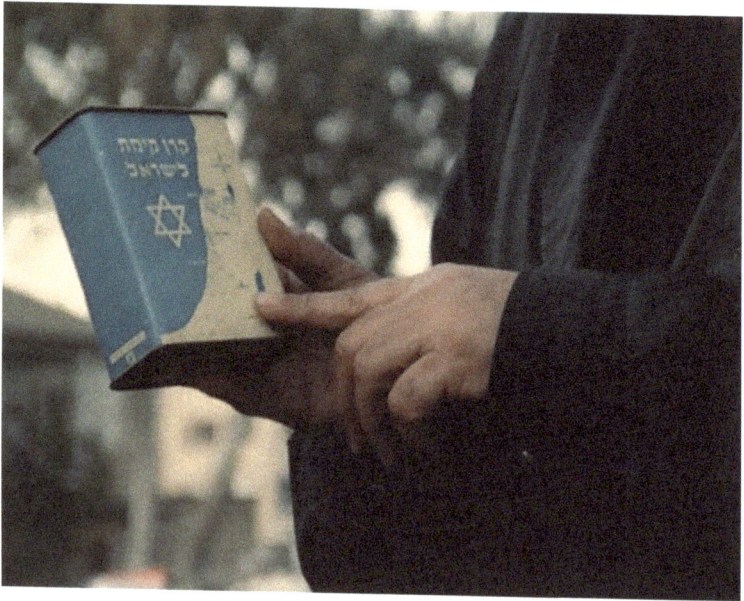

Figure 3.5 Ruth Beckermann (dir.), *Towards Jerusalem*, 1991.
© Ruth Beckermann Filmproduktion.

tissue of voices and sounds, linking this film with the final shots of *Paper Bridge* – most obviously in the recurrent image of walls covered with photographs, like that behind the multilingual mother-and-daughter couple, with its map of Israel and its photocopied pictures of landscapes and sculptures. Photocollage operates as a prevalent representational code figuring the wider social bricolage of late 1980s Israel amid the first Intifada (which, lasting from December 1987 until 1991, coincided with Beckermann's filming there). Collaged images are present from the opening scenes, in which a notice board adorned with posters and photographs is visible behind the action, to the closing sequence in an Elvis-themed gas station, with its rack of tourist postcards and walls covered with pin-up glossy Elvis pictures (Figure 3.6), another version of 'religious' or cultish devotion, echoing the shrine to the prophet Samuel seen a few moments earlier, the prophet, we are told, who emphasised most the importance of prayer – another form of vocal expression. The photocollage metonymises the processes of memorialisation (the construction of a usable past, and its encoding in images that act as guarantors of its 'reality' as well as in narratives and sites of memorial investment) which have accompanied the historical development of the Israeli state. Israel, in turn, is presented to the viewer through stylistic devices associated with the road movie, through (for example) long travelling shots along busy city streets (usually moving, as if reading Hebrew or Arabic script, from right to left), their signage emphasising again the densely polysemic and multilingual cosmopolitanism of the nation; and through the multilayered voices constituting prominent elements of the film's auditory landscapes. In contrast with the prevailing melancholic drift of *Paper Bridge*, the experience of watching *Towards Jerusalem* is one of sensory overload, of multiple media and codes operating simultaneously – a disordered trek through a forest of signs, momentarily literalised in the plethora of TV aerials visible atop the blocks of municipal residences past which the camera travels.[66]

The film's concern with the material image (photographs, postcards) grounds its analysis of the ideological 'image' of Israel, its questioning of the official historical and cultural version of the country constructed for international consumption by state machinery and media discourses. In her interview with Rebhandl, Beckermann described the "aesthetics" of Israel in 1990 as "a mixture of

Figure 3.6 Ruth Beckermann (dir.), *Towards Jerusalem*.
© Ruth Beckermann Filmproduktion.

American, Eastern Bloc, and Third World", and commented on its evident contemporary, slightly seedy decrepitude, a revelation which, she says, "shattered [*erschüttert*] my childhood dreams"[67] of a shining modern nation. Interviewed by Kantor, Beckermann expands on her childhood "dream" and its relation to the "dream" embodied in Israel itself: "[*Towards Jerusalem*] is a very pragmatic film. I mean, going to Israel to find out what became of 'the dream', because I was brought up with the dream, with the dancing and the songs and the kibbutz, and so on."[68] The suggestion that Israel is not just a version of the utopian "American Dream" (emphasised in the Elvis-themed gas station where the journey towards Jerusalem effectively ends), but also a "dream-state", echoes the intermittently oneiric mood of *Paper Bridge*, with one important difference – nostalgia for the Bukovina of the *entre deux guerres* is replaced by the anticipatory, forward-oriented, utopian desire of Israel, with Jerusalem as the endlessly displaced object of that desire, "ein Sehnsuchtswort [...] und eine Metaphor für Sehnsucht" ("a word of longing, and a metaphor for longing"), as Beckermann phrased it in 1991. The onward trajectory of the road movie form thus parallels the ostensible ideological progress of the nation-in-formation depicted in the film. This forward-facing aspect is, however, constantly undermined by the narratives Beckermann hears, in which memories of the recent or, sometimes, distant past are a repeated refrain; the Palestinian workers lamenting the lack of work compared to eight years earlier, the schoolgirl remembering her childhood after her family's adoption of strict religious practices. This is countered, in turn, by narratives of escape and arrival into safety in Israel, like the toy sellers, who recount each other's tales, he a German-speaking Polish survivor of Auschwitz and Dachau, she a Romanian survivor of a Transnistrian camp.

This personal historical revisionism – a reconstellation of the defining points of memory – corresponds to shifts in the wider processes of historical narrativisation of Israel, not addressed in Beckermann's film but significant elements of its historical context. Alongside its filming amidst the Intifada ("surely one of the great anticolonial insurrections of the modern period", according to Edward W. Said),[69] *Towards Jerusalem* also appeared in the wake of a wave of scholarly publications offering renewed revisionist interpretations of Israeli history, and particularly of the circumstances of the nation's origin in the late 1940s. Prompted by Maxime Rodinson's 1967 article "Israël: fait colonial" (published in Jean-Paul Sartre's *Les Temps modernes*, and expanded into a book published in English in 1973 as *Israel: A Colonial Settler State?*), books like Tom Segev's *1949, The First Israelis* (1986), Simha Flapan's *The Birth of Israel – Myths and Realities* (1987), and Benny Morris's *The Birth of the Palestinian Refugee Problem, 1947–1949* (1988) offered a counter-discourse to the origin myths constructed and perpetuated by successive Israeli governments and their supporters in the West. These revisionist arguments constituted what Zachary Lockman describes as "a breaking free of Israeli consensus history",[70] a development framed in part by responses by left and liberal Israelis to the invasion of Lebanon in 1982. The resulting counter-discourse scrutinised the establishment of what Lockman calls "a relatively homogenous Jewish state" on "the ruins of Palestinian Arab society".[71] As Said discusses at length, that society was itself characterised (despite ideologically motivated efforts to redefine it otherwise) by its own internal religious and cultural diversities and differences, and incorporated "a respectable Palestinian professional and intellectual class, the beginnings of small industry, and a highly developed national consciousness."[72] Jerusalem, central to three major religions, exists as the paradoxically 'absent centre' of the circulating signs and narratives and histories explored in Beckermann's film. The city exists as unattainable destination and endlessly displaced signified, beginning with the film's ambiguous, deictically gesturing title, which echoes the despairing, suspensive final paragraph of Amos Oz's 1971 novella *Crusade*: "Not turning homeward: they had given up all thought of human habitation. Not even toward Jerusalem, which is a place of disembodied love".[73] Jerusalem-as-sign becomes a contested figure, just as the real city is literally contested, fought over by warring communities (in 1990, Jerusalem had been annexed by the Israelis for 23 years, "its topography, environment and historic aura massively intervened in, forcibly changed, demographically tampered with" as a result, as Said argued in 1995).[74]

These discursive renegotiations of Israel's history frame the relations of Beckermann's film to earlier documentary engagements with the nation. Principally tracking the movement of German, Eastern European, and Russian Jewish migrants to Israel, *Towards Jerusalem* relates closely to precursor documentaries such as Claude Lanzmann's first feature film, *Pourquoi Israël* (1973), and Beckermann's montage of signs clearly echoes that of Chris Marker in his essay film on Israel, *Description d'un combat* (*Description of a Struggle*, 1960), the narration of which begins:

Signs,
this land first speaks to you in signs.
Signs of land,
signs of water,
signs of man,
signs –
This is the promised land,
this is Jerusalem on earth,
this is Israel.[75]

Eric Zakim has argued of Marker's film that it presses at the generic limits of the essay film, exploiting the ambiguity inherent in the form to attempt (*essai*) "to free language and the image from the historical and political confines"[76] of contemporary Israel. Zakim reads Marker's film in terms foregrounding its influence on Beckermann:

> *Description of a Struggle* emphasises an Israel that is a place of infinite signs, symbols in constant motion, where meaning never settles into a firm image. Rather, signs circulate, interact and constantly take on new meaning with the changes observed by the movie camera. The film's chiastic structure, which opens and closes with reference to the notion of signs themselves, reflects a transitory semantics from the very beginning [...].[77]

Towards Jerusalem also formally echoes Susan Sontag's first documentary, *Promised Lands* (1974), made immediately after the Yom Kippur war (and promptly banned in Israel on its release). Coinciding with, and deeply informing, Sontag's writing of *On Photography* (1977),[78] the concern of *Promised Lands* with a traumatised, war-torn culture is thematically connected to her analysis of photography as a discourse of *mementos mori*, an analysis on which Marianne Hirsch's arguments about photographs as media of memorialisation are, in turn, grounded. Hanan Toukan has described Sontag's film as

> a Godard-influenced lamentation of the psychological effects of the multilayered complexities binding the Israeli state. These include above all the collective consciousness of a beleaguered, paranoid, and terrified nation grappling with the traumas of persecution, war, pain, and death.[79]

In *Towards Jerusalem* Beckermann traces a different but analogous configuration of cultural trauma. She follows Sontag's film in (largely) refusing to mediate overtly the society, scenes, images, and narratives depicted. Eschewing both first person narrative and voice-over soliloquy-narration (the mediating forms of her previous films), the film thus avoids any simple authorial framing. Instead, it is edited as a series of self-supporting, interlocking scenes, Beckermann appearing in many as interviewer-questioner but never offering commentary, while music, particularly the deep violin notes of *Serenade mélancolique*, emphasises and emotionally orchestrates key moments in the film.

The single exception to this occurs early in the film, as the narrator (the actor Nina Kunz) reads a short poem, which encapsulates much of the film's ideological position, against a long tracking shot of the Tel Aviv beachfront and the east Mediterranean Sea:

> What did you dream of?
> In Tarnopol, Czernowitz, Berlin and Vienna?
> A country of your own, -
>
> Trees, plants, oranges and flowers.
> Milk and honey should flow – the same for everyone.
> Free people, new people on the old earth.
> No more ridicule, no more misery and no more shame.
> A people like any other people – homeland, earth, fatherland.
> Gone is the fear of soldiers and neighbours.
>
> So they dreamed in Tarnopol and elsewhere -
> the eye in the west, the heart in the east,
> in Jerusalem, where the Temple once stood.
>
> A flag was then sewn in Basel,
> blue and white, and said:
> If you want it, it's not a fairy tale.
>
> And then -
> Under the winter sun over the sea –
> erase fear, forget fear,
> burned from survival.
>
> What did you dream of?[80]

Alongside its overt echoes of Psalm 44 and its citation of Felix Salten's 1925 Palestine travelogue *Neue Menschen auf alter Erde: Eine Palästinafahrt,*[81] this poem alludes to a short lyric by the poet Yehuda HaLevy:

> My heart is in the east, and I in the uttermost west.
> How can I find savour in food? How shall it be sweet to me?
> How shall I render my vows and my bonds, while yet
> Zion lieth beneath the fetter of Edom, and I in Arab chains?
> A light thing would it seem to me
> to leave all the good things of Spain -
> Seeing how precious in mine eyes
> to behold the dust of the desolate sanctuary.[82]

Balancing references to Western and Palestinian literary and religious traditions, the poem is a significant statement of the film's productive ambivalence in relation to the politics of contemporary Israel.

The fractured and fragmented world presented in *Towards Jerusalem* can be read as a refusal of what Said calls the "ideology of difference" of the Israeli state (a monological ideology embodying that state's monotheistic religious basis, but not its multiple ethnic and linguistic composition). Instead, a subtle aesthetic alignment is implied. In representing its version of Israeli–Jewish social realities, the film adopts a poetics resembling that critically associated with the experience of the one community, Palestinians, specifically excluded from those social worlds but (as the film insistently reveals) economically and culturally supplementary and thus necessary to them, underpinning and sustaining through their labour their economic viability. Members of this labour community appear throughout the film as signifiers of this excluded supplement, constant reminders of the reliance of Israeli society on Palestinian labour. In doing so, a degree of shared experience is implied, a level of social commonality between Israeli settlers and the Palestinian community they have displaced, a commonality officially refused by the "ideology of difference" that dominates Israeli society.

Similarly the 'road movie' form of *Towards Jerusalem* underlines an essentially nomadic and itinerant interaction with Israeli life on the part of the film crew, one that conflicts with the narratives of new-found rootedness the film records. This rootedness is constantly asserted, and just as constantly critiqued, throughout the film. To take one example of its complex visual semiotics, after the café sequence, in the montage of street scenes presenting the bustle of urban life in Tel Aviv noted earlier, passengers and soldiers disembark from an arriving bus and disperse into the passing crowds, carrying bags, holdalls, and rifles. The camera pans, and then zooms and lingers for a few seconds on one blue bag carried by an elderly man, momentarily singled out from the crowd of bag-carrying pedestrians. Semiotically this moment links with the blue charity boxes and the recurrent blue star and stripes of the Israeli flag in a semantic thread of signifiers of national identity. It also echoes the insistence in Jean Mohr's photographs (in *After the Last Sky*) of *Palestinians* bearing luggage as a signifier of rootlessness and mobility, of movement and itinerance. As Said puts it in his text accompanying Mohr's pictures, "the Palestinians are a people who move a lot, who are always carrying bags from one place to another".[83] The bags carried by Israeli soldiers and other passengers become markers of a similar kind of internal mobility, suggesting a nomadic, rootless dimension within the ostensible 'rootedness' of Jewish–Israeli society.

In their attempts to establish roots, the recent immigrants to the region brought with them, and recount for the camera, memories and traditions that straddle the borders between personal history and cultural myth, establishing utopian traditions and physical memorials as embodiments of their new transplanted rootedness and of their sense of nationhood and belonging. The best known of these is the Yad Vashem Holocaust Memorial, opened in 1957 on the Hill of Remembrance in West Jerusalem (and site of the opening scene of Lanzmann's *Pourquoi Israël*). Despite all the personal narratives recorded in *Towards Jerusalem*, no narrative equivalent in mythic or parabolic force to the tales of Hagazussa or the "paper bridge" is forthcoming. Where *Paper Bridge* explored contemporary memories of the lost modernity of central Europe, *Towards Jerusalem* discovers in Israel the apparent rootlessness of Jewish postmodernity, a condition figured not in the cutting down of a tree or a cemetery carving of a lopped tree but in footage (almost exactly

Figure 3.7 Ruth Beckermann (dir.), *Towards Jerusalem*, 1991.
© Ruth Beckermann Filmproduktion.

half-way through the film) of a tractor transporting an uprooted tree along a road. A sequence late in the film shows the ceremonial unveiling of a small memorial, veil and monument bearing trees, "a symbol" (the ceremonial host declares) "of Jewish rootedness and a symbol of Jewish life". "Nothing represents peace as well as a tree", she continues, as (in a profoundly dystopian moment) loud gunfire is clearly heard in the background, echoing across the desert landscape[84] (Figure 3.7). Said notes, however, that, for the Palestinians under Israeli occupation, "To plant a tree required a permit".[85] The Palestinians Beckermann encounters, mostly male workers waiting for labour or, engaged in their jobs, reluctant to speak to the camera (all are self-consciousness before the film crew; their fear of legal reprisals – "*You* can go to jail", one man jokes as he pushes his friend before the film crew – is a recurrent motif in the film), are an insistent presence, a reminder of the other, uprooted, and dispersed diversity on the repression of which the Israeli version of Jewish national identity is founded.

Figure 3.8 Ruth Beckermann (dir.), *Towards Jerusalem*, 1991.
© Ruth Beckermann Filmproduktion.

Reprising the cart moving forward into fog of *Paper Bridge*, *Towards Jerusalem* ends in a car journeying along a foggy motorway between Purim and Pessach, towards Jerusalem (Figure 3.8). Amazingly, snow is falling, a sign that apparently impossible things may still happen. The film's images dissolve in this closing sequence into the blur of the windscreen; Israel, and Jerusalem, remain unattained objects, indefinitely projected and deferred locales and identities, the journey interstitially suspended, its movement continuing between incompletely composed potential homelands. Beckermann's double quest for a sense of belonging or of utopian resolution in the contrasting, territorial and genealogical, contemporary Jewish communities of *Paper Bridge* and *Towards Jerusalem* remains likewise incomplete, unresolved, dialectically in suspension as the latter film ends.

Notes

1 Ruth Kluger, *Landscapes of Memory: A Holocaust Girlhood Remembered* (London: Bloomsbury, 2003), pp. 74–5.

2 " 'Die Gegend, wo Menschen und Bücher lebten', ist heute 'der Geschichtslosigkeit anheimgefallen', sagte Paul Celan, der ebensowenig in die Stadt seiner Jugend zurückkehrte wie die anderen alten Czernowitzer. Sie würden eine Stadt finden, die nur von ferne, durch die Scheiben eines fahrenden Autos ihrer Erinnerung gleicht." Beckermann, "Erdbeeren in Czernowitz", in Christoph Ransmayr (ed.), *Im blinden Winkel: Nachrichten aus Mitteleuropa* (Frankfurt am Main: Fischer, 1987), p. 109.

3 Daniel Boyarin and Jonathan Boyarin, "Diaspora: Generation and the Ground of Jewish Identity", in Jana Evans Braziel and Anita Mannur (eds), *Theorizing Diaspora: A Reader* (Oxford: Blackwell, 2003), pp. 85–118; p. 103.

4 Daniel Boyarin and Jonathan Boyarin, *Powers of Diaspora: Two Essays on the Relevance of Jewish Culture* (Minneapolis, MN: University of Minnesota Press, 2002), p. 12.

5 "Die Montage folgte der Logik der Reise, den Assoziationen, die sich durch die Bilder ergeben und den Geschichten, die im Film vorkommen." Christa Blümlinger, "Im Gespräch mit Ruth Beckermann", 11 January 1991. Promotional flier, *21 Internationales Forum des jungen Films 26 / 41 Internationale Filmfestspiele Berlin* (Berlin, 1991), n.p.

6 Kadya Molodowsky, 'My Paper Bridge', *Paper Bridges: Selected Poems* (ed. and trans. Kathryn Hellerstein) (Detroit: Wayne State University Press, 1999), p. 237.

7 See Marc Sagnol, "Bukovina and Its Poets: A Country Where Men and Books Lived", *Social Sciences* Vol. 11 No. 5 (2022), 283–90. Beckermann mentions Celan, Ausländer, and other writers in her essay on Czernowitz, "Erdbeeren in Czernowitz", pp. 107, 109.

8 Katya Krylova, "Melancholy Journeys in the Films of Ruth Beckermann", *Leo Baeck Institute Yearbook* Vol. 59 (2014), 249–66: 256.

9 Ruth Beckermann, untitled text (dated 02/1987), *Ruth Beckermann Film Collection* box set, DVD booklet, *Die papierene Brücke*, p. 3.

10 Christina Guenther, "The Politics of Location in Ruth Beckermann's 'Vienna Films'", *Modern Austrian Literature* Vol. 37 Nos. 3–4 (2204), 33–46: 41.

11 Beckermann, untitled text (dated 02/1987).

12 *War and Remembrance* (mini-series, Disney / ABC Domestic Television), dir. Dan Curtis, 1988. First broadcast November 1988 – May 1989.

13 "Interview with Rebhandl", 2007.

14 Tzvetan Todorov and Arnold Weinstein, "The Structural Analysis of Literature: The Tales of Henry James", in David Robey (ed.), *Structuralism: An Introduction* (Oxford: Clarendon Press, 1973), pp. 73–103; p. 73.

15 Christa Blümlinger, "Meanderings of an Austrian Traveller", in Lendl (ed.), *Ruth Beckermann Film Collection – Texte/Texts/Textes*, p. 73.

16 Dagmar C. G. Lorenz, "Ruth Beckermann's Journey to Czernowitz: Displacement and Postmemory in *Die papierene Brücke*", *Journal of Austrian Studies* Vol. 53 No. 3 (2020), 77.

17 Katya Krylova, *The Long Shadow of the Past: Contemporary Austrian Literature, Film, and Culture* (Rochester: Camden House, 2017), p. 38.

18 Florence Heymann, *Le Crépuscule des lieux: Identités juives de Czernowitz* (Paris: Stock, 2003), p. 109.

19 Guenther, "The Politics of Location in Ruth Beckermann's 'Vienna Films'", 39.

20 For a detailed summary survey of the history and cultural diversity of Bukovina and Czernowitz, see Amy Diana-Colin and Andrei Corbea-Hoisie, "Paul Celan's Bukovina-Meridians", in Michael Eskin, Karen Leeder, and Marko Pajević (eds), *Paul Celan Today: A Companion* (Berlin: De Gruyter, 2021), pp. 9–15. See also Ransmayr, *Im blinden Winkel: Nachrichten aus Mitteleuropa*.

21 Marianne Hirsch and Leo Spitzer, *Ghosts of Home – The Afterlife of Jewish Memory in Czernowitz* (Los Angeles, CA: University of California Press, 2010), p. 9.
22 Hirsch and Spitzer, *Ghosts of Home*, pp. 36–7.
23 Cited in Hirsch and Spitzer, *Ghosts of Home*, p. 19.
24 Hirsch and Spitzer, *Ghosts of Home*, p. 10.
25 Cixous, Hélène, "How to Film Becoming Invisible" (trans. Eric Prenowitz), in Lendl (ed.), *Ruth Beckermann Film Collection: Texte/ Texts/Textes*, p. 88.
26 Helga Mitterbauer and Carrie Smith-Prei, "Introduction: Crossings and Encounters", in Mitterbauer and Smith-Prei (eds), *Crossing Central Europe: Continuities and Transformations, 1990 and 2000* (Toronto: University of Toronto Press, 2017), p. xi.
27 Heymann, *Le Crépuscule des lieux*, p. 73.
28 Beckermann discusses the relation of resemblance between Czernowitz and Vienna in her essay "Erbeeren in Czernowitz", in Ransmayr (ed.), *Im Blinden Winkel*, pp. 98ff.
29 See Adriana Madej-Stang, *Which Face of Witch: Self-representations of Women as Witches in Works of Contemporary British Women Writers* (Newcastle-Upon-Tyne: Cambridge Scholars Publishing, 2015), pp. 3ff.
30 Hillary Hope Herzog, "The Global and the Local in Ruth Beckermann's Films and Writings", in Hope Herzog, Todd Herzog and Benjamin Lapp (eds), *Rebirth of a Culture: Jewish Identity and Jewish Writing in Germany and Austria Today* (New York: Berghahn, 2008), p. 103.
31 Andrea Reiter notes the "almost verbatim" quoting of this passage in the film. Reiter, *Contemporary Jewish Writing*, p. 114.
32 Manès Sperber, *God's Water Carriers* (trans. Joachim Neugroschel) (New York: Holmes and Meier, 1987), p. 31.
33 Included on Bulgarian State Television Female Choir, *Les mystères des voix bulgares* Vol. 1, Philips 1975/4AD CD 1986.
34 A version of *Fratres* recorded in 1997 by the Hungarian State Orchestra was used by the BBC in Laurence Rees' 2005 documentary *Auschwitz: the Nazis and the 'Final Solution'*. Beckermann also uses passages from Pärt's *Tabula Rasa* (1977) in *Die papierene Brücke*.
35 Hillary Hope Herzog points out that this shot reveals to the viewer that Beckermann "is, quite literally, going in circles" in trying to tell the story she sets out to tell. Hillary Hope Herzog, "The Global and the Local in Ruth Beckermann's Films and Writings", in Hope Herzog et al. (eds), *Rebirth of a Culture*, p. 103.
36 "Interview with Rebhandl", 2007. Beckermann fleshes out this extraordinary narrative in great detail in this interview.

37 Hirsch and Spitzer recount seeing similar gravestones in the cemetery in Czernowitz: "A few large gravestones were carved to resemble severed tree trunks, symbolizing the tree of life cut short by death and usually used to mark children's graves." *Ghosts of Home*, p. 23.

38 Molodowsky, *Paper Bridges*, p. 32.

39 Krylova, "Melancholy Journeys in the Films of Ruth Beckermann", 257.

40 Matti Bunzl, "Political Inscription, Artistic Reflection: A Recontextualisation of Contemporary Viennese-Jewish Literature", *The German Quarterly* (Spring 2000), 163–70: 168.

41 See Robert Schindel, *Born-Where* (trans. Michael Roloff) (Riverside: Ariadne Press, 1995), pp. 275–85.

42 Lukas Stepanik, *Gebürtig*, 2009.

43 "Es schneit Geschichte, las ich in einem Roman. Je weniger Geschichte, desto leichter kann man an Ereignissen vorbei oder durch sie hindurchgehen."

44 Posthofen, "Ruth Beckermann: Re-activating Memory", p. 268.

45 Philip Davis, *Bernard Malamud: A Writer's Life* (Oxford: Oxford University Press, 2007), p. 252.

46 Bernard Malamud, *The Fixer* (Harmondsworth: Penguin, 1968), pp. 281–2.

47 Améry, *At the Mind's Limits*, p. 3.

48 "Interview with Rebhandl", 2007.

49 "Interview with Rebhandl", 2007.

50 Krylova, "Melancholy Journeys", p. 42.

51 Lorenz, "Post-Shoah Positions", 162.

52 Hirsch, *Family Frames*, p. 101.

53 Heymann, *Le Crépuscule des lieux*, p. 185.

54 Amos Oz, "Universal Redemption", *TIME*, 15 May 1978, p. 61.

55 Arnold Zweig, letter to Sigmund Freud, 1 September 1935, in Ernst L. Freud (ed.), *The Letters of Sigmund Freud and Arnold Zweig* (trans. Elaine and William Robson-Scott) (New York: New York University Press, 1970), p. 108.

56 "*Nach Jerusalem* hat nicht mehr als 121 Einstellungen, und trotzdem werden in dem Film 23 individuelle Geschichten angerissen. Ich glaube, daß der Film sehr voll und schnell ist, ohne Fünf-Sekunden-Schnitt-Techniken anzuwenden." "Beckermann im Gespräch mit Christa Blümlinger" (n.p.).

57 Hamid Naficy, *An Accented Cinema – Exilic and Diasporic Filmmaking* (Princeton, NJ: Princeton University Press. 2001), p. 31.

58 For a discussion of the diverse ethnic, national, and class constitution of Israeli society in the early 1970s, see Haim Hanegbi, Moshe

Machover, and Akiva Orr, "The Class Nature of Israeli Society", *New Left Review* 1–65 (Jan–Feb 1971), 3–26.

59 Lorenz, "Post-Shoah Positions", 165.

60 Hana Morgenstern, "A Savage Corpse: Colonialism, Anticolonialism, and the Hebrew Avant-Garde", *Modernism/modernity* Vol. 28 No. 4 (November 2021), 661–86: 665.

61 "[D]espite the fact that most Hebrew modernists were in active support of the national-colonial project, modernist practices such as collage were at stylistic odds with the crude representations, teleologies, and linear trajectories of nationalism." Morgenstern, ibid., 665.

62 See Susan Buck-Morss, *The Dialectics of Seeing: Walter Benjamin and the Arcades Project* (Cambridge, MA: MIT Press, 1989), p. 74: "the kaleidoscopic, fortuitous juxtaposition of shop signs and window displays".

63 Writing of his visit to Tel-Aviv in 1992, Edward W. Said observed that "The national snubbing of Palestinians by Israel is evident in road signs, all of which are in Hebrew, of course, some with English translations, only a few in Arabic." See Said, "Return to Palestine-Israel", in *The Politics of Dispossession: The Struggle for Palestinian Self-Determination 1969–1994* (London: Vintage, 1995), p. 176.

64 These boxes figure frequently in Israeli literature. See, for example, Amos Oz, *To Know a Woman* (trans. Nicholas de Lange and Amos Oz) (London: Vintage, 1992), pp. 120, 197, 200.

65 "Interview with Rebhandl", 2007.

66 This scene echoes Jean Mohr's photograph "Jerusalem, 1979. A forest of television antennae", reproduced in Edward W. Said and Jean Mohr, *After the Last Sky: Palestinian Lives* (London: Vintage, 1993), p. 147.

67 "Interview with Rebhandl", 2007.

68 Kantor, "Ruth Beckermann – Documentarian of the Present", 231.

69 Edward W. Said, "Introduction", *The Politics of Dispossession*, p. xxvii.

70 Zachary Lockman, "Original Sin", in Lockmann and Joel Beinin (eds), *Intifada: The Palestinian Uprising against Israeli Occupation* (London: IB Tauris, 1990), p. 189.

71 Lockman, "Original Sin", p. 190.

72 Edward W. Said, "The Question of Palestine", in *The Question of Palestine* (New Edition) (London: Vintage, 1992), p. 12.

73 Amos Oz, "Crusade", in *Unto Death* (trans. Nicholas de Lange) (London: Flamingo, 1986), p. 81.

74 Edward Said, "The Current Status of Jerusalem", *Jerusalem Quarterly* 45 (2011), 57–72: 59.

75 www.markertext.com/description_of_a_struggle.htm, accessed 21 March 2023.

76 Eric Zakim, "Chris Marker's *Description of a Struggle* and the Limits of the Essay Film", in Elizabeth Papazian and Caroline Eades (eds), *The Essay Film* (London: Wallflower Press, 2016), p. 160.

77 Zakim, "Chris Marker's *Description of a Struggle* and the Limits of the Essay Film", p. 146.

78 See Jerome Boyd Maunsell, *Susan Sontag* (London: Reaktion, 2014), pp. 115–17.

79 Hanan Toukan, "Lacan, Sontag, and Israel on Screen", in Viola Shafik (ed.), *Documentary Filmmaking in the Middle East and North Africa* (Cairo: The American University in Cairo Press, 2022), p. 280.

80 Wovon hat man geträumt / In Tarnopol, Czernowitz, Berlin und Wien? / Ein eigenes Land, / Bäume, Pflanzen, Orangen und Blumen. / Milch und Honig sollten fließen – für alle gleich. / Freie Menschen, neue Menschen auf der alten Erde. / Kein Spott mehr, kein Elend und keine Scham. / Ein Volk wie jedes Volk – Heimat, Erde, Vaterland. / Vorbei die Angst vor Soldaten und Nachbarn. / So hat man in Tarnopol und anderswo geträumt – / das Auge im Westen, das Herz im Osten, / in Jerusalem, wo einmal der Tempel stand. / In Basel wurde dann eine Fahne genäht, / blau–weiß, und gesagt: / Wenn ihr wollt, ist es kein Märchen. / Und dann – / Unter der Wintersonne übers Meer – / Angst auslöschen, / Angst vergessen, / vom überleben gebrannt. / Wovon hat man geträumt?

81 Felix Salten, *Neue Menschen auf alter Erde: Eine Palästinafahrt*, Königstein: Athanäum, 1986 (first published Berlin: Paul Zsolnay, 1925).

82 This poem is also alluded to by Yehuda Amichai in his *Poems of Jerusalem* 1: "My Heart. Myself. East. West" (in *A Life of Poetry 1948–1994*, trans. Benjamin and Barbara Harshav [New York: HarperCollins, 1995], p. 79).

83 Said, "On Palestinian Identity", p. 115.

84 This moment echoes the concentration camp funeral filmed in Falkenau by Sam Fuller in 1945 and fictionalised in Sam Fuller, *The Big Red One* (1980). See also Emil Weiss and Sam Fuller, *Falkenau, The Impossible* (1988). See Georges Didi-Huberman, "Opening the Camps, Closing the Eyes: Image, History, Readability", in Griselda Pollock and Max Silverman (eds), *Concentrationary Cinema: Aesthetics as Political Resistance in Alain Resnais's Night and Fog (1955)* (Oxford: Berghahn, 2011), pp. 84–125: pp. 100–103.

85 Edward W. Said, "Intifada and Independence", in Lockman and Beinin (eds), *Intifada*, p. 6. See also Said and Mohr, *After the Last Sky*: "Laws 1015 and 1039 [...] stipulate that any Arab on the West Bank and Gaza who owns land must get written permission from the military governor before planting either a new vegetable – for example, an eggplant – or fruit tree. Failure to get permission risks one the destruction of the tree or vegetable plus one year's imprisonment" (p. 28).

4

Intolerable images – *East of War* and *The Waldheim Waltz*

Waldheim showed me where I really lived. [...] He forced me to confront my own illusions. He, who was the biggest repressor of all, showed me how much I myself had repressed in order to justify living in this country. (Leon Zelman, Director of the Jewish Welcome Service)[1]

In this part of the story we recognise the *return* of the repressed, which (along with the immediate effects of the trauma and the phenomenon of latency) we have described as among the essential features of a neurosis. (Sigmund Freud)[2]

The photo- and image-collages depicted at various points in *Paper Bridge* and *Towards Jerusalem* emphasise the importance of the image, as a repository of memory and identity, to Beckermann's enquiries into Jewish identity and into her own experience of unbelonging in Austria. The two films addressed in this chapter focus on particular forms and uses of the image through recent theories (particularly those developed in several works by Jacques Rancière and Georges Didi-Huberman) of how images work in relation to history, memory and politics. Following Rancière in his analysis of images of atrocity, for example, we might provisionally characterise the images Beckermann addresses in these films as dealing, in two ways, with "intolerable" realities: first, in the implication that the images depict a reality "too intolerably real to be offered in the form of an image"[3] and are therefore unacceptable (excessive, overdetermined, too offensively graphic) as documents of that reality; and second, in the sinister political manipulations involved in the image's construction and use to *conceal* intolerable elements of reality. Each film offers a different analysis of the deconstruction at the end of the twentieth century of the historical lie of non-involvement and non-culpability in Nazism and its atrocities that defined post-war Austrian politics, a lie constitutive of the social, political and cultural conditions of unbelonging as theorised by Beckermann.

The photographic images of wartime atrocities displayed in the exhibition *Vernichtungskrieg: Verbrechen der Wehrmacht 1941–44* (*War of Annihilation: Crimes of the Wehrmacht*), shown in Vienna in the Autumn of 1995, provide the basis for an enquiry into the relations between Austrian memory, history, identity and politics in Beckermann's film and book project *East of War* (1996) and *Jenseits des Krieges: Ehemalige Wehrmachtssoldaten erinnern sich* (*East of War: Recollections of Former Wehrmacht Soldiers*, 1998).[4] The "intolerability" of these images – their intolerability *as* images, alongside that of the reality they represent ("the intolerable in the image", as Rancière puts it)[5] – is proven by many of the responses recorded in Beckermann's film, which reject outright, or protest the alleged falsity or indeterminacy of, or attempt to excuse, the photographs and the implications of what they depict. In *The Waldheim Waltz* (2018), a related enquiry develops from Beckermann's exploration of the media-discursive construction of the Austrian politician Kurt Waldheim during his successful 1986 campaign for the country's presidency amidst high-profile revelations of his previously concealed Nazi past. The "intolerable" image here is the smooth, media-manufactured appearance of Waldheim as legitimised figure of a historically amnesiac state authority, a construction embodied in the DVD cover-image of Waldheim, seated erect, his head turned awkwardly downwards to watch an equerry's hand brushing his suit clean in preparation for a television appearance – an image (to which we'll return later) capturing the manufacturing of an image. The film examines the processes and motivations, as well as the political implications, of this image-manufacturing, which is simultaneously an erasure (as the grooming brush suggests) of tenacious traces of another, less tolerable image.

The historical events explored in these films mobilised a visual anamnesis or "lifting of repression"[6] which transformed Austrian engagement with the recent past but also laid bare the anachronistic persistence of disturbing elements of that past. Both films offer diagnostic surveys of conditions producing Beckermann's experience of 'unbelonging' (itself an attempt to grasp the intolerability of a kind of intolerance) in late twentieth-century Austria, an experience heightened and sharpened by the re-emergence in Austrian society of fascism as a viable, and indeed electable, political force exploiting to the full the politics of the image to create the conditions of its electability. Beckermann traces the ideological contours of this resurgent fascism by scrutinising its distorting and deforming effects on public and critical perception and debate over different varieties of image and their effects, alongside the incitement of differing degrees of social tolerance or intolerance. Both films, in different ways, offer snapshots of and critical interventions into the evolution of Austrian public (self-) perception and opinion in relation to how images mediate and manipulate cultural and historical events, distorting points of view and opinions, and disruptively re-animating and foregrounding anachronous topics and events by inserting them unpredictably into contemporary discourse, which is rendered unhomely and inhospitable by these distortions.

The disrupted temporal sequence defining the conditions of production of these two films is a formal and constitutive expression of this inhospitableness. The twenty-two-year gap between the films emphasises their anachronous relations regarding their respective concerns, the earlier film addressing the historically later event, the later film exploring the earlier event. These concerns are, in turn, connected by their analogous thematic and ideological content. International political scandal and scandalous photography exhibition thus become intertwined, comparable expressions of a double, and doubly intolerable, national trauma: that of repressed historical events and the revelation, in the contemporary, of the persistence of the social attitudes underpinning them; and that of the fragility of the myth of victimhood with which the nation sought to conceal that repression and that persistence. The belatedness implicit in the very notion of the historical resurgence or return in the late twentieth century of Austrian fascism is further concretised in the two-year gap between film and book of *East of War*, and in the belated making of *The Waldheim Waltz*, appearing over thirty years after the events it documents (and recycling some of the footage of demonstrations in Vienna in 1986 that Beckermann had used at the end of *Paper Bridge*), so that the film itself both registers and performs a kind of traumatic aftershock, and can thus be read as a manifestation of Freudian *Nachträglichkeit* or "afterwardsness", the delayed response to damaging traumatic events – a delayed response also clearly evident in some of the witness testimony Beckermann records in *East of War*. This extended historical perspective enables us to read these films as mapping Austria's painful but necessary process of redistributing cultural responsibility, a redistribution accompanying the anamnesis.

Together, these two films explore the discernible effects upon late-twentieth-century Austrian history of the public experiences of and responses to what Heidemarie Uhl, in her detailed history of the politics of post-war Austrian memory, calls Austria's "divergent cultures of remembrance".[7] This period came to an arguably inevitable conclusion with the election in 1999 of a coalition government including Jörg Haider's far-right and openly fascist Freedom Party (FPÖ), a moment (in the future of *East of War* and framing the retrospective gaze of *The Waldheim Waltz*) in which the conflicting truth-regimes mapped in each film found an unsettling resolution in the effective 'return' to power of the political ideology underpinning the cause of the trauma.[8] Temporal disorder and delay are thus intrinsic elements of these films' engagements with the disrupted, recursive psychological sequences of post-war Austrian political history, in which, as each film was released, the nation returned disturbingly to its repressed Nazi past by electing figures or parties overtly connected to, or publicly re-enacting attitudes and policies characteristic of, that past. It is these distinct but closely connected moments of political regression – symptoms of Austrian trauma – which Beckermann's films perceive as distorting ideological convulsions within the body politic. The past, in turn, exists in each film in distorted, semi-concealed versions of itself, presented in different configurations of the image and its (political and ethical) intolerability: in *East of War*, the photographic image as record of (disputed) events and as (disputed) record of events, and, in *The Waldheim Waltz*, the constructed media image as screen that both conceals and bears projections of contested versions of Austrian history.

Discursive contestations: image and history in *East of War*

"Wo waren die Mörder geblieben?"

"*Die Mörder sind unter uns.*"[9]

These images, I did not take them, I do not know anything about them. I do not recognize anything at all about where they were taken either.[10]

Vernichtungskrieg: Verbrechen der Wehrmacht 1941–1944, held initially in Hamburg in 1995, showed ostensibly amateur photographs of torture and other atrocities, images taken by Wehrmacht soldiers on the Eastern Front during World War II. Nadine Fresco's *On the Death of Jews*, first published in French in 2008 and dealing principally with atrocities committed in Libau, Latvia by German and, later, Latvian soldiers, discusses a comparable sequence of photographs shown at trials in Berlin and Hannover in 1971. Fresco provides some context for these photographs (and, by extension, those exhibited in Hamburg a quarter of a century later), particularly in relation to the easy portability of the camera and consequent wide availability of photographic technology during the war:

Photography has been very popular in Germany since the 1920s, most notably thanks to Leica, the pioneer of film cameras in 24 × 36 mm, Minox, and Zeiss Icon (in 24 × 24) – formats that make the cameras particularly easy to transport. Soldiers often carry them in their military bags. So, while they are contributing to the collections the Propaganda Kompanien send to Berlin, they can also keep some for themselves, to send to their spouses or fiancées – images that for some, perhaps, are bound to enhance the family album, alongside the memories of birthdays and marriages and other 'precious life moments'.[11]

Fresco details the long-running tension in wartime German military communications between the imperative to prohibit photography of atrocities perpetrated against non-combatants and combatants alike (executions, mass killings, hangings or shootings) and the evident prevalence of both practices – committing atrocity and documenting it in photographs – among Wehrmacht soldiers.[12] "The myth" (she writes) "of a Wehrmacht free of all responsibility for the atrocities committed in the East – for which the SS alone would be found guilty – was going to last in the post-war period."[13]

The *Vernichtungskrieg* exhibition toured to numerous German and Austrian cities including Vienna, where Beckermann filmed public responses to the displayed images over several weeks of October and November 1995. Initially comprising over 1400 photographs, the show came under critical scrutiny when it was revealed that

several pictures had been mis-captioned or misattributed, laying the
entire display open to contestation by opportunistic sceptics. A cor-
rected and drastically pared-down version was relaunched in 2001,
accompanied by a larger and more textually detailed catalogue.[14]
Presenting interviews with, discussions between, and monologues
from visitors to the exhibition, sometimes individually, sometimes
in pairs or small groups, Beckermann's *East of War* was filmed
exclusively in the Viennese exhibition space of the first run of the
exhibition. The film thus takes place entirely within a restricted
indoor arena and presents a dramatically curtailed visual field, contrasting with the expansive international journey-narratives of the
films addressed in the previous chapter. The film also restricts its
purview within this already restricted field by avoiding direct or
close-up documentation of the photographs exhibited, following
the formal and stylistic decisions taken by Claude Lanzmann in
his *Shoah* (1985), in which (as Karoline Feyertag phrases it) "oral
testimonies evoke extremely intense imagery in the imagination of
the individual onlookers which can in a certain sense only be read
from the eyes of the witnesses who are given a chance to speak in
the film".[15] The focus of attention is thus on the speakers – their
faces, their gestures, their eyes – as they talk to the camera.

Expanding on this evocation, Beckermann's "Shooting Journal"
for *East of War* records, among other things, her daily emotional
reactions to the interviews she documents (thus constituting a
remarkable real-time record of her visceral experience of "unbelonging" in relation to the exhibition attendees). On 8 November
1995 she notes Roland Barthes' comment (at the beginning of his
Camera Lucida) on seeing, in a photograph of Napoleon's younger
brother, "eyes that had seen the emperor".[16] This provides her with
an analogy for the experience of filming those who both perpetrated
and witnessed wartime atrocities: "I see the eyes of those who had
seen the tortured, hanged, humiliated."[17] She immediately follows
this insight with a sentence debunking the entire public response
to the exhibition: "Of course we knew that the Wehrmacht was
not innocent, but quite involved in executing the NS annihilation-
policies."[18] Beckermann's assertion of this 'common knowledge'
comes several years after the Austrian Chancellor Franz Vranitzky's
July 1991 broadcast to the nation in which he apologised for wartime atrocities committed by Austrians – the first public political

acknowledgement of this national guilt.[19] Vranitzky's address, delivered in the wake of the Waldheim scandal (discussed later in this chapter), marked a crucial shift in the nation's political relations to its history and signified the end in official political terms of the myths of Austrian 'victimhood' which had defined the entire history of the Second Republic, and the introduction instead of the "co-responsibility thesis" which posited Austria as sharing responsibility for Nazism and the Holocaust. "Thereby", writes Helga Embacher of the address, "National Socialism was no longer seen as foreign rule imposed from outside but as a genuine part of Austria's history."[20] The implications of this revised historical awareness were made clear at the beginning of the introductory text to the catalogue accompanying the 'Wehrmacht exhibition': "In 1945, immediately following the defeat of Nazi Germany, the former generals began to fabricate a legend – the legend of the 'clean Wehrmacht'."[21] However, reviewing the revised exhibition in 2002, Gabriel Fawcett emphasises a potential distinction between public and academic kinds of awareness, noting that "graphic photographs of ordinary German Army or Wehrmacht soldiers involved in war crimes and genocide in the East" were "nothing new to German historians" but "hit the German public like a bombshell".[22] Assuming that "German" here also refers to 'Austrian', this distinction suggests that Vranitzky's acknowledgement in 1991 of Austrian culpability in Nazi crimes was, a decade later, being selectively received.

Beckermann's film engages with the tensions and the anamnesis generated in mid-1990s Austria by this fifty-year-old myth and its apparent contradiction by the intolerable images exhibited in the 'Wehrmacht exhibition'. The film is spare and minimalist, devoid of music, almost wholly reliant on ambient and sometimes intrusive sound (at one point the trill of a telephone interrupts an interview), with transparent, sometimes clumsy camera movements, zooms, pans, and other devices drawing attention to its 'authenticity', set within an exhibition space filmed from constantly shifting perspectives but always eschewing any direct depiction of the images themselves. The restricted documentary arena allows violently contested, partially repressed narratives to come into play through conversation and social interaction, dispute over political and experiential similarities and differences spreading from one commentator to the next, in a discursive process analogous to the "epidemic power" of photography itself, as described by Georges Didi-Huberman in *Images malgré tout* [*Images in Spite of All*]: "Photography works hand in glove with image and memory and therefore possesses their notable epidemic power."[23] The resulting *agon* of public debate pits contrasting truth regimes into direct conflict as people rehearsing different narratives and different interpretations of history struggle to transform memory into testimony, and questions of rumour and hearsay counter the documentary force of the silent, unreadable images and wall texts in the background. The discursive positions taken up by the men and, occasionally, women Beckermann films include speculation and assertion about (for example) *why* (and, in the most extreme denials, *whether*) the acts documented were actually performed; argument about the validity or otherwise – the *truth value* – of the content of the images; and a range of emotional responses, veering from fury to grief, to the events and scenes depicted.

East of War presents, then, a series of *in-situ* arguments between members of the viewing public brought together by the exhibition (or, sometimes, arguments individuals are acting out with themselves as they struggle to articulate to the camera their own responses). This series resolves within the first ten minutes into several broad positions, some apparently prompted by Beckermann's questioning, others assumed in relation to overheard statements or descriptions (several times, arguments begin after unprompted interventions or comments): first, one of denial from personal experience or personal disbelief ("I didn't see it" / "I refuse to accept that this happened"); second, admission of limited truth ("It happened, but only in isolated cases"); third, comparative exoneration ("It's true, but the Russians/Polish did equally bad or much worse things"); and fourth (and most infrequently), admission of general truth ("It's all true" / "I witnessed mass slaughter"). Recurrent phrases like "It was different then" are used to distance or substantiate positions. Strikingly, witnessing is repeatedly couched in terms of experience ("*Das habe ich erlebt*" / "I experienced that", or "*Das habe ich nicht erlebt*" / "I didn't experience that") rather than seeing, a sensorial shift from particular to general suggesting that, even in the moment of confession, the intolerability of the image (or of what has been seen, which has been recorded in the photographic images) persists. In her "Shooting Journal" Beckermann diagnoses these positions in terms of character-types: "The Coward and Follower", "The Unbroken/Unbowed", "The Schwejk-Type (a Viennese type in a positive sense)", and "The Outsider"[24] – suggesting a reading of the film as a kind of modern morality play. The recurrence of this limited social scope means that the film's discursive patterning is one of circularity and rhetorical constriction, as each argument defines and then covers and re-covers territories of dispute. Individuals deploy strategies of denial, contestation, revelation, confession, shame, guilt, refusal, disbelief, admission – all of which define the emotional and ideological affect of the intolerable imagistic and discursive field, and by extension the intolerable cultural field, with which the film is concerned. Out of these responses key ethical tensions develop between different claims of seeing and not seeing, remembering and not remembering.

The visual and discursive intolerability of the Wehrmacht images thus grounds the public dispute documented in *East of War* and its enactment in miniature of the wider social argument about the exhibition. The resulting arena of debate provides, the film implies, an allegory of the wider social field of the Austrian nation confronted with intolerable, unacceptable, but (for most, but not all, of the film's interlocutors) undeniable pictorial evidence of its repressed past. The nation is thus also implicitly faced with the belated recognition that its past, and its present as based on that past, are themselves intolerable. The film marks a shift in Beckermann's analyses of Austrian and Jewish identities and histories, towards scrutinising elements and manifestations of the ideologies that comprise late twentieth-century Austrian society, and which through their expression, overt or otherwise, in public discourse generate the experience of unbelonging that underpins her own critical relation to the country. The nation's gradual and reluctant re-assessment of its history in the wake of public political and cultural controversies generates a series of discursive spaces into which Beckermann intervenes in order both to demonstrate and to analyse the grounds of unbelonging, the 'becoming-hostile' of the nation-space.

As noted in the Introduction, Beckermann's concept of unbelonging draws on the writings of Jean Améry. The German title *Jenseits des Krieges* echoes that of Améry's 1966 book *Jenseits von Schuld und Sühne: Bewältigungsversuche eines Überwältigten*,[25] which compiled transcripts of radio talks broadcast in Germany during the Frankfurt Auschwitz trials of 1965–6, including the essay "How much home does a person need?" in which Améry meditates on the question of home and hospitality. In 1994 Beckermann had published a polemical essay titled "Jean Améry and Austria" (its title echoing W. G. Sebald's 1988 essay "Verlorenes Land: Jean Améry und Österreich")[26] in which she examines Améry's account of his experience of exile, torture, incarceration in Auschwitz and Bergen-Belsen, and return to an irredeemably hostile homeland – an account informing her own experience of being Jewish in post-war Austria: "Austria's relationship with Améry", she argues, "reflects the country's character"[27] (a trope of comparison that will return later in this chapter). In its echoes of Améry, *East of War* uses the Wehrmacht exhibition responses as a template for a provisional mapping of expressions or elements of that national character as it existed in the mid-1990s.

The disputes Beckermann documents chart the expression of opinions and prejudices while sustaining a critical camera-eye relation to their performances. These performances, in turn, feed into the field of critical discourse and dispute around the exhibition itself, of which critical responses to Beckermann's film constitute a significant part. For critics like Frances Guerin (writing in 2017), the strategy of *East of War* of engaging with the public response, rather than with the photographs themselves, indicated the power of the photographs to spark debate and discussion. The exhibition, Guerin argues, was defined by "ambiguity" (by which she means the tensions generated by the photographs between visible/invisible and audible/inaudible, or spoken/unsaid) and "provocation", embodied in the controversy caused by the difficulty of defining what the photographs represent, and of deciding what was their function (i.e. why were they taken?):

> I would argue that what gave these amateur photographs the capacity to challenge the not-yet-laid-to-rest narratives of German [sic] history was their ambiguity. Their most impressive provocation was not simply that they made visible what had always been kept invisible. Rather, it was that they ignited a public controversy. Ageing soldiers, their adult children, museum curators, the German public, international audiences, Jewish survivors, and Polish bystanders all

had different opinions regarding the meanings of the photographs. It was the vociferous debates spawned by these amateur photographs that effectively gave them the power to make audible what had never previously been heard.[28]

In an earlier (2011) chapter on the 'Wehrmacht exhibition', Guerin makes a series of points that are crucial to grasping Beckermann's project in *East of War*, arguing (using terms – "unwanted details", "uncensored" – reminiscent of descriptions of the contents of the Freudian unconscious) that the amateur photographs offer a legally significant register of historical 'truth' distinct from those of professional photographers:

> Due to their status as amateur and private photographs, they were taken and processed with abandon, with little attention paid to technical mistakes, unwanted details, or uncensored inclusions. Thus the events they depict can be seen as, on some level, historical truth. There may be other truths, particularly those that do not appear in any of the photographic images, which are only ever fragments of the time and place of which they are traces. And their truths must not be privileged above any others. Nevertheless, the photos in existence are, in a legal sense, evidence of the events at which their authors were once present.[29]

This is the same historical and legal dimension of "presence" that grounds Beckermann's experience of unbelonging when looking into the eyes of the perpetrators as she films them.

Karoline Feyertag connects the debates around the Wehrmacht exhibition with later comparable controversies like that sparked by the 2001 Paris exhibition *Memoire des camps*, which showed four photographs covertly taken in 1944 inside Birkenau, by members of the Sonderkommando (these photographs were the subject of Didi-Huberman's *Images in Spite of All*). Feyertag concludes that the public debate resulted in an aporia: "[...] both sides did not succeed in understanding – or at least analyzing – the other side's motives, perhaps even ulterior motives."[30] Kerstin Mueller Dembling argues for a reading of the Wehrmacht photographs through Marianne Hirsch's concept of the "family album" (touched on at the end of the previous chapter, and reinforced by Nadine Fresco, as noted earlier),[31] a position expressly countered by Christine R. Nugent's analysis of these "contentious debates about the Nazi past". Nugent summarises the findings of Welzer et al.'s analysis of multigenerational German memory of the Holocaust:

> Perhaps not surprisingly, Welzer and his team found that the Holocaust did not appear in the 'family album' at all. That is to say, while the Holocaust dominated cultural memory in post-reunification Germany, meaning that it occupied much space in the 'lexicon', there were only blank spaces in the 'family album' where the Holocaust should have been. Instead, victim and hero narratives dominated those spaces.[32]

Chloe Paver's comparative and careful analyses in two essays of the display strategies of the two Wehrmacht exhibitions offer more detailed criticism and engage at length with Beckermann's intervention in *East of War*. Paver focusses on Beckermann's short essay "Das Photo der jungen Frau", published in the 1998 book accompanying her film, in which Beckermann speculates on a particular image of a crowd of people from which the face of a young woman in a headscarf returns the viewer's gaze. Of this choice of image Paver writes:

> [T]he Jewish-Austrian filmmaker Ruth Beckermann, in her response to a particular photograph in the first Wehrmacht Exhibition, somewhat wilfully constructs an imaginary soldier-photographer who casually exercises his power over a group of Jewish victims by taking a snapshot of them (I say 'wilfully' because the photograph in question was part of a series taken by a propaganda-corps photographer and because it ought to have been possible to recognize it as such). Beckermann's description of this act suggests that the imagined figure of the soldier-photographer, whose defining characteristic is his readiness to photograph the suffering of others without intervening on their behalf, was already sufficiently common currency by the late 1990s for her to conjure him up in a few brief words.[33]

Paver's issue ("perhaps unfairly", she later concedes)[34] is with Beckermann's implication that the photograph was taken by an amateur soldier-photographer. In claiming that the exhibition catalogue attributes the image to a propaganda corps photographer,[35] she also considers Beckermann's apparent error in attribution in the context of the exhibition's "muddled" and "careless" organisation,[36] and, in her earlier essay, furthermore points out that the identities of the photographers were, crucially, difficult to ascertain:

> In the wake of Fotofeldpost there has been further empirical research into the practicalities of photography in the Wehrmacht, notably two

articles by one of the organizers of the first Wehrmacht Exhibition, Bernd Boll, who both uses Fotofeldpost as a source and adopts its working methods. Among other things, Boll demonstrates that the dividing line between propaganda photography and amateur photography was surprisingly porous: that the army often used soldier-photographers to do the work of the propaganda corps and that the propaganda corps regularly sold photographs to the troops.[37]

Paver's criticisms highlight the ethical difficulties involved in responding to the Wehrmacht exhibition and imply that the truth-value of the photographs themselves demands careful consideration in the context of questions of provenance and ownership, origin, and purpose. Beckermann's film is, however, clearly less interested in the photographs themselves – for her, their truth-value is never in dispute, regardless of whether they were taken by professional Nazi soldier-photographers or amateur Nazi soldier-photographers. Her concern is rather with the distorting effects on public debate of their existence and exhibition, and what that debate reveals of contemporary Austrian society, its repressions, and its political make-up.

Figure 4.1 Ruth Beckermann (dir.), *East of War*, 1996.
© Ruth Beckermann Filmproduktion.

Figure 4.2 Cover of Bernd Boll, Hannes Heer, Walter Manoschek,
Hans Safrian and Christian Reuther (eds), *Vernichtungskrieg:
Verbrechen der Wehrmacht 1941 bis 1944* (Hamburg:
Hamburger Institut für Sozialforschung, 1996).

In using a shallow depth of field and thus depicting the photographs only as largely indecipherable or undetailed blurs inci-
dentally visible in the background of the various talking heads or
arguments and confrontations recorded in the film (Figure 4.1),
Beckermann follows the curators of the exhibition, who chose for
the cover image of the 1996 catalogue a distinctly blurred, indeterminate image of a human figure running, apparently away from a

line of equally indeterminate figures located in the background of the image (Figure 4.2). This cover image magnifies a detail from a photograph reproduced on p. 44 of the catalogue, captioned "Vulkisova Kostić-Garibović auf dem Weg zur Erschießung, Šabac, November 1941". In cropping, enlarging, and exaggerating the blue tint of this photograph the editors emphasise distortion over clarity, the blur over sharpness, photographic dynamism over documentary precision, gesturing towards modernist distortions of the human figure.[38] The cover photograph embodies in its dynamic blur the evident ideological difficulties of seeing and interpretation generated by its very existence among hundreds of other often blurred, badly framed snapshots, difficulties whose effects are manifest in the public disputes over the exhibition and its contents. Such an image, the catalogue cover suggests, requires a particular way of looking, akin to what Slavoj Žižek calls (in relation to Lacanian film theory) "looking awry",[39] in order accurately to discern the content in its distorted form and thus to begin to apportion to it elements of meaning.

The comparable distortions of the cultural field exposed by the exhibition, the film suggests, are symptomatic of, and indeed affirm the anachronic persistence of, Austria's distorted, "awry" view of its history, a view which dramatically affects its moral legitimacy and contemporary ethical standing as a nation-state. In order to scrutinise this view, *East of War* focusses attention on what is said, and how it is said, by the people it depicts, leaving the viewer to mull over what they may be seeing in the images they see. "The only possible form for the film: Enter, exit; a series. A hearing", the "Shooting Journal" concludes.[40] Prefiguring Frances Guerin's argument, cited earlier, that "the photos in existence are, in a legal sense, evidence of the events at which their authors were once present", Beckermann's definition of the film's form as a "hearing" (*Anhörung*, shifting attention from seeing, from the eye to the ear) suggests a dramatic response to the legal discourse already threateningly invoked by some of the voices protesting at the intolerability of the images and the exhibition which, they claim, performs a "slander" (*Verleumdung*, 'defamation') against the 'innocent' Wehrmacht soldiers who were also their husbands, fathers, uncles, grandfathers – that is, a 'slander' by extension against the 'Austrian' people *in toto*. Beckermann's "Shooting Journal" cites three uses by visitors of the word "slander". On 22 October, two people who "were outraged without even having seen the exhibition [...] stayed at the entrance and carried on about slander".[41] The next day a woman claims "Slander. [...] [M]y husband was also in the war and he is not a criminal [...]. It is well known that the SS dressed in Wehrmacht uniforms."[42] And on 27 October the exhibition is visited by the notorious Holocaust denier and anti-pornography protester Martin Humer (1925–2011; Beckermann calls him "Pornojäger", porn-hunter), who, Beckermann writes, "barely looks around and begins to fret about 'slandering' ...".[43]

In the background of these accusations (made in some cases, Beckermann suggests, despite not actually seeing the images), perhaps, lurks a cultural memory of Simon Wiesenthal's libel case in 1975 against Austrian Chancellor Bruno Kreisky in response to Kreisky's highly charged reaction to Wiesenthal's releasing of information about the alleged SS history and involvement in mass killings of the then leader of the Austrian Freedom Party, Friedrich Peter (Wiesenthal had already exposed the Nazi and Waffen-SS pasts of four members of Kreisky's cabinet, leaving Kreisky "furious with the embarrassment that Wiesenthal had caused", according to Hella Pick).[44] This legal dispute, between an assimilated and popular Jewish Austrian Chancellor and an internationally renowned Austrian Jewish Nazi-hunter, centred on perceived Jewish interference in Austrian democratic processes. It reached its nadir when Kreisky notoriously stated his opinion in a press conference that "If the Jews are a people then they are a wretched people", a phrase he later insisted "had been distorted and blown out of all proportion".[45] In the context of Austrian political history, the word 'slander' (its direction reversed in 1995, used by reactionary responses to the exhibition) is thus freighted with symbolic force, and laden specifically with anti-Semitic implications.

Understood as a transitory linguistic act (rather than the written or recorded act of libel), the charge of "slander" wielded by the exhibition viewers presumably nevertheless refers to the statements and details of the exhibition's wall texts, which, the accusation implies, deliberately and falsely impute to specific people ("My husband ...") responsibility for the actions depicted in the photographs. "Slander" thus accuses the exhibition of mis-identifying the perpetrators of photographed actions which, in the accusation of slander, nevertheless remain substantially 'true'. To accuse the exhibition of "slandering" is to accuse it of maliciously distorting the truth about responsibility, but not the truth of the events depicted. Such accusations can be read as defensive acts that seek to reverse those distortions of the truth necessary to repress or ignore the photographs and the historical realities to which they testify – part of the "machinery of *disimagination*" analysed by Georges Didi-Huberman, the "silence and smothered information" by which the SS sought to conceal the realities of the Holocaust.[46] In documenting these moments of (counter-)accusation by some of those offended by the exhibition, Beckermann focusses on a discursive process – the speech act of accusation – performed by particular figures, in order to draw attention to the ethical contortions (and factual distortions) necessary to sustain the viewpoint of denial.

The accusation of slander by some of those who found the exhibition intolerable is, in this sense, merely another attempt to rationalise through legal clichés the social and cultural distortions of history apparently revealed by the exhibition and the images. These distortions were also revealed in the debate they stimulated, which demonstrated the persistence into the contemporary of attitudes and prejudices officially and contradictorily both abandoned to history and never held in the first place, but which nevertheless re-entered the cultural arena in the form of blurred amateur photographs proving the occurrence of fifty-year-old, unspoken and unacknowledged, events. For all its pared-down documentary verisimilitude, *East of War* ultimately presents an image of a society undergoing severely distorting convulsions in its efforts to navigate the sudden (but wholly predictable, even inevitable) exposure of historical and ideological contradictions that threaten its symbolic order. The film's image of Austria demands that we 'look awry' at its scarcely perceptible details, its apparently marginal features and concealed qualities (or the "technical mistakes, unwanted details, or uncensored inclusions" that, Guerin argues, now characterise both the 'Wehrmacht' photographs and the 'image' the nation constructed of its history), in order to discern the real contours of Austria in the 1990s.

Looking awry: *The Waldheim Waltz*

Those real contours had emerged even more convulsively a decade earlier in the international scandal (a word etymologically linked to the word "slander") surrounding the campaign and eventual election in 1986 of former United Nations Secretary-General Kurt Waldheim (1918–2007) to the Austrian Presidency. Waldheim was revealed during the campaign to have both concealed and misrepresented (that is, distorted) details of his wartime military service in the Balkans and Greece, suppressing and transforming knowledge in relation both to the extent of his wartime experience and to the campaigns and 'administrative' roles and procedures with which he had been involved. Initially, articles in German and Austrian magazines from 1985 onwards had raised doubts about the narrative Waldheim had constructed concerning his past. As his election campaign progressed through early 1986, research into Waldheim's military service conducted by the World Jewish Congress (WJC) in New York led to a drip-feed of further details, revealing among other things that Waldheim's long-held claim he had spent the bulk of the war in Vienna convalescing from an ankle injury was false, and that in July 1942 he had instead been awarded a medal in Croatia for "service under enemy fire" under the command of the notorious war criminal General Alexander Löhr, who had been executed by firing squad in 1947 but (as Beckermann's film details) was still revered as a war hero by many in Austria at the time of the Waldheim scandal.[47]

These revelations, and the public debate surrounding them, provide the historical narrative structuring *The Waldheim Waltz*, a film made entirely of found footage organised by the device of dialectical montage, as Beckermann juxtaposes segments offering versions of the official narrative with alternative or critical arguments and contradictory 'facts' from a variety of sources. Through this procedure the film reveals how the series of repeated disclosures of newly discovered documents indicating Waldheim's presence at, and personal involvement in, events of which he had previously denied all knowledge, created images of his character, history, and candidacy radically diverging from those he was attempting to portray. While this divergence eventually led to the effective collapse of the illusions sustaining Austria's post-war 'victim myth', the international (but not Austrian) media campaign against Waldheim during the election generated increasingly acrimonious dispute and stimulated the mobilisation in Austria of a far-right nationalist exceptionalism that counter-protested against perceived international interference in the nation's electoral processes, and launched publicly anti-Semitic attacks on those questioning Waldheim's candidacy. Helga Embacher summarises the political atmosphere and the legalistic language of the controversy, which prefigured the accusations of slander surrounding the 'Wehrmacht' exhibition:

> When, in spring 1986, the debate about Waldheim's 'missing years' in the Balkans threatened to spin out of control, the ÖVP plastered Austria with a yellow poster bearing the following message: 'We Austrians elect whomever we want! Now more than ever Waldheim.' The hidden message was that Austrians have to thwart a Jewish conspiracy by voting for Waldheim. [...] Politicians from the ranks of the ÖVP also dealt in anti-Semitic undertones by calling representatives of the WJC a 'dishonourable lot' and 'a slander-spewing mafia'.[48]

On 8 June 1986, Waldheim was elected to the Presidency with 53.87 per cent of the vote.[49]

During the election campaign in 1986, Beckermann had filmed public anti-Semitic disputes disrupting a pro-Waldheim demonstration, including a verbal attack on her own father, in Vienna's Stefansplatz, using some of this footage (as we noted earlier) in *Paper Bridge* but not engaging in that film directly with the political events generating the conflicts she recorded. *The Waldheim Waltz* returns to the wider national and international contexts of those events to perform a documentary archaeology of the political identity of late-1980s Austria. Centring on the mediated figure of Waldheim itself, the film uses material from a wide international variety of mainly television sources to examine the processes of political image-construction amidst emergent debates about historical truth and responsibility comparable in intensity and urgency to those discussed nine years later in relation to *East of War*. As in the earlier film, the key questions motivating Beckermann's enquiry centre on issues of representation and misrepresentation: "For me", said Beckermann in a 2018 interview, "it is a film about lying".[50]

These questions generate a deeply contested discursive field circulating first around Waldheim's conflicting representational and representative functions, and second around the question of truth and falsity in relation to a body of information that was, due to almost daily media revelations through press conferences and news articles, constantly changing but always expanding. The film's thematic focus is thus on the extensive mediation in a range of national and international contexts – in the USA (where the WJC pursued its research to expose Waldheim's past and the Congressional hearings on his case were conducted), in various European countries linked to the controversy through Waldheim's past career at the United Nations, and in various cities and towns in Austria – of what Waldheim stood for in political and ethical, as well as ideological and electoral, terms, and what these terms implied about the Austrian electorate. Those implications constitute the film's symbolic focus, as its charting of the process of exposure of and national resistance to Waldheim's past parallels the revelation of the depth and extent of Austria's allegiance to its own repressed history.

Tracing a largely chronological narrative countdown of events leading up to Waldheim's election, Beckermann's film counterpoints media footage from news reports and other documentary sources, interviews, archive material, and the director's voice-over narration to encompass the range of positions and discursive strategies through which the figure of Waldheim was simultaneously (self-) constructed as, and revealed to be, a deeply ambiguous sign representing in subtle and contradictory ways a deeply ambivalent national self-consciousness. *The Waldheim Waltz* furthermore contextualises the Waldheim affair in relation to political and cultural events like the 1985 Reder controversy (when the FPÖ politician Friedhelm Frischenschlager was photographed welcoming, with a public handshake, the convicted Austrian war criminal Walter Reder, returning to Vienna after his release from an Italian prison)[51] and the public reception in 1985 of Lanzmann's *Shoah*, a film which (Beckermann comments in her film) "changed the climate" in Austria. Through such contexts, her film emphasises how Waldheim's ambiguity, the complexity of which is due to its being manufactured by forces pulling in conflicting directions, depends upon ambiguities inherent in the mediated image itself and evident also in the manufactured self-image of the Austrian nation. As events progress in the narrative, Waldheim becomes virtually synonymous with this national self-image, a double-edged attribute which is crucial to the political force of the film, which itself constitutes a belated contribution to a debate that persisted long after the election was resolved.[52] Walter W. Moser argues that *The Waldheim Waltz*'s focus on a person rather than a place lends it a unique position in Beckermann's oeuvre.[53] The processes by which that "person" is constructed are crucial to the film's argument, and, in Waldheim's case, much of the controversy surrounded the construction of his image and what it represented, a construction in which he actively participated (Brian Urquhart, in his United Nations "Character Sketch" of the former UN Secretary-General, notes that "Waldheim worried a great deal about his 'image', as he called it").[54] We see the journalist Hubertus Czernin (whose research initially exposed Waldheim's previously concealed wartime activities) stating: "[Waldheim] represents, and I'm sad to say this, the Austrian country perfectly [...]. He is the real Austria" – two sentences summarising a range of rhetorical conflations of person and nation found in many of the journalistic and critical writings on the Waldheim affair. Most of these writings were critical of Waldheim's evident concealment of his past and true involvement in Nazi atrocities. Hella Pick, for example, asserts (in 2000) that "Waldheim's character was also Austria's character: expert in the art of forgetting, with a lack of moral fibre, opportunism, servility, a reluctance to undertake self-criticism. [...] Indeed the country acquired a new image, synonymous with Waldheim's."[55] Pick quotes American newspapers like the *Washington Post* asserting that "President Waldheim will remain an unwelcome symbol of Austria's least attractive side"; and the *Buffalo Times* declaiming (in a passage mobilising the waltz metaphor that Beckermann also uses) that "the Austria revealed by the Waldheim controversy is not a place unburdened by history, moving happily through time to the graceful strains of the waltz".[56] In his 1988 essay 'The Waldheim within us' Anton Pelinka asserted: " 'Mr Waldheim is Mr Austria. [...] The candidate transmits what is, to be sure, a genuine picture of Austria, but for that very reason also a particularly poor one. [...] Kurt Waldheim is a piece of Austria: he represents the disorder of our past'."[57] Citing this analogy, Andrea Reiter goes on to paraphrase Robert Menasse's critique of Waldheim as "the first postmodern president", "a symbol of Austria's reluctance to acknowledge its Nazi (and Austro-fascist) past" who "came to personify Austria's forgetfulness for the whole world to see."[58] Such critical assessments evaluate the man in terms also indicating what Waldheim's supporters saw in him – as American reporter Robert Edwin Herzstein (who appears briefly in Beckermann's film on a WJC press panel) points out, "Waldheim's career, writings, and behaviour serve as marvellous examples of the self-serving national compact. [...] 'I am you', said Waldheim to his fellow citizens, so do not turn your backs on me and your fathers."[59]

These descriptions reveal the variety of significatory and rhetorical functions perceived in Waldheim's relation to the nation by both his supporters and opponents, from "perfect" representation to "synonymous" image to "symbol" to "personification" to "genuine picture" to synecdochic "piece of Austria" to "marvellous example", and (at its most extreme) the implication of absolute identity between Waldheim, his supporters, and their version of Austria. *The Waldheim Waltz* offers a variety of cinematic versions of this extended tropism: in one interview Beckermann compares Waldheim to Woody Allen's Zelig, calling him a "chameleon".[60] She is particularly intrigued, for example, by Waldheim's hands, which, as he speaks in public, perform their own kind of gesticulatory dance, a synecdoche of the political dance traced by the film. This expressive process is usually conciliatory and entreating, drawing the audience together with the speaker (hands raised, fingers straight and then curling in as the hands are drawn towards the speaker's body) in a rhetorical/gestural unity, a version of the "I am you" rhetoric noted by Herzstein. While Waldheim's hands performed highly choreographed movements emphasising his articulate denials (for example, in the long interview around 17 minutes into the film), only once, momentarily in a BBC interview in English shown late in the film, do we see his smooth persona crack, when he suddenly slams his left hand on the table before him and shouts to override and silence the questioner. Moser notes the comparison in Andreas Pittler's 2020 crime novel *Schatten aus Stein* (*Shadows of Stone*) between Waldheim and Max Schreck's eponymous vampire in F. W. Murnau's *Nosferatu* (1922), with his distinctive elongated claw-like fingers.[61] Beckermann complies a long montage of passages cut from various television interviews with Waldheim, animatedly protesting (via a complex array of gestural movements employing both hands) his innocence and asserting his not having seen deportations and other events, suggesting comparison might also be made with the over-emphatic gesticulatory style of Adolf Hitler, whose carefully choreographed hand movements were a key part of a repertoire of semiotically powerful gestures which has been subject to detailed movement-analysis by Martha Davis, Dianne Dulicai and Ildiko Viczian.[62]

This range of comparisons indicates the cultural function of Waldheim as malleable *sign* operating within a complex and fluid relation to the signified of the nation, and within a discursive field in which the viability and usefulness of representation, in both semiotic and political senses, were themselves at stake. In his contradictory status as simultaneously electable (to his supporters) and intolerable (to everyone else), Waldheim confirms Umberto Eco's insight that signs comprise "everything which can be used in order to lie".[63] His function as sign affirmed in virtually identical terms an absolute and irresolvable ambiguity: the "truth" of his statements to his supporters, and their simultaneous "falsity" to his opponents. In exploring this process of semiosis from the perspective of 2018, Beckermann's film makes implicit comparisons between the Waldheim affair and the election of Donald Trump to the US presidency two years earlier in 2016 (as well as the return to the Austrian government in 2018 of the FPÖ, under the leadership of Christian Strache), a point she emphasised in discussion with Katya Krylova after a screening of the film in Aberdeen in 2019.[64]

In *The Waldheim Waltz* these diverse critical constructions of Waldheim-as-trope ultimately combine in the image of "the candidate" (as she calls him throughout the film, following Pelinka) as ambiguous screen/mirror, a medium receptive to whatever is projected upon it, reflecting back that which it needs to in order to prevail, a space repeatedly shape-shifting (hence the Zelig comparison) according to the pull of expediency and exigency – he could (Herzstein argues) "turn himself into a German officer and, when the source of authority change[d], into a victim of the Nazi regime".[65] As *screen*, Waldheim functioned simultaneously as receptor of Austria's projected fantasies of its own past and identity (or "the deep-seated prejudices of the Austrian electorate", in Joseph W. Moser's words),[66] concealer of the truthful aspects of that past and that identity, and screen memory, a defence against the nation's repressed historical guilt. As *mirror*, he reflected throughout his career (as Herzstein argues) whatever qualities were required in order for that career to progress smoothly, without interruption, regardless of extraneous historical realities. *The Waldheim Waltz* tracks the carefully syncopated movements of these complementary and contradictory functions as a kind of circular dance of signification ('waltz' derives from the German word 'walzen', to revolve), a dance in which the Austrian people and the world were unwitting partners.

'Leading someone on a dance' is, of course, deceiving them. Exposing and scrutinising Waldheim's role in extending and, for a while, reinforcing the mass deception surrounding Austria's 'Victim myth' (a deception Beckermann calls in her narration the "österreichische Lebenslüge" ["Austrian life-lie"]) is the ultimate concern of the film. The film's narrative and its teleological drive to a historically inevitable conclusion imitate the circular, repetitive movements of the waltz (and echo the equally circular, repetitive argument-denials of *East of War* and the earlier narrative circularities of *Paper Bridge*, itself reprised in the re-used footage of the pro-Waldheim demonstration in Vienna). In a sequence that functions as a *mise-en-abîme* of the entire film, a press conference on Austrian television, at which Waldheim's former superior in Salonika describes "the candidate's" work for him as assembling this "Mosaik aus kleinen Steinen" ("mosaic of small stones" – an image that by unconscious synonym inserts Judaism and its symbolic regime into the discourse), is interrupted by masked protesters, one of whom is Beckermann, wielding placards demanding (among other things) Hitler be called as witness for Waldheim's defence. Echoing her earliest films of Austrian strikes and protests, Beckermann includes monochrome footage of the meetings discussing and planning this protest.

Revoking the intolerable image

Among the multiple interviews and expository sequences (in many of which Waldheim is given space in the film to speak at length and thus, as David Perrin notes, "to incriminate himself"), photographic and painted images constitute another central thread in the narrative of exposure Beckermann constructs.[67] Images constantly subvert the narratives Waldheim and his supporters construct. Czernin's *Profil* article of 3 March 1986, which effectively sparked the controversy, included an image reproducing Waldheim's military service card, disclosing his membership of the SA and the Nazi German Students' League. Beckermann dwells on the significance of German photographer Walter Dick's (1914–76) shots of the Nazi deportation to Auschwitz-Birkenau and Bergen-Belsen in March 1943 of around 50,000 Jews from Salonika in Greece, a quarter of the town's population, a process Waldheim claims not to have noticed ("Ich habe sie nicht gesehen", he states in one interview) during his time as an administrative officer of the district.[68] Dick's photographs mutely contradict Waldheim's claims of ignorance and non-involvement.

The Waldheim Waltz includes archive footage from 1978 of Waldheim's wife Elisabeth (named after the Empress Elisabeth, subject of *A Fleeting Passage to the Orient*, and like her known as "Sisi") (1922–2017) giving a press tour of their New York apartment, with its walls adorned with artworks on loan from the Metropolitan Museum of Art, including a Corot, and Monet's *The Seine at Vétheuil* (1880), which, Elisabeth pointedly tells the cameras, is "[Waldheim's] favourite picture". This painting is shown hanging in the darkened apartment, partly obscured by a table lamp, its romantic–pastoral conventionality evoking a series of tropes concerning art, tradition, taste and judgement, values which, Elizabeth Waldheim's comments imply, accrue by association to her husband's character and to the Waldheim family (the youngest daughter of the Waldheims, Christa, is an artist). The film emphasises the coincidental opening of the *Vienna 1900* exhibition at the Museum of Modern Art in New York.[69] Earlier, a series of haunting pastoral stills from Lanzmann's *Shoah*, the film which (Beckermann's narrative states) "changed everyone's awareness", subtly counterpoints the bland, conventional aesthetic taste implied by Waldheim's liking for these impressionist pastorals: "And forever death is inscribed in the beauty of the Polish woods, the beauty of Austrian nature", she states over a still from *Shoah* of Simon Srebnik pacing out the visible traces of the perimeter of KZ Chelmno.[70]

As with the *Vernichtungskrieg* exhibition nine years later, the documentary force of photography proved central to the evidence surrounding Waldheim. A crucial photograph emerged during the media turmoil around the affair, showing him on an airfield in Podgornica (in the former Yugoslavia, a country he claimed, on a UN diplomatic visit in the late 1960s, never to have previously visited) on 22 May 1943 (at a time when he had previously claimed he was convalescing and studying in Vienna). In the photograph he is in discussion with Italian General Ercole Roncaglia (later accused by Yugoslavia of war crimes, but not convicted), Colonel Hans Herbert Macholz, and Romanian General Artur Phleps, commander of the 7th SS Freiwillige Gebirgs Division *Prinz Eugen*, which (according to Valdis O. Lumans) "left in its wake a legacy of rapine and a shameful record of atrocities".[71] Waldheim was Phleps' interpreter at the meeting in Podgornica. The (re-)appearance of this photograph and its documenting of Waldheim's proximity to figures involved in or connected to action and atrocities in the Balkans, and by implication his involvement in what her narrative calls "eine ganz korrekte, anständige Tätigkeit" ("a wholly correct and decent job") exemplifies how Beckermann's use of dialectical montage relentlessly exposes the tension between what is claimed by Waldheim's narrative and what is shown in such photographs. As in *East of War*, the photographic image demonstrates the return of the historical reality that has been repressed by myths; it offers evidential proof of a history radically different from that claimed by the narrative Waldheim constructed and sought to embody. And, like the earlier film, contesting narratives generated contested legal accusations centring on the distortion or misrepresentation of the truth, accusations emanating not least from Waldheim himself, who was reported in the *New York Times* in 1987 to be planning, despite all the proven revelations of his long dissembling, to sue the WJC for slander.[72]

As noted earlier, the closing sequence shows the newly elected Waldheim being groomed in preparation for a television appearance, footage (which, Beckermann informed Katya Krylova in 2019, was unbroadcast material retained by a former ÖRF employee who contacted her during the making of the film)[73] that depicts the manufacturing of a mediated image, Waldheim as embodiment of the nation, his brushed and sanitised appearance as simulacrum of the Austrian body politic. Its function in terms of the logic of the film's narrative is to summarise the processes by which the image has replaced, and now stands in for and overrides, the man and the history – that is, the reality. Before Waldheim arrives at his chair (which, it seems, has been moved forward to increase his comfort), a woman cleaner, dressed in a yellow smock, vacuums around and under the desk. Taking his seat beside the Austrian flag, Waldheim checks the appearance of his tie in the camera; his right hand, a clenched fist, rests on the desk, his left raises a glass of water, while a man brushes the left lapel of his suit (Figure 4.3).

This closing sequence enacts an uncanny return of images seen earlier in the film. At the end of US Congresswoman Patricia Schroeder's long and eloquent address to the House as it debates whether to put Waldheim on the Watch List, another Congress member in a bright yellow jacket takes her seat in the background. A few minutes later, waiting for the run-off result, Beckermann describes Vienna as "in eine Bühne verwandelt" ("transformed into a stage"); she films random street scenes, posters and graffiti condemning Waldheim, and, in a short sequence, a pair of women talking, one picking dust off the black jacket of the other. Prefiguring the

Figure 4.3 Ruth Beckermann (dir.), *The Waldheim Waltz*.
© Ruth Beckermann Filmproduktion.

grooming of Waldheim's TV persona, this recurring set of motifs – a yellow jacket, someone being groomed – forces us to look awry at the Waldheim affair, and view its semiotics as both permeating and prefiguring the wider visual and media landscapes it inhabited. The "stage" of the city pre-emptively frames the "staging" of Waldheim's media image, while the intrusion into the frame of the yellow-jacketed Congress member and its repetition in the Austrian cleaning woman performs a symbolic 'staining' of the politicised realm of simulation, inserting into the sanitised image the historical trace of anti-Semitism embedded in the colour yellow, connoting the yellow Star of David, of which Victor Klemperer writes:

> the Jewish star, the six-pointed Star of David, the yellow piece of cloth which today still stands for plague and quarantine, and which in the Middle Ages was the colour used to identify the Jews, the colour of envy and gall that has entered the bloodstream; the yellow piece of cloth with 'Jew' printed on it in black, the word framed by the lines of two telescoped triangles, the word consisting of thick block capitals, which are separated and given broad, exaggerated horizontal lines to effect the appearance of the Hebrew script.[74]

The mannered artificiality of the closing sequence of *The Waldheim Waltz* summarises the film's concern with the construction and dissemination of the candidate's intolerable political image, tainted always by the traces of symbols gesturing to the reality it seeks to repress and erase.

Both *The Waldheim Waltz* and *East of War* address the intolerable persistence of images as documentary traces of the real, endlessly contradicting the denials of cultural repression. Like the rotations of the waltz, images return, refusing to disappear, recycling their evidential force into public consciousness, undermining the efficacy of manufactured narratives of forgetting and images constructed to conceal, and affirming their effectiveness in relation to the mediating force of memory. In this relation, the intolerable presence of images confirms the existence of an unrepresented (repressed, intolerable) historical reality and thus affirms the condition of unbelonging which Beckermann's films explore. In her next film, Beckermann approaches the question of the relation between history and the image in a different way – via an exploration of how the *absence* of images mobilises and affirms an *over-represented* history.

Notes

1 Leon Zelman (with Armin Thurnher), *After Survival: One Man's Mission in the Cause of Memory* (trans. Meredith Schneeweiss) (New York: Holmes and Meier, 1998), p. 148.

2 Sigmund Freud, *Moses and Monotheism: Three Essays*, in *The Pelican Freud Library Vol. 13: The Origins of Religion* (ed. Albert Dickson, trans. James Strachey) (London: Penguin, 1985), p. 323.

3 Jacques Rancière, "The Intolerable Image", in *The Emancipated Spectator* (trans. Gregory Elliott) (London: Verso, 2009), p. 83.

4 Ruth Beckermann (ed.), *Jenseits des Krieges: Ehemalige Wehrmachtssoldaten erinnern sich* (Vienna: Döcker, 1998).

5 Rancière, "The Intolerable Image", p. 84.

6 See Suleiman, *Crises of Memory and the Second World War*, pp. 123–4.

7 Uhl, "From Victim Myth to Co-Responsibility Thesis", p. 57.

8 Some of the effects of the 1999 coalition government on Viennese life will be explored in Chapter 7.

9 "Where had all the murderers gone?" (Ulla Hahn, *Unscharfe Bilder* [Munich: Deutsche Verlags-Anstalt, 2003], p. 43); "*The Murderers Are Amongst us*" – title of the first German film made after the end of World War II, directed by Wolfgang Staudte in 1946.

10 Former SS-Oberscharführer Carl-Emil Strott, under cross-examination in Hannover, 1971. Cited in Nadine Fresco, *On the Death of Jews: Photographs and History* (trans. Sarah Clift) (New York: Berghahn / United States Holocaust Memorial Museum, 2021), p. 58.

11 Fresco, *On the Death of Jews*, p. 32.

12 Fresco, *On the Death of Jews*, pp. 33ff.

13 Fresco, *On the Death of Jews*, pp. 33–4.

14 For a detailed account of the first exhibition and responses to it, see Hannes Heer and Jane Caplan, "The Difficulty of Ending a War: Reactions to the Exhibition 'War of Extermination: Crimes of the Wehrmacht 1941 to 1944", *History Workshop Journal* 46 (Autumn, 1998), 187–203.

15 Karoline Feyertag, "The Art of Vision and the Ethics of the Gaze: On the Debate on Georges Didi-Huberman's Book *Images in Spite of All*" (trans. Camilla Neilson), at https://transversal.at/transversal/0408/feyertag/en (accessed 5 May, 2023), np.

16 Beckermann, "*East of War*: Shooting Journal, October to November 1995", in Lendl (ed.), *Film Collection: Texte/Texts/Textes*, p. 100. Barthes writes "Je vois les yeux qui ont vu l'Empereur" (*La chambre*

claire: note sur la photographie) (Paris: Gallimard Seuil, 1980, p. 13) / "I am looking at eyes that looked at the emperor" (Roland Barthes, *Camera Lucida* [trans. Richard Howard], London: Vintage, 2000, p. 3).

17 "Ich sehe die Augen, die die Gemarterten, Gehängten, Gemütigten gesehen haben." Beckermann, "Shooting Journal", pp. 42, 100.

18 "Sicher wussten wir, dass die Wehrmacht nicht unschuldig war, sondern sehr wohl beteiligte an der Durchführung der NS-Vernichtungspolitik." Beckermann, "Shooting Journal", pp. 42, 100.

19 See Pick, *Guilty Victim*, pp. 198–201.

20 Helga Embacher, "Controversies over Austria's Nazi Past: Generational Changes and Grassroots Awakenings Following the Waldheim Affair and the 'Wehrmacht Exhibitions' ", *Nationalities Papers* Vol. 51 No. 3 (2023), 644–64: 654.

21 "1945, kaum daß Nazi-Deutschland besiegt war, begannen die ehemaligen Generäle mit der Fabrikation einer Legende – der Legende von der 'sauberen Wehrmacht'." Bernd Boll, Hannes Heer, Walter Manoschek, Hans Safrian, and Christian Reuther (eds), *Vernichtungskrieg: Verbrechen der Wehrmacht 1941 bis 1944* (Hamburg: Hamburger Institut für Sozialforschung, 1996), p. 7.

22 Gabriel Fawcett, "The Wehrmacht Exhibition", *History Today* Vol. 52 No. 4 (April 2002), 2–3: 2.

23 Georges Didi-Huberman, *Images in Spite of All* (trans. Shane B. Lillis) (Chicago, IL: University of Chicago Press, 2008), p. 23.

24 Beckermann, "Shooting Journal", p. 102. "Der Feigling und Mitmacher", "Der Ungebrochene", "Der Schwejk-Typ: Wiener Typ im positive Sinn", "Der Aussenseiter", p. 44.

25 Jean Améry, *Jenseits von Schuld und Sühne: Bewältigungsversuche eines Überwältigten* (Munich: Szczesny Verlag, 1966) (translated as *At the Mind's Limits*). Victoria Fareld suggests that the book's German subtitle, omitted from the English version, might be translated as "attempts to master [something] by one who has been overpowered [by that thing]". See Fareld, "Ressentiment as Moral Imperative: Jean Améry's Nietzschean Revaluation of Victim Morality", in Jeanne Roue and Mary Gallagher (eds), *Re-Thinking Ressentiment: On the Limits of Criticism and the Limits of its Critics* (Bielefeld: Transcript, 2016), pp. 53–70; p. 54.

26 W. G. Sebald, "Verlorenes Land: Jean Améry und Österreich", in *Unheimliche Heimat: Essays zur österreichischen Literatur* (Frankfurt am Main: Fischer, 1995), pp. 131–44.

27 Beckermann, "Jean Améry and Austria", p. 75.

28 Frances Guerin, "The Ambiguity of Amateur Photography in Modern Warfare", *New Literary History* Vol. 48 No. 1 (2017), 53–74: 63.

29 Frances Guerin, "On the Eastern Front with the German Army", in *Through Amateur Eyes: Film and Photography in Nazi Germany* (Minneapolis, MN: University of Minnesota Press, 2011), pp. 37–92; p 50.

30 Feyertag, "The Art of Vision and the Ethics of the Gaze", np.

31 Kerstin Mueller Dembling, "Staging the German Family Photo Album: The *Wehrmacht* Exhibit and Thomas Bernhard's *Vor dem Ruhestand*", *Journal of Austrian Studies* Vol. 48 No. 2 (2015), 1–24: 5.

32 Christine R. Nugent, "The Voice of the Visitor: Popular Reactions to the Exhibition *Vernichtungskrieg: Verbrechen der Wehrmacht 1941–1944*", *Journal of European Studies* Vol. 44 No. 3 (2014), 249–62: 249, 254. See Harald Welzer, Sabine Moller and Karoline Tschuggnall, '*Opa war kein Nazi': Nationalsozialismus und Holocaust im Familiengedächtnis* (Frankfurt am Main: Fischer, 2002).

33 Chloe E. M. Paver, "Ein Stück langweiliger als die Wehrmachtsausstellung, aber dafür repräsentativer": The Exhibition *Fotofeldpost* as Riposte to the 'Wehrmacht Exhibition'", in Anne Fuchs, Mary Cosgrave, and Georg Grote (eds), *German Memory Contests: The Quest for Identity in Literature, Film, and Discourse since 1990* (Rochester, NY: Camden House, 2006), pp. 107–125; p. 111.

34 Chloe E. M. Paver, *Refractions of the Third Reich in German and Austrian Fiction and Film* (Oxford: Oxford University Press, 2007), p. 74.

35 Paver, *Refractions of the Third Reich*, p. 72. The photograph appears, uncaptioned, as the 22nd in an uncredited sequence of 27 photographs in a section titled "Lubny, 16.10.1941: Die jüdische Bevölkerung vor ihrer Erschießung" ("Lubny, 16.10.1941: Jewish people prior to their being shot"). *Vernichtungskrieg: Verbrechen der Wehrmacht 1941 bis 1944*, pp. 81–3. Beckermann cites this title at the beginning of her essay, see "Das Photo der jungen Frau", p. 7. At no point does the 1996 catalogue credit the photograph or those it appears among; Paver is possibly referring to the revised, 2001 edition of the catalogue, which Beckermann obviously could not have seen while preparing the book of *Jenseits des Krieges* published in 1998.

36 Paver, *Refractions of the Third Reich*, p. 73.

37 Paver, "Ein Stück langweiliger als die Wehrmachtsausstellung, aber dafür repräsentativer", 120.

38 See, for example, Marcel Duchamp's *Nude Descending a Staircase* of 1912) and, more disturbingly, more recent works like Gerhard Richter's blurred photo-painting *Hunting Party* (*Jagdgesellschaft*, 1966).

39 Slavoj Žižek, *Looking Awry: An Introduction to Jacques Lacan through Popular Culture* (Cambridge, MA: MIT Press, 1991).

40 Beckermann, "Shooting Journal", p. 102. "Die einzig mögliche Filmform: Auftritt, Abtritt; eine Serie. Eine Anhörung" (p. 44).

41 "Shooting Journal", p. 94. "... ohne sie auch nur anzusehen [...]. Also bleiben sie beim Eingang und schimpften von Verleumdung", p. 36.

42 "Shooting Journal", p. 95. "Eine Frau sagt: 'Verleumdung ... Mein Mann war auch im Krieg und ist kein Verbrecher ... Man weiß ja, dass sich die SS Wehrmachtsuniformen anzog" (p. 37).

43 "Shooting Journal", p. 97. "... schaut sich kaum um und regt sich schon über die 'Verleumdungen' auf", p. 39.

44 Pick, *Guilty Victim*, pp. 106–7; p. 106. See also Uhl, "From Victim Myth to Co-Responsibility Thesis: Nazi Rule, World War II, and the Holocaust in Austrian Memory", pp. 59–60; Andre Reiter, *Contemporary Austrian Writing: Austria after Waldheim* (London: Routledge, 2013), pp. 18–19.

45 Quoted in Pick, *Guilty Victim*, p. 107.

46 Didi-Huberman, *Images in Spite of All*, p. 20.

47 See David Art, *The Politics of the Nazi Past in Germany and Austria* (Cambridge: Cambridge University Press, 2010), pp. 116–17.

48 Helga Embacher, "Controversies over Austria's Nazi Past", p. 653. The posters appear in *The Waldheim Waltz*.

49 Pick, *Guilty Victim*, p. 161.

50 David Perrin, "Not Reconciled: Ruth Beckermann discusses *The Waldheim Waltz*" (27 March 2018), at https://mubi.com/notebook/posts/not-reconciled-ruth-beckermann-discusses-the-waldheim-waltz (accessed 7 June 2023).

51 See Pick, *Guilty Victim*, pp. 155–6; Allmer, *The Traumatic Surreal*, p. 116.

52 David Art points out that the media and public debate around Waldheim continued after the election. See *The Politics of the Nazi Past in Germany and Austria*, p. 118.

53 Joseph W. Moser, "Ruth Beckermann's Reckoning with Kurt Waldheim: *Unzugehörig: Österreicher und Juden nach 1945* (1989) and *Waldheims Waltzer* (2018)", in Frauke Matthes et al. (eds), *Edinburgh German Yearbook* Volume 14: *Politics and Culture in Germany and Austria Today* (Cambridge: Cambridge University Press, 2021), pp. 207–21; p. 215. Moser has forgotten the focus of *Ein flüchtiger Zug nach dem Orient* on the Empress Elisabeth.

54 Brian Urquhart, "Character Sketch: Kurt Waldheim", at https://news.un.org/en/spotlight/character-sketches-kurt-waldheim-brian-urquhart (not dated) (accessed 1 June 2023).

55 Pick, *Guilty Victim*, p. 164.

56 Pick, *Guilty Victim*, p. 164.

57 Reiter, *Contemporary Jewish Writing*, p. 11.

58 Reiter, *Contemporary Austrian Writing*, p. 25.

59 Robert Edwin Herzstein, "The Present State of the Waldheim Affair: Second Thoughts and New Directions", in Günter Bischoff and Anton Pelinka (eds), *Austrian Historical Memory and National Identity* (*Contemporary Austrian Studies* Vol. 5) (New Brunswick: Transaction Publishers, 1997), pp. 116–34: pp. 120–1.

60 Horwath and Omasta, "A Conversation with Ruth Beckermann", p. 41. Woody Allen, *Zelig* (1983).

61 Moser, "Ruth Beckermann's Reckoning with Kurt Waldheim", p. 216.

62 Martha Davis, Dianne Dulicai, and Ildiko Viczian, "Hitler's Movement Signature", *TDR* Vol. 36 No. 2 (1992), 152–72.

63 Umberto Eco, *A Theory of Semiotics* (Bloomington, IN: Indiana University Press, 1976), p. 7.

64 *The Director's Cut: Interview with Ruth Beckermann*, University of Aberdeen (25 May 2019), at https://youtu.be/W9DbITD_xkw (accessed 28 May 2023).

65 Herzstein, "The Present State of the Waldheim Affair", p. 123.

66 Moser, "Ruth Beckermann's Reckoning with Kurt Waldheim", p. 213.

67 Perrin, "Not Reconciled: Ruth Beckermann Discusses *The Waldheim Waltz*". For a detailed discussion of the use of images in media coverage of the Waldheim affair, see Ina Markova, "Visualizing Waldheim: Mediale Schlüsselbilder der 'Affäre Waldheim'", *Journal of Austrian Studies* Vol. 49 Nos. 1–2 (2016), 71–89.

68 Giuliana Tedeschi's Holocaust memoir *There Is a Place on Earth* records her mixing in Birkenau in 1944 with Greek Jews from Salonika, from where "two or three years before, the whole Jewish population had been deported en masse"; she recalls their "peculiar way of speaking, that smack of cosmopolitanism typical of many Greek and Oriental cities". Giuliana Tedeschi, *There Is a Place on Earth: A Woman in Birkenau* (trans. Tim Parks) (London: Lime Tree, 1993), p. 66.

69 See Kirk Varnedoe, *Vienna 1900: Art, Architecture, and Design* (New York: Museum of Modern Art, 1986).

70 "Und für immer ist der Tod nun eingeschrieben in die Schönheit der polnischen Wälder, in die Schönheit der österreichischen Natur."

71 Valdis O. Lumans, "The Ethnic Germans of the Waffen-SS in Combat: Dregs or Gems?", in Sanders Marble (ed.), *Scraping the Barrel: The Military Use of Sub-Standard Manpower* (Fordham University Press, 2012), p. 231.

72 Henry Kamm, "Waldheim Plans Slander Suit", *New York Times* (8 May 1987), at www.nytimes.com/1987/05/08/world/waldheim-plans-slander-suit-aginst-jewish-group-s-chief.html (accessed 26 May 2023).

73 *The Director's Cut: Interview with Ruth Beckermann.*

74 Victor Klemperer, *The Language of the Third Reich* (New York: Continuum, 2000), p. 155.

5

Home as constellation of mobility – *A Fleeting Passage to the Orient*

I shall travel the whole world over [...]. The Wandering Jew shall seem a stay-at-home compared to me. I will cross the seven seas by ship, a female Flying Dutchman, until one day I drown and am forgotten. (Elisabeth, Empress of Austria)[1]

The complex intersections of image, myth, and unbelonging are among the many concerns of *A Fleeting Passage to the Orient* (1999). Based on the travels to Egypt in the late nineteenth century of the Austrian (but Bavarian-born) Empress Elisabeth (1837–98), this film explores and recontextualises the experience of unbelonging via the structures of desire that organised Austria's colonial history. It traces connections between Egyptian and Austrian cultures at the *fin de siècle* and, in the travels of the Empress to Egypt in 1885 and 1891, finds new configurations of home and of feminine identity, contrasting with (and yet strangely resembling) those afforded to Beckermann by post-war Austria. Key themes of travel and mobility relate in turn to a concern with the technology of cinema, rapidly developing during the period addressed in the film. Beckermann frames these themes with an enquiry into the geopolitics of nascent modernity and its links to the exoticising colonial gaze of western Europe. In this chapter, we consider each of these aspects and examine the importance of the Austrian Empress in post-war Austria's cultural and political imaginary. Our approach centres on the insistent concern of *A Fleeting Passage* with the complex relationship between the Empress and her image, a theme linking this film to Beckermann's interest in the functions of the image in Austrian history.

Elisabeth, popularly known as Sisi, famously refused to be photographed or painted after 1868 (and had refused to be depicted with her husband or children since 1860). Consequently, no official photographs exist of the Empress performing her duties, or engaged in family or leisure activities, in the decades with which *A Fleeting Passage* is concerned. During this period, however, she collected images of women on which (Beckermann suggests in the film) she modelled herself: "She studied the details of beauty as if in a catalogue from which she chose what suited her purpose. What she herself wanted to look like. Who she wanted to be."[2] The absence of images corresponds at times to an absence from history; one sequence in the film dwells on Sisi's failure to attend the opening of the Suez Canal in 1869. In this sequence the camera pans across the walls and seating areas of the foyer of the former Palace of Gizeh, now a Marriott Hotel. "The international hotels" (Beckermann narrates of contemporary Cairo) "function as western enclaves and are meeting places for rich Arabs, serving as substitutes for palaces, clubs, and coffee houses."[3] A contemporary space of principally masculine social transience, the Cairo hotel is also a site of colonial and historical significance, its lobby adorned with murals depicting the Suez Canal opening (on which the camera momentarily lingers) (Figure 5.1), "the most important social event of the era", Beckermann reports, attended by royalty and other dignitaries from the whole of Europe but not by the Austrian Empress:

> Elisabeth had failed to attend [...]. She would have been the second most important female person after Eugénie of France, and she let the emperor travel to Egypt alone. And so, in the illustrations and photographs that went around the world, one sees Eugénie and Franz Joseph as a couple.[4]

This complex intermeshing of geopolitics, gender, and the image centres on Sisi's absence from the event and thus from the archive of historical images. The effects of this absence are the basis for the film's examination of the political functions of the image of woman in Austrian history and, more broadly, of the nation's self-image in the post-war period.

Figure 5.1 Ruth Beckermann (dir.), *A Fleeting Passage to the Orient*, 1999. © Ruth Beckermann Filmproduktion.

Sisi as myth

Sisi occupies a crucial, even definitive role in the mythology of post-war Austria, assuming mythical stature herself in the nation's imaginary ("How does one become a myth?" asks Beckermann).[5] After 1945, successive Austrian governments manipulated the image of the Habsburg past (generating a complex network of conflicting elements of exoticising distance and kitsch intimacies, intensities of nationalist emotion alongside imperial nostalgia) to mobilise a series of powerful associations that worked (as we've seen) to mask, or erase, more recent historical events. The constructed and heavily mediated image of the Empress Elisabeth personified those elements of Austrian, and specifically Habsburg, history selected to present a particular version of the nation to the world via a highly successful and ubiquitous marketing strategy. Consequently, post-war Austria became closely identified with the image of the Empress and thus, in a move that effectively erases the intervening decades, with the residual cultural memory of the Habsburg empire and its social and political agendas – a situation that still persists. As Sabine Wieber notes, "It is virtually impossible to visit Vienna and not encounter Sisi – be that in the form of her portrait on chocolate boxes, her full-length silhouette beckoning us to visit the Sisi Museum in the Hofburg or tourist guides inviting us to follow Sisi's footsteps."[6] Through this proliferation of commercial manifestations, Sisi has come to embody a particular version of post-war Austria's imaginary relation to its past.[7]

Because no images exist of her in later life, Sisi's presence in Austrian popular culture since about 1870 has been as a permanently fixed, ageless, nostalgically motivated icon of aristocratic youth and beauty, a mythic version of the Empress perpetuated by an extensive industry of ingeniously photomontaged images, combining elements of earlier photographs with imagined or constructed contextual features as markets demanded new, updated but non-existent imagery of the Empress and her family. In her 1996 essay "Elisabeth – Sisi – Romy Schneider" Beckermann critiques the mobilisation of Sisi as myth and emphasises her "Blickphobie" or "gaze-phobia": "Blicke streichelten Elisabeth nicht, sondern verletzten" ("Looks didn't caress Elisabeth, they hurt her"). She argues that, in exercising control over her image, Sisi effectively became director of her own film ("Sie wurde zur Filmregisseurin ihres eigenen Lebens").[8] *A Fleeting Passage* emphasises the technical aspects of this cultural procedure of image-manufacturing alongside its gradual visual distortion of the "ideal" of the imperial couple:

> Photography [the film's narrative tells us] was also not safe from the techniques of forgery. Photographs of the Empress had to continue to circulate: so her face was retouched, her head mounted on different clothes, she was put into family groups, at her husband's side. Montages, collages. Nobody noticed that in these assiduously circulated photographs a youthful Elisabeth stood at the side of an ageing Franz Joseph.[9]

Olivia Gruber Florek has analysed how these techniques produced an extensive corpus of faked works – an entire visual mythology – that circumvented the absence of new images of Sisi. Gruber Florek connects Sisi's refusal to be depicted with postmodern pathologies of celebrity (which, she argues, partly originate in Elisabeth's popularity) and with the contemporary ubiquity of the celebrity image (even in spaces rarely or never visited by the depicted person; for example, the Elvis-themed gas station of *Towards Jerusalem*).[10] Sisi's refusal to be portrayed, she argues, constituted "evasive manoeuvres" aimed at asserting "control over her photographic image".[11] Post-war Austria's enthusiasm for the Empress's disavowed image thus offers Beckermann another example of how willingly the nation has substituted historical reality with deceptive myth.

Sisi as dialectical image and mobile icon

In its cinematic consideration of Sisi *A Fleeting Passage* presents her as a dialectical image, a visual entity refracting a complex series of symbolic functions. Susan Buck-Morss, discussing the concept as introduced by Walter Benjamin, understands dialectical images as "a modern form of emblematics" from which "politically instructive" analytical perceptions may be derivable.[12] The "interruptive" juxtaposition and temporised sequencing of elements in cinematic montage, providing a version of this "recognition of relatedness" for the viewer, offers (Buck-Morss argues) one manifestation of this constellatory logic.[13] The dialectical image is thus "a way of seeing that crystallises antithetical elements by providing the axes for their alignment" in "a transitory field of oppositions that can perhaps be pictured in terms of coordinates of contradictory terms"[14] – a suggestive definition for analysing the contradictory functions of the image, and specifically the image of Sisi, in *A Fleeting Passage*.

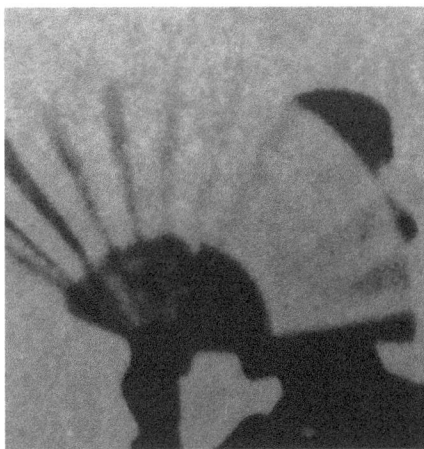

Figure 5.2 Anonymous, *Elisabeth of Austria on horseback* (detail), 1879 or 1881.

Figure 5.3 Eadweard Muybridge, *Woman Jumping over a Chair*, 1887.

Figure 5.4 Lumière brothers (dir.), *Train Arriving at La Ciotat*, 1896.

In the treatment for the film Beckermann identifies three pictures she considers essential to her film's portrayal of the Empress – a cropped photograph from 1879 or 1881, generally considered to be the first paparazzi image, of Sisi on horseback concealing her face behind a fan (Figure 5.2);[15] Eadweard Muybridge's (1830–1904) stop-motion images titled *Woman Jumping over a Chair* (1887) (Figure 5.3); and a still from the Lumière brothers' film of the arrival of a train at La Ciotat in 1896 (Figure 5.4). Together these historically proximate images offer a visual archaeology documenting the transition from still to moving (cinematic) photography via the intermediate, experimental procedure of stop-motion photography. They work dialectically in their relations to each other and to their roughly shared historical context to present a constellation of associations definitive of early modernism and its technological redefinitions of movement in time and space: the Empress's gesture of refusal of the image, ironically captured in an image freezing her in the activity of riding a horse; the dynamism of female movement through space and time in the Muybridge sequence (Muybridge himself, a near-contemporary of Sisi, offers in his well-documented *wanderlust* an interesting parallel with the Empress); and the arrival of a railway train, iconic of modernity and movement, and indicative of cinema's potential as a kind of visual time-travel. Beckermann situates Sisi within this constellation, in which she becomes a dynamic element, both emblem and product of its dialectical effects (the only image of Sisi in the film appears near the beginning held by Beckermann while travelling on a train) (Figure 5.5).

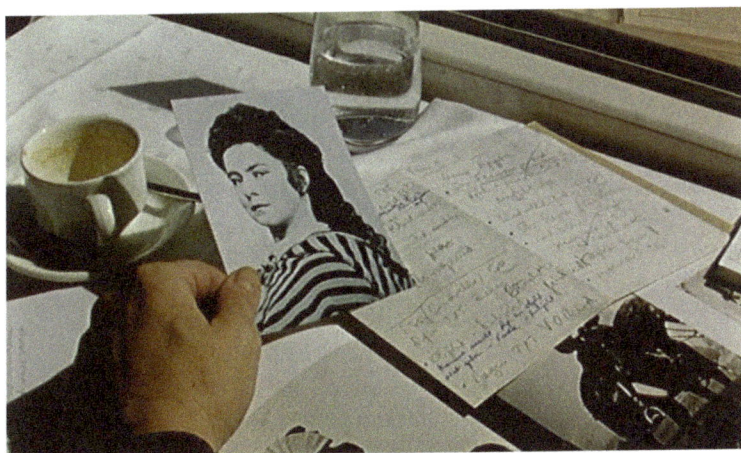

Figure 5.5 Ruth Beckermann (dir.), *A Fleeting Passage to the Orient*, 1999. © Ruth Beckermann Filmproduktion.

Each of these images marks a stage in the historical transition from still to moving images, establishing Sisi within this process as a mobile icon of the technological and cultural dynamism of nascent European modernity – as constantly moving evader of the fixity of images (refusing, for example, to sit for portraits), as controlling agent of her own mobility (understood as extending beyond mere physical movement to include social and cultural mobility) and as traveller (by train, among other modern forms of transport). As Anthony W. Lee has argued, Muybridge's experiments with photography "were part of a much larger historical transformation in which certain forms of motion were given significance and accrued value".[16] *A Fleeting Passage* meditates at length on the potential values in terms of women's freedoms of this emergent paradigm of modernity in motion. The film explores the complex intersection of photography, nascent cinema, and the imperial and gendered gaze of the Empress, geographically and historically locating in her (Austrian and thus European, colonial, aristocratic) perception of Egypt in relation to the development of image technology, and locating the Empress herself within what Tim Cresswell calls "a constellation of mobility" comprising evolving modes of transport and travel alongside increasingly mobile technologies of image-making.[17] Beckermann's narration emphasises the importance of this modern mobility as a parallel to the narrative trajectory her film explores, "a journey out from the static world of the Habsburgs and into the imagery of modernism. The destinations of the first cameramen overlapped with Elisabeth's itinerary: Côte d'Azur, Switzerland, Italy. They went where modern, busy life was".[18]

Sisi's embodiment of "the mobility of life" provides the framework of Beckermann's film. Historical displacement (or movement through time) parallels geographical movement, as the film finds in Cairo a series of scenes, encountered through the cinematic gaze of Beckermann-as-*flâneuse*, drifting through Cairo's urban spaces. The film's title embraces the notion of the "fleeting" or transitory moment evoked by Walter Benjamin and Charles Baudelaire as expressive of the condensed and constellated experience of modernity. It attempts to crystallise in a series of images the complexity of a multitude of historical frames that evoke the Benjaminian inflection of the word "passage" which Beckermann emphasises in her interview with Karen Schiefer,[19] where the word suggests movement, intermediality and intermediacy, and textual duration. Nurith Aviv's camerawork is conspicuously oneiric and reinforces this sense of passage and mobility – long tracking shots along streets and bazaars or through the windscreens of moving vehicles offer a constantly mobile perspective, alongside a notable emphasis on locations of temporary residence – coffee bars, hotels, streets, markets, spaces of itinerancy facilitating Said's "fleeting moments of freedom". The camera embodies Cairo as an image-space comprised of a complex and mobile amalgam of documentary realism and western fantasy, contemporary perception and historical palimpsest, a city of memory and desire constructed by many passages and displacements, simultaneously (for Sisi) colonial and (from Beckermann's late twentieth-century perspective) decolonial, accompanied by a speculative, meandering narrative that constantly emphasises movement and displacement as both condition and effect of the narratives of desire under scrutiny. Egypt appears through the binocular effect of a double 'tourist-imaginary' gaze deeply informed by this contexture – that of the late twentieth-century film-maker and that of the nineteenth-century travelling Empress. Via this double presentation, the specifically Austrian and Jewish experience of unbelonging expands into a wider western and modernist alienation, situated amidst the exemplary socio-economic environment of "colonial modernity"[20] experienced by Sisi in late-nineteenth-century Cairo and doubled in Beckermann's travels through the city a century later. "I would like to travel through the ages", Beckermann's narrative states, "but I can only ever film the one that is mine. I can't travel back in time, only to faraway places, in foreign lands … But perhaps the past is a foreign country."[21] This sinuous interfolding of time and space, movement and restriction, indicates some of the film's complexities.

'Oriental' Cairo

Critics have focussed on *A Fleeting Passage*'s apparent construction of Cairo as a potential, if not fully realised, site of exotic and sometimes threatening difference. Dagmar Lorenz describes the film as offering "an extremely unromantic impression of the Orient",[22] while Karen Remmler points out the complexity of the interplay of different constructions of Egypt in the film: "The underlying irony of the voiceover reminds us that we are making assumptions about the landscapes in the so-called Orient that are themselves only reflections of nineteenth-century fantasies."[23] Lorenz emphasises gender and its intersections with the apparently hostile ethnic otherness of Cairo: "[t]he precarious situation", she writes, "of the Jewish woman filmmaker roaming the streets and bazaars of Cairo provides insight into a problematic past and an uncertain present in a non-European setting." Consequently, "The filmmaker and her camerawoman move in a latently hostile space where they, doubly marginalized, are either barely tolerated or patronized."[24]

One effect of placing femininity at the centre of the film's double vision of Cairo is that the city's exotic unfamiliarity becomes strangely ideologically *familiar* to the Western viewer, as the camera lingers on sights and locations in which versions of the conventional gender and class hierarchies of Western capitalism and patriarchy seem evident. "Something I notice immediately … the luxury of leisure is reserved for men",[25] Beckermann comments as the camera pans along a street, views into coffee bars revealing men, individually or in groups, lounging with newspapers, while women appear as images adorning the city's surfaces. Lorenz emphasises how Beckermann's journey to Egypt revises the travel narratives of films like *Paper Bridge*, in that Beckermann "discovers [in Egypt] a hidden history paralleling her own, and she shows a cultural break less frequently discussed than the Holocaust but just as violent as that in Austria of the 1930s: the expulsion of Jews and Europeans from Egypt and the Arab world".[26] These historical contexts constitute one dimension of this film's complex navigation of an insistently doubled and interlinked cultural history – Austria/Egypt, Vienna/Cairo, Sisi/Beckermann.

This interlinked history becomes evident in a sequence in which Beckermann visits a spice market in a Cairo version of a Parisian passage. We see several women shopping while the tradesman identifies and shows Beckermann samples of the variety of spices on offer. The camera pans across sacks full of spices and other foodstuffs. The handfuls of spice she is offered echo the "handful of sand" in the parable of the desert nomad Beckermann has just related: "Scooping up a handful of sand, the nomad says: '*This is my life*', and repeating the gesture with the other hand he says: '*And this is my death. Everything else is fata morgana*'."[27]

A few minutes later Beckermann quotes a passage from Sisi's writings expressing the Empress's western perception of Egyptian women:

'*What can I say about the women? We saw very little of them. Shrouded from head to foot in white linen, a number of them trudged listlessly past, conveying the impression of walking sacks*'.[28]

In the echoes and repetitions of this sequence of interlinked images and narrative fragments, the film establishes a symbolic network connecting meditations on sand and mortality (the *Book of Common Prayer*'s "dust to dust", and, in a modernist echo, T. S. Eliot's "fear in a handful of dust"),[29] spice and the exotic, the near-invisibility of Egyptian women to Elisabeth's nineteenth-century imperial–colonial gaze, and the resemblance of those women she does see to "walking sacks", echoing the sacks of spice in the market and thus implicitly commodified, reduced to depersonalised, marketable objects. "Among the exotic spices", Beckermann narrates during this sequence, "I notice a bright blue powder. Somebody explains that it's for bleaching white laundry"[30] (Figure 5.6).

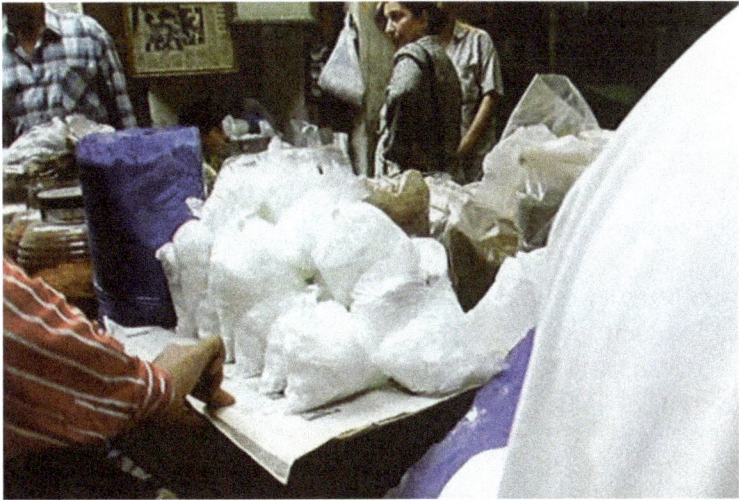

Figure 5.6 Ruth Beckermann (dir.), *A Fleeting Passage to the Orient*, 1999. © Ruth Beckermann Filmproduktion.

This "bright blue powder" sharpens the eye-catching and apparently exotic signscape of the Egyptian city; it offers an apparently innocuous but significantly incongruous detail – not an exotic spice but a bleaching agent, a substance whose function is to erase traces of usage and presence, a material connoting concealed female labour ("laundry") and momentarily (fleetingly) making manifest the colonial ideology implicit in Elisabeth's restricted perception of the Egyptian women, who she sees dressed "head to foot in white [i.e. bleached] linen".

Crystallised within this momentary encounter in the marketplace of modern Cairo is a complex set of relations operating within the historical, economic, cultural, and gender codes surrounding Egypt's colonial history and Austria's relations to it. The bleaching agent metonymises Egypt's burgeoning economic significance for Europe by the 1880s, which was due largely to its status as a cotton-producing country. As Timothy Mitchell notes in his analysis of the colonial construction of Egypt-as-image, by the late nineteenth century

> Egypt was turning into a country whose economy was dominated by the production of a single commodity, raw cotton, for the global textile industry of Europe. By the eve of the First World War, cotton was to account for more than ninety-two per cent of the total value of Egypt's exports.[31]

The exporting of cotton from Egypt offers a concrete commercial and economic expression of the colonial power embodied in the visits to Egypt of an imperial European empress. Furthermore, Egyptian cotton was a vital raw material for the Viennese textile industry in which, in the twentieth century, Salo Beckermann worked (and which provided the economic–industrial pressure motivating the occupation of the arts centre in *Arena Squatted*). The bright blue laundry powder, a fleeting image stimulating a range of connotations, thus embeds within *A Fleeting Passage* a constellation of relations connecting the film's themes and linking them to earlier moments in Beckermann's oeuvre.

The polysemy of this image also gestures towards the ambiguities of the version of Egypt constructed by the western, and principally masculine, gaze. Mitchell argues that

[v]isitors to the Orient conceived of themselves as travelling to 'the East itself in its vital actual reality'. But [...] the reality they sought there was simply that which could be photographed or accurately represented, that which presented itself as a picture of something before an observer. A picture here refers not just to a visual illustration, but to what stands apart as something distinct from the subject and is grasped in terms of a corresponding distinction between representation and reality. In the end the European tried to grasp the Orient as though it were an exhibition of itself.[32]

Sisi's refusal of the image, and her efforts through various strategies (such as travelling incognito, as Beckermann narrates, under the names Countess Hohenembs or Mrs Nicholson) to sustain this 'invisibility' while in Egypt, contribute to this orientalist position. Mitchell points out that the sustaining of Oriental difference required the constant erasure of European 'presence': "To establish the objectness of the Orient, as something set apart from the European presence, required that the presence itself, ideally, become invisible."[33] Sisi's desire to "become invisible" is thus, in the contexts of her Egyptian travels, a conventional European desire to exercise the privilege of seeing without being seen, to bleach out her visible presence from the fabric of Egyptian social life. In Egypt, Sisi looks, but resists being seen. For Beckermann, the Occidental concept of Oriental "self-exhibition" – Cairo's presentation to the western gaze of images of itself – counters Elisabeth's refusal of the image, generating a tension the film navigates partly by displacing its visual analysis into textuality and specifically the relations between written and visual signs.

Sisi in Egypt: image and text

Biographies of Elisabeth largely omit reference to her subsequent travels in Egypt, which were undertaken several years after the 1869 Suez opening, privately and without official functions. Hamann echoes Egon Corti in noting a comment by the Austrian Chargé d'affaires in Cairo about Sisi's remarkable capacity for daily walks.[34] Corti offers a little more detail: "In November [1891 – her 1885 visit is unremarked] the palace in Corfu was deserted and the yacht

Miramar sailed for Egypt. Here the Empress spent nearly three weeks at Shepherd's Hotel in Cairo."[35] Searching for this location in 1998, Beckermann finds that "it stood on the site of what is today a gas station. On a black Saturday in 1952, it was burnt down by nationalists, as were hundreds of foreign-owned cinemas, bars, banks, casinos and department stores."[36] This event, a key element of the thread concerned with Egyptian decolonial independence that runs through *A Fleeting Passage*, occurred during the 23 July Revolution, which marked the end of British colonial rule in Egypt. Sisi's evident political leanings (in particular her identification and alignment with the Magyar element of the Austro-Hungarian imperial arrangement) may have drawn her towards sympathising with the extensive political agitation during the 1880s for Egyptian independence from the newly imposed British imperial rule, which began with the military-colonial occupation in 1882, a date marking the beginning (Zeinab Abul-Magd argues) of "a period of failed empire and an unfinished nation".[37] Sisi's visit to Cairo in 1885 took place amidst a historical period of intensive and highly controversial colonial nation-formation. The British were engaged in Egypt in developing (and imposing) a unified capitalist market, a process of economic modernisation and rationalisation aimed at optimising Egyptian cotton and sugar production for European markets (as noted earlier) but extending to institutional 'modernisation' involving legal and governmental restructuring of the nation, processes that led to widespread social and juridical contestation and unrest.[38]

Despite her presence in the country amidst this politically volatile atmosphere, Elisabeth's stay in Egypt seems to have been largely undocumented. Beckermann narrates:

> What is a matter of record, evidenced in documents, preserved in the Austrian state archives, and thus certain, is that in October 1885 and November 1891, she sailed from Trieste to Corfu and from there over the Mediterranean to Egypt. On her second journey she was 54 years old. Her ship, the *Miramar*, remained in the harbour at Alexandria while she travelled to Cairo for about two weeks with an entourage of only 13 people, on the ordinary fast train, refusing the offer of a special saloon car.[39]

The second of these journeys was recorded by the captain of the yacht *Miramar*, who titled his narrative *Ein flüchtiger Zug nach dem Orient*;[40] the railway journey to Cairo recalls, of course, the still from the Lumière brothers' film discussed earlier. Beckermann's film thus frames incomplete Austrian cultural memory through an imagined (and cinematically imaged) version of the Cairo visited by Sisi. This film version of the city, which emphasises what Beckermann has called the "visual pleasures"[41] of Egypt as image, masks the absence of images of Sisi in Cairo, an absence compensated for by the film's emphasis on reading and interpreting *written* signs. A *Fleeting Passage* opens and closes with different explorations of the relation between word and image. The narration begins with a citation from the published recollections of the Empress's Greek tutor Constantin Christomanos (1867–1911), describing his first encounter with the Empress (and echoing the paparazzi photograph noted earlier):

> Her Greek reader writes: "*She stood before me, bending forwards slightly; her head stood out against the background of a white parasol through which the rays of the sun penetrated, forming a bright nimbus around her head. In her left hand she held a black fan inclined towards her cheek. One thought only filled my head. This is 'she'. A feeling of amazement came over me: how little she resembled the pictures of her that I was familiar with!*".[42]

Reading and writing, and the ekphrastic rendering of image and visual appearance in words, are thus foregrounded from the outset. Beckermann's narrative collages quotations from Sisi's writings alongside other sources, referring throughout to Christomanos's book ("In my bag, I have the record kept by Constantin Christomanos",[43] she tells us), itself an exercise in heavily romanticised hagiography.[44] His narrative version of Sisi is predicated on how the real Empress exceeds both her image and his ability to describe her in words (his brother, who meets her first, tells him "Elle est indescriptible").[45] Both image and language fail to match the 'reality' of the Empress. Nevertheless, Christomanos seeks to compensate for this failure through an extended performance of what W. J. T. Mitchell calls "the utopian desire of ekphrasis" – an effort to ensure "that the beautiful image be present to the observer".[46] In a further ekphrastic sequence at the end of the film, Beckermann encounters a fortune teller, Mdme Warda, a reader of coffee grounds and people's palms, who 'reads' Sisi's character from the portrait photograph Beckermann shows her, constructing in words an imaginary version of the Empress, and diagnosing her as (like Beckermann, and like the fortune-teller her-self) a reader: "She reads a lot of books, stories, English stories, French stories, American stories, she is always reading."[47]

Different kinds of *verbal* representation thus bookend the film's "visual pleasures", emphasising the ways Sisi's image mobilises different narratives. In *A Fleeting Passage* she exists largely as a product of these verbal representations, which generate a set of associations which, extended via her own writings and Beckermann's quoting from and commenting on them, elaborate a wider commentary (always refracted through the film's questioning Western gaze) on Egypt's sense of its own colonial history and how this relates to Beckermann's Austrian unbelonging.

Sisi in post-war Austria

Beckermann's film is predicated on the significance of Sisi in post-war Austria, as a cultural icon and as a cinematic construction, both performing complex ideological functions. As Gundolf Graml has argued, post-war Austrian political and cultural institutions have worked hard to construct in image and narrative a specific kind of 'Austria' for international consumption, seeking (only partially successfully) to erase evidence of the "inconvenient past"[48] and establish "a counter-image of Austria as unified, whole, and innocent [which] began to emerge in the discourse of tourism, complementing political efforts at presenting Austria as Hitler's first victim".[49] Austrian history is not merely contested but fully revised in the process of its re-figuring, in which several narratives of national becoming were combined and mobilised – racial, ethnic, moral and ethical, and, above all, gender. Graml argues that this process produced a markedly 'feminine' image of Austria. The nation's (exclusively male) leaders identified a set of qualities associated with femininity as potentially definitive of a newly modelled national identity that sought to distance itself from what were perceived as historically 'German' and masculine qualities of militaristic aggression, and thus to minimise association with recent events.

The resulting image of the nation as 'feminine' passive victim was actively reinforced (Graml notes) by the bizarrely gendered rhetoric deployed in allied documents of the 1950s to explain recent history: "It should be remembered that Austria yielded with so little opposition and afterwards accepted her violator with such enthusiasm that it was legitimate to wonder whether it was a case of rape or seduction."[50] The new self-image of Austria was epitomised in photographs used to promote the country in the best-selling *Österreich Buch* (*The Book of Austria*) (1948), with its prominently positioned image of the 'Venus of Willendorf', a c.29,500-year-old oolite fertility figurine unearthed in Lower Austria in 1908. This ancient female figure mobilised a series of nebulous and evasive ideological associations. Its exaggerated feminine features and its stylised, semi-seated mimetic form emblematised the new, passively feminine and victimised, post-war version of the nation. Its undatable origins in prehistory, along with its uncertain function, also conveniently and pointedly transcended (and thus implicitly evaded, if not erased) the immediate, narrow confines of recent history, suggesting a vague timescale way beyond that of recent memory, which is, in turn, reduced in scale and significance, narrowed in relation to the expanded historical perspective of prehistory.

During the decades after the war, Austrian cinema (which, for international economic and linguistic reasons, overlapped significantly in industrial and generic features with German cinema) provided a series of texts instrumental in the process of constructing the wider contours this feminised tourist imaginary version of the country. The *Heimatfilm* genre (related to *Bergfilm* and other nature-based film genres and hugely popular in the post-war period), in particular, was characterised by its emphasis on *Heimat* or home as not merely a territory but also what Raymond Williams would call a "structure of feeling",[51] a broader but indeterminate sense of belonging and belief in "home" as both experience and condition, embodiment of a set of immutable (and thus static, immobile) values.[52] Johannes Von Moltke argues that

> Heimat in the Heimatfilm functions in two ways simultaneously: on the one hand, it affords a colourful flight from a reality deemed lacking into an apparently unrelated fantasy world; on the other hand, it serves as a metaphoric displacement of that reality, whose lack remains legible at different levels of the film text.[53]

The legibility of this lack is evident in the use in *Heimatfilme* of a series of conventional tropes: human and social proximity to the land, rural (often Alpine) lives and notions of folklore and seemingly 'eternal', changeless traditions, and associated conventional gender roles (masculinity and labour, femininity in the domestic sphere, and the landscape as feminised by a male gaze. Austrian *Heimatfilme* were characterised above all by their ambivalent rejection of modernity (but some films, von Moltke suggests, celebrated the cultural dynamism of the post-war period while still promoting older, traditional and patriarchal, values). The genre constructed what Maria Fritsche calls an "unspoilt and seemingly apolitical" version of Austria as *Heimat* which "arguably answered a deep desire for stability, rekindled a sense of pride in the homeland, [and] 'purified' the nation from the violence of war and assuaged collective guilt".[54]

Among other features, *Heimatfilme* offered fictional portrayals of figures from periods of Austrian history predating, and thus 'uncontaminated' by, the Nazi past, in order to establish in the post-war context usable historical narratives as grounds on which to build a revised contemporary version of the country. Films like Franz Antel's musical comedy *Ideale Frau gesucht* (*Ideal Woman Sought*) (1952), adapting an 1894 operetta by Karl Zeller, focused audiences on the romantic intrigues of the Habsburg aristocracy which, despite ending in the chaos of the years immediately after World War I, nevertheless provided Austrian cultural memory with a historically fixed set of events, characters, and relations that proved immensely seductive, driving the powerful wave of imperial nostalgia experienced by post-war audiences (and shared, as noted earlier, by Beckermann's father in his own recollections in *Paper Bridge* of Habsburg-ruled Czernowitz).

The Empress Elisabeth was a key figure in the construction of this imperial nostalgia. Her highly mythologised life and (ironically) ubiquitous image were ideologically powerful presences in post-war Austria. Anita McChesney outlines cinema's importance in establishing the identification of the Empress with the nation:

> The qualities associated with the Empress have been repeatedly mapped onto those of Austria, whether in the late nineteenth-century Austro-Hungarian Empire in which she ruled or in the Republic of Austria that followed. A few prominent examples are the Sisi monument in the Volksgarten in Vienna from 1907, Ernst Marischka's three Sisi films from 1955 to 1957, and the numerous portrayals of the Empress in the 1990s that culminated in the "Sisi Year" in 1998

[when Beckermann was filming *A Fleeting Passage*] commemorating the one-hundredth anniversary of her death. Despite their differing media and time periods, these representations all create a sentimentalized image of the Empress and, with it, an idealized image of Austrian history and culture.[55]

Marischka's "Sisi" trilogy, depicting highly romanticised versions of Sisi's life and contributing significantly to the post-Nazi reconfiguration of Austrian history, starred the Vienna-born German-French actor Romy Schneider (1938–82).[56] While most critics subsume them into the *Heimatfilm* category, Maria Fritsche argues that these films should be seen instead as "historical costume films", a genre that "sought to instil a sense of pride in Austria by emphasising the highly cultured nature of the society".[57] Heidi Schlipphacke points out both the generic uncertainties and the conflicted ideological agenda at work in these films:

> Shot in glossy Agfacolor, the Sisi films are usually read as representing a hybrid genre of Heimatfilm, historical drama, melodrama and even fairytale: the innocent princess marries the Emperor, and their union signifies a liaison between Germany and Austria that reimagines the unsuccessful 'marriage' between the two countries following Hitler's annexation of Austria. [...] Rather than offering the simple pleasures of a fantasy of national harmony to traumatized West German and Austrian spectators, these films reflect deep-seated anxieties about home and historical continuity that haunt post-Nazi Germany and Austria.[58]

For Schlipphacke, the overdetermined feminine iconography of these films tips over into the "hyperperformance and excess"[59] of camp. The demand that Sisi embody the values of conventional (heterosexual) femininity in contributing to the nation's (feminised) reconstruction is undermined, Schlipphacke argues, by the films' prevailing mood of "melancholy and loss", a mood she connects to the "queering" effects of Sisi's wilful narrative displacement from family, homeland, and duty, displacements and evasions that repeatedly conflict with the ostensible ideological imperatives of the films' narratives, which demand of the Empress the public performance of wifely and maternal duties alongside national and international responsibilities of state. "Queering", Schlipphacke points out, suggests an "askance" or "skewed" quality in a relationship, an "obliqueness" and "displacement" (reminiscent of the "looking awry" demanded by *The Waldheim Waltz*) which she productively links to Freudian notions of mourning and melancholia and their connections with "ambivalence and shame".[60] The Sisi films and their immense popularity become, in this reading, symptoms of cultural evasion and distortion, the movies suspending any direct engagement with the recent past in their elaboration of mythical histories long predating, and ideologically distant from, that past. Their generic and ideological ambiguities figure analogous uncertainties and contradictions at work in the national psyche as it seeks to evade troubling historical realities.

Discussing these films, Beckermann points out important historical and film-industry continuities which the mythologisation of Sisi sought to gloss over:

> The ingenious casting in *Sisi* simulates a break with the ideology of the Nazi era which is actually a full continuity: Romy Schneider is the daughter of the actors Magda Schneider and Wolf Albach-Rety, who were celebrated from 1933–45. Karl-Heinz Böhm's father was the star conductor of the Third Reich. For the cliques of actors and directors, life really went on as before.[61]

Another problem lies in tensions between the ideological functions demanded by the mythic version of Sisi's life and the historical realities of that life, significant elements of which were embroidered out of the films' narratives: her long-term avoidance of imperial duty, her clear identification with the Hungarian (i.e. minority) element of the Austro-Hungarian empire, her extensive travels over many years away from her husband and family, her chronic mental and physical illnesses (in particular her apparent anorexia nervosa),[62] and, in particular, her "Blickphobie", which deprived the Austrian public of images of their Empress performing her symbolic roles of mother, wife, and national icon.

Eliding these tensions, Marischka's films offered instead narratives of national heroism and redemption embodied in Sisi as performer of internationally significant acts of diplomacy and resolution, ultimately constructing imperial loss as (Fritsche argues) "meaningful sacrifice"[63] and thus an ideologically legitimate spur for Austrian nostalgia. The broadly *international* dimension of these films' appeal, furthermore, problematises their ostensible focus on specifically *Austrian* historical perspectives and contexts; as Fritsche points out, the first Sisi film "implies – through its characterisations of the protagonists as well as the Alpine setting in Bavaria and the Austrian Bad Ischl – that Austrians and Bavarians are essentially the same people",[64] a conflation suggesting the unconscious proximity of historical assertions of German-Austrian unity. Erica Carter furthermore outlines the "binational trade dispute" and "full-blown diplomatic row" that developed in early 1957 over the alleged appropriation by German distributors of commercially successful Austrian films, including the first instalment of Marischka's Sisi trilogy. "The space of German-language film production in Western Europe", Carter argues, "and specifically Austria and West Germany after 1945 [was] a territory united in matters of popular film aesthetics and social affect, which later took the form in the trilogy [...] of an affective drift toward imperial nostalgia and the melancholy of territorial loss."[65]

Beckermann's essay film resists the ideological and emotional associations mobilised so powerfully in Marischka's dramatic trilogy. Against "the melancholy of territorial loss", *A Fleeting Passage* presents Egypt, a territory of semiotic plenitude ("visual pleasure") and insistent, defamiliarised presence. Against Sisi's conventional embodiment of Austrian *Heimat* values of tradition, home, and belonging, she posits the Empress as a symbol of unbelonging, a *flâneuse* inhabiting a mobile condition located always outside itself, in spaces exotic to the ostensible but abandoned home. That home is defamiliarised in spatial and historical terms, so that Elisabeth feels "at home" in precisely the location – Cairo – in which she is an anonymous visitor. The narrative quotes from Elisabeth's writings: "*I feel extraordinarily at home in Cairo* [...]. *Even in the greatest crush of porters and donkeys I feel less oppressed than at a ball at court, and almost as happy as in a forest.*"[66] This relation echoes Charles Baudelaire's description of the situation of the (explicitly male) flâneur (epitomised for Baudelaire in the painter Constantin Guys):

To be away from home, and yet to feel oneself everywhere at home; to see the world, to be at the centre of the world and yet to remain hidden from the world – such are a few of the slightest pleasures of such independent, passionate, and impartial natures [...]. The spectator is a *prince* who everywhere rejoices in his incognito.[67]

The experience of feeling at "home" afforded by being an Austrian *Empress* incognito in a foreign city signifies, in Sisi's writings, a feminisation of this spectatorial position, along with a distancing from the familiar class territory of imperial Austria, and a kind of secret proximity instead to those of the lowest classes, servants and beasts signifying an extreme degree of social otherness – introducing into the film's exploration of Sisi via the dynamics afforded by modern mobility a desire for *social* mobility, a freedom of movement between classes. This suggests (in the context of the conventionally rigid class boundaries of the higher levels of Habsburg society) a markedly unhomely version of homeliness, in which Elisabeth's privileged status as wealthy imperial Westerner sojourning in the East insists, reinforcing Mary Jacobus' point that "Home is always lined (and aligned) with the unhomely that bounds it."[68]

Egypt in Vienna: *unheimliche Heimat*

As suggested above, *A Fleeting Passage* marks a distinct shift in cinematic style and form, moving from the visual sparsity and compressed numbers of shots characteristic of the earlier documentaries and essays to the director's "throwing [her]self into visual pleasure and truly creating images".[69] Presenting Egypt as a tourist space composed of cinematically seductive images (the country as "exhibition of itself" for the western viewer/traveller), the film engages with aspects of the country's colonial history, in particular its construction as spectacle to be consumed by western travellers, a construction it seeks to problematise by ironising its own (contemporary) view of Cairo, rendering the city via a look that undercuts questions of colonial visibility and the operation of the imperial gaze. It also interacts with the long tradition of Western constructions of Egypt as image, explored (for example) in Maria Golia's *Photography and Egypt* (2010). Golia emphasises Egypt's significance at the origins of photography, historically coincident with Sisi's birth in 1837. While announcing to the Académie des Sciences in 1839 the invention of the new daguerreotype process, the Académie's permanent secretary François Arago lamented the production, before such photographic technology was available, of the compendious French colonial documentation of the country in the *Description de l'Egypte* (1810–28). Golia notes the "urgency associated with photography from the start, the desire to capture the ephemeral", including "preserving a record of a civilisation's [i.e., Egypt's] past",[70] a past evident in archaeological traces perceived to be on the brink of vanishing. This 'fleeting' but immense past and its diversity are markers of Egyptian difference: Edward Said writes of "Egypt's ungraspably long past, pharaonic, Hellenistic, Coptic, Fatimid, Mameluke, Ottoman, European".[71] Egypt thus existed in European colonial consciousness as a space simultaneously transient and eternal, its conflicting, ancient but uncannily *modern* temporalities needing to be documented in images, to be recorded, tabulated, and enclosed by the power of the image to record and fix reality. It also constituted a significant influence on and element of the cultural history of Austrian modernism, which was not immune to the waves of "Egyptomania" that entranced several generations of Europeans and Americans.

Sisi's visits to Cairo can be interpreted in relation to the popular prominence in Viennese cultural life of the late nineteenth-century of elements of Egyptian culture that performed specific ideological functions and were facilitated by historically contingent political and economic systems of exchange, generating their own socially symbolic networks of cultural significance. As Said argues, "[T]he taste for Egypt and the images that derive from it are part of the political history of our time, as changeable and shifting in their meaning as any other of the icons with which our ideological perspectives are propped up."[72] Austria participated, like all of Europe, in the "Egyptomania" of the time, a craze that saturated first-world cultural production with a huge range of tropes and styles drawing (Jean-Marcel Humbert writes) "on many sources":

> from ancient originals that were copied or adapted, with varying degrees of fidelity depending on the ear, in travellers' narratives, explorers' sketches, and the documentary and scientific works that result from the archaeological research of Egyptologists; [and from] forms derived from earlier Egyptianizing production dating from the Roman period to the present day.[73]

These "many sources" fuelled stylistic innovations in a wide variety of contexts across the whole range of Austrian cultural production – for example, Egyptian-style scenery (designed by artists like the French Marcel Multzer and the Germans Karl Friedrich Schinkel and Simon Quaglio) and costumes were extensively used for Viennese productions of Mozart's Masonic-influenced *The Magic Flute*, while the Viceroy of Egypt's pavilion at the 1873 World's Fair in Vienna was promoted as "a pearl of oriental architecture".[74] The 7th International Congress of Orientalists was held in Vienna in 1886, a year after Sisi's first visit to Cairo. The Austrian imperial family was directly and deeply involved in these crazes. The Egyptian collection of Vienna's Kunsthistorisches Museum was expanded by the addition of articles procured by Sisi's son, Crown Prince Rudolph, on his travels in Egypt in 1881, and the Museum's website notes further contemporary acquisitions, indicating the extensive imbrication of "Egyptomania" within the networks of international imperial power:

> Several years later the collection received a generous gift from the Egyptian government. These were coffins and coffin ensembles found in a hiding place – a so-called cachette – in Thebes. Towards the end of the 19th century the Miramar collection of almost 2,000 objects from the possession of Emperor Maximilian of Mexico was added to the inventory of the imperial collections.[75]

Diane O'Donoghue has explored a further complication of the relationship between Vienna and Egypt found in the influence on the early development of Freudian psychoanalysis of the popular genre of "Egyptian dream books", pamphlet-guides to oneirocriticism widely sold on the streets of Vienna and promoting strategies of dream-analysis derived from ancient Egyptian traditions of dream-interpretation. These cheap publications were "ubiquitous in Vienna" while Freud was elaborating his own early theories of dream-interpretation.[76] As O'Donoghue points out:

> At least ten publishers were producing these texts in Vienna in 1900 [the year Freud published *The Interpretation of Dreams*], and the one that sold most widely, Stock's *Persisch-Egyptisches Traum-Buch*, uncannily, was printed at Berggasse 31, only a few doors away from Freud's now-famous residence and consulting room at Berggasse 19.[77]

In her essay "Freud's Uncanny Egypt", Mary Bergstein discusses Freud's long and complex relation to Egypt, a country he never visited but which was mediated to him via the texts and imagery circulated by Austria's "Egyptomania", from which he gleaned an early sense of the country's potential *unheimlich* qualities:

> From the daydreams of early childhood, to musing over his collections of books and ancient sculpture in maturity, through the adventure of *Moses and Monotheism* in old age, Egypt – biblical, ancient, and modern – was a place of uncanny 'otherness' in Freud's visual and historical imagination.[78]

Egypt had, furthermore, a palpable impact on the theoretical development of psychoanalysis. Egyptian hieroglyphics, "already uncanny and [requiring] interpretation",[79] provided Freud with a usefully exotic metaphor for the functions of the image in dream-logic, in which (he argued) the unconscious processes of condensation and displacement resulted in compressed, rebus-like signifiers reminiscent of hieroglyphic writing. Bergstein argues that Freud's versions of Egypt and its history derived largely from images he collected – in particular, photographs of mummies, with their uncanny connotations of life after death – and culminated in the provocative arguments of his last book, *Moses and Monotheism* (1939), in which he constructed Moses as an Egyptian aristocrat.

Freud's controversial arguments in this book have generated much scholarly debate, but the historical moment of its production – amid the rapid aggressive pre-war expansion of Nazi Germany and resulting panic among European (and specifically Austrian) Jewish communities – is significant. Jan Assmann, for example, points out that

> Freud wanted to discover the roots of anti-Semitism. Strikingly enough, his question was not how the Gentiles, or the Christians, or the Germans came to hate the Jews, but "how the Jew had become what he is and why he has attracted this undying hatred".[80]

Yosef Hayim Yerushalmi describes Freud's book as "a public statement about matters of considerably wider consequence – the nature of Jewish history, religion and peoplehood, Christianity and anti-Semitism – written at a tragic historical juncture".[81] Bergstein reads Freud's attempts to redefine the Jews as "remnants of the Mediterranean peoples and heirs of the Mediterranean civilisations" as "a racialist absurdity" which (like Yerushalmi) she ascribes to "a conscious or unconscious response to Nazi racial policies and the *Anschluss* of 1938".[82] These complex intersections between Freudian and psychoanalytic interest in Egypt and its (contested) place in both Jewish history and Austria's traumatic Nazi history haunt *A Fleeting Passage*, constituting vital elements of the wider cultural contexture on which Beckermann's analysis of Sisi draws.

Beckermann clearly gestures to Freud's book, and locates her film in relation to it, in her discussions of *A Fleeting Passage*: "To my mind, it is no coincidence that I went to Egypt, the land of ancient gods that had to be abandoned by Moses' people to attain monotheism."[83] The film itself contains no direct allusion to *Moses and Monotheism*, but Lorenz's insight (quoted earlier) that it indirectly alludes to "the expulsion [in the 1950s] of Jews and Europeans from Egypt and the Arab world" suggests Beckermann's awareness of how *A Fleeting Passage* might resonate in relation to questions of Jewish history and identity despite, as Lorenz notes, being "void of any images of Jewish life"[84] – an absence that echoes the thematic concern with the 'absent' image of Sisi. Sisi (Lorenz suggests, in a reading that reinforces the intersection of women's and Jewish experiences of unbelonging in the film) comes to figure Jewishness, assuming "stereotypical Jewish traits",[85] specifically in her modern mobility, errancy, and homelessness. Beckermann's narration quotes her (in the epigraph to this chapter) comparing herself to the stereotype of the Wandering Jew. Her prohibition of images of herself corresponds suggestively, of course, to the prohibition of the image of God in the Jewish religion.

Sisi's embodiment of the cliché of Jewish migrancy adds a further element to the complex "constellation of mobility" constructed in *A Fleeting Passage*. It figures the Empress's highly mobile quest for belonging amid the unhomely, uncanny (to European aristocratic eyes) spaces of nineteenth-century Cairo, adding Jew and Gentile to the list of oppositions structuring the film and emphasising the subtle interplay, at the heart of this instalment of Beckermann's enquiry into the roles played by images in Austrian history, of homely and unhomely experiences of migrancy and residence. The latter of these two conditions is one focus of the texts addressed in the next chapter.

Notes

1 Beckermann, "Commentary" to *A Fleeting Passage to the Orient*, in Ruth Beckermann, *Film Collection: Texte/Texts/Textes*, pp. 104–14; p. 104. This is the text of the film's narrative and is reproduced in German, French, and English; quotations will be taken from the English version.

2 Beckermann, "Commentary", p. 108.

3 Beckermann, "Commentary", p. 109.

4 Ibid.

5 Beckermann, "Commentary", p. 115. Lorenz calls her an "almost mythical figure". "Post-Shoah Positions", 167.

6 Sabine Wieber, "Vienna's Most Fashionable Neurasthenic: Empress Sisi and the Cult of Size Zero", in Wieber and Gemma Blackshaw (eds), *Journeys into Madness: Mapping Mental Illness in the Austro-Hungarian Empire* (New York: Berghahn, 2012), pp. 90–108; p. 91.

7 Recent texts extending Sisi's cultural afterlife into the 21st century include Marie Kreutzer's film *Corsage* (2022), which fictionalises Sisi's life in 1877–8; and Linda Stift's novel *Stierhunger* (2007) (trans. Jamie Bulloch as *The Empress and the Cake* [London: Peirene, 2016]), an allegory of bulimia in which a modern, elderly counterpart to Sisi bears her travelling pseudonym Frau Hohenembs.

8 Ruth Beckermann, "Elisabeth – Sisi – Romy Schneider", in Beckermann and Christa Blümlinger (eds), *Ohne Untertitel: Fragmente einer Geschichte des österreichischen Kinos* (Vienna: Sonderzahl, 1996), p. 313.

9 Beckermann, "Commentary", p. 105.

10 Olivia Gruber Florek, *The Celebrity Monarch: Empress Elisabeth and the Modern Female Portrait* (Newark: University of Delaware Press, 2023), p. 14. See also Rudolf Bernd, who compares Sisi to Garbo and Dietrich. *Ruth Beckermann und das Sichtbarmachen des Verschwindens: Der Beitrag der Autorin und Filmemacherin zur Medien- und Kommunikationsgeschichte in den Jahren 1978–2008* (unpublished MPhil thesis, University of Vienna, 2008), p. 147.

11 Gruber Florek, *The Celebrity Monarch*, p. 109.

12 Buck-Morss, *The Dialectics of Seeing*, p. 170.

13 Buck-Morss, *The Dialectics of Seeing*, p. 67.

14 Buck-Morss, *The Dialectics of Seeing*, p. 210.

15 Hamann reproduces this image in her biography of Elisabeth. See Brigitte Hamann, *The Reluctant Empress: A Biography of Empress Elisabeth of Austria* (trans. Ruth Hein) (Berlin: Ullstein, 1986), plate 33f.

16 Anthony W. Lee and Tim Cresswell, *Muybridge and Mobility* (Oakland, CA: University of California Press, 2022), p. 4.

17 Tim Cresswell, "Visualizing Mobility", in Lee and Cresswell, *Muybridge and Mobility*, p. 13.

18 Beckermann, "Commentary", p. 112.

19 Karin Schiefer, *"American Passages: Interview with Ruth Beckermann"*, 24 February 2011, at www.ruthbeckermann.com/en/publications/texts/american-passages/ (accessed 12 January 2023).

20 See Zeinab Abul-Magd, *Imagined Empires: A History of Revolt in Egypt* (Berkeley, CA: University of California Press, 2013), p. 12; and Timothy Mitchell, *Colonising Egypt* (Irvine, CA: University of California Press, 1991), *passim*.

21 Beckermann, "Commentary", p. 104.

22 Lorenz, "Post-Shoah Positions", 168.

23 Remmler, "Geographies of Memory", 223.

24 Lorenz, "Post-Shoah Positions", 159, 168. The DVD of *Ein flüchtiger Zug* includes an extra titled "Photogallery: Women in Egypt".

25 Beckermann, "Commentary", p. 105.

26 Lorenz, "Post-Shoah Positions", 169. Bert Rebhandl argues, in contrast, that the film's images "persistently dissolve the boundaries of the spoken word – and thereby also dissolve the person behind the film, the director as author, the woman, who inscribes herself with the camera." Rebhandl, "At another place", in *Ruth Beckermann Film Collection: Texte/Texts/Textes*, p. 68.

27 Beckermann, "Commentary", p. 110. Italics in original.

28 Ibid. Italics in original.

29 T. S. Eliot, *The Waste Land*, in *Collected Poems* (London: Faber and Faber, 1974), p. 64.

30 Beckermann, "Commentary", p. 110.

31 Mitchell, *Colonising Egypt*, p. 27.

32 Mitchell, *Colonising Egypt*, p. 38.

33 Mitchell, *Colonising Egypt*, p. 36.

34 Hamann, *The Reluctant Empress*, p. 354.

35 Count Corti, *Elisabeth: Empress of Austria* (trans. Catherine Alison Phillips) (London: Thornton Butterworth, 1936), p. 345.

36 Beckermann, "Commentary", p. 111.

37 Abul-Magd, *Imagined Empires*, p. 123.

38 Abul-Magd, *Imagined Empires*, pp. 126–7.

39 Beckermann, "Commentary", p. 110.

40 August von Almstein, *Ein flüchtiger Zug nach dem Orient: Reise der allerdurchlauchtigsten Frau Gräfin von Hohenembs im Herbste des Jahres 1885, an Bord der kaiserlichen Yacht 'Miramar'* (Vienna: Alfred Hölder, 1887).

41 Horwath and Omasta, "A Conversation with Ruth Beckermann", p. 15.

42 Beckermann, "Commentary", p. 104. Italics in original.

43 Beckermann, "Commentary", p. 105.

44 Constantin Christomanos, *Élisabeth de Bavière, Impératrice d'autriche* (trans. Gabriel Siveton) (Paris: Mercure de France, 1986). Corti writes of Christomanos's book: "The facts are enveloped in such sentimental vapourings that it is difficult to disentangle what the Empress actually said and did from the mass of empty verbiage" (Corti, *Elizabeth – Empress of Austria*, p. 343 n.1).

45 Christomanos, *Élisabeth de Bavière*, p. 34.

46 W.J.T. Mitchell, *Picture Theory* (Chicago, IL: University of Chicago Press, 1994), p. 172.

47 Beckermann, "Commentary", p. 117.

48 Gundolf Graml, "We Love Our Heimat, but We Need Foreigners! Tourism and the Reconstruction of Austria, 1945–55", *Journal of Austrian Studies* Vol. 39 No. 3 (2013), 51–76: 52.

49 Graml, "We Love Our Heimat", 54.

50 Caccia to Eden, Nov. 16, 1951, Foreign Office 371/93597, Public Record Office; cited by Graml, 72 n.7.

51 "The structure of feeling, as I have been calling it, lies deeply embedded in our lives; it cannot be merely extracted and summarized; it is perhaps only in art—and this is the importance of art—that it can be realized, and communicated, as a whole experience." Raymond Williams, "Film and the Dramatic Tradition", in Williams and Michael Orrom, *Preface to Film* (London: Film Drama Ltd, 1954), pp. 1–55. Quoted from Scott Mackenzie (ed.), *Film Manifestos and Global Cinema Cultures* (Berkeley, CA: University of California Press, 2014), p. 613.

52 Elizabeth Anthony notes that many Austrian Holocaust survivors refer to Vienna as 'home' but not 'Heimat', due to the word's corrupted meaning after its Nazi usage. See *The Compromise of Return*, pp. 12–13.

53 Johannes von Moltke, *No Place Like Home: Locations of Heimat in German Cinema* (Berkeley, CA: University of California Press, 2005), p. 5.

54 Maria Fritsche, *Homemade Men in Postwar Austrian Cinema: Nationhood, Genre, and Masculinity* (New York: Berghahn, 2013), p. 103.

55 Anita McChesney, "Imagining Austria: Myths of 'Sisi' and National Identity in Lilian Faschinger's *Wiener Passion*", in Maureen E. Hametz and Heidi Schlipphacke (eds), *The Empress Elisabeth in Memory and Myth* (London: Bloomsbury, 2018), pp. 278–9. Faschinger's novel is another contemporary Austrian text in which Sisi figures

prominently. See Lilian Faschinger, *Vienna Passion* (trans. Anthea Bell) (London: Headline, 2001).

56 *Sisi* (1955), *Sisi: Die junge Kaiserin* (*Sisi: The Young Empress*) (1956); *Schicksalsjahre einer Kaiserin* (*The Fateful Years of an Empress*) (1957). See von Dassanowsky, *Austrian Cinema: A History*, ch. 4 "Post-War and Second Republic Boom 1946–59" (pp. 113–77) for a wider discussion of *Heimatfilm* and the 'Sisi' films.

57 Fritsche, *Homemade Men in Postwar Austrian Cinema*, p. 64.

58 Heidi Schlipphacke, "Melancholy Empress: Queering Empire in Ernst Marischka's *Sisi* Films", *Screen* Vol. 51 No. 3 (2010), 232–55: 232–3

59 Schlipphacke, "Melancholy Empress", 238.

60 Schlipphacke, "Melancholy Empress", 236.

61 "Durch die geniale Besetzungs-Idee wird in *Sisi* der Bruch mit der Ideologie der Nazizeit bei voller Kontinuität simuliert: Romy Schneider ist die Tochter der von 1933–45 gefeierten Schauspieler Magda Schneider und Wolf Albach-Rety. Der Vater Karl-Heinz Böhms war der Stardirigent des Dritten Reichs. Für die Cliquen der Schauspieler und Regisseure ging das Leben wirklich weiter wie bisher." Beckermann, "Elisabeth – Sisi – Romy Schneider", p. 320. Karl-Heinz Böhm (1928–2014) played the young Emperor Franz Joseph in the three Sisi films,

62 Hamann, for example, writes: "Modern medicine would speak less of a mental than of an emotional illness. The Empress's excessive drive to physical activity, her constant refusal to eat indicate (with all due reservations against such retrospective diagnoses) a neurotic anorexia nervosa, which is often coupled with (somewhat pubertal) rejection of sexuality. This theory would also explain the fact that Sisi seemed to recover at once whenever she removed herself from Vienna and her husband" (Hamann, *The Reluctant Empress*, pp. 102–3).

63 Fritsche, *Homemade Men*, p. 84.

64 Fritsche, *Homemade Men*, p. 93.

65 Erica Carter, "Sisi the Terrible: Melodrama, Victimhood, and Imperial Nostalgia in the Sisi Trilogy", in P. Cooke and M. Silberman (eds), *Screening War: Perspectives on German Suffering* (Rochester, NY: Camden House, 2010), pp. 81–101; pp. 81–2. Italics in original.

66 Beckermann, "Commentary", p. 110.

67 Charles Baudelaire, "The Painter of Modern Life", in *The Painter of Modern Life and Other Essays* (ed. and trans. Jonathan Mayne) (New York: Phaidon, 1964), p. 9.

68 Mary Jacobus, *On Belonging and Not Belonging: Translation, Migration, Displacement* (Princeton: Princeton University Press, 2022), p. 35.

69 Horwath and Omasta, "A Conversation with Ruth Beckermann", p. 15.
70 Maria Golia, *Photography and Egypt* (London: Reaktion, 2010), pp. 13–14.
71 Said, "Egyptian Rites", in *Reflections on Exile*, p. 170.
72 Said, "Egyptian Rites", in *Reflections on Exile*, p. 167.
73 Jean-Marcel Humbert, "Egyptomania: A Current Concept from the Renaissance to Postmodernism", in Humbert, Michael Pantazzi, and Christiane Ziegler (eds), *Egyptomania: Egypt in Western Art 1730–1930* (Paris/Ottawa Vienna: National Gallery of Canada, 1994), p. 21.
74 https://en.worldfairs.info/expopavillondetails.php?expo_id=4&pavillon_id=1577 (accessed 4 July 2023).
75 Kunsthistorisches Museum Wien, Egyptian and Near Eastern Collection: History of the Collection, at www.khm.at/en/visit/collections/egyptian-and-near-eastern-collection/history-of-the-collection/ (accessed 4 July 2023). Sisi sailed to Egypt on the yacht *Miramar* in 1891.
76 Diane O'Donoghue, "The Magic of the Manifest: Freud's Egyptian Dream Book", *American Imago* Vol. 66 No. 2 (2009), 211–30: 215.
77 O'Donoghue, "The Magic of the Manifest", 222.
78 Mary Bergstein, "Freud's Uncanny Egypt: Prolegomena", *American Imago* Vol. 66 No. 2 (2009),185–210: 186.
79 Bergstein, "Freud's Uncanny Egypt", 188.
80 Jan Assmann, *Moses the Egyptian: The Memory of Egypt in Western Monotheism* (Cambridge, MA: Harvard University Press, 1997), p. 167.
81 Yosef Hayim Yerushalmi, *Freud's Moses: Judaism Terminable and Interminable* (New Haven: Yale University Press, 1991), p. 2.
82 Bergstein, "Freud's Uncanny Egypt", 194.
83 Horwath and Omasta, "A Conversation with Ruth Beckermann", p. 15.
84 Lorenz, "Post-Shoah Positions", 168. The film's narration states: "There are no Greeks, no Jews, no Armenians any more in Alexandria" (p. 120).
85 Lorenz, "Post-Shoah Positions", 169.

6

Home, ritual, life – *homemad(e)*, *Zorro's Bar Mitzvah* and *Leben!*

We are all fellow-citizens: and if so, we have a common city. The universe, then, must be that city; for of what other common city are all men citizens? (Marcus Aurelius)[1]

A Fleeting Passage to the Orient uses Sisi's historical sense of unbelonging as a template to help define and explore Beckermann's contemporary experience of the condition. The film cements the idea of 'home', insistently central to Beckermann's oeuvre, as both a question of belonging ('what qualities or experiences constitute the acceptable condition of being-at-home?') and the elusive object of a geographical and historical quest ('where, and when, might home be found?'). Seeking 'home' in her travels, Sisi embodies a kind of summary of Beckermann's concerns thus far. Her unbelonging echoes and condenses into a single figure the movements and displacements traced in *Paper Bridge*, the potential, constructed homelands or social utopias (historical and contemporary) of *Arena Squatted*, *Return to Vienna*, and *Towards Jerusalem*, and the hostile hospitalities found in the late twentieth-century Austria of *East of War* and *The Waldheim Waltz*. Insistently locating possible homelands in utopian spaces outside the time and place she inhabits, Beckermann's enquiries repeatedly encounter in the search for homely accommodation the political and emotional discomforts of the *unheimlich*, a condition expressed in melancholic or nostalgic disconnection, articulated by many of her interviewees and addressed by several critics.

The works explored in this chapter simultaneously extend these enquiries while refocussing their range through imposing specific constraints in relation to subject matter. In doing so, Beckermann shifts focus firmly onto the ontological question of what constitutes 'home' and even whether 'being-at-home' is any longer a desirable situation. In the film *homemad(e)* (2001) she opts (perhaps in dialogue with Felix Salten's "Die Wiener Straße" ["The Viennese Street"], the opening section of his 1910 book *Das österreichische Antlitz* [*The Face of Austria*])[2] for a narrow, restricted vision concentrating on a specific urban space. *Zorro's Bar Mitzvah* (2006) addresses the practice of ritual and rites of passage in different Jewish communities in Europe and Israel. The exhibition of Hungarian Margit Dobronyi's (1913–2009) photographs, *Leben! – Jews in Vienna after 1945* (Jewish Museum, Vienna 2008) (the curation of which Beckermann undertook while filming *Zorro's Bar Mitzvah*) focusses this attention to community and ceremony on images of Jewish life in post-war Vienna. These works are linked by their shared exploration of clearly defined groups whose structures of social and kinship ties – family, neighbourhood, community – afford different kinds of potential belonging within the rapidly shifting networks of postmodern urban-metropolitan and transnational social organisation. Twentieth-century questions of modern cosmopolitanism, central to histories of Europe's Jewish communities and ideologically coded by the melancholia of Austrian post-imperial nostalgia, are reframed in these twenty-first-century texts as questions of the possibilities for belonging offered not by nostalgic or utopian imaginary homelands but by convivial relations between distinct but geographically proximate or overlapping cultures, or by a specifically Jewish convivial culture.[3] Addressing each work in turn, this chapter will trace the shared themes and devices through which Beckermann articulates a renewed awareness of the continuities and postmodern cosmopolitan potentials of Jewish culture and traditions.

homemad(e): Hostility and/of Home

Marc-Aurel Straße in Vienna's 'innere Stadt', the street on which Beckermann lives, provides both scene and subject of *homemad(e)*, and stands (Katya Krylova argues) "allegorically for her homeland".[4] This double function – both home and allegory of home – reinforces the ambiguity indicated in the film's English title, its bracketed 'e' simultaneously asserting and undercutting the association of the home with multiple connotations – (family) domesticity, (national) insanity, (personal) anger – specifically rage at the 'insanity' of the 1999 Austrian elections, which saw Jörg Haider's far right FPÖ assuming shared governmental power, winning 27 per cent of the vote on an explicitly racist and anti-immigrant ticket. As Beckermann stresses in the film, one in three Austrians and one in four Viennese voted for Haider; any notion of 'home' conveyed by the film must therefore be read in relation to this dramatic intrusion of a new reality that transforms the local and national political climate, rendering Austrian society (again) hostile and 'unhomely'.

Marc-Aurel Straße is named after Roman Emperor and Stoic philosopher Marcus Aurelius, who died either in Vindobona, now Vienna, or at Sirmium, in Serbia, in 180, and whose conceptions of "citizens of the universe" and of the universe as a single state in which human "brotherhood" is grounded in "fellowship or the common welfare" and "based not on blood or seed, but on mind" underpin much modern cosmopolitan thought.[5] Marcus Aurelius also connotes the imperial reach of ancient Rome as far as the territories of modern Austria, and the implicit echo of Roman imperial power in the country's modern Nazi history and its potential repetition in the election of the FPÖ. The Vienna street named for him thus assumes a subtly complex symbolic and ironic function in the film. It apparently constitutes what Berthold Schoene (critiquing versions of cosmopolitan optimism he finds in theorists like Ulf Hannerz and Paul Gilroy) has called a "comfortably inhabitable 'Third Space' enabling mutual encounter" between different communities and identities; but it also becomes momentarily the "perilous rift or gap, an *ou*-topia or non-place" Schoene imagines might divide them.[6] It stands simultaneously for an abstract ideal of the wider nation and a condensation of its actuality, while evoking, through its name, a double tradition of cosmopolitan thought and imperial occupation. The former's contemporary Viennese manifestation is deeply compromised by the emergent political reality echoing the latter. Both are carefully scrutinised in Beckermann's film.

This scrutiny is itself necessarily double-edged. While *homemad(e)* situates its interlocutors in relation to each other and their neighbourhood, the wider frame of Austrian politics – the affairs of the world made manifest in the locales of the city, as it were – remains implicit for much of the film, moving into the foreground only in the last section, which explores the responses of the interviewees to the newly emergent (but alarmingly familiar) political landscape of an FPÖ-ÖVP coalition government, resulting in sanctions being imposed on Austria by the EU (the country thus economically ostracised, distanced by the international community it nevertheless inhabits). Christina Guenther argues that *homemad(e)* responds to this new reality through its representing of "an alternative site of intercultural exchange. Jews, Muslims, and Christians, a mix of Eastern European and Middle-Eastern immigrants, local pensioners and professionals, share this street in which they have constructed a modern-day Leopoldstadt".[7] But it is also clear that the apparently hospitable and neighbourly qualities of Marc-Aurel Straße's community take on a different light in this new context, which throws the street's ethnic diversity into sharp relief, exposing in the process some of the fissures in its social veneer. The film's exploration of the street's multicultural diversity counterpoints the nation's political lurch towards the politics (if not, yet, the practical reality) of monocultural nationalism. Its constrained, narrow focus (its visual field mainly comprising brief establishment shots and interviews of varying lengths with many of the street's various inhabitants, some- times alone, sometimes in pairs or larger groups, often indoors, with handheld cameras and against back-lighting that sometimes casts their faces into obscurity) mirrors the political narrowing of Austrian cultural horizons taking place in the wider political and historical frame, while the social world depicted expands in cultural and (in particular) historical diversity, as successive interviewees introduce and elaborate on their own pasts and perspectives. The resulting historical, geographical, political, professional, emotional and other frames of reference provide discursive contexture that expands the film's restricted spatiality. The dynamics of everyday (unscripted, impromptu) communication – jokes, banter, anec- dotes, questions asked of the film crew and a constant refrain of ironic self-referentiality – add further expansive embellishments to a film in which disparities of scale are self-consciously empha- sised: "Having returned from a long journey with a large camera [Beckermann narrates] I take my small camera on short journeys no further than my street, in the centre of Vienna."

The emphasis of *homemad(e)* is thus on the local rather than the international, but its version of the local is revealed to be a space striated by the economic and ideological forces of transnational postmodernity, its sense of community dependent on varieties of labour and leisure (as well as disparities of origin and historical experience) which seem, as the film progresses, to be increasingly precarious and in conflict with each other, paralleling the conflicting narratives and myths of identity inhabited by its residents and visitors. An underlying question of the film, never directly addressed, concerns the status of Marc-Aurel Straße as simultaneously a locale characterised as a residential and trade/labour district (and thus inhabited by permanent or temporary, working, residents) and as a thoroughfare facilitating passage between different city districts (and thus a conduit of urban movement and circulation). Caren Kaplan has argued for a fluid conception of this kind of indeterminacy, suggesting that

> the 'local' is not really about a specific intrinsic territory but about the construction of bundles or clusters of identities in and through the cultures of transnational capitalism. Whether the 'local' is seen to be fluid and relational or fixed and fundamentalist depends upon one's position or enunciatory situation vis-a-vis economic, political, and cultural hegemonies. This is, perhaps, one of the greater paradoxes of the global-local nexus: The local appears as the primary site of resistance to globalization through the construction of temporalized narratives of identity (new histories, rediscovered genealogies, imagined geographies, etc.), yet that very site prepares the ground for appropriation, nativism, and exclusions. This condition may be paradoxical but it is by no means mysterious or ineluctable.[8]

homemad(e) enacts in its portrayals and interviews many of the tensions outlined here, and the possibility that the local may constitute a "site of resistance" to nationalist extremism (understood as a reaction against, and therefore product of, the impacts of globalisation on Austrian self-consciousness) becomes a key concern in the film's final section.

The film extends a long Austrian cinematic and literary tradition of texts dealing with the tensions between local and national/international, resident and itinerant, private and public, through the allegorical form of interlinked lives connected by an urban street, which functions as a simplifying metonymy of a larger, more

complex social entity. Notable examples include Viennese-born
Jewish director Karl Grune's film *Die Straße* (*The Street*, 1923), in
which the protagonist, lured out of his home by the phantasmagoria of the night-time city, becomes "no more than a particle swept
along in the maelstrom of a busy metropolitan street at nightfall".[9]
Die Straße explores constructions of Jewish duality – the tension
between public and private identities, between interior safety and
exterior threat, and the conflicted bourgeois character who is (Ofer
Ashkenazi argues) "rooted in a place to which he does not, and
cannot, belong" – that resonate in relation to Beckermann's film.
This resulted in a "spatial encoding of identity" which, Ashkenazi
suggests, "enabled Jewish filmmakers to envisage an intricate
sense of personal and collective identity, in which different elements, different strata, are reconciled in a way that resembles – or,
at least, could be imagined as – the coexistence of different urban
spheres."[10]

The co-existence of distinct urban spheres also pre-occupies
Veza Canetti's story-compilation *Die gelbe Straße* (*Yellow Street*,
1932–3), a modernist city-text in the tradition of Alfred Döblin and
Veza's partner Elias Canetti. The text uses Canetti's real-life experience of living in Ferdinandstraße in Vienna's Leopoldstadt (just a
fifteen-minute walk across the Danube from Marc-Aurel Straße) to
explore the interconnections linking human lives within this predominantly Jewish urban community, despite being constructed (as
Elias Canetti points out in his comments on this novel) of narratives exclusively addressing non-Jewish characters.[11] Lisa Silverman
documents the connections between Canetti's text and the Jewish
community of the Leopoldstadt (and its destruction):

> She lived not far from the Leopoldstadt temple at the corner of
> Ferdinandstraße and Tempelgasse, and near the Zirkusgasse, the
> location of the Sephardic temple, built by her maternal grandfather,
> where she and Elias were married. According to unpublished material
> in the Canetti archive in Zurich, this temple, which was destroyed in
> November 1938, along with all the others in the Leopoldstadt, bore
> two plaques honouring the founder and his wife, Veza's grandmother
> and namesake, Veneziana.[12]

Die Straße and *Die gelbe Straße* thus present distinct but overlapping models of how metropolitan Jewish communities might be

modelled in film and fiction. Each offers a version of double coding, in which the multiplicities inherent in the experience of the modern metropolis allow the articulation of (but offer no resolutions to) the conflicted experience of being Jewish and metropolitan.

The attention of *homemad(e)* to the impact of national events on the local neighbourhood offers (like the ambiguous title) another form of this doubling of perspective, which relates closely to these specifically Jewish and Viennese cultural traditions. A further set of intertextual frames derives from Beckermann's own 'double' identity, as a Viennese-born resident of Vienna and Paris. Interviewed about her film, Beckermann notes her reading while living in Paris of the OuLIPO writer Georges Perec (1936–82), whose experimental analyses of Parisian locales in texts like *Espèces d'espaces* (1974) and *Tentative d'épuisement d'un lieu parisien* (1975)[13] demonstrate (Jacob Soule argues) "fiction's capacity [...] to capture the impact of abstract economic models on the material configuration of social space".[14] At least one critic has argued that Perec's stoical attempts to exhaust through intensive description the spaces and objects he perceives ("Note down what you can see", he instructs in the 'Street' section of "Species of Spaces")[15] are analogous with Marcus Aurelius' efforts to transcend habitual thought, and thus find new forms of accommodation in the world, through varieties of defamiliarisation.[16]

Agnès Varda's *Daguerreotypes* (1976), which provides *homemad(e)* with another crucial formal model, is roughly contemporary with Perec's urban writings. Like *homemad(e)* Varda's film depicts the shopkeepers of her home street, Rue Daguerre in Paris, in this case to scrutinise the impact of the modernisation of Paris on the experience of everyday life. Rebecca J. DeRoo emphasises the connections between Varda's film and the critical urban sociology of theorists like Henri Lefebvre, providing frames for thinking about how Beckermann adapts models like those of Perec and Varda to early twenty-first century Viennese contexts:

> Like Lefebvre Varda recognizes [in *Daguerreotypes*] that the burdens of everyday urban life are experienced unevenly, due to gender, age, race, class, and other social categories. Varda's filmic depictions subtly suggest this unevenness – she represents a broad spectrum of her neighbours, ranging from post-colonial immigrant laborers to comfortable middle-class shop owners – and lays bare the often unacknowledged divisions of labour and urban experiences.[17]

homemad(e) presents a comparable social spectrum of shopkeepers on, residents of, and itinerant visitors to Marc-Aurel Straße, each with their own relation to the street and its facilities (principally its coffee shops and restaurants), and each with their own history, narratives which emerge anecdotally in interviews and conversations. Key among them are the Jewish textile merchant and Holocaust survivor Adolf Doft and his wife, Helene. Doft (earlier filmed briefly by Beckermann in *Paper Bridge*) is the last of the textile merchants still trading on the street. In between comments on how the street has changed, he repeatedly recalls his traumatic family history (his parents and brothers were executed by the Nazis in 1941). Other important figures include the essayist Franz Schuh, who offers sibylline theoretical commentary on political events, adding intellectual weight to the film; and the Iranian hotelier Djavad Alam, who rebukes Beckermann for never having eaten in his restaurant despite living virtually next door but also asserts the cosmopolitan ideal when he describes his relations with his fellow residents: "Good neighbours [*Gute Nachbarn*], that's important." The poet Elfriede Gerstl appears several times, constantly on the move, unable or unwilling to stop and talk for long. The theatre manager Dieter Haspel waxes lyrical about his late friend, the hotelier Ernst Göschl, as do others, including Göschl's wife Erika. Housewife Senta Segall recalls her difficulties as a returning Jew in adjusting to the new, postwar, social realities of Vienna but still claims the city as home ("But somehow I felt at home here", she says). The artist and film-maker Lisl Ponger documents "acts of resistance" against the new government, thus providing another link to the protest cultures recorded in Beckermann's earliest documentaries. "The universities" (she tells Beckermann) "are occupied (*Besetzt*), and the art school, and what the students are doing is interesting."

The Viennese coffee house

Haspel's friend, the late owner of Café Salzgries, Ernst Göschl (1943–97) (Figure 6.1), emerges as a central but absent figure (another embodiment of the "missing image"), clearly (from their reminiscences of him) an important community symbol for many of the film's interlocutors. Present only in images and recollections, Göschl personifies the district, acting as a kind of conduit for reminiscence and nostalgia and an embodiment of socially cohesive and cosmopolitan ideals which are already, as the film progresses, undergoing nostalgic reification. At the table of his regular customers, Dieter Haspel recalls, there was no prejudice against race or religion, "or who you are or what your status is"; his symbolic function as a modern, idealised version of Marcus Aurelius is thus clear. His café, surviving under his wife's management, provides one of the film's social foci. A newly installed road sign indicates its address as 1 Ernst-Göschl Platz (thus symbolically replacing Marcus Aurelius as marker of the urban territory) (Figure 6.2); and Haspel recalls fictionalising him in a cabaret as "Die Grocer Ernst Göschl": "We gave him life transposed as a cabaret figure but it was [actually] Ernst Göschl himself with his characteristic remarks." Göschl exists in the film as a nostalgically personified ideal of community imagined as a shattered screen memory, a momentary figure of brokenness and loss: "Maybe" (Haspel speculates) "from hundreds of small fragments you could make up a picture of his personality".

The significance of Göschl and the contemporary Austrian version of the cosmopolitan ideas of Marcus Aurelius his memory embodies for the street's community points at a central theme in *homemad(e)*. The film focusses on the symbolic importance of his coffee house and, by extension, of the café as a general locus

Figure 6.1 Ruth Beckermann (dir.), *homemad(e)*, 2001.
© Ruth Beckermann Filmproduktion.

Figure 6.2 Ruth Beckermann (dir.), *homemad(e)*, 2001.
© Ruth Beckermann Filmproduktion.

of Viennese and Jewish social life and a significant "site of urban modernity and cultural exchange".[18] Charlotte Ashby argues that the Viennese coffee house, characterised by its informality within a city environment organised by conventionally strict and rigid codes and hierarchies, provided a space tolerating temporary transgressions, and thus "a 'home' for more marginalised groups within the city". For Stefan Zweig the Viennese coffee house was a "democratic club" affording "intellectual mobility" and "international orientation" within which the customer could access newspapers from, and thus become informed about, the entire world.[19] Cathy S. Gelbin and Sandor L. Gilman emphasise the specifically Austrian qualities of the coffee house, its importance in cultural constructions of Jewishness, and its prominence in Jewish writers' version of Austrian society:

> Viennese intellectuals and writers of the period practically lived in the coffeehouse, where they worked, ate and drank, and conducted private affairs. The coffeehouse, which represented the essence of urban Viennese lifestyle, was a specifically Austrian institution. [...] The idea's somewhat clichéd implications today result precisely from the numerous literary references to the coffeehouse in writings by Zweig, Roth, and Franz Werfel, to mention but a few, who made it the salient signifier of Austro-Hungarian society.[20]

Thanks in part to this nexus of associations, cafes subsequently came to be associated closely with the city's Jewish communities,[21] and, as a result of the annihilation of these communities by Nazism, had (like much of the rest of Austrian culture) to be nostalgically reinvested with cultural resonances that erased, or repressed, the historical rupture of the Holocaust. Café Salzgries (as Beckermann points out in her interview with Bert Rebhandl) exemplifies this redefinition, symbolically extending the tradition, and performing a series of ideal functions that resonate with the film's themes. About a decade old when *homemad(e)* was filmed, it had been decorated to look a century old, and, a few years after its owner's death, has clearly already generated a variety of myths of cosmopolitan inclusivity. In *homemad(e)* it is equally clearly frequented by contemporary versions of the "Viennese intellectuals and writers" Gelbin and Gilman mention – theatre managers and writers, essayists and film-makers – a substantial proportion of the milieu Beckermann interviews in seeking to understand the nature of the 'home' offered by the café and the street (as well as by the Austria they stand for). In using Café Salzgries as a principal location in the film, Beckermann again echoes texts in the Jewish Viennese literary tradition like Veza Canetti's *Die gelbe Straße*, one story of which is set in a café, thus asserting an important continuity of Jewish tradition across the divide of the Nazi period. The café's function as a kind of home-outside-the-home (Krylova notes that it occupies 49 of the film's 84 minutes)[22] offers, furthermore, an indirect commentary on the notion of *Heimat* and the genre of *Heimatfilm*; 'home', in *homemad(e)*, exists implicitly in the transient accommodations offered by public spaces like cafés and streets, and is thus inhabited by those who eschew the nostalgic rootedness embodied in the notion of *Heimat*.

Belonging as performance

Haspel's description of his cabaret version of Göschl as "actually …himself" reinforces the suggestion throughout the film that Austrian identity exists substantially in the ambivalence generated and sustained by its continuous performance. The café becomes an arena for performances, even a kind of theatre, its interior mirroring the exterior social space of the street (with which, through outside seating, it also substantially overlaps), allowing certain kinds of identity and positionality to undergo constant performance as they are narrated and filmed. Performativity is, indeed, a crucial shared quality of the majority of the film's protagonists, suggesting that a level of concord and social unity exists, beyond the level of cultural differences and distinctions, in the common act of performing oneself. But performance is also closely linked to its neoliberal redefinition as a measure of labour productivity, suggesting another troubling ambiguity within the film's construction of the Marc-Aurel Straße community, a question pinpointed by the Café Salzgries waiter, Peter Ferber, who tells Beckermann "I always wanted to be an actor and now I am one – salesperson and actor. [...] Sometimes I think the ways one has to act in a café ... I'd be good enough for Max Reinhardt."

This individual performativity is implicitly connected to the wider nation's contemporary performance of itself. Franz Schuh diagnoses the entire post-election national condition as a kind of spectacular performance and, in doing so, identifies one aspect of the new configuration of hostile socio-political environment and consequent magnification of unbelonging that characterises Austria under the FPÖ:

> The performance of those in power is likely to be a philosophical spectacle reflecting the state of the country. A kind of sociological experiment they're acting out in front of us free of charge. OK, they're paid extremely well, but they're not paid to mime our mentalities in a kind of dumb-show. I say that advisedly because they're dumb as well, what they say is scandalously simple-minded ... an artificial simple-mindedness intended to hide what they actually 'think' [...]. It's a perfect performance of what I would term a terrible vacuity. I ask myself – Is this my country? How does it relate to me?

At the end of the film, Adolf Doft, having locked up his shop for the night, turns to the camera: "I'm an actor, a director, I do everything ... Life's a theatre. Everything passes [Alles vergänglich]." The film's position regarding this statement is ambiguous. On the one hand, while it is partially framed and thus validated by the longer perspective of Doft's personal traumatic history, it also explicitly echoes the stoicism of Marcus Aurelius ("How swiftly all things vanish. How the corporeal forms, are swallowed up in the material world, and the memory of them in the tide of ages")[23] while carrying Biblical echoes (for example, 1 John 2:17: "And the world passeth away, and the lust thereof: but he that doeth the will of God abideth for ever"). On the other, Doft's position of resigned stoicism implies an acceptance of the new status quo, however temporary, which rests uncomfortably with the need to mobilise political resistance articulated by people like Lisl Ponger. Doft offers only fragile consolation, reinforcing the film's ambiguous relation to the ostensibly cosmopolitan Marc Aurel-Straße. When he (possibly humorously?) castigates his Iranian neighbour Djavad Alam and his friends for not speaking German – "Don't speak Persian. You're eating Austrian bread, speak German!" – it's difficult not to hear (despite Krylova's reading of the film as "optimistic")[24] a troublingly nationalist and monocultural echo in the performed moment of ostensible neighbourly banter – the haunting presence of the *Unheimlich* within the *Heim*.

Krylova calls Doft a "unifying figure" offering "insightful remembrance",[25] and Beckermann has affirmed in interview his centrality to the film in his embodiment of the conflicting questions of identity, connectivity, and difference explored in *homemad(e)*.[26] Another key person in this context, whom Beckermann eventually finds drinking a coffee in the Café Salzgries, is the poet Elfriede Gerstl (1932–2009), a major figure in the post-war Austrian avant-garde and editor of the important interview-anthology *eine frau ist eine frau ist eine frau … Autorinnen über Autorinnen (a woman is a woman is a woman … female Authors on Authorship)*.[27] Gerstl's elusive mobility (we first meet her dashing down Marc-Aurel Straße, unable to stop and talk), is a significant trope in the film, dramatically counterpointing the fixed presences of the other characters. If Ernst Göschl and Adolf Doft represent contemporary versions of Marcus Aurelius, Gerstl suggests a modern version of Sisi as "Wandering Jew" or "Flying Dutchman". Her wartime experience of hiding in various Viennese locations to escape the occupying Nazis closely echoes that of Beckermann's grandmother, whose tale was recounted in *Paper Bridge*. This traumatic experience extends to the post-war difficulties Gerstl recalls in finding settled accommodation in Austria for herself and her family. This enforced migrancy, or (in Elfriede Jelinek's coinage) her "Niederlassungsscheu" ("reluctance to settle"),[28] has left its own traumatic residues in her contemporary behaviour as a kind of itinerant, evasive collector of second-hand clothes, choosing to inhabit other people's discarded spaces and costumes and thus a constant 'performer' of her own mobile identity. Her costumes, indeed, provide a focus of curiosity and eccentricity for the community of the street. Gerstl's performance of herself embodies the film's ambivalence; it signifies both the cosmopolitan freedom and the threatening instability of identities as temporary, unfixed conditions of being.

Gerstl's problematic relations to both 'home' and hospitality preoccupy her interview in the film and figure its wider concerns with Beckermann's questioning of the varieties of 'home' available in early-twenty-first-century Vienna – in particular the director's alertness to the kind of unbelonging that characterises her own experience of the city. "I'm not a good guest", Gerstl tells Beckermann, "I rarely tie myself down to an appointment or to staying in one place [...]. I spend enough time at home." Elfriede Jelinek's speech honouring the award of the 2007 Erich Fried Prize to Gerstl emphasises how she embodies in her life feminine versions of some of the tropes of Walter Benjamin's theorisations of fleeting urban modernity (the *flâneuse*, the collector, the rag-picker).[29] If her itinerancy makes her only intermittently a neighbour, she nevertheless embodies potential community links in other ways. Her 1995 collection *Kleiderflug* [*Lost Clothes*] includes an 'Afterword' by fellow Marc-Aurel Straße resident Franz Schuh,[30] suggesting the possibility that avant-garde networks and shared textual spaces, overlaying those of street and neighbourhood, might afford at least an intellectual form of community (and the possibility of resistance) amid the post-election turmoil. This possibility is, however, fragile; *Kleiderflug* also features Gerstl's essay "The Home of the Collector", in which she considers how collecting "owes its existence [...] to some sense of deprivation" and can, in extreme situations, transform the collector's home into an inhospitable space, the collection squeezing out the collector, whose identity becomes fixed in its displacement, attached to the all-consuming collection which defines her.[31]

Gerstl's collections of clothes (which link her, of course, to textile merchants like Adolf Doft and Salo Beckermann, asserting a further set of community bonds) and her multiple, strikingly original hats and costumes suggest, on the other hand, a conception of identity as

flexible and changeable, as a kind of continuous and portable performance, a subversion challenging the ritualisation of identity into
repetition and asserting a kind of belonging *within* the unhomely
homeliness of Vienna's café and street cultures. In *homemade(e)*, it
is the female, Jewish, avant-garde poet who embodies most fully
the subtle ambivalences of Beckermann's critique of home and
Heimat, which (through Gerstl's echo, in her wanderings and her
costumes, of Sisi) is also a deconstruction of the visual ideology of
the *Heimatfilm* genre (with its elaborate costumes and over-ornate
settings), a subversive performance of a hostile home (un)made.

Zorro's Bar Mitzvah: interruption and ritual

Some of the connections explored in *homemad(e)* – those, for example, between dressing up as a ritualised performance of identity and
the experience of being-at-home in commemorated tradition – are
central themes of *Zorro's Bar Mitzvah*, which premiered in Paris in
2006. Examining the experiences of four Jewish families preparing
for their children's bar or bat mitzvahs, Beckermann also focusses
in this film less on community bonds and the pervasive impact
of national politics and international economic forces, and more
on family dynamics and the symbolic and material importance of
religious and cultural rituals in contemporary Jewish life. The different ways of sustaining of these religious rituals represented in
the film express in turn various embodiments of the underlying
"categorical imperative" of post-Auschwitz Judaism asserted by
Theodor Adorno – "to arrange [...] thoughts and actions so that
Auschwitz will not repeat itself, so that nothing similar will happen".[32] *Zorro's Bar Mitzvah* is thus initially readable as an allegorical exploration of how the continuity of repetition-with-variation
afforded by religious ritual, its persistence through practice into the
future, thus performs a cultural desire for, and hopefully ensures,
the non-repetition or "interruption", in Josh Cohen's phrasing,[33] of
traumatic history.

Nick Pinkerton describes *Zorro* as "a small, unprepossessing
film",[34] but this underplays its place in the oeuvre and its subtle
navigation of themes linking it to Beckermann's earlier works.
Underlying its attention to preparation, rehearsal, and performance

is this deeper concern with tradition and continuity, and (ultimately) with survival experienced specifically as a relation of continuity with the past, a relation which the film reinterprets in the context of Jewish life two generations after the Holocaust. Emmanuel Levinas argued in 1951 (a year before Beckermann was born) that "The existence of Jews who wish to remain Jews [...] depends on Jewish education", while also insisting on the inadequacy of religious instruction alone for effecting this continuity.[35] In another essay Levinas laments the apparent withering of Jewish education, and thus of what survives of Jewish civilisation, in the middle of the twentieth century:

> Jewish civilization, laid down in its entirety in books that henceforth become inaccessible, allowed no resonance to emerge from the phrases taught since the Emancipation in the fusty religious instruction classes, classes which were reduced to a few hours a week in the whole life of a pupil, during which, for his *bar mitzvah*, he learned the basic elements in reading and a few quickly forgotten gestures.[36]

In her 2013 memoir–essay "Growing up Jewish in Austria: A Personal Testimony" Beckermann explores the generational frictions she experienced in Vienna in the 1970s, and connects her education and relation to Jewish traditions enacted as parental demands and familial pressures:

> We were meant to find a Jewish partner so that the traditions and religion could be upheld and a certain harmony in the household left undisturbed. We were supposed to get married as young as possible so that we would not be led into various temptations. At the same time we were supposed to make our way in the world out there and not let ourselves be held back by our Jewishness. Worthy respectable members of the middle class were what we were supposed to become, preferably doctors and lawyers.[37]

Half a century after Levinas, *Zorro* explores some of the results of this pressure to bourgeoisify and sustain traditions: a cosmopolitan and international Jewish culture flourishing in its wide range of interpretations of ritual and education, highly mobile and flexible in its adaptive relations to inherited religious and cultural codes and practices, and innovative in its responses to the freedoms and constraints of contemporary global culture. The film's focus on different Jewish Viennese families of multiple ethnic and national origins (Georgian, Iraqi, Iranian, American and Israeli, as well as Austrian), speaking a wide range of languages (German, Yiddish, English, Iranian), affirms Howard Wettstein's point (in 2012) that Jewish ritual is centrally concerned with "human flourishing",[38] a notion carrying both ethical force and wider symbolic significance in the context of the histories addressed in Beckermann's wider oeuvre.

The film affirms above all Beckermann's shift of interest (stated in her 2020 interview with Dèbora G. Kantor) toward examining the diversity of *living* Jewish culture:

> people [have] already talked about what happened [in] the Holocaust and the Jews and so on, and everybody here in Austria and in Germany talked about dead Jews. So I was angry about that and wanted to show that we are still alive. That's why I made a film about bar mitzvah, and about the very modernity of bar mitzvah. I mean, the connection between religion and youth culture, how this mingles. So that's why, I wanted to say that the Jews are still alive and are very diverse.[39]

This is a version of the theoretical reaction against rendering Jews as tropes, the tendency (critiqued by Shia Ginsburg, Martin Land and Jonathan Boyarin) "to perceive the Jew primarily as figure and only secondarily (and rather abstractly) as living being".[40] In its focus on families and children preparing for and performing rituals around the liminal moment of accession to adulthood and thus to full community participation, *Zorro* seeks to evade both the reductive fixity of tropes and stereotypes and the 'abstraction' (or generalisation) often associated with portrayals of living Jewish people. It offers instead Jewish identities as lived, as complex, multi-dimensional and processual lives, existing in and as processes of becoming which are partially constituted within mobile or fluid ritual and traditional frameworks.

(Mis)reading tradition

Beckerman finds someone analogous both to her own position as film-maker and to that of the Viennese poet, collector and *flâneuse* Elfriede Gerstl in the Jewish film-maker André Wanne, whose filming of bar mitzvahs provides a loose framing narrative for *Zorro*'s survey of contemporary Jewish rites of passage. The film opens with André filming Tom and his Rabbi rehearsing elements of his upcoming bar mitzvah – the wearing of the prayer shawl, and the reading and reciting of the instructions, before unrolling and chanting (following the Rabbi's lead) from the Torah scroll, as André films (and, on occasion, intervenes directorially to ensure a better camera angle on the performance). Reading, ritual and (filmed) performativity are thus foregrounded, establishing the film's core interrelated concerns.

André speculates that his career recording bar mitzvahs is an extended compensation for having missed his own ceremony due to his parents' illnesses (thus echoing Gerstl's argument that adult collecting offers a form of excess that compensates for childhood experiences of deprivation). This notion of compensation for historical lack recurs throughout the film – Sophie's Hungarian grandfather missed his own bar mitzvah in Budapest in spring 1945 when "conditions were such that it was impossible to hold one", while Tom's Iraqi-born grandfather, arriving with his family as a refugee in Israel in 1951 and subsequently living in a kibbutz, also missed his ritual, instead donning borrowed prayer bands for a makeshift simulated bar mitzvah at the Wailing Wall years later in 1967, after fighting in the Six Day War (Tom's bar mitzvah is also held by the Wall). The adult generation's missed bar mitzvahs thus becomes a repeated trope, a symbolic marker of interrupted Jewish tradition, suggesting that *Zorro's* focus on living Jewish communities masks a deeper concern with how contemporary practices mobilise semi-conscious responses to the processes of mourning deeper historical traumas of loss and lack. The interruptions experienced by the parental and grandparental generations become signifiers of interruptive moments (Holocaust, migration, war) in Jewish history. They signify momentary failures of tradition which (as the sometimes-extravagant celebrations of the ceremonies planned for the current generation imply) must be seen to be temporary and wholly compensable through the adaptation and implementation of tradition as restoration and ritual as repair.

How living communities and their restorative rituals adapt to, and reinterpret, influences from the cultural environments they inhabit is a key theme of the film, particularly in its analysis of the tensions between religious ritual and tradition (and thus between generations) and the semiotic and ideological pressures of contemporary western capitalism. As with all traditions, questions of reading and misreading haunt the intergenerational relations mapped in the film. In learning what they must recite, each child stumbles verbally, an inevitable process of corrective absorption the film is careful to permit and record. Beckermann's filming of André's filming of the preparations for Sharon's bar mitzvah offers, however, an altogether different example of cross-generational misreading, which both lends the film its title and constitutes its most detailed narrative. Sharon's mother wants to stage, at vast expense, a re-enactment of scenes from Martin Campbell's film *The Mask of Zorro* (1998) with Sharon in the title role. While admitting her own fondness for it ("I like Zorro so much", she confesses), she is also drastically misreading her son's liking for the film, a misreading which provides the central *mise-en-abîme* of comic misinterpretation around which Beckermann's film revolves, as it becomes apparent that Sharon's apparently childish interest in Antonio Banderas as Zorro centres on one scene that foregrounds Zorro's (and Sharon's developing, adolescent) sexual desire for Elena (Catherine Zeta-Jones), rather than on the mother's preferred performance of the extended romance of Zorro as swashbuckling hero. As Sharon's mother organises an elaborate, time-consuming, and expensive spectacle involving costumes, horsemen, makeup artists, and André's film crew doing repeated retakes of the increasingly sulky and reluctant Sharon leaping heroically from his horse, the symbolic gap between the fabricated, ritualised spectacle of the romanticised rite of passage and its overlaid reality (of passage to [sexualised] adulthood) becomes ever more apparent, and Beckermann's core concern with the performing of contemporary Jewishness, and the varieties of spectatorial positioning enforced by this performing, takes centre stage.

Sharon's family, Georgian-Viennese with "Spanish roots", wealthy, and coded in their relations to tradition by the mother's fondness for Hollywood production values, offers one version of contemporary Jewishness in which are manifest the tensions surrounding the rite of passage as an ambivalent accession to multiple, not necessarily overlapping, potentials – to sexual and spectacular, as well as traditional and ethically effective, forms of adult Jewish identity. In mapping different family negotiations of this passage,

Zorro establishes possible and thinkable (if not quite utopian) futures that contrast radically with Beckermann's earlier explorations of the residues of unthinkable, unrepresentable pasts. In the case of Moishe and his Chasidic version of Judaism, the bar mitzvah provides an arena for a highly ritualised performance of traditional Judaic devotion, dramatically contrasting with the romance of Zorro (but equally rooted in spectacle and performance). Tom's bar mitzvah, performed in Israel, affirms another established Jewish future (reprising aspects of *Towards Jerusalem*); while Sophie, who usually insists on speaking American English, seems the most 'modern' of the film's four protagonists but, in her bat mitzvah, reveals how traditional gender codes demanding the exclusion of women from the ritual impose a form of spectatorial censorship that sits uneasily with her family's progressive contemporaneity. "I wish that the women didn't have to go upstairs", one woman complains; "I rather like it", responds Sophie's grandfather, the only man in the room, "because I can concentrate on my reading and prayers." "What a joke", replies his wife Elaine. Affirming this exclusion, the women of Moishe's family watch the dancing at his orthodox ceremony from behind a hedge, and dance together in a separate room.

The film-about/within-a-film structure of *Zorro* allows Beckermann to explore both different configurations of ritual (and, underlying them, the flexibility of ritual as structure within the international diversity of Jewish communities) and the forms of spectatorship mobilised by their performance. *Zorro* is above all concerned with Jewish rites of passage as forms of spectacle invested with socially symbolic meanings – "a particularly modern manner of image-making", as Pinkerton writes of the film.[41] As the case of Sharon's Zorro suggests, how each generation reads and interprets these meanings provides the film's dynamic. Sophie's arguments with her mother about the style and colour of her dress provide another example. "Here's the pink", says her mother, "because you love pink, and everything is in pink." "But I don't like that", she replies. Her mother, exhausted, has recently survived the 2004 Sri Lankan tsunami; they are organising Sophie's bat mitzvah because "our religion says we have to" (thus affirming the etymological meaning of 'mitzvah' as 'commandment' or 'law'). The film André makes of Tom becomes a version of a tourist guide to Vienna, as Tom 'performs' his typical day in the city. Tom's (non-Jewish) father has wholly invested in the idea of his son's bar mitzvah; his Jewish mother, speaking in halting German, seems less convinced but looks forward to having a man in the family able to read the prayers and perform the religious rituals which she, as a woman, is prohibited from doing. Sophie's father narrates his family history and the transmission of ethical values between generations – his mother's conversion to orthodox Judaism ("very strict") after his parents' return to Austria in the 1950s, the motives for which remain unclear to him; his (Jewish) father's suffering during and after the war (not least because his family opposed his marriage to a non-Jew); and the "tolerant atmosphere" in which his parents raised him, which he has tried to pass on to his own children. Moishe's parents explain to Beckermann the elaborate symbolic functions of the phylacteries and banding Moishe correctly but laboriously dons; Moishe himself (the most 'adult' of the four children, and the most deeply involved in the purely religious aspects of the ritual) explains the changes in fashion, favouring leather bands and the "newest model", among the children.

In each case the contemporary tension between tradition and change expresses the deeper theme of cultural continuity after disastrous interruption. Adherence to religious rules acts as a guarantor of the community's future, and each version of the mitzvah ceremony involves the performance of Jewishness-as-identity as (re-) interpreted by each family and negotiated by their various generations. Moishe's alertness to changes in fashion, which is prefigured more fully earlier by Sophie's discomfort with the 'Empire line' of the dress she tries on, emerges as a crucial insight in the film, introducing into its exploration of the process of continuity between generations the question of fashion as an expression of interruption, its shifts of taste and style ostensibly marking generational differences rather than shared identities. This ambivalence links the performances of the children in the film to figures like Elfriede Gerstl (who, as noted earlier, represents a modern version of Sisi). As a collector and wearer of vintage clothes (i.e. those of previous periods and generations), Gerstl short-circuits fashion's cyclical, consumerist historical modes, offering (Elfriede Jelinek writes) "a more comfortable, but still not entirely harmless, form of subversion".[42] For Jelinek, the individualism of Gerstl's style subverts the oppressive conformity imposed by 'fashion' in the commercial sense. In *Zorro*, fashion (in its repetitive reviving and recycling into the contemporary of decontexualised fragments of older, historical styles like the 'Empire line' of a modern bat mitzvah dress) gestures towards the cyclical progression of history while encoding into inter-generational differences its linearity (hence the tensions between Sophie and her mother) and thus its potential interruption, the consequence of breaks in the line or gaps in historical continuity.

A single image in the film expresses this complex set of concerns. When, at Sophie's bat mitzvah, her parents project over the stage a photograph of Sophie as a young child wearing a Gap shirt, the company logo onomastically embeds into the film the idea of the "generation gap" (the inter-generational experience of interruption and distance) spelt out by the (conspicuously American but globally resonant) brand name (Figure 6.3). Sophie's comfort within semiotic (post)modernity, notable in a film deeply concerned with tradition and ritual, points us towards the 'gap' that the religious ritual of the bar and bat mitzvah is expressly designed to elide, a 'gap' (echoing both the potential utopic 'gap' of the local in *homemad(e)* and the traumatic gaps and absences Beckermann identifies in the Jewish-Viennese history of *Die Mazzesinsel*) which nevertheless insists in the inter-generational conflicts mapped by the film. The moment

Figure 6.3 Ruth Beckermann (dir.), *Zorro's Bar Mitzvah*, 2006.
© Ruth Beckermann Filmproduktion.

(in ritual) when each child achieves adulthood and becomes a full member (in life) of the Jewish community is thus also the moment of the bridging of the 'gap' between generations and between different historical experiences, as the bar and bat mitzvah ceremonies assert community and continuity despite, and in order to overcome and ensure the non-recurrence of, the traumatic historical gaps and interruptions suffered by parental and grandparental generations.

Leben! Juden in Wien nach 1945

My work is not about, it is after. (Christian Boltanski)[43]

Zorro's focus on ways of ensuring cultural continuity offers contemporary Judaic ritual practices as forms of overcoming the past, embodying conceptions of time and history that exist in tension with their lived experiences through the processes of learning traditions, adapting fashions, and passing on or compensation for lost historical experiences. While making the film, Beckermann worked on the curation of an exhibition of photographs documenting Jewish life in Vienna after the war by Budapest-born Margit Dobronyi (1913–2009), who fled Hungary for Vienna when the Soviet troops invaded in 1956. *Leben! Juden in Wien nach 1945* (*Life/Living! Jews in Vienna after 1945*) was held at the Jewish Museum in Vienna between March and June 2008 (marking the 70th anniversary of the Anschluß) and accompanied by an extensively illustrated catalogue reproducing several hundred of the photographs exhibited, initially monochrome and later colour, along with an essay by Beckermann, her interview with Dobronyi, and several passages recording the memories of some of those appearing in the pictures. The photographs exhibited, selected from some 130,000 made by Dobronyi now archived in Vienna's Jewish Museum, record leisure and festival events in post-war Viennese Jewish life – bar and bat mitzvahs, weddings, parties, celebrations for notable visitors – and thus depict a community engaged over several decades and in a wide variety of social spaces in repeated celebrations of its own continuity. Beckermann describes Dobronyi's oeuvre as depicting "a unique testimony of the existence and development of a Jewish community after the Shoah".[44] In contrast with *Die Mazzesinsel* (discussed in Chapter 3), which documented a community soon to be virtually destroyed, *Leben!*, like *Zorro's Bar Mitzvah*, records a Jewish society both diverse and thriving, offering an extended response to the rhetorical question Adolf Doft asks in *homemad(e)*: "What is 'life'? [Was heißt 'Leben']? Life is a very varied thing ...".

In *Family Frames*, Marianne Hirsch addresses the functions of family portraiture in preserving cross-generational memory. Discussing the 'Tower of Faces', a space in the US Holocaust Memorial Museum in Washington devoted to "several hundred photographs of the Lithuanian shtetl of Ejszyzski", she emphasises the dearth of images of Jewish life that survived the Holocaust:

> Many survivors, in fact, have no photographs that precede the war years; it is as though the museum collection were trying to repair this irreparable loss. The family and community pictures, particularly, provide a part of a record and a narrative about the Jewish world lost in the Holocaust and thus place the images of destruction into a needed contextual framework.[45]

In *Die Mazzesinsel* Beckermann contributed to this act of historical compensation by exhibiting images of pre-war Viennese Jewish life alongside texts offering narrative descriptions and recollections of that life. *Leben!* performs a different kind of compensation for the "irreparable loss"; it offers images that (adjusting Christian Boltanski's phrase) document a world explicitly 'after', and thus also 'about', the overcoming of historical loss. Jewish community roots had to be re-established by returning exiles, a small constituency that (as we've seen) included Beckermann's parents, both of whom appear in Dobronyi's photographs, Salo dancing with Zwi Ben Shalom at a wedding in the Hotel Intercontinental in 1969 and at a ceremony in the Stadttempel in 1970, Bety posing with friends after a meal at a wedding in 1971.[46]

People insistently fill the frames of Dobronyi's sometimes disingenuously amateur-looking photographs, their gestures and postures indicative of vivaciousness and exuberance, an insistent physicality that constantly threatens to overspill the image, just as the repeated scenario of the party table, replete with bread, food, bottles of drink, full glasses and plates, gestures towards lives being fully lived in the moment. People interact with the camera, smiling, laughing, gazing seductively at the lens or captured with eyes shut as they blink; in performing themselves for the camera's gaze they confirm their existence as individuals and as elements of a social fabric existing in and through the act of its performance. A striking feature of many of the photographs is the variety and extravagance of women's hats on show, markers of luxury and prestige but also of a comfortable and socially sanctioned form of feminine performativity.[47] Internationally significant figures, often asserting political and cultural links between Vienna's Jews and Israel, mingle with the local Viennese Jewish community – Nazi-hunter Simon Wiesenthal poses for the camera with his plate of food, and outside on a balcony with a glass of orange juice, in 1975; former Israeli Minister of Foreign Affairs Moshe Dayan is caught on his visit to Vienna in 1980, in the process of sitting on a stool, surrounded by a crowd of Viennese notables including Vienna's Chief Rabbi Akiba Eisenberg and literary critic and Holocaust survivor Gisela Fried; and writer Hilde Spiel is captured deep in conversation with Ivan Hacker, a survivor of Auschwitz, at the Israeli Embassy in 1982.[48] In merging social and leisure ritual with evident political and cultural networking, these images affirm Pierre Bourdieu's argument that photography "supplies the means of solemnizing those climactic moments of social life in which the group solemnly reaffirms its unity". Group portraits like the wedding photographs Dobronyi captures are, Bourdieu suggests, processes that fix "for eternity" forms of consecration of community identity: "In the case of the wedding, the picture that captures for eternity the group that has been brought together, or rather the bringing together of two groups, is necessarily implied within a ritual whose function is to consecrate."[49]

If the function of these photographs is to help consecrate the ritual assertion of community, their insistent message announces 'presence' – that of the community and that of the artist, borne out by one testimonial to Dobronyi's ubiquity at Jewish social events: "You didn't need to hire her. She always knew when all the events were. She was here! Always!"[50] The photographer's presence guarantees the social and community sense of 'presence' afforded by the images she records. Photographing individuals, pairs, groups and families, Dobronyi documents a community existing in the repeated performance of its rituals of continuity. Intergenerational relations appear not as conflicts but as repetitions (of son in father, daughter in mother, and of the cycle of bar and bat mitzvahs, birthdays, weddings, and other social events she photographs) and re-enactments of conventional group poses. Beckermann writes of these photographs:

> Life! That also means taking up space. Going out of the private sphere, out of the protected social spaces and into the fabric of the city. Only when this now integrated community can look itself in the mirror and talk and laugh about its beginnings, and finally show itself to the others as Margit Dobronyi photographed it, will it have truly arrived in Vienna.[51]

This suggests an extended act of territorial reclamation (another kind of 'Return to Vienna') in which the passage from history to presence recorded in *Leben!* coincides with the passage from private to public life. Elizabeth Anthony's analysis of how Jewish communities re-established themselves in Austria after the Holocaust reinforces this sense of reclamation as an assertion of homecoming and belonging:

"Vienna was home", writes Anthony; Jewish returnees "chose to stay and reroot in the post-Nazi society of their hometown, all with eyes wide open to their charged surroundings and the city's recent past".[52] The assertion by the surviving fraction, only 3 per cent of the pre-war Jewish community, of its social presence in the process of self-recognition and self-definition is expressed most effectively in the exhibition's title, ambiguously asserting both 'life' and 'living'. Its emphatic exclamation mark responds to several contemporary intertexts, for example, the more tentative and historically located title (with its past tense 'gelebt') of Tanja Eckstein and Julia Kaldori's book *Wie wir gelebt haben: Wiener Juden erinnern sich an ihr 20. Jahrhundert* (*How We Lived: Viennese Jews Remember Their Twentieth Century*),[53] the final section of which documents (like *Leben!*) aspects of post-war Viennese Jewish life.

A key reference point of Beckermann's curatorial and editorial strategy is the immense work by Berlin-born artist Charlotte Salomon (1917–43), first exhibited in Amsterdam in 1961 with an accompanying publication titled *Charlotte: A Life in Pictures*, and later published and exhibited under its own title *Leben? Oder Theater? (Life? Or Theatre?)*.[54] Described by Griselda Pollock as "a modernist cycle of paintings that challenges all our conceptions of each of those terms while being structured by the double helix of historical events and the gendered traumas of the everyday and the home",[55] *Leben? Oder Theater?* comprises 784 paintings, with 330 accompanying texts presented as transparent graphic overlays, constituting a remarkably complex work hovering generically between veiled dramatised autobiography and transmedial bildungsroman. Salomon trained as an artist in 1930s Berlin, concealing her Jewishness by signing the work (which she left behind in southern France when the Nazis deported her to Auschwitz, and to her death, in October 1943) only with the monogram CS.

The affirmative title *Leben!* responds to the questioning uncertainty posed by Salomon's title. Post-war Jewish Vienna, Beckermann asserts via Dobronyi's photographs, emphatically lives on, *within* and *because of* its continued performance in the overt theatricality of social and religious rituals. But it is a life still haunted by the traumas of history. In one photograph from 1982 of Ivan Hacker, Paul Chaim Eisenberg, and Paul Grosz addressing a room we cannot see, a poster on the wall behind them is partially concealed by the seated figure of Eisenberg. The poster advertises the 1938 French release of the immensely popular 1937 Yiddish film *Le Dibbouk* (*Dybuk* / *The Dybbuk*) by the Polish Jewish director Michał Waszyński (1904–65),[56] based on the 1920 play by S. Ansky, a text which, argue Debra Caplan and Rachel Merrill Moss, offered "a porous theatrical conduit for a wide range of discourses about Jews, belonging, and modernity over the past century".[57] J. Hoberman points out that this film was made at the same time as "preparations for the Nazi propaganda exhibition *Der ewige Jude* (*The Eternal Jew*), which opened in Munich in November 1937 and was shown, the following year, in Vienna and Berlin". *The Dybbuk* is readable in this context as "an act of Jewish solidarity".[58] Nevertheless, it was screened by Joseph Goebbels in 1942 as an anti-Jewish propaganda film, an act indicating the distorting power of Nazi strategies of interpretation. The film's history, contexts, and legacy are laden with resonances. Hoberman notes, for example, that "the Jewish inhabitants of Waszyński's birthplace of Kovel were massacred *en masse* in June 1942";[59] many of the film crew involved in making *The Dybbuk* were also murdered in the Holocaust. The poster captured in the background of Dobronyi's 1982 photograph thus condenses into a single incidental image a series of allusions to the contribution of Europe's Jewish community to film history and, simultaneously, to that community's near-eradication – a trauma that is insistently both remembered and repudiated in the photographs of *Leben!*.

Notes

1 Marcus Aurelius, *The Meditations of the Emperor Marcus Aurelius Antoninus* (ed. James Moore and Michael Silverthorne, trans. Francis Hutchinson and James Moore) (Indianapolis, IN: Liberty Fund, 2008), Book IV article IV, pp. 48–9.

2 Felix Salten, *Das österreichische Antlitz – Essays* (Berlin: Fischer, 1910), pp. 9–23.

3 For a discussion of cosmopolitanism and conviviality in relation to British culture, see Paul Gilroy, *After Empire: Melancholia or Convivial Culture?* (London: Routledge, 2004).

4 Krylova, *The Long Shadow of the Past*, p. 46.

5 G. R. Stanton, "The Cosmopolitan Ideas of Epictetus and Marcus Aurelius", *Phronesis* Vol. 13 No. 2 (1968), 183–95: 188–9.

6 Berthold Schoene, *The Cosmopolitan Novel* (Edinburgh: Edinburgh University Press, 2009), p. 4.

7 Guenther, "The Politics of Location in Ruth Beckermann's 'Vienna' Films", 41.

8 Caren Kaplan, *Questions of Travel* (Durham, NC: Duke University Press, 1996), pp. 159–60.

9 Anton Kaes, "29 November 1923: Karl Grune's *Die Straße* inaugurates 'Street Film', Foreshadows Film Noir", in Jennifer M. Kapszynski and Michael D. Richardson (eds), *A New History of German Cinema* (Rochester: Camden House, 2012), p. 124.

10 Ofer Ashkenazi, "The Jewish Places of Weimar Cinema: Reconsidering Karl Grune's *The Street*", in Steven E. Aschheim and Vivian Liska (eds), *The German-Jewish Experience Revisited: Contested Interpretations and Conflicting Perceptions* (Berlin and Jerusalem: Leo Baeck Institute/DeGruyter, 2015), p. 139.

11 See Julian Preece, *The Rediscovered Writings of Veza Canetti: Out of the Shadow of a Husband* (Rochester: Camden House, 2002), pp. 68–71; and Silverman, *Becoming Austrians*, p. 137.

12 Silverman, *Becoming Austrians*, p. 137.

13 Georges Perec, *Species of Spaces and other Pieces* (ed. and trans. John Sturrock) (London: Penguin, 2008); *An Attempt at Exhausting a Place in Paris* (trans. Marc Lowenthal) (Cambridge, MA: Wakefield Press, 2010). The bracketed '(e)' of *homemad(e)* recalls the notorious

avoided 'e' of Perec's *La disparition* (1969; *A Void*, trans. Gilbert Adair [London: Harvill, 1995]), while the brackets echo the bracketed ellipsis in *W, ou le souvenir d'enfance* signifying the disappearance in the Holocaust of Perec's mother (Perec, *W or the Memory of Childhood*, trans. David Bellos [London: Harvill, 1988], p. 61).

14 Jacob Soule, "The End of the City and the Coming of the Urban: Georges Perec's *An Attempt at Exhausting a Place in Paris*", *Novel: A Forum on Fiction* Vol. 55 No. 2 (2022), 324–38: 326–7.

15 Perec, *Species of Spaces and other Pieces*, p. 50.

16 See Austin Sarfan, "The Conversion of the Gaze in the Work of Georges Perec", *The Comparative Literature Undergraduate Journal* (Spring 2016), np, at https://ucbcluj.org/the-conversion-of-the-gaze-in-the-work-of-georges-perec/ (accessed 2 September 2023).

17 Rebecca DeRoo, *Agnès Varda between Film, Photography, and Art* (Oakland, CA: University of California Press, 2018), p. 88.

18 Charlotte Ashby, "Introduction", *Austrian and Habsburg Studies 16: The Viennese Café and Fin-de-Siècle Culture* (New York: Berghahn, 2016), p. 3.

19 Zweig, *The World of Yesteryear*, pp. 61–2.

20 Gelbin and Gilman, *Cosmopolitanisms and the Jews*, p. 125.

21 Ashby, "Introduction", pp. 3–4.

22 Krylova, *The Long Shadow of the Past*, p. 43.

23 Marcus Aurelius, *Meditations* III: xii, p. 36.

24 Krylova, *The Long Shadow of the Past*, p. 47.

25 Krylova, *The Long Shadow of the Past*, p. 45.

26 "Interview with Rebhandl", 2007. The DVD includes an extra "Photogallery Adi Doft 1921–2006".

27 Vienna: Promedia, 1985.

28 Elfriede Jelinek, "Elfriede Gerstl", speech delivered 28 November 1999 at the award of the Erich Fried Prize to Gerstl, np, at www.elfriedejelinek.com/fgerstl.html (accessed 3 September 2023). Gerstl's text "Mein Prater Dein Prater: gemischte gefühle oder ein phobienparadies" features (along with Elfriede Jelinek's 'Pratertext") in Ulrike Ottinger's documentary *Prater* (2007).

29 Jelinek, "Elfriede Gerstl", np.

30 *Kleiderflug – Texte – Textilien – Wohnen* (with photographs by Herbert Wimmer and 'Afterword' by Franz Schuh) (Vienna: Edition Splitter, 1995).

31 Gerstl, "The Home of the Collector", in Will Bellamy "*lost clothes* by Elfriede Gerstl, translated from the German with an Introduction and a Translator's Note" (unpublished MA thesis, Wesleyan University, 2019). p. 49.

32 Theodor W. Adorno, *Negative Dialectics* (trans. E. B. Ashton) (London: Routledge and Kegan Paul, 1973), p. 365.

33 Josh Cohen, *Interrupting Auschwitz* (London: Continuum, 2005), p. xviii.

34 Nick Pinkerton, "The Present Absence", p. 8

35 Emmanuel Levinas, "Reflections on Jewish Education", *Difficult Freedom: Writings on Judaism* (ed. and trans. Seán Hand) (Baltimore, MD: Johns Hopkins University Press, 1990), pp. 265–8; p. 265.

36 Levinas, "Antihumanism and Education", *Difficult Freedom*, pp. 277–87; p. 280.

37 Beckermann, "Growing up Jewish in Austria: A Personal Testimony" (trans. Adrian Sewell) *Jewish Culture and History* Vol. 14 Nos. 2–3 (2013), 165–70: 166 (translation modified).

38 Howard Wettstein, "Ritual", in *The Significance of Religious Experience* (Oxford: Oxford University Press, 2012), p. 204.

39 Beckermann, in Kantor, "Ruth Beckermann: Documentarian of the Present", 234.

40 Shia Ginsburg, Martin Land and Jonathan Boyarin, "Introduction" to *Jews and the Ends of Theory* (New York: Fordham University Press, 2019), pp. 8–9.

41 Pinkerton, "The Present Absence", p. 8.

42 "... einer gemütlicheren, aber trotzdem nicht ganz ungefährlichen Form von Subversion". Jelinek, "Elfriede Gerstl". Jelinek cites Walter Benjamin's description of fashion in "On the Concept of History", XIV: "It is the tiger's leap into the past". (Benjamin, "On the Concept of History", in *Selected Writings* Volume 4 (1938–1940) (ed. Howard Eiland and Michael Jennings) (Cambridge, MA: Belknap Press of Harvard University Press, 2003), p. 395.

43 Georgia Marsh, "An Interview with Christian Boltanski", in Boltanski, *Reconstitution* (exh. cat.) (London: Whitechapel Gallery, 1990), p. 10.

44 "[...] ein einmaliges Zeugnis der Existenz und der Entwicklung einer jüdischen Gemeinde nach der Schoa". Beckermann, "Das Leben packen: zum Fotoarchiv der Margit Dobronyi", in Ruth Beckermann (ed.), *Leben! Juden in Wien nach 1945* (exh. cat.) (Vienna: Mandelbaum, 2008), p. 8.

45 Hirsch, *Family Frames*, p. 251.

46 *Leben!*, pp. 100, 121, 227.

47 See, for example, *Leben!*, pp. 104, 110, 125, 144, 184, 301.

48 *Leben!*, pp. 253 and 255, 262, 258.

49 Pierre Bourdieu, *Photography: A Middle-brow Art* (trans. Shaun Whiteside) (Oxford: Polity, 1990), p. 21.

50 "Man hat sie nicht engagieren brauchen. Sie hat immer gewusst wann alle Veranstaltungen waren. Sie war da! Immer!" Sylvia Segenreich, in *Leben!*, p. 50. Dobronyi appears in several of her own group photographs: see, for example, *Leben!* p. 254.

51 "Leben! Das heißt auch, Raum einnehmen. Hinausgehen aus dem Privatbereich, hinaus aus den geschützten Gesellschaftsräumen und hinein in das Gewebe der Stadt. Denn erst, wenn sich diese inzwischen integrierte Community selbst in den Spiegel schauen und über ihre Anfänge reden und lachen kann und sich schließlich auch den anderen so zeigt, wie Margit Dobronyi sie fotografierte, ist sie wirklich in Wien angekommen." Beckermann, "Das Leben packen: zum Fotoarchiv der Margit Dobronyi", in *Leben!*, p. 16.

52 Anthony, *The Compromise of Return*, p. 2.

53 Vienna: Mandelbaum, 2008.

54 Charlotte Salomon, *Life? Or Theatre?* (ed. Judith C. E. Belinfante, Christine Fischer-Defoy, Ad Peterson and Norman Rosenthal, trans. Leila Vennewitz) (London: Royal Academy of the Arts, 1998).

55 Griselda Pollock in conversation with Nicholas Chare, *RACAR – Canadian Art Review* Vol. 42 No. 1 (2018), 63–80: 64.

56 See Joel Rosenberg, "The Soul of Catastrophe: On the 1937 Film of S. An-sky's *The Dybbuk*", *Jewish Social Studies* Vol. 17 No. 2 (2011), 1–27, for a critical discussion of the film.

57 Debra Caplan and Rachel Merrill Moss, "Introduction: One Hundred Years of *The Dybbuk*", in Caplan and Merrill Moss (eds), *The Dybbuk Century: The Jewish Play that Possessed the World* (Ann Arbor, MI: University of Michigan Press, 2023), p. 7.

58 J. Hoberman, "*The Dybbuk*: the movie(s)", in Caplan and Merrill Moss (eds), *The Dybbuk Century*, pp. 128–9.

59 Hoberman, "*The Dybbuk*: the movie(s), p. 131.

7

Threads and traces – *American Passages* and *Those Who Go Those Who Stay*

Les migrants n'errent pas à la surface du globe, ils ne violent pas les frontières, ils n'agressent pas le bel ordonnancement géopolitique des nations. Ils font au contraire advenir un monde là où il n'y avait qu'un globe, ils en composent les partages en trouant les lignes de séparation de points de passage et de lieux de vie où éclosent les mondes et se rencontrent les peuples. Plus il y a de migrants, d'exilés et de transgressions, plus il y a de monde et plus il y a de mondes. (Étienne Tassin)[1]

homemad(e) and *Zorro's Bar Mitzvah* explore contrasting possibilities of 'home' as location and concept facilitating belonging, and its relations to memory and tradition within distinct national and international political frames of reference. Both located and mobile, a product of residence within an urban space and of religious and cultural practices, 'home' emerges as a complex, endlessly negotiated, and precarious condition, its apparent security constantly threatened by historical and political forces, insistently tempered by its interdependence with the barely repressed and always-returning threat of homelessness or unhomely unbelonging, a product of the often 'hostile hospitality' afforded by the wider community. The two films discussed in this chapter – *American Passages* (2011) and *Those Who Go Those Who Stay* (2013) – present new and different developments in contrasting but complementary directions of this analysis which, of course, underpins all Beckermann's works. One shift concerns thematic and spatial focus; where the earlier films centre on a particular place (the street) or social ritual (the bar/bat mitzvah) to provide narrative and structural coherence, the films addressed in this chapter share a conspicuous *lack* of such organising principles, turning instead to new, wide parameters of

scale, distance, and resulting mobility as Beckermann develops the
cinema of drift of her earlier essay films into a discernible poetic
through which to analyse some of the geopolitical dimensions of
the contemporary, early twenty-first-century world.

These chronologically sequential and closely interrelated films
share many incidental features; both are titled in English and mainly
comprised of exchanges in that language, and both are structured
as journeys resonating with powerful western myths. Via these
mythic echoes and the shared formal patterning that results from
such organisation, each addresses through a distinctive cinematic
rhetoric of documentary editing, rhythmic montage and contrastive scenic juxtaposition, the relations between varieties of 'home'
as belonging and the distorting, alienating effects of contemporary
economic and political events, which exist in both films as abstract
but directly affective forces influencing lives. 'Passage' in these films
becomes the extended process of identification, articulation, and
following of specific, semi-imposed and semi-voluntary trajectories
through and between locations and events, all linked by their inter-
relations within the film's contexture but existing also in complex
symbolic relations to the economic and ideological forces of which
they are expressions. 'Passage' is something experienced, sought,
negotiated, and (in some cases) endured by the people Beckermann
encounters while filming; from this complexity of experience emerge
new configurations of "hostipitality" indicative of newly emergent
social and economic structures, the barely discernible outlines of
which each film strives to encompass. These peoples' narratives,
which establish their positions in relation to the wider narratives the
films construct, become the textual substance counterpointing the
images and tracking sequences Beckermann arranges in each film.

American Passages

It was October, home, and work again. The first cold winds rattled
the windowpane, and I had made it just in time. Dean had come
to my house, slept several nights there, waiting for me; spent after-
noons talking to my aunt as she worked on a great rag rug woven of
all the clothes in my family for years, which was now finished and
spread on my bedroom floor, as complex and as rich as the passage

of time itself; and then he had left, two days before I arrived, crossing my path probably somewhere in Pennsylvania or Ohio, to go to San Francisco. (Jack Kerouac)[2]

In one of the more surreal moments in the frequently comically surreal *American Passages*, an Elvis impersonator climbs out of his huge pink Cadillac, a reproduction of the 1950 Eldorado (the real Elvis owned four such vehicles), and walks self-consciously across the brightly sunlit street into a shady Las Vegas bar, passing the camera without a glance (Figure 7.1). The contrastive logic organising the entire film is condensed in this short sequence: the themes of auto-mobility and the exteriority of American social life alongside its containment in places of temporary habitation (the car, the street, and the bar, in this case); the embedding in masquerade of a unique but infinitely repeated, deeply mythologised popular-cultural history, itself inevitably a structure of imitation-as-repetition (Elvis had his first blue Cadillac painted pink in imitation of Sugar Ray Robinson; Aretha Franklin sang of "Ridin' on the freeway of love / In my pink Cadillac" in homage to both); and the allegorical exposure of the privacy of fantasy (the desire to transform oneself literally into a universally recognisable pop icon, with all its concomitant erasures of self, identity, individuality) to the pitiless glare of the Nevada sun.

Figure 7.1 Ruth Beckermann (dir.), *American Passages*, 2011.
© Ruth Beckermann Filmproduktion.

American history-as-performance constitutes a key node of thematic and critical organisation of Beckermann's film, the journey of which passes through carefully arranged real-life scenarios and performed or represented actions, static views and travelling shots, and dramatically contrasting situations of deep poverty and huge wealth. The film visits several museums dedicated to American historical events which are performed by actors (or, in the case of "the moment of the signing of the Constitution" in Signer's Hall in the National Constitution Center in Philadelphia, statically restaged by forty-two life-sized statues). America's obsession with its own history, an infolding of self-attention repeatedly manifest in the act of permanent performance or representation, is an insistent trope (the film's title echoes at least one standard textbook of American history).[3] History provides less a ground sequence of formative events from and on which narratives of home and belonging might be constructed, and more a set of imaginary or utopian scenarios of belonging-within-tradition, to be constantly re-enacted; versions of history are endlessly repeated even as the spaces staging this repetition have demonstrably shifted due to historical changes. "We try to be as historically accurate as possible", state the owners of a museum located in a house built by slaves, before arguing over the date of its building.

In other vignettes, historical experience is perspectivised, individuated, its general (or social) significance trammelled to the singular point of view of the perceiver. A German teacher describes the term paper of one of her students on "The way Germans viewed the American Dream"; an African-American cab driver recalls his childhood memories of segregation in Mississippi; a teenage girl stands on stage in Atlanta's Museum of Slavery, an individual example in a lesson about how slavery involved reducing humans to possessions, a statue behind her of an African-American couple and baby in bondage. People launch unprompted into their repetitive performances, assuming their roles amid the proliferating representations of historical figures (one man, working in the American Village theme park in Montevallo, Alabama, "is" Benjamin Franklin; his long, bizarrely theatrical segment is immediately followed by a view of the statue of Moses the Lawgiver over the courthouse in Hinds County, Mississippi). A woman, Lynette Lyon, gives a tearful, heartfelt, and clearly well-practised rendition of and speech about the history of the "Star-Spangled Banner" before a crowd of ageing veterans, ending with a request that "every day be a memorial tribute for those that have fought for our freedoms".

A stray black balloon floating aimlessly in the street, blown back and forth by the breeze, offers a random but obvious metaphor linking all these threads; equally buffeted by seemingly inescapable economic forces, a painter, half-Creek Indian, narrates (in the film's first extended segment) his failure to sell his house and move a hundred miles to where he now works. He laments America's racial identity laws and the "rights" they afford certain categories of people, assuming they possess the correct documents. Home as displacement, a pressure towards constant transience, alongside normalised bureaucratic hostility, are thus established early as defining conditions of residence in American society. The human types accumulate as the film moves westward, marking the inscription into American space of social difference and diversity alongside constantly shifting identities and uniformities, inviting capitalised denominations – the Black Woman Judge of Hinds County, the Elderly Professor (analysing the American dream) of Oxford, Mississippi, the Gay Adopting Parents, the Liberty Evangelists, the Evicted Woman, the Reformed Addict, the Gambling Addict. These figures, each performing their role in the national narrative, combine in the film's passaging around America to form an allegorical social patchwork, a version of "the great rag rug woven of all the clothes" of which Jack Kerouac writes (in the epigraph to this chapter) in *On the Road*, a novel published in 1957 but written in 1951, 60 years before the release of *American Passages*. Beckermann's film closely aligns itself formally and politically with the mood evoked by Kerouac and what Michael Hrbeniak calls his "narrative principle of inclusiveness – voices, moods, speeds, points of view, modes of lighting – to confront the problem of presentation".[4]

Centrelessness: America on the move

American Passages adapts formal precursors in addressing this "problem of presentation", which it encounters most clearly at the level of form. While its form suggests the road movie and its associated narrative myths (like Kerouac's novel) as a template, it lacks the overt linearity and teleological drive most often associated with the genre, and evident in its immediate documentary precursor, Robert Kramer's *Route One USA* (1989), which maps a north–south journey from the Canadian border to Florida's Key West, tracing the American outlines of what Caroline Boué calls "community multiplicities and singular identities"[5] (a distinction that equally applies to the structural relations between Beckermann's various interviewees). Beckermann's film is compiled instead as a circulation of fragments without centre, eschewing the north-south or east-west structure conventional to the genre for the looser form of the "associative journey",[6] echoing influential postmodern readings of late-twentieth-century America like that of Jean Baudrillard. In *America* Baudrillard critiques the USA as "the zero degree of culture, the power of unculture" which nevertheless (in its fragmented totality) exceeds the possibility of its own representation: "even though every detail of America may be abject or insignificant, it is the whole which passes our imagining".[7] Bert Rebhandl notes an analogous sense in Beckermann's film: "The country is too big to be summarized in one concept, and so the passages are the only adequate form: a passing of momentum that could well remain unconnected."[8]

Interviewed in 2011, Beckermann emphasises this evasion of the generic conventions:

> In this film, we do not travel from East to West. We are going in all directions, and specifically through the southern and central states of the country. I avoid the East and California, which are too often shown. I don't specify where we are. I also film a parking lot, an airport tarmac, a highway, what I would call "non-places". This film shows American architectural signs. They are identical everywhere and provide the link, the "connection" in every sense of the word, across this vast country. What is striking for a European is the total absence of centres. In a European city, there is a square, a church, a centre to which everything leads. In the American West, you are lost in the tangle of roads, the successive kilometres of suburbs, or, as in Las Vegas, in a flat basin surrounded by desert. This notion of centrelessness is fundamental.[9]

This emphasis on "centrelessness" and "non-places" (a marked contrast to culturally resonant European centres like Vienna) suggests a version of America existing interstitially, in spaces and places in-between those other locations and sites which may be invested with socially symbolic meaning, thus becoming in some way 'significant'. Many of the film's scenes take place in or near such non-places – bars, gas stations, airport aprons, rehearsal rooms, waiting rooms, diners (like the "Waffle House", an American version of the Viennese coffee house), domestic storage facilities. Such sites evoke the work of French anthropologist Marc Augé, whose "ethnology of the near"[10] emphasises the symbolic construction of socially significant spaces through lines, intersections, and points of intersection, which correspond to routes, crossroads, and centres (the latter, Beckermann asserts, are absent from the America she films; routes and crossroads, on the other hand, proliferate).[11] Beckermann clearly alludes in the statement cited above to Augé's conception of "non-place" as designating "two complementary but distinct realities: spaces formed in relation to certain ends (transport, transit, commerce, leisure), and the relations that individuals have with these spaces".[12]

In her 2020 interview with Débora G. Kantor Beckermann defines *American Passages* in relation to a series of "utopian concepts" explored in earlier works (notably *Towards Jerusalem*, which it formally resembles), and in particular her interest in using moments of "change" as catalysts for her films:

> This was a long project for me. I'm interested in memory but also in utopian concepts, if you want. Like Zionism or the United States, that was also a utopian concept, in a way. So, when Barack Obama was elected – I had always wanted to make a film about the United States – I thought maybe this was the right moment to make the film. Because I think for documentaries it's always good when something changes, it's a good moment to make a film when there are changes in politics or whatever; that's why I made the film after the election.[13]

"Those moments where something is just starting to break open are always the most exciting", she reiterates in her interview with Horvath and Omasta.[14] In order to explore the effects of these utopian moments of transformation, *American Passages* presents its "associative journey" through the United States via a sequence of interview-vignettes with representative Americans linked by establishment shots and short tracking shots from car windows. Opening in Harlem on election night, and capturing something of the mood of jubilation among the African-American community at that moment, the film moves southwards and westwards across America towards the Californian coast (which it doesn't reach, ending its journey, as we've seen, in Las Vegas), documenting accounts and experiences across the social and racial range of the country.

The "associative journey" suggests a corresponding psychoanalytic reading of the nation, in which the film's speakers and the visual signage it portrays reveal to the viewer concealed or repressed dimensions of American consciousness. The vignettes are organised in a system of delayed echoes and oppositions, subtle repetitions, and the endless displacements and condensations of passage, all rhetorical tropes characteristic of the Freudian unconscious and of the dream logic or phantasmagoria that characterises what Beckermann calls "American space":

> I wanted to avoid the postcard, the tourist approach and the sequences with the long traveling shots that you would expect. All of this is too obvious for American space. Above all, it must be said here how much the entire production and distribution circuit of a documentary – from television channels to the CNC – is formatted, and conditions the financing of projects on compliance with standardized forms and concepts. We must get out of this formatting. I had a hard time finding funding for this film. I hope that with *American Passages,* everyone can make their own collage from the fragments I offer. What is fundamental for me is to invent a device that allows the viewer to think, to develop their own perception of the world through images.[15]

The audience-constructed collage, conspicuously non-sequential and narratively non-contiguous, can thus be read as a short-circuiting and subversion of media-industry conventions and as an invitation to the viewer to engage in the shared process of making meaning from "the fragments I offer". The film's abrupt and uncaptioned shifts of location – in which the simultaneous urgency and temporal delay of actual movement and travel are largely replaced by the instantaneity of cutting – contrasts sharply with the highly articulate "rhetorical capacity"[16] and linguistic flow demonstrated by many of the people filmed. This tension between smooth and staccato progression is expressed at different levels of *American Passages* – notably in its use of music (to which we'll return), but also in the relations between moving and still images.

Modern America as image

Pervasively present in its mythologising performance, history also impacts directly on *American Passages* as a series of real, if intangible, forces generated by national and international events, affecting the daily lives of Americans. Beckermann's cinematic exploration of the USA occurs at a specific historical juncture, the coincidence of the election of the first African-American president, Barack Obama, in 2008 with the emergent social effects of the global economic crash of that year. This immediate context is constantly haunted, throughout the film, by the longer historical perspective of the continuing wars in Iraq and Afghanistan. Several of the film's scenes directly address the impact of these wars on daily lives back home: in one long sequence the singer in a punk band narrates his wartime service and its disastrous and long-term psychological effects on his life, revealingly mixing into the tale cryptic allusions to "what really happened" on 9/11.

The film thus explores in part what Bert Rebhandl calls "The hope for a new beginning of national history [...] [which] manifests itself in the vastness of the country and its inhabitants, products of a diaspora",[17] alongside the weary sense (again) of history repeating itself, Iraq and Afghanistan as new Vietnams. A further dimension is provided by Beckermann's *Arbeitsbuch* (*Workbook*) for the film, extracts from which were published in 2016, opening with the question (dated 13 October 2008): "What would my life have been, if my parents had gone to the United States?"[18] This speculative autobiographical reading remains largely implicit throughout the film but (like the wider geopolitical reality of a nation at war) haunts many of the scenes and interviews, investing some of Beckermann's directorial choices and interviewer questions with deeper resonances.

Central to Beckermann's inquiry into the impacts of this nexus of events is the question of America-as-image, and the distortions and transformations of that image as it reworks itself to accommodate (or evade) new political and economic realities. *American Passages* is dedicated to Swiss-American and Jewish photographer Robert Frank (1924–2019) and marks in its earliest filmed segments the 50th anniversary of his photographic collection *The Americans* (published in France as *Les Américains* in 1958 and in the US by Grove Press a year later, with a short 'Introduction' by Jack Kerouac). Frank documented the Americans he encountered during three Guggenheim Fellowship-funded journeys across numerous states in 1955–6, attempting, as he phrased it in a short 1958 essay "A Statement", "to show a cross-section of the American population".[19] A selection of Beckermann's own monochrome photographs of Americans and American scenes, made in New York in 1975–6, was published in the German-language Synema book of essays on her work, and reveals some of the evident influence of Frank (among others, including, in Beckermann's interest in dramatic self-portraits, Cindy Sherman) on her own photographic practice.[20]

Jonathan Day situates the 83 photographs in *The Americans* intermedially, emphasising their "poetic / prophetic truth" in terms of the American culture of Beat writing and jazz with which they coincided: "The photographs are the truth as Frank saw it. They are as honest, as poetic and as prophetic as Jack Kerouac's prose, Allen Ginsberg's poetry, Willem de Kooning's painting or John Coltrane's tenor saxophone playing."[21]

Day's reading of Frank stresses through a variety of metaphors the complex interconnectedness of the photographs, their working in sequences and parallels, with "linking motifs or notions" in the manner of "architectural devices" or "the interwoven trunks of a yew tree", "themed examinations" with which Frank "stitches his book together", a book nevertheless "in many ways structured like music".[22] In "A Statement" Frank situated his work somewhat less diversely, in relation to American (Walker Evans) and English (Bill Brandt, Hamburg-born to a British father) photographic traditions and to a quote (or rather, a fragment) he attributes to French novelist, art critic, politician and Resistance fighter André Malraux (1901–76): "To transform destiny into awareness",[23] suggesting photography's transmutative power in relation to questions of fate and perception. This triangle of influences notably excludes several potentially key contemporary references – Frank does not, for example, mention Edward Steichen and his recent and hugely influential photographic exhibition *The Family of Man* (MoMA, 1955, and subsequently a worldwide success), with its ambition to represent what Steichen called "the gamut of life from birth to death with emphasis on the daily relationships of man to himself, to his family, to the community and to the world we live in".[24] Instead, he locates his work in a documentary–realist pictorial tradition aesthetically leavened by Malraux's sense of the historical power of art to transform human perception. This power, Malraux insistently argues, works in explicit opposition to the destructive impetus of the Nazism against which he fought in the French army and the Resistance.

Beckermann takes several visual and organisational cues from Frank. *American Passages* captures in its emphasis on the disastrous effects on individuals and families of addiction, poverty, and bereavement, something of his humanist emphasis on photographic and documentary realism ("There is one thing the photograph must contain", Frank wrote in 1961, "the humanity of the moment. This kind of photography is realism. But realism is not enough – there has to be vision, and the two together can make a good photograph").[25] The film also follows his attention to a diverse social range of 'ordinary' people, who become emblematic in their testimonies of specific kinds of experience – simultaneously specific and personal in their responses to the world, and representative of general conditions and ranges of experience implicitly shared with many others; and it imitates Frank's careful patterning and organisation of images, its scenes presenting a rhythmic oppositional and repetitive patterning of themes and visual symbols that bind together to produce the overall effect of passage through a particular moment in space and time. From the opening footage of celebrations in the streets of Harlem and Times Square on Obama's election night, cries of "We're free!" echoing amid the partying (a traffic sign in the background reads "No Stopping Anytime"), the camera cuts to a long shot of a flock of pigeons circling in the sky over the city, and then to a shot of a road at dawn, and then to grids of lights punctuating the darkness of an airport runway. A silhouette reveals itself as a German-speaking man looking through a telescope. "People ask me if I look into other people's houses," he says. "But the image is upside down and back to front. Not much to see." Such moments locate the viewer in the film's generic version of the non-place, "Irgendwo zwischen Dokumentarischem und Fiktion" ("somewhere between documentary and fiction"), writes Beckermann in the *Arbeitsbuch*.[26]

Ending: Alabama in Vegas

The journey of *American Passages* ends in Las Vegas, short of the road-movie convention of west coast-California but a final location (the ultimate non-place) replete with intertextual significance. The camera travels along its facades of advertising signage, evoking Tom Wolfe's enraptured descriptions in 1965 of the Vegas signscape: "But such signs! They tower. They revolve, they oscillate, they soar in shapes before which the existing vocabulary of art history is helpless."[27] Beckermann films a contemporary avatar of Wolfe's Raymond, the amphetamine-fuelled gambling addict he tracks through the Vegas casinos; Beckermann's gambler, barely able to stay upright, spews his racism freely across the roulette table, a bizarre and disturbing performance of damaged masculinity (in marked contrast with that of the punk singer). Addiction, an insistent trope in the versions of America Beckermann documents, becomes in this scene an allegory of America itself, a nation addicted to repeating fantasies of its own past and endlessly repeating outmoded relations of race, class, and power.

Besides the Elvis impersonator noted earlier, Vegas provides the stage for other performances, notably a young African-American woman giving a practice-rendition in a barber's shop in Las Vegas of Brecht and Weill's 'Alabama Song' (a counterpoint to the earlier performance of the national anthem). Several strands of the film coalesce in this scene; the theatricality of her performance ("Is this water or real?" she asks, of the whisky she's offered, while passersby wave to her through the window), the non-place of its setting, the poverty thematised in the song, and, linking all, the thread of song itself and its expressive or gestural power. Chosen by Weill to illustrate the notion of 'gestural' (*gestische*) music (which allows expression of an attitude) as elaborated in Brecht's theory of drama, 'The Alabama Song' was first performed by Weill's wife Lotte Lenya and, in its "outlandish mixture of German beer-drinking ditty and American ballad",[28] epitomised the *song* element of Brechtian epic. It was written by Brecht in 1925, translated by Elisabeth Hauptmann, set to music by Weill, and published in Brecht's *Hauspostille* (*Home Devotions*, a parody of Martin Luther's sermons) in 1927, and became one of the songs in *Aufstieg und Fall der Stadt Mahagonny* (*Rise and Fall of the City of Mahagonny*,

1930), a cabaret-opera about a mythical Midwest American city which lures people into a life of disastrously indulgent sin. Alex Ross describes *Mahagonny* as "Brecht's uncanny prophecy of Las Vegas", and argues that its libretto, while "widely understood as a protest against rampant capitalism [...] reads just as well as a critique of the fake utopia of the Soviet Union".[29]

In its enactment of destructively addicted desire – what Daniel Albright characterises as "a combination of boredom and yearning [...], a constricted circuit of wish-whisky-wish-boy-wish-dollar-wish-whisky, a state of No Exit from the banality of thirst"[30] – the song enacts the rhythmic pattern and staccato movement onwards towards an elusive, endlessly compromised utopia that characterises the entirety of *American Passages*, while importing into Beckermann's version of American a passage of *echt* German modernism that both contrasts dramatically with and thematically reinforces the tension between the utopian and realist elements she repeatedly finds in Obama's America. The song's abrupt formal shifts between pressing urgency and swooning lyricism, and its relentless non-arrival and incompletion (the impossibility of satisfying its insatiable thirst), mimic the film's rhythmic oscillation between abrupt montaging of images and the lyrical fluency of its narratives. In the singing of 'The Alabama Song', Beckermann finds a performance that momentarily embeds into *American Passages* not the rootless floating signifiers of Baudrillardian postmodern America or the drifting idealism of Kerouac, but the critical utopian drive of Brechtian modernism, its historical framing by the collapsing Weimar Republic echoing also the disintegration, 80 years earlier, of 'Red Vienna', narrated by Franz West in *Return to Vienna*.

Those Who Go Those Who Stay: threads, traces, passages

After seeing Herzl's 1894 play, *The New Ghetto*, Freud noted in 1898 that "the Jewish problem" was a "concern about the future of one's children, to whom one cannot give a country of their own, concern about educating them in such a way that they can move freely across frontiers". Freud's phrase is both metaphor and fact – one must be trained to respond to the trauma that can occur when crossing frontiers.[31]

The link to Brechtian modernism in *American Passages* is taken up in one of the segments of *Those Who Go Those Who Stay* (2013), which depicts a crowd of people outside the reception centre on Lampedusa in the southern Mediterranean, one of the remote sites used by the global north to administer migration into Europe and a site (Paolo Cuttitta argues) "more 'border' than other places".[32] The 'borderisation' of the extraterritorial Italian island of Lampedusa draws attention to how the Mediterranean itself has been redefined as a new kind of European border, isolating and distancing the continent and the political space of the European Union with frequently deadly efficiency. As Stathis Kouvelakis argued in 2018:

> The Mediterranean has become the most lethal of the EU's external borders. Its waters are the site of interlacing sovereign powers – those of the littoral states, but also those now superimposed on them in the form of the EU and its agencies, and notably those specifically charged with border control, whose operations transform the modalities of state action on which they rely.[33]

The migrant centre epitomises the 'borderisation' process – the redefinition of ostensibly neutral spaces like Lampedusa as border territories, a process involving several policies including the concentration of migrants on the island, appointing border guards and building the detention centre there, securitising the surrounding ocean, and importing humanitarian workers. It presents to Beckermann's camera a scene fraught with tension, as men shout, jostle, argue, and mill aimlessly around the restricted space. It's unclear which side of the border we are on. A man jogs up and down a narrow patch of grass. Two dogs evade an arriving truck carrying military police. Voices are heard, bodies can be seen, but little coherent action or meaning can be decoded from the scene; communication among the participants (differentiated by skin colour but little else), and between the film and the viewer, is frustrated by the border's very existence, which places on the Italian island an intangible barrier among the people it materially separates from Europe. The border appears as an arena of conflict between unclear antagonists, its architectural features blank and forbidding, its effects socially and communicatively disruptive.

Noting that Lampedusa was the site of two "exceptional" immigration crises in 2009 and 2011 (immediately prior to Beckermann's film), each a consequence of mis-management leading to over-crowding and rioting, Cuttitta considers the island as a paradigm of the contemporary state border as spectacle, defining the process of 'borderising' Lampedusa as "a 'theatre performance'", and "the Sicilian island as a theatre for the 'border play' represented by Italian migration control policies".[34] He reads the border as a performance of a five-act tragedy aimed at the audience of Italian voters and at the wider global north to demonstrate and empha-sise the 'reality' of the 'threat' posed by uncontrolled mass migra-tion and the effectiveness of the Lampedusa centre in managing it. Deploying a similar theatrical metaphor, Gabriel Popescu includes Lampedusa in his list (compiled in 2008) of "little-heard-of places" that "have come to embody the drama of the twenty-first-century security paradigm".[35]

Beckermann's scene, a fragment of this continuing contempo-rary humanitarian tragedy, is titled "Those in Darkness Drop from Sight", a translation of the final line of the last verse of "Mack the Knife", a stanza Brecht added to the song for the film version of *Die Dreigroschenoper* (*The Threepenny Opera*) directed by G. W. Pabst in 1931:

Denn die einen sind im Dunkeln
Und die anderen sind im Licht
Und man sieht nur die im Lichte
Die im Dunkeln sieht man nicht.
(There are some who are in darkness
And the others are in light
And you see the ones in brightness
Those in darkness drop from sight.)[36]

The added stanza develops the metaphor of (in)visibility to empha-sise the exclusionary effects of economic and class stratification as a matter of perception and thus of representation and agency. Cited at this moment in Beckermann's film, this quotation from Brecht draws attention to the complex roles played by vision and technologies of the visible in regulating and policing migrant bod-ies. Chiara Giubilaro (writing in 2018) notes the paradoxical con-struction of migrant bodies in terms of (in)visibility (a construction echoing that of the racialised 'other'): "Migrant bodies are differ-entially exposed to a politics of visibility that sometimes makes them (hyper)visible via the construction of scenes of exclusion or control, and at other times imprisons them in a zone of invisibility and disavowal."[37] *Those Who Go Those Who Stay* foregrounds in this scene what Giubilaro calls "the often-concealed relationship between the migrant-spectacle and the citizen-spectator";[38] we view people simultaneously apparently oblivious to the presence of the camera yet wholly coded by and enmeshed within the spectacular–visual paradigm of border security and its paradoxical regimes of excessive (in)visibility. The concern with the political functions of images explored in earlier films is elaborated in the attention here to the relations between state power and visibility. The Lampedusa scene is followed by one recording a car journey across Sicily with two undocumented Nigerian refugees, Alex and Good Luck, who discuss their hopes and ambitions, which centre mostly on Italian football and their desire to live in Italy; they pray for the Italian government "to help us out of this place". The segment offers an alternative version (a kind of mirror-image) of an earlier one in which Beckermann and cinematographer Peter Roehsler drive through Israel, a formal repetition comprising one of the many rhizomic ramifications of *Those Who Go Those Who Stay*.

Contemporary Europe and border consciousness

Brecht and Weill's "Mack the Knife" is one of many literary and cinematic works referred to in this complex and profoundly allusive text. It connects the film to Brecht's critique of capitalism in *Die Dreigroschenoper*, a critique updated in Beckermann's analysis of contemporary capitalist structures of global organisation and distribution in *Those Who Go Those Who Stay*. Structured into 24 distinct segments (listed in the film's credits by title, location, and film crew), the film comprises a complex, interlocking system of constellatory images depicting multiple facets of contemporary geopolitical diversity. Beckermann uses the contrastive and dynamic effects of montage to generate continuities and echoes across the film; each segment is reflected in the others, and many scenes and events reprise episodes from earlier works. She states in her interview with austrianfilms.com that "It's less a matter of wandering around lost and much more a case of sauntering through the labyrinth. [...] It's about moving the eyes, but it's also about the voluntary and involuntary movement of people." The "labyrinth" figures the world of routes, passages, and borders, criss-crossed by people engaged in constant movement or encountering arbitrary obstacles, both voluntary and enforced, all in different ways searching for home, their varied conditions and experiences summarised in a segment discussing the tonic structures of middle-Eastern music as "*Sehnsucht*" (yearning, longing, nostalgia).

The film's multiple themes and settings map a geographical range spanning sites in Europe, Israel, Buenos Aires and Arizona but centring on ports and locales of the Mediterranean Sea and specifically on Italy. They intersect in complex constellatory relations, generating via reiteration and reflection, conflict and reinforcement an ever-expanding series of associative readings as the film seeks ways of mapping emergent patterns and historical residues in contemporary geopolitical reality. The contexture of this reality is deepened historically in the segment showing a Salzburg conference with Palestinian activist Viola Raheb and Syrian-Palestinian sociologist Sari Hanafi comparing the contemporary refugee experience with that of Jews in the 1940s. Hanafi defines the refugee condition as "a transient experience which lasts forever". In another ironic counterpoint, Barbara Taufer (in the segment on music mentioned above) asserts the historical importance of middle Eastern culture for Europe – "Ohne dieser Kultur, hätte es keine Renaissance in Europa gegeben" ("Without this culture, there'd have been no European Renaissance") – before the film cuts to an FPÖ rally in Vienna, its Austrian attendees and music products (and probably celebrants) of the homogenising Western culture critiqued by Taufer. Through this thematic diversity the film presents images, narrative scenes, interviews and encounters, and further dramatic counterpoints that indicate, without necessarily explaining, some of the dynamic intersections of contemporary patterns of human and cultural movement (migration, displacement, exile) and those elements of human culture – borders, barriers, immigration control – by which they are both regulated and prevented.

Borders exist in the film in a variety of forms: as material (non-) spaces arresting the movement of people around the globe, as discursive spaces produced by the meeting-points between linguistic and other cultural differences, as ideological constraints interrupting processes of imagining totalities and interconnections and thus constituting the edges of imagined or utopian possibilities. Borders are internal (figured most dramatically in bird's-eye footage of a maze through which rats run, actually a video artwork by Peter Kogler projected onto a floor in Paris for children to play on); or external, thresholds between nations or political entities or different configurations of social space. One such threshold is seen in Prato, Italy, where Beckermann films a clothing factory housing illegal migrant workers from China (the contemporary industrial form of large-scale and globally outsourced mass production that has largely replaced the family-owned Viennese textile shops of Salo Beckermann and Adolf Doft). Forbidden from entering the factory, the camera lingers at the doors, offering a view of the cavernous interior behind one tired-looking man sat smoking on the threshold. Earlier, the film visits the border between Italy and Austria at the high mountain pass of Plöckenpass. This internal European Union border, which we see from the Austrian side, is deserted, its checkpoint kiosks empty, road traffic passing freely between two of the EU's Schengen states. The border exists merely as a sign marking the beginning of Italy; its silence and the absence of overt disciplinary machinery contrast dramatically with the crowded scenes and heavily policed fences and gates of Lampedusa, indicating the radically distinct distributions of power differentiating internal and external European borders.

One theme of the film addresses how borders redefine the identity of contemporary Europe, a fluid and indeterminate historical and political concept overlapping but not wholly coincident with a grouping of nation states. This conceptual fluidity is established in the contrast between internal and external borders, with their distinct forms of openness and potential flow suggesting the corresponding fluidity of the very concept of the 'border'. Writing in 2013, a year after the release of Beckermann's film, Nicholas De Genova addresses many of its themes and stresses the ideological basis of the border as a concept, arguing that

> the crisis of European borders is eminently political, in manifold ways. [...] [T]he borders of Europe are never reducible to anything resembling immutable, integral, internally consistent, or objective boundaries corresponding to any self-evident 'natural' fact of physical geography. Nor can these European borders be apprehensible

as simply the outward projections of a stable and coherent centre, whereby the sociopolitical, cultural, or civilizational identity, and spatial integrity of Europe may be presupposed in contradistinction with a variety of alterities beyond or outside the ostensible limits demarcated by those boundaries. Instead, Europe's borders, like all borders, are the materializations of sociopolitical relations that mediate the continuous production of the distinction between the putative inside and outside, and likewise mediate the diverse mobilities that are orchestrated and regimented through the production of that spatial divide.[39]

In his discussion of migratory passages across the Mediterranean, Iain Chambers articulates a similar sense of Europe's borders, describing the border-spaces constructed by the EU and by individual nation states as

a complex system of filters and channels that stretch outward into extraterritorial space, both on the waters of the Mediterranean Sea and over the horizon into the Maghreb. So Europe and the Mediterranean – how they come to be defined and regulated – emerge from a legal configuration in which human rights go largely unrecognized in the elaboration of juridical confines and citizenship. It is these that establish the borders between the "inside" and the "outside," between belonging and expulsion.[40]

The oppositional frames organising these arguments – inside/outside, centre/periphery, European/non-European, geography/politics, belonging/expulsion (or unbelonging) – recur, along with the titular opposition between going and staying or movement and stasis, as structures organising the episodes of Beckermann's film. The border thus constitutes a central, highly charged, and highly flexible metaphor through which Beckermann elaborates her version of Hamid Naficy's "border consciousness"[41] (discussed earlier in relation to *Towards Jerusalem*).

Naficy examines "accented cinema" and its representations of "border consciousness" in films made in a wide variety of contexts by an international diversity of film-makers. In *Those Who Go Those Who Stay* this diversity is reconfigured and internalised in the textuality of the film which, we suggest, re-articulates its concern with contemporary "border consciousness" by developing an elaborate intertextual (border) relations with other, precursor, texts in cinematic and other media, an interlinked textual field that includes earlier works in Beckermann's oeuvre. Intertextuality is understood here in the sense developed by Daniela Caselli, who conceives it (in her reading of Beckett's uses of Dante) as a "productive questioning" of "ideas of origin, stability, and repetition".[42] The intertextuality of *Those Who Go Those Who Stay* likewise propels its analysis of the effects of globalisation and its impact on notions of origin (or home), its generation of precarity as a persistent contemporary state of economic and ideological instability, and its imposition on a wide range of contexts of structural uniformity or repetition.

Palimpsestic intertextuality

Embodying the political realities of "border consciousness" in its thematic concerns with dispossession and invisibility and its close attention to the semiotics of border spaces (highly policed versions of the "non-places" Beckermann finds in America), *Those Who Go Those Who Stay* addresses the question of borders between texts and media and their functions in regulating cultural exchange and intercommunication. Intertextuality, in the form of cross-medial and cross-linguistic allusion, reference, citation and quotation, thus assumes political significance as a process allegorising the porosity (or otherwise) of real-world borders and embodying in its processes and effects a utopian vision of a (textual) cultural space free of border restrictions and their restrictive or definitive effects.

The thematic and structural coherence of *Those Who Go Those Who Stay* is reflected in this web of intertextual connections linking the film to other works, evident at its every level, from its title to elements of its structure. The film opens in Paris, with views from a window blurred by rain, the image fuzzy, indeterminate, the windowpane itself and the raindrops on it zooming into focus, and the city beyond fragmented and unidentifiable; layers of perception thus obscure the object of the gaze, drawing the viewer's attention to the layering itself as a motif that prefigures the film's palimpsestic layering of textual and historical allusions. This opening segment (which echoes the opening shots of *Paper Bridge*) is titled "A Flâneur in Paris", gesturing to an earlier unmade project with the working title *Die Flâneurin*,[43] some elements of which (notably in the opening Paris-based sequence) were retained for this film, and immediately introducing the Benjaminian and Baudelairean resonances associated with the Parisian *flâneur* which Beckermann has explored elsewhere. Shots of Parisian signscapes and their conflicting messages ("Zone Sensible", "Less=More"), and of ambulances with sirens wailing, suggest the bustling city, the frame constantly cut and crossed by passing traffic and strolling pedestrians. This is, however, a Paris intersected and redefined by multiple movements and displacements along trade and travel routes of the nineteenth and subsequent centuries. A flea market find reveals a Tel-Aviv-issued 1942 Palestinian identity card and an Israeli 500 Lirot banknote from 1975, featuring David Ben-Gurion's portrait. Shop-window dummies evoke Surrealism (as does the segment "The Doll Suitcase" with its images of vintage dolls) and the photographs of Eugène Atget. Some of the mannequins model hijabs, signifying the contemporary city's multiculturalism; much later in the film, three hijab-wearing women try to navigate the dangerously fast traffic of Alexandria while crossing a road, which becomes a threatening border.

The Paris represented in this segment links with the colonial history explored in *A Fleeting Passage to the Orient*; filming in the locale of Rue d'Alexandre and the Place and Passage du Caire, Beckermann invokes the colonial history of the Parisian passages via Egypt and its iconic functions in the urban architecture of the city. The Passage du Caire, the oldest of the Parisian passages, dates from Napoleon's campaign in Ottoman Egypt in 1798; its appearance in the film establishes European imperialism and cultural appropriation as one thread of links through the network of historical contexts. The camera dwells on one of the three distinctive carved sphinx-like heads of Hathor (an Egyptian goddess associated with love, motherhood and joy), renditions of a carving from the temple at Dendera and now in the Louvre, a trophy of French imperialism (Figure 7.2). Hathor's relevance to the film's themes of migration and border-consciousness is evident from her function in many representations as "Goddess of the West" welcoming the dead to the next life.

The film's title alludes to two modernist paintings, parts of the 1911 trilogy *Stati d'animo* (*States of Mind*) by the Italian futurist Umberto Boccioni (1882–1916), respectively titled *Quelli che*

Figure 7.2 Ruth Beckermann (dir.), *Those Who Go Those Who Stay*, 2013. © Ruth Beckermann Filmproduktion.

vanno and *Quelli che restano* (*Those Who Go* and *Those Who Stay*).[44] These paintings, depicting departure and arrival at a railway station, formally embody the "universal dynamism" of futurist art. In his 1914 book *Pittura, scultura futuriste* (*Futurist Painting and Sculpture*) Boccioni emphasised dynamism and the capturing of "velocity" in painting as key futurist aims: "Velocity will thus be something more than an object in swift motion, and we will perceive it as such: We will draw and paint velocity by rendering the abstract lines that the object in its course has aroused in us."[45] In titling her film after Boccioni's futurist paintings Beckermann implies the aesthetic dynamism of early Italian modernism as a metaphor for the rapid mobility of transit and displacement in contemporary Europe; but she also suggests, via the well-documented connections of the Futurists with Italian fascism, a critique of the contemporary Italian border policies she films at work in Lampedusa.[46]

Among the people acknowledged in the credits is the French feminist writer and theorist Hélène Cixous (b. 1937), whose essay celebrating *Paper Bridge* Beckermann describes in an interview in 2017: "It was as if I had posted a letter that was received by someone almost 20 years later."[47] In her novel *Si prés* (*So Close*) (2007) Cixous records versions of conversations with her ailing ninety-five-year-old mother about potentially revisiting her birth city of Algiers.[48] Cixous' plans are echoed and mirrored in the segment "Mother Remembers: Vienna", in which an elderly and hospitalised Bety Beckermann, prompted by her visiting daughter, recalls her escape from Vienna to Palestine via Brindisi in 1938. This interview and that with Elfriede Gerstl in the Café Salzgries reprise major scenes from earlier films (noted in Chapters 3 and 6), establishing intra-oeuvre cross-reference as a significant element of the inter- and intratextuality of *Those Who Go Those Who Stay*, and evident also in the sequence shot at an Aarhus screening of *East of War*, and in the link between Bety Beckermann's memories of fleeing Vienna and those of screenwriter and director and screenwriter Georg Stefan Troller (b. 1921), interviewed earlier in the Paris segment, who likewise fled Austria in 1938, later joining the US army and participating in the liberation of Dachau.

Underpinning these interlinked intertextual frames is the film's loosely mythic structure, indicated in the 24 chapters which echo the 24 books of Homeric epic. *Those Who Go Those Who Stay* alludes to a long tradition of reworkings of *The Odyssey*, from James Joyce's *Ulysses* (1922) to John Akomfrah's *The Nine Muses* (2010). An epigraph to Beckermann's film commemorates the death a few months before its completion of the Greek director Theo Angelopoulos (1935–2012), whose 1995 film *Ulysses' Gaze*, itself a revisioning of Homer's *Odyssey* as a journey round the Balkans in search of a lost film, shares many parallels with Beckermann's work. Angelopoulos was unable to film in Sarajevo due to the Bosnian war (just as Beckermann was unable to film any of *Paper Bridge* in Czernowitz; a passage of *Those Who Go Those Who Stay* is, however, filmed there, interviewing the artist Matthias Zwilling). The film includes a sequence showing a barge sailing down the Danube under Vienna's Donaustadt bridge, reprising the famous sequence in Angelopoulos' film where his protagonist (played by Harvey Keitel) stands at the prow of a ship carrying a huge statue of Lenin on the Danube in Romania. A linking landscape shot of lines of people traversing up snowy mountains reprises a visually similar sequence in *Ulysses' Gaze* (Figures 7.3 and 7.4). Beckermann's film uses the same incidental music as Angelopoulos' – the mournful "Ulysses' Theme" by the Greek composer Eleni Karaindrou.

Figure 7.3 Ruth Beckermann (dir.), *Those Who Go Those Who Stay*, 2013. © Ruth Beckermann Filmproduktion.

Figure 7.4 Theodoros Angelopoulos (dir.), *Ulysses' Gaze*, 1995.

As with Angelopoulos, episodes from the *Odyssey* inform several of the scenes in Beckermann's film. A Calypso-like girl, playing on a beach, asks Beckermann whether she films boys too, or only girls. Shots of bathers enjoying the quiet sea at Haifa suggest Proteus. In "Security!", filmed at an arms fair in Israel, Beckermann

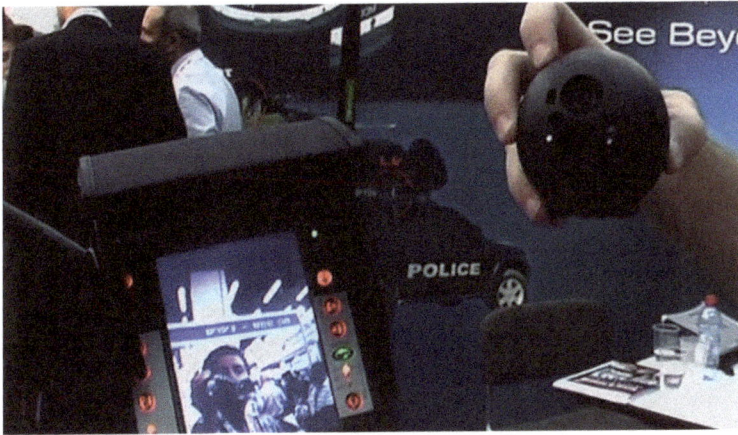

Figure 7.5 Ruth Beckermann (dir.), *Those Who Go Those Who Stay*, 2013. © Ruth Beckermann Filmproduktion.

encounters a mobile security camera, the "Eye Ball R1", made by Israeli defence company ODF Optronics (its motto: "See Beyond Vision") and designed as a small, portable ball to be thrown into potentially hostile spaces (Figure 7.5). "Where's the camera?", she asks the salesman, who shows her the single, Cyclops-like eye embedded in the metal ball. A sequence in Prato showing yards of white and green fabric being rolled and folded, followed by brightly coloured dresses hanging in the gentle breeze outside a shop, recalls the windy "Aeolus" episode in Homer and Joyce. The circular-homeward passage of Odysseus provides the underlying drive of the entire film; Vienna and Paris offer versions of Ithaca, while Odysseus himself, the returning warrior forced to circle the Mediterranean for a decade in search of home, seeking refuge in caves and on islands, personifies the condition of migrancy the film explores.

Threads and traces

The film's epigraph provides a clue to how we might read this web of mythic, cinematic, and literary allusions. Taken from the opening of Italian historian Carlo Ginzburg's book *Threads and*

Traces: True False Fictive (2006), it points to the intersection of myth and interpretation as a way of approaching Beckermann's procedure in the film:

> The Greeks tell us that Theseus received a thread as a gift from Ariadne. With that thread he found his bearings in the labyrinth, located the Minotaur, and slew him. The myth says nothing about the traces that Theseus left as he made his way through the labyrinth.[49]

In the segment titled 'Couple in a Park, Vienna', a young woman ties one end of her scarf around her partner's neck, in a gesture of affectionate affiliative connection that threads the couple together. Ariadne's thread (referencing another Greek myth) leads us forward into the labyrinth of similarly interconnected, mutually reflecting fragments constituting *Those Who Go Those Who Stay* and, simultaneously, backwards into intertextual passages of repetition and recurrence linking the film to Beckermann's earlier works. The thread itself works as a guiding motif linking this film with earlier engagements with the Viennese textile industry; its foregrounded recurrence here suggests an abiding tapestry metaphor linking the various interconnected themes and concerns of Beckermann's oeuvre, a network perhaps metaphorised in the "labyrinth" of the Greek myth. Versions of this labyrinth appear in the film in the aerial footage of Phoenix, Arizona, an immense conglomeration of cryptic characters inscribed into the American landscape; or, a few seconds earlier, in Peter Kogler's rat-trap floor maze in Paris. In the library at Alexandria (echoing the Rue d'Alexandre in Paris) Beckermann interviews the French architect Rudy Ricciotti, who propounds his radical Voltairean anticlericalism and points out the barbarism underpinning the Enlightenment ("We decapitated 20,000 in the Revolution ... some 'Enlightenment', eh?"). The library offers a material embodiment of the labyrinthine textuality of the film, its shelves and corridors policed by blue-clad security guards, its cubicles filled by internet and catalogue screens.

Together, the labyrinth and the web of intertextual links offer alternative ways of conceiving the complexity of the globalised economic system. Each image-sequence in the film engages a facet of that system and attempts to provide a fragmentary metonymy of it; each addresses in some way the labyrinthine legal and juridical structures and processes, the meshes of language and economics and culture and history relentlessly entrapping those on the wrong side of the borders, which recur throughout the film as insistent motifs of differentiation. Each allusion furthermore embeds into the film's textuality a series of threads leading to further potential resonances with a widening diversity of cultural traditions, like those scrutinised in the discussion in Jaffa (noted earlier) about different traditions of Arabic music and the differential evolution in various local middle-Eastern contexts of the pentatonic scale and its variations: "Jeder Ort hat seine eigene musikalische Sprache ... und seinen eigenen Rhythmus" ("Each place has its own musical speech ... and its own rhythm") – a conversation that rapidly mutates into an argument about the cultural uniformity apparently imposed by 'Americanisation'.

The quotation from Ginzburg, however, emphasises not the thread or the labyrinth but the "traces" left behind by the passage of Theseus. The film's focus is not on the guide or the site but on the act of passage itself and its effects on the 'labyrinth' passed through. Ginzburg's book engages with historical narratives as always provisional, mutative, indeterminate and constantly under revision. It develops in its argument "an awareness that our understanding of the past inevitably was uncertain, discontinuous, lacunar, based only on fragments and ruins".[50] The "fragments and ruins" of the past become, in *Those Who Go Those Who Stay*, elements of a contemporary experience of "Sehnsucht", components of a contemporary world of apparently endless dislocation and drift. Beckermann's film closes on a tram in Istanbul (outside Europe, in another former imperial centre), the camera tracking along the busy city streets as the carriage moves from stop to stop. We see several male passengers, and a young boy, silent but self-conscious before the camera, hitching a ride by sitting on the vehicle's rear access steps as it travels along its busy metropolitan route. The tram stops. The men go. The boy stays.

Notes

1 "Migrants do not roam the surface of the globe, they do not violate borders, they do not attack the beautiful geopolitical ordering of nations. On the contrary, they bring about a world where there

is only one globe, they compose its divisions by piercing the dividing lines of crossing points and places of life where worlds hatch and peoples meet. The more migrants, exiles and transgressions there are, the more people there are and the more worlds there are." Étienne Tassin, "Philosophie /et/ Politique de la migration", *Raison Publique* Vol. 1 No. 21 (2017), 197–215: 203.

2 Jack Kerouac, *On the Road* (New York: Viking, 1959), p. 63.

3 David Oshinsky, Edward L. Ayers, Jean R. Soderlund and Lewis Gould, *American Passages: A History of the United States* (New York: Houghton Mifflin, 2006).

4 Michael Hrbeniak, *Action Writing: Jack Kerouac's Wild Form* (Carbondale, IL: Southern Illinois University Press, 2006), p. 74.

5 Caroline Boué, "L'identité en marche dans *Route One USA* de Robert Kramer (1989)", *Tumultes* No. 10 (April 1998), 241–57: 244.

6 This phrase is used in the advertising blurb promoting the film.

7 Jean Baudrillard, *America* (trans. Chris Turner) (London: Verso, 1988), pp. 78, 104.

8 "Das Land ist zu groß, als dass man es auf einen Begriff bringen könnte, und so sind die Passagen die einzig adäquate Form." Bert Rebhandl, "Das ewige Thema: 'Judenkind, Flüchtlingskind, Wirtschaftswunderkind' – Die Identifikationen von Ruth Beckermann", in Horwath and Omasta (eds) *Ruth Beckermann*, p. 32.

9 "Dans ce film, on ne circule pas d'Est en Ouest. On va dans toutes les directions, et plus particulièrement dans les Etats du sud et du centre du pays. J'évite l'Est et la Californie, trop souvent montrés. Je ne précise pas où l'on est. Je filme aussi un parking, un tarmac d'aéroport, une autoroute, ce que j'appellerais des 'non-lieux'. Ce film montre les signes architecturaux américains. Ils sont partout identiques et assurent le lien, la 'connexion' dans tous les sens du terme, à travers ce pays si vaste. Ce qui est frappant pour un Européen, c'est l'absence totale de centres. Dans une ville d'Europe, il y a une place, une église, un centre à quoi tout mène. Dans l'Ouest américain, vous êtes perdus dans l'enchevêtrement des routes, la succession des kilomètres de *suburbs*, ou comme à Las Vegas, dans une bassine plate entourée de désert. Cette notion d'absence de centre est fondamentale. Dans le film, l'architecte Paolo Soleri évoque cela. Il dit: "Si on perd la ville, on perd la culture'." ("Entretien avec Ruth Beckermann, *American Passages*", *Journal du Réel* #7, 31 March 2011.)

10 Marc Augé, *Non-Places: Introduction to an Anthropology of Supermodernity* (trans. John Howe) (London: Verso, 1995), p. 10.

11 Augé, *Non-Places*, p. 57.

12 Augé, *Non-Places*, p. 94.

13 Kantor, "Ruth Beckermann: Documentarian of the Present", 235.

14 Horwath and Omasta, "A Conversation with Ruth Beckermann", p. 35.

15 "J'ai voulu éviter la carte postale, l'approche touristique et les séquences avec les longs travellings auxquels on s'attend. Tout cela est trop évident pour l'espace américain. Surtout, il faut dire ici combien tout le circuit de production et de diffusion d'un documentaire – des chaînes de télévision au CNC – est formaté, et conditionne le financement des projets au respect de formes et de concepts normés. Il faut sortir de ce formatage. J'ai eu beaucoup de mal à trouver un financement pour ce film. J'espère qu'avec *American Passages*, chacun peut réaliser son propre collage à partir des fragments que je propose. Ce qui est fondamental pour moi, c'est d'inventer un dispositif permettant à celui qui regarde de penser, d'élaborer lui-même sa perception du monde à travers des images." ("Entretien avec Ruth Beckermann" (*Journal du réel* #7).

16 "La capacité rhétorique des personnes qui s'expriment face à la caméra est stupéfiante [...]." ("Entretien avec Ruth Beckermann").

17 "Die Hoffnung auf einen Neubeginn der nationalen Geschichte [...] bricht sich in der Weite des Landes und seiner Bewohner, die alle wirken, als wären sie in einer Diaspora." Rebhandl, "Das ewige Thema", p. 32.

18 "Was aus meinem Leben geworden wäre, wenn meine Eltern in die USA gegangen wären?" Beckermann, "*American Passages*: Auszüge aus dem Arbeitsbuch", in Horwath and Omasta (eds), *Ruth Beckermann*, p. 96.

19 Robert Frank, "A Statement", *US Camera 1958* (New York: US Camera Publishing Corporation, 1958), p. 115.

20 Horvath and Omasta (eds), *Ruth Beckermann*, pp. 34–40.

21 Jonathan Day, *Robert Frank's* The Americans: *The Art of Documentary Photography* (Bristol: Intellect, 2011), p. 11. Day later compares the photographs in *The Americans* to the 'gestural painting' of Jackson Pollock and other artists, and to "jazz improvisation" (p. 49).

22 Day, *Robert Frank's* The Americans, pp. 11–12.

23 Robert Frank, "A Statement". The phrase seems to originate in Edwin Honig's review, "Malraux's Psychology of Art", *New Mexico Quarterly* Vol. 21 No. 4 (1951), 488–94: 493. The full quote, ostensibly from André Malraux's *The Psychology of Art*, reads: "For, while history seeks merely to transform destiny into awareness, art seeks to transmute it into freedom." Honig is misquoting Gilbert's translation of Malraux: "... while history aims merely at transposing destiny onto the plane of consciousness, art transmutes it into freedom."

(André Malraux, *The Voices of Silence* (trans. Stuart Gilbert) (St Albans: Paladin, 1974), p. 623. Malraux's original French reads: "... car l'histoire tente de transformer le destine en conscience, et l'art de le transformer en liberté". (Malraux, *Les Voix du silence* [Paris: La Galerie de la Pléiade, 1951], p. 621).

24 Edward Steichen, quoted in Gerd Hurm, Anke Reitz, and Shamoon Zamir (eds), *The Family of Man Revisited: Photography in a Global Age* (London: Routledge, 2020), p. 1. *The Family of Man* appears briefly in *The Waldheim Waltz*; it was included on the information disks on the NASA Voyager spacecraft along with an address by Waldheim as Secretary General of the United Nations.

25 Robert Frank, quoted in Edna Bennett, "Black and White are the Colours of Robert Frank", *Aperture* Vol. 9 No. 1 (1961), 20–2: 22.

26 Beckermann, "Auszüge aus dem *Arbeitsbuch*", p. 96.

27 Tom Wolfe, *The Kandy-Kolored Tangerine-Flake Streamline Baby* (London: Picador, 1981), p. 20.

28 Marc Blitzstein, quoted in Kim H. Kowalke, "Singing Brecht vs. Brecht Singing: Performance in Theory and Practice", *Cambridge Opera Journal* Vol. 5 No. 1 (1993), 55–78: 63.

29 Alex Ross, *The Rest Is Noise: Listening to the Twentieth Century* (London: Fourth Estate, 2008), p. 205.

30 Daniel Albright, *Untwisting the Serpent: Modernism in Music, Literature, and Other Arts* (Chicago, IL: University of Chicago Press, 2000), p. 118.

31 Gelbin and Gilman, *Cosmopolitanisms and the Jews*, pp. 82–3.

32 Paolo Cuttitta, " 'Borderising' the Island: Setting and Narratives of the Lampedusa 'Border Play' ", *ACME: An International E-Journal for Critical Geographies* Vol. 13 No. 2 (2014), 196–219: 199.

33 Stathis Kouvelakis, "Borderland: Greece and the EU's Southern Question", *New Left Review* 110 (March–April, 2018), 5–33: 18.

34 Cuttitta, " 'Borderising' the Island", 205; 200–1.

35 Gabriel Popescu, *Bordering and Ordering the Twenty-First-Century: Understanding Borders* (Washington, DC: Rowman and Littlefield, 2011), p. 105.

36 Quoted in Hannah Arendt, *Reflections on Literature and Culture* (ed. Susan Young-ah Gottlieb) (Stanford: Stanford University Press, 2007), p. 246.

37 Chiara Giubilaro, "(Un)framing Lampedusa: Regimes of Visibility and the Politics of Affect in Italian Media Representations", in Gabriele Proglio and Laura Odasso (eds), *Border Lampedusa: Subjectivity, Visibility and Memory in Stories of Sea and Land* (Cham: Palgrave Macmillan, 2018), pp. 103–17; p. 104.

38 Giubilaro, "(Un)framing Lampedusa", p. 106.

39 Nicholas De Genova, "Introduction: The Borders of Europe and the European Question", in De Genova (ed.), *The Borders of Europe: Autonomy of Migration, Tactics of Bordering* (Durham, NC: Duke University Press, 2017), pp. 20–1.

40 Chambers, *Mediterranean Crossings: The Politics of an Interrupted Modernity*, p. 4.

41 See Naficy, *An Accented Cinema*, p. 31.

42 Daniela Caselli, *Beckett's Dantes: Intertextuality in the Fiction and Criticism* (Manchester: Manchester University Press, 2005), p. 6.

43 A draft of the proposed project is published in Horwath and Omasta (eds), *Ruth Beckerman*, pp. 60–5.

44 Elena Ferrante's novel *Storia di chi fugge e di chi resta* was published in Italy in 2013, and as *Those Who Leave and Those Who Stay* (trans. Ann Goldstein) in 2014.

45 Umberto Boccioni, cited in Ester Coen, *Boccioni* (New York: Metropolitan Museum of Art, 1988), pp. 118–20.

46 See, for example, Andrew Hewitt, *Fascist Modernism: Aesthetics, Politics, and the Avant-Garde* (Stanford, CA: Stanford University Press, 1993), esp. Ch. 5 "Avant-Garde and Technology: Futurist Machines – Fascist Bodies", pp. 133–60; and Francesca Billiani, *Fascist Modernism in Italy: Arts and Regimes* (London: Bloomsbury Academic, 2021).

47 Horwath and Omasta, "A Conversation with Ruth Beckermann", p. 27. Cixous, "How to Film Becoming Invisible".

48 Hélène Cixous, *So Close* (trans. Peggy Kamuf) (London: Polity, 2009).

49 Carlo Ginzburg, *Threads and Traces: True False Fictive* (trans. Anne C. Tedeschi and John Tedeschi (Berkeley, CA: University of California Press, 2012), p. 1.

50 Ginzburg, *Threads and Traces*, p. 24.

8

Where fascism begins – *The Dreamed Ones, MUTZENBACHER* and *The Missing Image*

Whatever is unnamed, undepicted in images, whatever is omitted from biography, censored in collections of letters, whatever is misnamed as something else, made difficult-to-come-by, whatever is buried in the memory by the collapse of meaning under an inadequate or lying language — this will become not merely unspoken, but unspeakable. (Adrienne Rich)[1]

I really wanted to transform the words, the words themselves, into film. (Ruth Beckermann).[2]

Interconnections between performance, interpretation and the analysis of cultural memory are explored in the three works discussed in this chapter. Despite their apparent distinction in formal and structural terms from her preceding works, Beckermann's recent films (including *The Waldheim Waltz*, discussed in Chapter 4) develop the long-running preoccupation with the politics of performance evident in the presence in earlier works of storyteller-performers like Franz West, Herbert Gropper and Adolf Doft, a thread emerging more prominently in the thematisation of performance-as-spectacle in works like *American Passages*. The documenting of performance, and the potential political and generic transformation or translation of the text in its being performed, emerges as a significant focus in the recent films, becoming an explicit thematic preoccupation through which Beckermann explores how Austrian literary and cultural traditions frame the politics of gender relations, a ground which emerges as central to the analysis of questions of unbelonging. This exploration focusses furthermore on texts not specifically intended for performance, and thus involves a deliberate staging which is transformative of the text in question.

The Dreamed Ones (2017) dramatises the reading of passages from letters exchanged between the authors Ingeborg Bachmann (1926–73) and Paul Celan (1920–70), two authors whose extended, closely interconnected, and profoundly complex responses to the post-war condition of living within the German language offer analogies with Beckermann's own analyses of unbelonging.[3] *MUTZENBACHER* (2022)[4] presents a series of men in casting performances and interviews for roles in a film version of the notorious erotic novel *Josefine Mutzenbacher oder Die Geschichte einer Wienerischen Dirne von ihr selbst erzählt* (*Josefine Mutzenbacher, or the Story of a Viennese Prostitute, as told by Herself*), a book published anonymously in 1906 and banned in Austria until 1971. These dialogic engagements with texts from Austria's literary tradition are prefigured in the 2014 installation *The Missing Image*, located in Vienna's Albertinaplatz, which will be discussed in conclusion. Together these works constitute a merging of media – letters, literary texts, dramatic adaptations, film, installation, music – offering a variety of new responses to Beckermann's recurrent theme of the legacies of Austria's fascist history.

In one sense, the Bachmann–Celan letter exchange and the novel *Mutzenbacher* constitute polar opposites. The former (which provoked a minor scandal in German literary circles when it was published in 2008) is the product and one of the principal mediations of an intense historical love affair over many years between two of the greatest post-war German-language poets (neither of whom was actually German), a relationship characterised by brief or missed encounters amid long periods of separation. The latter presents pornographically detailed accounts of sexual encounters written from the point of view of a fictional female narrator. Beckermann's interest in these texts, however, lies less in their shared scandalous nature, and more in their potential as pretexts or grounds for analyses of the (gender and sexual) politics of performance within the distinct but interlinked generic frames of (high-cultural) romance and (low-cultural) pornography. Both films emphasise the relations between sexual–textual difference and performativity in distinct social arenas, and each explores the ambiguities resulting from the mediating effects of these different varieties of performance – a dialogic performance of a controversial epistolary text in the case of *The Dreamed Ones*, and a polyvocal performance of an ostensibly monologic (that is, first-person narrative) text in *MUTZENBACHER*. The passage between the fluid, emotionally intense, dialogic exchange of letters and voices in *The Dreamed Ones* and the relentlessly repetitive intensities of the male voices in *MUTZENBACHER* is also the passage of (written, performed) language from negotiated to imposed identities and histories, and from plural to authoritarian–monologic discourses of power – language as the medium of free expression versus language as the means of silencing all expression other than the voice of power. Each film opens the space for a different set of audience responses to this passage, which is offered as a movement between different poles of an ambiguity or tension integral to the cinematic form Beckermann has used. In *The Dreamed Ones*, the ambiguity centres on the repeated assertion by both writers, in writing, of the impossibility of writing, an impossibility reified in the act of filming, which generates its own ambiguities as the film maps two sets of relations, that between Bachmann and Celan, and that between the film's performers, the latter offering a subtle but pointed commentary on the former. In *MUTZENBACHER* it inheres in the performative assertion of male power and its simultaneous undercutting by the repeated revelation of male frailty. In both cases, gender relations emerge as the field on which Beckermann's critical attention is most firmly focussed. Both films derive their force from the tensions and instabilities of meaning, and the distances and interruptions, resulting from these inherent ambiguities – as Peter Szondi wrote of Paul Celan's poetry, "The ambiguity is not a defect nor mere stylistic contrivance, it is the structure of the poetic text."[5]

Correspondences: *The Dreamed Ones*

> The amorous subject suffers anxiety because the loved object replies scantily or not at all to his language (discourse or letters). (Roland Barthes)[6]

Ambiguity, the distance between conflicting potential meanings within a single word or phrase, is the central trope of *The Dreamed Ones*, as it is a crucial trope in the wholly distinct but deeply interlinked oeuvres of Paul Celan and Ingeborg Bachmann. Co-scripted with Bachmann biographer and literary critic Ina Hartwig,[7] the film adapts epistolary passages from a text whose publication in German in 2008 (under the title *Herzzeit*, 'Heart's-time', and translated into English by Wilfred Hoban as *Correspondence* in 2019)[8] revealed the extent and intensity of the relationship between Romanian, Czernowitz-born Celan[9] (whose letters are read by actor Lawrence Rupp) and Bachmann (born in Klagenfurt in Carinthia, whose letters are read by experimental musician and composer Anja Plaschg, who later provided compositions for Beckermann's 2019 Salzburg Festival installation *Joyful Joyce*). *Herzzeit* documents (and analyses in its extensive editorial material) the affair that took place, over a number of years beginning in May 1948, largely via what Alice James calls "a poetics of correspondence" in which long-term emotional and gender-political dynamics are played out, along with an imbedded aesthetic debate about the difficulties for writing presented by the post-war German language and its political contexts, through the to-and-fro of an extensive and heavily interrupted letter-exchange. James argues that the correspondence between Bachmann and Celan is "situated at the crossroads of poetic and practical language",[10] a placing in which potentially conflicting linguistic functions play out in a dialogic exchange which centres increasingly on the impossibility of expressing in writing that which is being experienced. This impossibility, expressive also of the emotional difficulties inherent in conducting a relationship at distance, relates directly to the historical situation of the German language in the period in which the letters are written, compromised as it was by its recent and persistent Nazi associations. Echoing James's "crossroads" metaphor, Barbara Wiedemann and Bertrand Badiou emphasise the sense of a linguistic *agon* conveyed in the letters: "The struggle for language and the conflict within the word assume a central role in the correspondence", within which each phase of the affair is characterised by "points of intersection of a highly varied dialogue of letters characterised by its discontinuity".[11] This linguistic difficulty is expressed in Beckermann's film through her decisions to include or allude to specific poems by Celan and, through contingent elements of the film's *mise-en-scène*, to Bachmann's use in her writing of musical metaphors. These become integral to the thematic development of *The Dreamed Ones* and link it to her next film.

Translation/performance: waiting for an answer

Distance and discontinuity thus characterise the communicative difficulties explored in the film and, indeed, constitute much of its distinctness *as* film in relation to the published book on which it is based, in which the immediacy of epistolary directness and the continuity of narrative sequentiality are more obviously editorially constructed and imposed. Formally, *The Dreamed Ones* shifts away from (or distances itself from) the entirely 'found-footage' experiment of *The Waldheim Waltz* and the drifting, migratory camera movements and narrative structures of the earlier essay films, and towards a stricter application of cinema as dramatic (rather than documentary) form (as Beckermann notes, this is her first cinematic use of actors).[12] This is particularly evident in the careful use of shot-reverse-shot and of hand-held close-cropped shots of the performers (whom Beckermann describes as "voice-artists"),[13] and in the conspicuous use of lighting, extended pauses, and cut-aways; textually, it involves, at some points, close editing of the source document (particularly, at certain moments, removing all contextualising epistolary signifiers like dates and places of writing), and changing the historical sequence of some of the letters to sharpen key aspects of the narrative (which is occasionally foregrounded and progressed by intertitles). At times these processes transform (or translate) the letters into exchanges resembling dramatic dialogue (just as the film translates the published letters into a dramatic text) through which the relationship between Bachmann and Celan is played out. This generic translation draws attention to the film's underlying concern with questions around translation itself and its (im)possibilities, questions that haunt critical writings on Bachmann and (in particular) Celan.[14]

Marko Pajević points out that the 'dramatisation' of the letters in Beckermann's film focusses explicitly and extensively on its staging. Filmed mainly in and around Studio 3 in the ORF radio broadcasting building at Vienna's Funkhaus in the city's 4th district, this staging is foregrounded by the studio environment and the incorporation at several points in the action of technical dimensions of the recording (for example, a sound technician enters the studio at one point to adjust the microphone position and recording levels).[15] The process of recording and filming is thus a constituent element of the emotional drama performed in the film. Performance and acting are, furthermore, insistent themes in the Bachmann–Celan letters, which constitute along with their literary and romantic dimensions a joint enquiry into the conditions of post-war existence as a kind of drama of alienation, as experienced by two consummate artists. Celan writes on 7 July 1951: "I have the feeling [...] that, in Vienna, it is extremely rare for someone to actually be what they present themselves as being",[16] while Bachmann is extensively occupied during the period of the affair with writing and producing plays (including works by T. S. Eliot and Jean Anouilh) for the radio station Rot-Weiss-Rot.[17] In foregrounding this thematised performativity, and focussing also on what seem to be off-camera or 'behind-the-scenes' passages in which the two performers interact in apparently unscripted, informal exchanges, often commenting on the letters and the developing narrative (thus generating an extended parallel or 'shadow' metatextual narrative alongside the scripted performances, in which their own interactions take centre stage), Beckermann emphasises the complexity of relations mobilised by the film's structure and narrative. The viewer consequently engages in the relationship of correspondence between the voice-artists reading the letters nearly as much as that between the authors of the letters. The resulting structure recalls the doubling of the historical moments inhabited by Beckermann and the Empress Elisabeth in *A Fleeting Passage to the Orient*, as parallel narratives establish a series of symbolic echoes and reflections that develop and reinforce the film's themes.

Expanding the focus of precursor films like Agnès Varda's short *Elsa la rose* (1966), which explored the relationship between French writers Louis Aragon and Elsa Triolet, *The Dreamed Ones* exemplifies the dialogic and diegetic characteristics of epistolarity characteristic of Naficy's "accented cinema", which, he argues, is "intensely dialogic" and structured by varieties of addresser-addressee relations, from the letter writers and readers, to the film's address to its audience via intertexts and captions, making such films "both epistolic and calligraphic texts".[18] Read in these terms, the film's dramatisation of the Bachmann–Celan relationship becomes also an analysis of the act of reading/interpreting it. Beckermann and Hartwig's editing of the published text focusses on key elements of the exchange, their selections emphasising the film's generic hybridity (drama/romance/aesthetic meditation/epistolary text) as personal and wider historical concerns coexist in the written exchanges alongside private dialogue and more general commentary on ideas about writing and art. The intermeshing of private and public in the act of performance becomes crucial to the emotional dynamic organising the film's narrative and to the emotional investment of the performers in the work they are performing. This is clear in the response in particular of Plaschg to some of the passages she performs; she asks for breaks in filming when the act of reading becomes too upsetting, and is twice filmed lying, apparently exhausted, stretched out on the studio's conspicuous red couch. As Laura Rascaroli points out, the letter is "a form that radically mixes and merges private notations and commentary on public matters, the record of both everyday life and momentous events".[19] At the same time, the letter implies dialogue in its demand for a reply: "Like desire", writes Roland Barthes (in a book invoked by at least two reviewers of *The Dreamed Ones*), "the love letter waits for an answer."[20]

Beginning: "In Egypt"

The exchange of letters between the two writers begins in June 1948 with Celan's gift to Bachmann of a poem and a book, or rather of a poem, dedicated to Bachmann, written into a book (the first of four similar gifts; more will follow, in 1957). Celan's poem "In Ägypten" ("In Egypt") is inscribed in a copy of Henri Matisse's *Peintures 1939–46*, with a dedication to Bachmann.[21] The Matisse book, a limited-edition portfolio of 16 lithographs, reproduces works made across the war years and briefly into the post-war period, a time when the elderly and ill Matisse (whose relationship with the Nazi occupation of France and the Vichy régime is critically contested)[22] resided mostly in the south of France, distant from the wartime art world of occupied Paris. "In Ägypten", a poem drawing on Biblical narratives of exile and displacement, is retained by Beckermann at the film's beginning, its geographical connotations alerting us to intra-oeuvre links with earlier works like *A Fleeting Passage to the Orient*. Celan's poem was published (John Felstiner points out) three times before being included in a book, the poet's first collection, *Mohn und Gedächtnis* (*Poppy and Memory*) in 1952. It was one of those recited by Celan at his *Gruppe 47* reading in Hamburg in May 1952 (a reading instigated by Bachmann, who was a *Gruppe 47* member and, unlike Celan, would, a year later, win its prestigious literary prize).[23]

In the context of Celan's then-burgeoning relationship with Bachmann, "In Ägypten" performs a deal of symbolic labour, simultaneously establishing the primacy in the relationship of an aesthetics of verbal and physical intimacy, asserting in its vatic-declamatory and didactic tone a subtle elevation of Celan-the-poet over Bachmann's literary status, and allegorically positioning Bachmann as "the strange woman" (unlike Celan, she was not Jewish: her father was, furthermore, an early member of the NSDAP) addressed in the poem, in whose "eye" the male poet instructs himself to appear. The poem's language inaugurates a modality of ambiguous and compressed religious symbolism which seems to position Bachmann intimately in relation to the speaker while also distancing her mythically – she is not named, but implicitly identified and certainly indirectly addressed, in the poem, which performs a highly ritualised repudiation of Biblically named (Jewish) female archetypes in order to claim a new position – "Seht, Ich schlaf bei ihr!" ("Behold, I sleep by her!") – redolent of sexual ownership. Beckermann films Rupp's reading of this letter entirely through a tight headshot focussed on Plaschg, who listens intently through-out to the off-screen recitation, and smiles faintly as the reading ends. Not the performance of the letter's reading but the performed reaction of its recipient is thus foregrounded at the start of *The Dreamed Ones*; the film begins with an evocation via Celan's poem of Biblical narratives of exile, and an off-screen, displaced male voice defining in highly formalised poetic terms a woman's position in relation to his discursive world.

Beckermann's choice of title clearly differentiates her film from the *Herzzeit* of the published letters, recalibrating the romance they record from the physical-temporal and rhythmic (as well as the clichéd romantic) implications of "Heart-time" to the imaginary, immaterial space of dreaming. In doing so, it opens the letters to processes of interpretation closely associated with those of psycho-analysis, a framework within which the writings of both Bachmann and Celan have frequently been discussed. Karl Ivan Solibakke (for example) argues that Bachmann's oeuvre "succeeds in projecting the deficiencies of the post-war era onto a textual screen that is a montage of images originating from the collective unconscious",[24] while Charlotte Ryland's analysis of Celan's relations with Surrealism addresses his extensive uses of and resistances to Freudian psychoanalytic frameworks.[25] The phrase "The Dreamed Ones" is taken from the same stanza in Celan's poem "Köln, am Hof" (which comprises Letter 47, 20 October 1957, to which the poem is also dated) as that of the published volume:

> Herzzeit, es stehn
> die Geträumten für
> die Mitternachtsziffer.[26]

– which John Felstiner translates as:

> Heart time, those
> we dreamt stand up for
> the midnight cipher.[27]

This letter–poem is third in a sequence of four poems sent by Celan around this time (the others are "Weiss und leicht", on 17 October, "Rheinufer [Schuttkahn II] sent the next day, and "In Mundhöhe", on 26–27 October).[28] Individually, they receive no reply (like Barthes' love letter, they "wait for an answer"), and thus perhaps indicate a crisis (one of several) in the relationship, a momentary switch to unidirectional communication. As critics have noted, the condition of crisis is endemic in the post-war lives and writings of both Celan and Bachman. Áine McMurtry describes Bachmann's writing as "a radical project to develop a viable linguistic mode through which to express an inextricable condition of subjective and cultural crisis intimately bound up with the recent experience of historical atrocity";[29] while Felstiner offers Celan as one of the "few modern poets in whom the life and the work cleave so closely, so traumatically".[30]

In this apparent crisis of October 1957, their dialogue momentarily becomes his monologue, and the letters become a stream of poetically encrypted dedications ("For you, Ingeborg, for you", Celan writes before transcribing the first poem). Dedication (as Andréa Lauterwein points out) is a striking feature of the Celan-Bachmann literary matrix, in which individual poems and passages in novels function as vehicles bearing "a message or a psychological transfer".[31] The *Correspondence* editors note (perhaps following "Mitternachtsziffer" as a clue) that the phrase "Am Hof" ("At the Station", a site of "transfer" analogous to the linguistic "crossroads" deployed by Alice James above, and furthermore specifically indicating in this case a district in Cologne associated in the Middle Ages with the city's Jewish community) functioned as "a sort of code word" between Bachmann and Celan in two other letters. One of these (Letter 118, 11 February 1959) is accompanied by a card bought (Celan writes in Letter 120, on 18 February 1959) "at almost the same spot [in Paris] where the poem ["Köln, am Hof"] occurred to me over a year ago".[32] These letters were sent from Paris to Vienna; the card was "an old Viennese postcard" found in Paris; the poem is sited in Köln, by the railway station, a recurrent trope connoting dream-displacement in psychoanalysis that becomes for the two writers a "code word" (Celan will later write the major poem "Schibboleth", the Hebrew word meaning "password" or "code word"), and is thus laden with excess significance within the Bachmann–Celan exchange.

The Dreamed Ones emphasises these epistolary and semiotic displacements from city to city, country to country, signifier to code word, via letters and cards and poems and dedications, which perform versions of the displacements of distance and discontinuity that more extensively structure the letters (and the film). Letters constantly cross or are mis-delivered, remain unsent (Bachmann's first letter to Celan, dated Christmas 1948, was not sent), or exist only as drafts (one discussion between the performers concerns another unsent draft by Bachmann), or articulate anxiety about the failure of the other to reply promptly or even at all, or respond to earlier letters out of sequence; the correspondence is fractured by long periods of frequently mutually unaccountable silence on both sides (something the film enacts in the extra-performance passages, which often involve movement outside or elsewhere in the building, away from the studio). The film script, furthermore, adapts and interrupts Celan's "Köln, am Hof" letter-poem by intercutting or displacing into it fragments from his later letters (for example, the mention of finding Bachmann's poems published in the *Frankfurter Zeitung* in Letter 53 of 31 October)[33] and repetitions of lines from Bachmann's (non-poetic) response of 28 October

1957. His (possible) description of himself and Bachmann as "Die Geträumten" is twice countered by her sceptical question of a week later, "Aber sind wir nur die Geträumten?" ("But are we only the dreamt ones?"), the word "only" indicating a sudden note of plaintive or protesting intensity (extended in her question "and have we not already despaired at life?").[34] This moment occurs amid her effort to comprehend in this letter what she calls "the addition", meaning the facts of Celan's marriage in 1952 to Gisèle Lestrange and their child, both obvious obstacles to the easy continuity of any Celan-Bachmann relationship. These "code-words" and editorially compressed textual passages point towards a reading of *The Dreamed Ones* (Beckermann has omitted from her film's title Bachmann's "nur" / "only" qualifier, so that it cites both Celan and Bachmann) as a multi-dimensional text organised by the ambiguous and contradictory architecture of the dream-logic of displacement and condensation along with its invitation to endless interpretation. Such critical engagement is indeed implicit from the opening near-abstract shots of a roughly painted wall, its surface colours bleak and industrial, inviting a Rorschach-like analysis by the viewer, to the actors as they argue like critics over the motives behind different and sometimes contradictory or heavily cryptic statements in the letters they recite.

Orchestration

The Dreamed Ones orchestrates these dream-like complexities partly through reference to Bachmann's extensive and critically well-documented use in her writing of musical forms, references, and notation, which is reflected in Plaschg's status as musician and composer (under the performing persona Soap&Skin). Music assumes significance through the incidental context of the studio location, as an orchestra is working in another recording studio, which the two voice-artists visit and incorporate into their non-performed discussions. During the third break from filming, we see the pair walking through the building and entering the auditorium in which we hear rehearsals of the 1992 opera *Die Eroberung von Mexico* (*The Conquest of Mexico*) by German composer Wolfgang Rihm (b. 1952). *Die Eroberung von Mexico*, part of Rihm's extended engagement with Antonin Artaud's 'theatre of cruelty' (and directly responding to Artaud's planned 1933 performance also titled *The Conquest of Mexico*, among numerous other intertexts), offers an interesting parallel with the Bachmann–Celan letters. The opera's colonial Mexican setting (which functions, Alastair Williams argues, "more as a place where encounters with the Other can be played out in a mysterious, mythical setting than as a modern nation" – that is, as an oneiric or dreamed location)[35] frames an exploration of the relations between self and other that offers an alternative version of the gender opposition of Beckermann's film.

In this sequence Plaschg articulates in conversation with Rupp her problematic relation to the official music culture of Austria, which, she feels, fails to understand or properly accommodate her creative work. This grievance evolves into a critique of the bureaucratic process ("Für alles gibt's eine Form" ["there's a form for everything"]) of generic definition, and the tension in orchestral performance between the liberating potentials of aesthetic and formal talent and their control and regulation by musical convention and the authority of the conductor. "There is no more obvious expression of power than the performance of a conductor," wrote Elias Canetti in his analysis of the masses and authority, *Masse und Macht* (*Crowds and Power*, 1961); Canetti's orchestral conductor is "faced by a small army of professional players, which he must control".[36] Plaschg and Rupp comment on the orchestral performers as "the civil servants amongst the artists" ("das sind die Beamten unter den Künstlern"), referring to the way they are only allowed to execute the instructions they are given, lamenting the "do-as-you're-told mentality" ("führen das aber nur so aus"). This fascination with the orchestral balance of virtuoso creativity with the discipline imposed by the conductor becomes a potential allegory of the critic's relation to both film and letters. While the multitude of levels of textual and metatextual relations Beckermann puts into circulation in *The Dreamed Ones* presents an orchestrated textual space analogous to the musical work the orchestra is rehearsing, the unresolved aesthetic, romantic, and gender–political tensions expressed and explored in the performed Bachmann–Celan letters offer, in the arguments, silences, and failures to communicate fully, versions of textual disjunction, narrative discontinuity and non-orchestrated emotional disunity, contrasting productively and conspicuously with the potentially unified performance symbolised by the orchestra.

Beckermann's incorporation as incidental discussions within the diverse correspondences of *The Dreamed Ones* of these critiques of orchestration as a form of imposed bureaucratic conformity connects the film to her earlier explorations of unbelonging as the experience of intolerable social difference. Plaschg's definition of the psychological–emotional effect of her treatment by the musical community of Vienna – "Es ist gar nichts so konkret, aber man spürt es permanent" ("It's not really tangible, but you can constantly feel it") – encapsulates the intangible but constant pressure of Austrian "hostipitality" with which Beckermann's oeuvre has repeatedly grappled, and which finds a new form of expression in the orchestrated call-and-response structure of her next film, *MUTZENBACHER*.

MUTZENBACHER: critiquing Austrian masculinity

Men have learnt from wolves. [...] The pack wants its prey; it wants its blood and its death. [...] It urges itself on with its joint clamour, and the importance of this noise, in which the voices of all the individual creatures unite, should not be underrated. (Elias Canetti)[37]

The presence of a human voice structures the sonic space that contains it. (Michael Chion)[38]

Mitgrölen ist angesagt. (Olga Neuwirth)[39]

MUTZENBACHER is principally a critique of contemporary Austrian masculinity and can provisionally be situated within a strong feminist avant-garde tradition of such critiques. The film's call-and-response structure, for example, echoes a work by a key figure of the Austrian feminist avant-garde art, Renate Bertlmann's text for her work *7 Soldaten* (*7 Soldiers*, 1980/2004), a parodically obscene military marching chant accompanying a work comprising seven white dildoes clad in nappies and black neoprene sheaths adorned with tiny blue and white medals, all laid in a glass vitrine.[40] This work, exhibited recently in the Viennese Pavilion at the 2019 Venice Biennale, is part of Bertlmann's extended deconstruction of the iconography and accoutrements of male power and its integral and violent obscenity, an analysis performed in works of detournement and disempowerment of the symbolism of male authority (military, in this work and related pieces like *Der Patronenegürtel* [*The Ammunition Belt*, 1976]), and religious or bureaucratic in other works).[41] Such pieces (argues Peter Gorsen) "twist men's arrogant sexual prestige into metaphors of their failure".[42]

MUTZENBACHER adapts this feminist artistic engagement with male obscenity into a subversive staging of ritualised patriarchal violence performed in language, in which the aggression and obscenity is explicitly orchestrated to evoke historical echoes that resonate disturbingly in the context of the film's Viennese location. The film's analysis is predicated on an exploration of how (as Robin Ann Sheets puts it, discussing the English writer Angela Carter (1940–92)) "Pornography becomes a display of male power, expression and cause of men's aggression against women."[43] Its action is grounded in the narrative of a notorious novel still considered "Austria's most (in)famous piece of child pornography".[44] *Josefine Mutzenbacher*, anonymously written but widely credited to the Hungarian-born Austrian novelist and creator of Bambi, Felix Salten (1869–1945), was published in Austria in 1906. Beckermann's film uses this novel as a pretext that lends longer historical perspective to its extended feminist analysis of the contemporary linguistic and performative violence of patriarchy. The performance it documents is staged in an enclosed, post-industrial space (a former coffin factory) almost devoid of women but saturated by male fantasies of them, a space echoing throughout the film with the sound of loud male voices. Within this constrained *mise-en-scène MUTZENBACHER*'s action also evokes the narrative claustrophobia of films like Alexander Grasshoff's *The Wave* (1981), an analysis of fascism as an inescapable social tendency prone to spinning out of control given appropriate circumstances. The metaphor is politically ambivalent: Elias Canetti likened the anti-fascist protesting Viennese crowds of 15 July 1927 (at the burning of the Palace of Justice which Franz West also recalls) to a "wave", to the comprehension of which he was to devote a substantial part of his intellectual life: "The roaring of the wave was audible all the time [...] and only if this wave could be rendered in words and depicted, could one say: really, nothing has been reduced."[45] Beckermann's film identifies and explores comparable potentials in contemporary Austrian society.

Banned in Austria until 1971, the book *Josefine Mutzenbacher* has nevertheless significantly influenced the sexual socialisation of Austrian men and women across several generations. It has been reworked in numerous film versions and sequels (Wikipedia lists fourteen, all directed by men), and was anonymously translated into a bowdlerised English version in 1931, reappearing in a second, equally unreliable, English translation by Rudolf Schleifer in 1967. The novel's translation and adaptation histories thus affirm via uncertain authorship and unreliable texts in different languages its ventriloquial potential, its susceptibility to adaptation and transformation. Beckermann's film, which she calls "a kind of field experiment",[46] exploits the various dimensions of this indeterminacy. It takes its cue from a casting call posted in the press for men aged between sixteen and ninety-nine to perform in a proposed film of the novel. Shot exclusively within the coffin factory setting, the film initially depicts men, sometimes alone, or in pairs or groups of three or four, reading aloud (and in many cases actively performing rather than simply reading) and discussing short passages from the book which they have been assigned. The film presents the men before, during, and after their performances, offering what reviewer J. Hoberman calls "miniature psychoanalytic sessions"[47] in which they talk of what they anticipate before, and what they feel after, their casting calls. These elements of *MUTZENBACHER* bear comparison with the letter-recitations and dialogue sequences of *The Dreamed Ones*. The potential comparisons change, however, as the film develops, and we see sequences (which lack analogies in the earlier film, except in the passage where the orchestra rehearses, discussed above) in which the entire male cast, co-ordinated and conducted by Beckermann, engages in call-and-response routines in which, in unison, they shout lines and phrases from the novel – graphic descriptions of the sexual act, or lists of male terms of obscene 'endearment'. Characterised by a kind of relentless, obtuse repetition, a structure it shares with much pornographic literature and film, *MUTZENBACHER* offers through these different modes of performance a forensic dissection of Austrian masculinity and its relations to the verbal expression of sexual power. The parade of male performances furthermore constitutes, in its entirety, a psycho-social diagnosis of contemporary Austria in microcosm, figured as a limited geopolitical space dominated by a restricted number of orchestrated (male) voices engaged in a repetitive chanting that inevitably conjures up ghosts of the nation's past.

The novel *Josefine Mutzenbacher* graphically and at great length details the sexual exploits from a very young age of its titular protagonist. Or rather, it details a male imaginary version of these exploits, an act of male impersonation of the feminine which Beckermann's film lays bare in its contribution to long-running feminist debates about pornography and male power. As Andrea Dworkin comments in her 1981 study *Pornography: Men Possessing Women*, "Most writers of pornography are male. The female name on the cover of the book is part of the package, an element of the fiction. It confirms men in their fantasy that the eroticism of the female exists within the bounds of male sexual imperatives."[48] Canonical literary texts affirming this tradition of impersonation include Sade's *Justine* (1791), Alberto Moravia's *The Woman of Rome* (1947) and Frank Wedekind's *Lulu* plays (*Erdgeist* [1895] and *Pandora's Box* [1904]) – works in which a male author assumes a female subject position, and indeed names his text after that assumed identity (or, in Moravia's case, with an epithet assigned to that identity), in order to articulate and "explore" a male conception or fantasy of female sexuality, in the absence of any actual or authentic *female* manifestation or expression in the text of that sexuality. Such texts, including the novel *Josefine Mutzenbacher*, impersonate female experience in order to erase it, replacing it with a male-fantasised version of itself which is then presented as the 'authentic' version of that experience. As one exchange in *MUTZENBACHER* highlights, arguments justifying the textual politics of this supplanting representation – that (for example) the impersonation is legitimised because the character apparently "enjoys" what is done to her – are meaningless because the character does not exist outside the fiction; "she" is a cipher, a vacant space enabling the articulation of an exclusively male set of fantasies which are then projected into and through the fictional narrative. In recruiting only male voices for the filmed readings, Beckermann both highlights the procedure of erasure of the feminine and undercuts it, revealing in the process some of the operations of power underpinning the wider social silencing of female voices. The film's exposure and exploration of how male performance and the male voice erase and silence femininity, and what they construct to fill in the resulting emptiness, will be the focus of our discussion.

Masculinity on the couch

Impersonation-as-erasure is, then, inherent in *Josefine Mutzenbacher*: an unknown, but almost certainly male, author writes a text in the assumed first-person voice of a female narrator, into which are projected an extensive range of clearly male fantasies about female sexuality. In the case of *Josefine Mutzenbacher* these fantasies seem (one critic has argued) to derive at least in part from Sigmund Freud's *Three Essays on the Theory of Sexuality*, published in Austria in 1905 (a year before *Josefine Mutzenbacher*).[49] This intertextual connection resonates with a prominent element of Beckermann's film, its central prop, the suggestively pink, flowery couch on which the men are invited to sit as they perform and then discuss their responses to the passages they read. This couch, which reprises the (red, not pink) one Anja Plaschg lies on in the studio in *The Dreamed Ones*, organises much of *MUTZENBACHER*'s spatial and visual rhetoric, centring and softening the empty post-industrial *mise en scène* with its superficially domestic, chintzy-floral presence (Figures 8.1 and 8.2). A version of the Hollywood casting couch, it clearly also invites analogies with Freudian psychoanalysis and its central stage of the analyst's couch, and specifically Freud's own couch, which, Nathan Kravis argues, "is both Ruhebett (daybed) and Turkish divan, carrying the twin identities of sanatorium and asylum fixture on the one hand, and romantic symbol on the other".[50] Around this deeply ambivalent and polysemic prop the film sets in motion series of psychoanalytic connotations, a range of polymorphously perverse gender relations, entanglements, echoes, proximities, continuities, and ruptures between current and historical Austrian national and cultural fantasies and histories of violence against women.

In the post-performance moments, as we witness men reacting to their own performative capabilities, one of the functions of the couch emerges. It provides a kind of symbolic architecture, a motif of symbolic stability that temporarily structures the potentially unstable parade of male enactments. Its multiple upholstery

Figure 8.1 Ruth Beckermann (dir.), *The Dreamed Ones*, 2016.
© Ruth Beckermann Filmproduktion.

Figure 8.2 Ruth Beckermann (dir.), *MUTZENBACHER*, 2022.
© Ruth Beckermann Filmproduktion.

buttons form a regular and insistently present pattern against which each performance occurs. In his seminar on the psychoses, Jacques Lacan evokes these quilting points or *points de capiton*.[51] The buttons holding in place the stuffing of the couch stand, in Lacanian terms, for the points at which the symbolic structure is anchored to the Real over which it lies as a protective layer, buffering the subject from the potential trauma of any direct encounter with the Real. The buttons symbolically represent how performed subjectivities, both masculine and feminine (in this film, feminine-as-performed-by-men), might be temporarily pinned down within the symbolic structure, fastened to positions within the play of signs from which their significance emerges. Within this socially symbolic framework, the violent structure of impersonation-as-erasure, established from the film's beginning, is extended in *MUTZENBACHER* into an explicitly male performative masquerade in which the apparent circularity and interchangeability of social roles in the symbolic world masks the underlying erasure of woman almost entirely from the field of discourse and representation – a process that effectively results in what the American feminist theorist Mary Daly calls "the absolute elimination of all vestiges of real female presence"[52] from the social and political world. This world is, in Beckermann's film, a synecdoche of post-war Austria; a contained and hostile space, a field of almost exclusively patriarchal presence, resonating with the noise generated by one specific set of identities, which drowns out and virtually excludes the possibility of any other kind of voice. As Michael Chion argues, "The man's shout delimits a territory."[53] In this territorialised patriarchal field, the male actors perform their versions of a male-imagined and male-authored 'female' voice. The variety of male voices in the film, the range of different Austrian accents, the assumption by some men of a sing-song, fairy-tale-like storytelling mode of delivery or, in one case, actual sung delivery – this range merely affirms the absolute dominance, in this space of fantasy, of the *male* voice in all its forms.

What is apparently suspended in this space of male performativity is, then, the female voice itself and any experience it might express. *MUTZENBACHER* explores how patriarchy silences the female voice and supplants female experience through a variety of processes including appropriation, imitation, exclusion, and drowning out, all of which centre on the voice and the language it performs. This language is, of course, that associated with an extremely successful example of a particular discourse, that of pornography. It is thus a language deeply structured by generically encoded and historically sanctioned expressions of verbal misogyny and by the imagined performing of violent acts on female bodies.

Above all, the film explores how such linguistic violence expresses, legitimises, regulates, and structures male fantasy and facilitates its imposition on that space in the patriarchal social symbolic in which woman is positioned. As the allegorical dimensions of the film (enclosed space as Austria, patriarchal violence as engendering the experience of unbelonging) suggest, this exploration raises implications that extend beyond the obvious gender relations, to encompass the ways linguistic violence works at cultural levels to distort and reconfigure gender identities as group, and by extension national, identities. As *MUTZENBACHER* progresses, its insistent and increasingly relentless repetition serves to delineate (Austrian) masculinity as an insistently present social formation that serves to channel power regardless of semantic content. The male act of speaking or shouting, not what is spoken or shouted, comes to dominate the enclosed geography of the film, defining the ideological contours of the space, and filling it with particular values and associations, while excluding others.

Woman as figure/voice

Beckermann's film mobilises a range of performances – of passages from the novel *Mutzenbacher*, of masculinity, of misogyny, of versions or narratives of sexual interaction and the sexual act, and (in the self-conscious awareness of several of the men interviewed) of the very act of *performing* itself – through which we encounter a specific form of mass psychology in action. These intersections of history and identity, representation and response, are investigated in *MUTZENBACHER* through a focus on the male reader, and pivot around two key processes: 'acting' (which assumes a variety of meanings, from the theatrical performance and the sexual act, to taking action and to acting upon one's fantasies); and 'reading' (interpreting narratives, but also performative and bodily aspects of the act of reading – focus, attention, the direction and movement of the gaze across the text, gesture to and participation in actions described in the text, and so on). Through this double focus, Beckermann offers ambivalent, troubling insights into the covert intersections between reading, performing masculinity, elements of Austria's cultural propensities to violent misogyny, as well as the connections between these propensities and the violent historical realities of mid-twentieth-century Austria. Almost completely absent from all these are the material presence and the voice of woman.

Present only as a discursive construct, an object of performed activity and of fantasy, woman-as-figure nevertheless saturates the film. No woman is seen in *MUTZENBACHER*, yet the female figure is implicit in every shot and every sound. Woman is also represented – spoken of and for – by the male voices with which the film is concerned. She is thus simultaneously central yet displaced, silenced, both focaliser and narrator of all the texts recited, subject and title of the film and the narrative which it ostensibly reproduces, and yet unheard, drowned out, wholly replaced by a plurality of male voices. A surface reading of the film would suggest that it apparently explores how the female figure is constructed – imagined, narrated, fantasised – by men, as a structural absence that grounds the fantasy on which patriarchy is built. But the *absence* of woman as image or agent from the film reroutes critical attention onto what is *present* – the men and their performances. Absence becomes a form of masquerade, a cinematic sleight of hand, through which attention is deflected away from the object of discursive projection (the female body and its sexualities), onto the *male* performativity, which becomes a performance not of male versions of the feminine but of different versions of masculinity itself as it imagines itself performing femininity. The film relentlessly exposes the spectacle of these performed masculinities as fantasy, or rather an endless series of shifting, performed fantasies, a set of roles enacted in the putative enactment of imagined versions of the feminine, as the men act out in voices and gestures, tones and registers, what they imagine Josefine Mutzenbacher to be thinking and feeling.

One woman's voice, that of the director, is heard in the film, marginal to the depicted action and performances, permanently off-screen and out of sight, but nonetheless insistently present beyond the frame in her questioning and relaying of instructions to the men she films. The film thus subverts the ostensibly absolute erasure of the feminine by inserting, outside its visual field but momentarily present in the auditory field, a female voice as an agent of power, offering an ironic marginal commentary on the male performances it orchestrates. Always operating under instruction by the director's female voice, the men are disempowered at the very moment their power seems to be asserted in the act of performing their fantasies of woman. At the moment of its assertion of total power – its absolute drowning out of the possibility of an alternative (female) voice – the putative agency of male power is deconstructed by the female voice of the director, symbol of authority and agent of creativity in the film. Under the guise of exploring male constructions of the feminine, *MUTZENBACHER* thus performs a discursive deconstruction of the masculine.

This deconstruction reveals, of course, the structural frailty of each performed version of masculinity, a frailty repeatedly exposed in and by the act of performing. That which the men perform – fragments of deeply pornographic verbal material articulated from the female perspective of a fictional prostitute – seems in some cases to compromise their masculinity, and in others to exert a kind of demand for that masculinity to be reinforced, reasserted (thus, of course, exposing its weakness). Some of the male readers seem almost contrite, even vulnerable, when they stop reading, and the camera lingers on them for a few seconds. Some, disturbingly, seem visibly to be aroused by their performances. Others stare back almost aggressively, as if completing the performance without actually *becoming* that which they have performed were some kind of minor triumph. To take one of these types of performances as an example: the assumption by some men of a 'fairy-tale' narrative voice presents a perversely out-of-tune register, a parodic version of the maternal bedtime-story voice, a male version of that voice which infantilises, and thus desexualises, the (adult) woman, while simultaneously investing the female child with excessive, perverse sexuality. This dimension of the performances turns the couch into a kind of stage, on which are enacted a series of imagined relations in which subject positions are pinned by discursive *points de capiton* to a patriarchal discourse through which they are spoken. The discursive modality, furthermore, is predominantly *imperative*; Beckermann's directorial voice instructs the men to perform individually, and, in groups, to repeat lines together, just as Mutzenbacher orders her clients to perform acts on her body; the act of repetition, and the imperative of successful performance, further erode any awareness of the *content* of what is performed, so that the performance itself becomes empty of semantic force. The group of men thus perform, in their unified chanting, a semantically meaningless, decontextualised ritualised chanting which is nevertheless overdetermined by its excessive ideological content. One effect of this aspect of the film is to foreground and overdetermine what Mary Daly calls "the unacknowledged noise of omnipresent male obscenities", which, she suggests, "constitutes the 'background noise' which continually confuses and fragments [female] consciousness".[54]

Some of the most disturbing sequences in the film happen when all the men are gathered together, facing the camera in front of them, and led (by Beckermann) in a series of call-and-response routines in which sets of words or lines from the novel are shouted in unison (Figure 8.3). These passages allude ironically to the famous sequence in Leni Riefenstahl's *Triumph des Willens* (*Triumph of the Will*) (1935) (Figure 8.4) in which individual soldiers declare their places of origin before shouting in unison "*Ein Volk! Ein Führer! Ein Reich! Deutschland!*" *MUTZENBACHER* replaces the Nazi declarations of *echt* German-ness and its declarative anchoring in the imaginary geography of the *Heimat* with obscenities and misogynistic epithets locating male subjectivity in relation to the imagined sexual geography of the female body. The effect, however, is similar, generating an ideological field through sound and repetition in which a particular identity asserts its power, in the process inhibiting the possibility of other voices being heard or able to articulate

Figure 8.3 Ruth Beckermann (dir.), *MUTZENBACHER*, 2022.
© Ruth Beckermann Filmproduktion.

Figure 8.4 Leni Riefenstahl (dir.), *Triumph of the Will*, 1935.

a critical response (an extreme form of the failure of meaning to contain the full power of the voice: "Faced with the voice", Mladen Dolar writes, "words structurally fail").[55]

Echoed in this chanting is the memory articulated by Franz West nearly forty years earlier in *Return to Vienna* and depicted in that film by silent footage of gangs of Nazi thugs marching and chanting in the streets of 'Red Vienna' in the 1920s, nearly a century before *MUTZENBACHER*. In her analysis of the political uses of sound in Nazi Germany, Carolyn Birdsall uses the concept of "affirmative resonance" to describe the effects of sound "in the creation of resonant spaces within urban environments, whether through collective singing and cheering, loudspeaker technology, or in the call and response interactions between a speaker and a crowd".[56] This "affirmative resonance", described by Jean-François Augoyard and Henry Torgue as "a myth of strength symbolised by the power of sound", is the basis (Birdsall argues) of the Nazi strategy of "acoustic occupation of public life and urban space",[57] a procedure through which auditory attention and emotional responses were manipulated by the constant distraction of excessive noise to foreground specific kinds of identity while excluding the possibility of others. "Affirmative resonance" accounts for the way the collective performance of noise (for example, in orchestrated musical singing and performance, as well as apparently spontaneous outbreaks of chanting and singing like those at sporting events) becomes a form of mass identification which functions to assert one group identity as dominant.

What these passages of the film also evoke is, of course, a cultural memory of another specific crucial and traumatic moment in Austrian history in which such "acoustic resonance" effects the establishment of a novel form of Austrian national identity. In her memoir of surviving the concentration camps, Vienna-born Holocaust survivor and Professor of German Ruth Kluger (1931–2020) recalls the day of the Anschluß in Vienna:

> In March 1938 I lay in bed with a strep throat and a warm compress. Below the window men were yelling in chorus. What they were yelling can be checked out in the history books. My nanny mutters, 'If those guys lose their voices, they won't get any chamomile tea from me', as she brings me a cup. It's the first political joke I remember hearing.[58]

Kluger's "strep throat" symbolically indicates the historical silencing of her voice (and by extension those of other women), to be replaced in her narrative by "men yelling in chorus" to mark the arrival of Nazism in Austria, an assertion of active and violent masculinity over a femininity rendered silent and passive ("I lay in bed") by illness, graphically affirming the insight of Mary-Elizabeth O'Brien who, in her study of Nazism and cinema, reminds us that "The patriarchal order, and National Socialism in particular, dictate an active male and a passive female as necessary components for social order."[59] Similarly, in *MUTZENBACHER*, the combined male voices drown out any possibility of hearing a female voice, and announce instead the absolute dominance of vocalised masculinity, and, simultaneously, its alarming proximity to the sonic strategies of acoustic resonance historically deployed to assert fascistic power. Any residual masculine frailty disappears in the sheer volume of noise generated by the combined male voices as they reverberate in the confined space of the film set. Male power, *MUTZENBACHER* demonstrates, resides in part in the effect of this combined voicing, its drowning out of any other – specifically feminine – modes of expression. As Kluger recalls, women are reduced in this barrage of sound to silence or "muttering" (with its implicit pun between English and German on the role of mothering).

What is enacted – performed – in these call-and-response passages is the political message of *MUTZENBACHER*: the recognition that the frailty of each individual male voice, of each individual performance of patriarchal power, is overcome in the barrage of combined shouting, which constructs an auditory version of the *fasces* or bundle of sticks (individually weak but strong in combination) on which the ideological structure of fascism is symbolically based. In *MUTZENBACHER* Beckermann affirms the assertion of Ingeborg Bachmann in 1973 that "Fascism comes first in the relationship between a man and a woman."[60]

Missing voices, missing images

In its analysis of strategies of silencing, *MUTZENBACHER* continues through the medium of sound Beckermann's extended artistic project of interrogating the "missing images" that, excluded or erased from historical discourse (like the female voice, and like the image of the Empress Elisabeth), nevertheless return to haunt contemporary Austrian culture. As we've seen throughout this book, her oeuvre insistently examines the forms of cultural violence enacted in complicity with these repressions. Her works have addressed a series of analogous and sometimes interlinked violent historical erasures: of Austrian history by processes of repression and selective remembering, of Jewish culture and experience by the Holocaust, of contemporary migrant experience by the economic expediencies of neoliberalism, and of African-American experiences by the dominant narratives of white America. As in the case of *The Dreamed Ones*, clear connections can be made between *MUTZENBACHER* and earlier films like *East of War* and *A Fleeting Passage to the Orient* (particularly in the latter's exploration of how Sisi's image has been invested with a mass-cultural afterlife that expressly contradicts, and thus erases and silences, her actual historical presence and voice). Common to all these texts is an underlying concern with documenting absence, omission, silence, the apparent erasure of that which nevertheless persists beyond the frame, demanding constant cultural repression.

As Beckermann states in an interview about *Those Who Go Those Who Stay*:

> One thing that film is particularly good at is showing the world through an 'objective' lens and presenting pictures we would otherwise not see, because we're distracted. [...] What's the point of making films when we're not allowed to film in the places where something is happening? It brings you up against the limits of the documentary film, and of observation in general. Lampedusa is just one example. It is necessary to make the 'hors-champ' [off-screen] much more powerfully visible. Maybe it would be a good idea to make a film about everything that you can't film.[61]

The most direct expression of this concern with the processes of historical erasure and their integral position in specifically Austrian history is perhaps Beckermann's installation *The Missing Image* (2015), which displayed in the public space of Vienna's Albertinaplatz a fragment of archive silent film footage from March 1938 of Jewish people forced by the newly arrived Nazis to scrub the city streets of anti-Nazi graffiti while a crowd of standing Viennese spectators, some wearing swastika armbands, look on, some smiling and laughing[62] (Figure 8.5). *The Missing Image* was an interventional installation, responding correctively to the city memorial erected in 1988 (after much political controversy) in the Albertinaplatz, the *Mahnmal gegen Krieg und Faschismus* (*Monument against War and Fascism*) by Alfred Hrdlicka (1928–2009). This multi-part work incorporates a statue of an orthodox Jewish man prostrate on the ground, holding a scrubbing brush, surrounded by mural elements depicting, among other features, Orpheus on his journey from the Underworld. It has caused much public debate and controversy; the evocation of the Orphic prohibition against looking back seems odd in the context of a memorial to historical events, while the figure of the Jewish man is of sufficiently small scale that tourists and passing shoppers were prone to using him as a footrest to tie their laces, or as a seat, before the city authorities intervened by encasing him in barbed wire in an effort to prevent such abuses, adding in doing so a further bizarrely inappropriate set of connotations to the monument.[63]

Absent from Hrdlicka's monument was any representation of the crowd of laughing Viennese onlookers. The erasure of their presence at and evident complicity in the memorialised Nazi humiliation of Vienna's Jews is the motivation for Beckermann's installation,

Figure 8.5 Ruth Beckermann, *The Missing Image*, 2015.

in which the Viennese crowd constitutes the "missing image" of Austrian history, the evidence of the reality of the nation's repressed past, which historian Matti Bunzl describes in his discussion of the history and politics of Hrdlicka's monument:

> In Vienna, the Anschluss was immediately followed by events resembling pogroms: public humiliation, abuse, beatings, murders and robberies on a mass scale – all perpetrated predominantly by the

civilian population. Especially notorious were the scrubbing-squads, where Jews were forced to clean the streets of Vienna with brushes and toothbrushes to the loud cheers of the city's inhabitants.[64]

Beckermann projected the silent film footage, slowed down, onto large screens in the Albertinaplatz while a sound-composition by Viennese composer Olga Neuwirth (b. 1968) was played from surrounding loudspeakers. 'Performing' here is multiple; the Jewish streetcleaners were forced to perform humiliating actions while the crowd, watching on, played to the camera in fascist assertions of power; the contemporary audience of passers-by was furthermore implicated by the installation into a strangely voyeuristic and performatively repetitive relation to the slowed-down historical image and the eerie amplified music. In the context of an open public space the arrhythmic washes and gentle shifts of Neuwirth's atonal soundscape (which extends the composer's engagement with the erasure of Austria's Jewish history, expressed, for example, in her soundtrack to the rediscovered Hugo Bettauer film *Die Stadt ohne Juden* [*City without Jews*, 1924]), added a disturbing and alienating dimension to the installation.[65] One effect of *The Missing Image* when encountered *in situ* was that the Viennese passer-by might experience momentarily a version of the disorienting "hostipitality" of the city, its generation of the experience of 'unbelonging', which has, in a multitude of ways, been the overriding and insistent theme of Beckermann's works.

Beckermann's oeuvre offers a complex multimedia meditation on how to represent such attempted historical erasures and repressions in ways that re-inscribe them into public consciousness and, in so doing, to draw attention to the omissions and silences that have characterised public discourse around Austrian history since the 1930s. From her early political documentaries onwards Beckermann's works have insistently contested the strategies, processes and devices by which traumatic but real historical presences and events have been transformed into officially 'forgotten' narratives and 'missing' images, markers of a historical catastrophe demanding constant vigilant attention and redress. Each work discussed in this book provides an element of this necessary attention, offering potential routes of passage, in its efforts to redress the injustices of history and at least attempt to compensate for, if not fully alleviate, the resulting condition of unbelonging. In

Unbelonging Beckermann describes unbelonging as an enduring effect of the Austrian evasion of historical guilt and its constant demand to render experience as unreal, whether in the "perfect derealisation" ("der perfekten Irrealisierung")[66] of his own history performed by Kurt Waldheim or the wider rendering "unreal" of the years of Nazi occupation, the "years between" 1938 and 1945 ("die Irrealisierung des Dazwischen"), by the whole nation.[67] As our discussions of her works have demonstrated, Beckermann's oeuvre insists on facing, and undoing, this denial, and instead making the "derealised" past real again, exposing to public and critical view the repressed histories that define the modern Austrian nation.

Notes

1 Adrienne Rich, "It Is the Lesbian in us", *Sinister Wisdom* Vol. 3 (1977), 6–9: 6.

2 Thirza Wakefield, " 'A Lovers' Discourse' – Interview with Ruth Beckermann", *Sight and Sound* Vol. 27 No. 1 (January 2017), 9.

3 Austrian cinematic engagements with Bachmann include Werner Schroeter's 1991 adaptation of her 1971 novel *Malina* (with Isabelle Huppert as Bachmann and a script adapted by Elfriede Jelinek) and Margerethe von Trotta's *Ingeborg Bachmann: Reise in die Wüste* (2023), which focusses on Bachmann's affair with Swiss author Max Frisch.

4 The film is titled in capitals, unlike the book.

5 Peter Szondi, " 'Engführung': An Essay on the Poetry of Paul Celan" (trans. David Caldwell and S. Esh), *boundary 2* 11.3 (1983), 231–64: 232.

6 Roland Barthes, epigram to section titled "No Answer – *mutisme / silence*", *A Lover's Discourse: Fragments* (trans. Richard Howard) (New York: Farrar, Straus and Giroux, 1978), p. 167.

7 Author of *Wer war Ingeborg Bachmann? Eine Biographie in Bruchstücken* (Frankfurt am Main: S. Fischer, 2017).

8 Ingeborg Bachmann and Paul Celan, *Herzzeit – Briefwechsel* (ed. Bertrand Badiou, Hans Höller, Andrea Stoll, and Barbara Wiedemann) (Berlin: Suhrkamp, 2008); Ingeborg Bachmann and Paul Celan, *Correspondence* (trans. Wieland Hoban) (London: Seagull Books, 2019). Both volumes also contain letters between Celan and Max Frisch, and Bachmann and Gisèle Celan-Lestrange.

9 Celan is a recurrent figure in Beckermann's writings; for example, she discusses his post-war relationship with Friedrich Torberg in *Unzugehörig*. See pp. 112–3.

10 Alice James, "Das Briefgeheimnis: Ingeborg Bachmann and Paul Celan's Poetics of Correspondence" (unpublished MA Thesis, Durham University, 2013), p. 7.

11 Barbara Wiedemann and Bertrand Badiou, "Commentary: 'Let Us Find the Words' – The Correspondence of Ingeborg Bachmann and Paul Celan", in *Ingeborg Bachmann – Paul Celan: Correspondence* (trans. Wieland Hoban, ed. Bertrand Badiou, Hans Höller, Andrea Stoll and Barbara Wiedemann) (London: Seagull Books, 2019), pp. 379, 381.

12 Beckermann, "This Love Has the Character of a Dream" (interview with Karin Schiefer), January 2016 (press release for *Die Geträumten*), n.p.

13 Wakefield, "A Lovers' Discourse", 9.

14 See, for example, on Celan: Jacques Derrida, *Sovereignties in Question: The Poetics of Paul Celan* (ed. Thomas Dutoit and Outi Pasanen) (New York: Fordham University Press, 2005), esp. Ch. 4, "Majesties", pp. 108–34); and, on Bachmann, Lilian Friedberg, ' "A Time Yet to Come …": Translation and Historical Representation in Ingeborg Bachmann's Poem "Night Flight / Nachtflug"', *The German Quarterly* Vol. 74 No. 2 (2001), 148–163.

15 See Marko Pajević, "Celan's Correspondence and Correspondence with Celan. Transfer Processes of Life", in Michael Eskin, Karen Leeder and Marko Pajević (eds), *Paul Celan Today* (*Companions to Contemporary German Culture* Vol. 10) (Berlin: De Gruyter, 2021), pp. 299–303.

16 Letter 19, *Correspondence*, p. 37.

17 See Letter 26, *Correspondence*, pp. 52–3.

18 Naficy, *An Accented Cinema*, p. 103.

19 Rascaroli, *What the Essay Film Thinks*, p. 146.

20 Barthes, *A Lover's Discourse*, p. 158. See Wakefield, "A Lover's Discourse"; and Wolfgang Hottner, "Einander-Schreiben verfilmen. "Die Geträumten"–Überlegungen zu Ruth Beckermanns Verfilmung des Briefwechsels von Ingeborg Bachmann und Paul Celan", *Zeitschrift für Germanistik*, Neue Folge Vol. XXX No. 3 (2020), 662–4: 662.

21 Henri Matisse, *Peintures 1939–46* (with an Introduction by André Lejard) (Paris: Les Éditions du Chene, 1946).

22 See, for example, Michèle C. Cone, *Artists under Vichy* (Princeton: Princeton University Press, 1992), pp. 50–5: "Overall", Cone writes, "it seems to me that Matisse's 'life as usual' attitude [at this time]

reflected a belief imbedded in the collective psyche of the French bourgeoisie concerning the apolitical nature of art and the political naïveté of artists" (p. 52).

23 John Felstiner, *Paul Celan: Poet, Survivor, Jew* (New Haven: Yale University Press, 1995), pp. 58–9, 65–6. In Siegfried Mandel's *Group 47: The Reflected Intellect* (Carbondale, IL: Southern Illinois University Press, 1973), Bachmann and Celan are discussed consecutively (see Chapter 3: Poetry – Acts of Memory and Provocation", pp. 84–143).

24 Karl Ivan Solibakke, review of Áine McMurtry, *Crisis and Form in the Later Writing of Ingeborg Bachmann*, *Journal of Austrian Studies* Vol. 46. No. 4 (2013), 129–31: 130.

25 Charlotte Ryland, *Paul Celan's Encounters with Surrealism: Trauma, Translation, and Shared Poetic Space* (Abingdon: Legenda-MHRA/ Routledge, 2010).

26 Letter 47, *Correspondence*, pp. 92–3. The *Correspondence* translation, on which the English subtitling of Beckermann's film draws, is: "Heart-time, / the dreamt ones stand for / the midnight numeral."

27 Felstiner, *Selected Poems and Prose of Paul Celan*, p. 111.

28 Letters 45, 46, 50, *Correspondence*, pp. 87–91, 96–7. "Schuttkahn II" is a variant of "Schuttkahn", later published in Celan's collection *Sprachgitter* (Berlin: Fischer, 1959).

29 Áine McMurtry, *Crisis and Form in the Later Writing of Ingeborg Bachmann: An Aesthetic Examination of the Poetic Drafts of the 1960s* (London: MHRA, 2012), p. 31.

30 Felstiner, "Preface" to *Selected Poems and Prose of Paul Celan*, p. xiii.

31 Andréa Lauterwein, *Anselm Kiefer, Paul Celan: Myth, Mourning and Memory* (London: Thames and Hudson, 2007), p. 197.

32 *Correspondence*, pp. 93, 184; Wiedemann and Badiou, "Commentary", p. 402.

33 *Correspondence*, pp. 102–3.

34 *Correspondence*, Letter 52, p. 98. Pajević describes the effect of this intercutting as creating "an echo chamber of dreams". Pajević, "Celan's Correspondence and Correspondence with Celan", p. 302.

35 Alastair Williams, "Voices of the Other: Wolfgang Rihm's *Die Eroberung von Mexico*", *Journal of the Royal Musical Association* Vol. 129 No. 2 (2004), 240–71: 249.

36 Elias Canetti, *Crowds and Power* (trans. Carol Stewart) (Harmondsworth: Penguin, 1973), pp. 458, 460.

37 Canetti, *Crowds and Power*, p. 113.

38 Michael Chion, *The Voice in Cinema* (ed. and trans. Claudia Gorbman) (New York: Columbia University Press, 1999), p. 5.

39 "Shouting along is the order of the day". Olga Neuwirth, *Bählamms Fest: Ein venezianisches Arbeitsjournal* (Vienna: Droschl, 2003), p. 107.

40 Work and text are reproduced in Renate Bertlmann, *Discordo Ergo Sum* (Vienna: Verlag für modern Kunst, 2019), pp. 114–17.

41 See Bertlmann, *Discordo Ergo Sum: Der Patronengürtel* (1976) (pp. 130–1), *Prega per noi (Bitte für uns)* (*Pray for Us – 7 Kardinäle* (7 Cardinals) (1982) and its accompanying text *Litane* (*Litany*) (pp. 118–21); and *Contemplatio* (1981) (pp. 124–5).

42 Peter Gorsen, "Remaining Serious Is Successful Repression", in Bertlmann, *Discordo Ergo Sum*, p. 114.

43 Robin Ann Sheets, "Pornography, Fairy Tales, and Feminism: Angela Carter's 'The Bloody Chamber' ", *Journal of the History of Sexuality* Vol. 1 No. 4 (1991), 633–57: 642.

44 Clemens Ruthner, "The Back Side of Fin-de-Siècle Vienna: The Infamously Infantile Sexuality of Josefine Mutzenbacher", in Ruthner and Raleigh Whitinger (eds), *Contested Passions: Sexuality, Eroticism and Gender in Modern Austrian Literature and Culture* (New York: Peter Lang, 2011), pp. 92–104, p. 101.

45 Canetti, *The Torch in my Ear*, p. 250.

46 "Ruth Beckermann introduces her film *Mutzenbacher*", *Notebook*, Column 16, February 2023, at https://mubi.com/en/notebook/posts/ruth-beckermann-introduces-her-film-mutzenbacher (accessed 8 November 2023).

47 J. Hoberman, "The Talking Cure: On Ruth Beckerman's *Mutzenbacher*", *LA Review of Books*, 10 January 2023. At https://lareviewofbooks.org/article/the-talking-cure-on-ruth-beckermanns-mutzenbacher (accessed 17 November 2023).

48 Andrea Dworkin, *Pornography: Men Possessing Women* (New York: Plume/Penguin, 1989), p. 34.

49 See Désirée Prosquill, "Pepi auf der Couch: Die Mutzenbacher und Freuds Drei Abhandlungen", in Ruthner, Clemens, Matthias Schmidt and Carolin Schmieding (eds), *Die Mutzenbacher: Lektüren und Kontexte eines Skandalromans* (Vienna: Sonderzahl, 2019), pp. 45–60.

50 Nathan Kravis, *On the Couch: A Repressed History of the Analytic Couch from Plato to Freud* (Cambridge, MA: MIT Press, 2017), p. 127.

51 Jacques Lacan, *Seminar Book III, 1955–56: The Psychoses* (ed. Jacques-Alain Miller, trans. Russell Grigg) (New York: Norton, 1997), pp. 258–71.

52 Mary Daly, *Gyn/Ecology: The Metaethics of Radical Feminism* (London: The Women's Press, 1979), p. 88.

53 Chion, *The Voice in Cinema*, p. 79.

54 Daly, *Gyn/Ecology*, pp. 323–4.

55 Mladen Dolar, *A Voice and Nothing More* (Cambridge, MA: MIT Press, 2006), p. 13.

56 Carolyn Birdsall, *Nazi Soundscapes: Sound Technology and Urban Space in Germany, 1933–1945* (Amsterdam: Amsterdam University Press, 2012), p. 28.

57 Cited in Birdsall, *Nazi Soundscapes*, p. 32.

58 Kluger, *Landscapes of Memory*, p. 22.

59 Mary-Elizabeth O'Brien, *Nazi Cinema as Enchantment: The Politics of Entertainment in the Third Reich* (New York: Camden House, 2004), p. 190.

60 "Der Faschismus ist das erste in der Beziehung zwischen einem Mann und einer Frau". Ingeborg Bachmann, *Wir müssen wahre Sätze finden – Gespräche und Interviews* (Munich: Piper, 1985), p. 144.

61 Schiefer, "Ruth Beckermann on Her Essay on Escape and Volatility, *Those Who Go Those Who Stay*".

62 A short documentary film on this installation can be seen at www.youtube.com/watch?v=fbHEEjQVqOQ (accessed 9 November 2023).

63 For a discussion of the Hrdlicka monument see Allmer, *The Traumatic Surreal*, pp. 137–40.

64 Matti Bunzl, "On the Politics and Semantics of Austrian Memory: Vienna's Monument against War and Fascism", *History and Memory* Vol. 7 No. 2 (1995), 7–40: 11.

65 For a discussion of these compositions by Neuwirth see Stefan Drees, "Erinnern als Verstehen: Zu einer grundlegenden Konstante von Olga Neuwirths Komponieren", in Ulrich Tadday (ed.), *Musik-Konzepte* 200/201 (IV/2023), 7–33: 21–6.

66 Beckermann, *Unzugehörig*, p. 29.

67 Beckermann, *Unzugehörig*, p. 27.

Bibliography

Films and installations by Ruth Beckermann

Asterisked films are available in *Ruth Beckermann Film Collection* (Vienna: Hoanzl // Ruth Beckermann Film Production, 2007).

Films

Arena Besetzt / Arena Squatted (Austria, 1977), Videogruppe Arena (Ruth Beckermann, Josef Aichholzer, Franz Grafl), 77 min, b/w.
Auf amol a Streik: Semperit Traiskirchen 17.4–11.5.1978 / Suddenly, a Strike (Austria, 1978, with Josef Aichholzer), 24 min, colour.
Der Hammer steht auf der Wies'n da draußen: Wie die VEW-Arbeiter um ihre Arbeitsplätze kämpfen / The Steel Hammer out There on the Grass (Austria, 1981, with Josef Aichholzer and Michael Stejskal), 40 min, colour.
Wien Retour: Franz West 1924–1934 / Return to Vienna (Austria, 1984), 95 min, colour and b/w.
Der Igel – Widerstand im Salzkammergut / The Hedgehog (Austria, 1986), 34min, colour; short made in collaboration with students at Salzburg University. *Die papierene Brücke / Paper Bridge* (Austria, 1987), 95 min, colour and b/w.
Nach Jerusalem / Towards Jerusalem (Austria, 1991), 87 min, colour.
Jenseits des Krieges / East of War (Austria, 1996), 117 min, colour.
Ein flüchtiger Zug nach dem Orient / A Fleeting Passage to the Orient (Austria, 1999), 82 min, colour.
homemad(e) (Austria, 2001), 85 min, colour.
Zorros Bar Mitzvah / Zorro's Bar Mitzvah (Austria, 2006), 90 min, colour.
Mozart Enigma (Austria, 2006), 1 min, colour, shown at international festivals through the Mozart anniversary celebrations.
American Passages (Austria, 2011), 120 min, colour.
Jackson/Marker 4am (Austria, 2012), 3.35 min, colour.
Those Who Go Those Who Stay (Austria, 2013), 75min, colour.

Die Geträumten / The Dreamed Ones (Austria, 2016), 89 min, colour.
Waldheims Waltzer / The Waldheim Waltz (Austria, 2018), 93 min, colour
and b/w.
MUTZENBACHER (Austria, 2022), 100 min, colour.

Installations/exhibitions

europaMemoria (29 August–28 September 2003), exhibition / installation,
Graz, Austria (European Capital of Culture).
Leben! Juden in Wien nach 1945 (19 March–22 June 2008), exhibition of
photographs by Margit Dobronyi, Jewish Museum, Vienna.
The Missing Image (12 March–12 November 2015), multi-channel video-
installation, Albertinaplatz, Vienna.
Joyful Joyce (8–28 August 2019), multi-channel video-installation, Salzburg
Festival.

Other films

Chantal Akerman, *News from Home* (1976).
Woody Allen, *Zelig* (1983).
Theodoros Angelopoulos, *Ulysses' Gaze* (1985).
Axel Corti, *Wohin und zurück – Teil 1: An uns glaubt Gott nicht mehr –
Ferry oder Wie es war* (1982); *Wohin und zurück – Teil 2: Santa Fé*
(1986); *Wohin und zurück – Teil 3: Welcome in Vienna* (1986).
Dan Curtis, *War and Remembrance* (mini-series, Disney / ABC Domestic
Television), 1988. First broadcast November 1988–May 1989.
Samuel Fuller, *The Big Red One* (1980).
Marie Kreutzer, *Corsage* (2022).
Claude Lanzmann, *Shoah* (1985).
Ernst Marischka, *Sisi* (1955); *Sisi: Die junge Kaiserin* (*Sisi: The Young
Empress*) (1956); *Schicksalsjahre einer Kaiserin* (*The Fateful Years of
an Empress*) (1957).
Chris Marker, *Description d'un combat* (*Description of a Struggle*) (1960).
Paul Martin, *Praterbuben* (*Prater Boys*) (1946).
Max Ophuls, *Letter from an Unknown Woman* (1948).
Carol Reed, *The Third Man* (1949).
Laurence Rees, *Auschwitz: the Nazis and the 'Final Solution'* (2005).
Christian Rouaud, *Les LIP – l'imagination au pouvoir* (2007).
Ernst Schmidt Jr., *P.R.A.T.E.R.* (1963–6).
Willy Schmidt-Gentner, *Prater* (1936).
Werner Schroeter, *Malina* (1991).
Susan Sontag, *Promised Lands* (1974).
Wolfgang Staudte, *Die Mörder sind unter uns* (1946).
Lukas Stepanik, *Gebürtig*, 2009.
Michał Waszyński, *The Dybbuk*, 1937.

Emil Weiss and Samuel Fuller, *Falkenau, The Impossible* (1988).
Margarethe von Trotta, *Ingeborg Bachmann: Reise in die Wüste* (2023).
Hans Wolff, *Im Prater blüh'n wieder die Bäume* (1958).
Bulgarian State Television Female Choir, *Les mystères des voix bulgares* Vol. 1, Philips 1975/4AD CD (1986).

Other media

Chris Marker, script of *Description of a Struggle*, at www.markertext.com/description_of_a_struggle.htm (accessed 21 March 2023).
Egyptian and Near Eastern Collection: History of the Collection, Kunsthistorisches Museum Wien, at www.khm.at/en/visit/collections/egyptian-and-near-eastern-collection/history-of-the-collection/ (accessed 4 July 2023).
The Director's Cut: Interview with Ruth Beckermann, University of Aberdeen (25 May 2019), at https://youtu.be/W9DbITD_xkw (accessed 28 May 2023).
The Missing Image (short documentary), at www.youtube.com/watch?v=fbHEEjQVqOQ (accessed 9 November 2023).
World Fairs and International Expos, at https://en.worldfairs.info/expopavillondetails.php?expo_id=4&pavillon_id=1577 (accessed 4 July 2023).

Print

Abul-Magd, Zeinab, *Imagined Empires: A History of Revolt in Egypt* (Berkeley, CA: University of California Press, 2013).
Adorno, Theodor W., *Negative Dialectics* (trans. E. B. Ashton) (London: Routledge and Kegan Paul, 1973).
Akomfrah, John, "Memory and the Morphologies of Difference", in Scotini and Galasso (eds), *Politics of Memory: Documentary and Archive*, pp. 23–36.
Albright, Daniel, *Untwisting the Serpent: Modernism in Music, Literature, and Other Arts* (Chicago, IL: University of Chicago Press, 2000).
Alexander, Phil, *Sounding Jewish in Berlin: Klezmer Music and the Contemporary City* (Oxford: Oxford University Press, 2021).
Allmer, Patricia, *The Traumatic Surreal: Germanophone Women Artists and Surrealism after the Second World War* (Manchester: Manchester University Press, 2022).
Alter, Nora M., *Chris Marker* (Urbana, IL: University of Illinois Press, 2006).
Alter, Nora M. and Timothy Corrigan (eds), *Essays on the Essay Film* (New York: Columbia University Press, 2017).
Améry, Jean, *Jenseits von Schuld und Sühne: Bewältigungsversuche eines Überwältigten* (Munich: Szczesny, 1966).
Améry, Jean, *At the Mind's Limits* (trans. Sidney Rosenfeld and Stella P. Rosenfeld) (London: Granta, 1999).

Amichai, Yehuda, *A Life of Poetry 1948–1994* (trans. Benjamin and Barbara Harshav) (New York: HarperCollins, 1995).

Anderson, Norman. D., *Ferris Wheels – An Illustrated History* (Bowling Green, OH: Bowling Green State University Press, 1992).

Anon, "Ein blutiger Sonntag im Burgenland", *Kronen Zeitung*, 31 January 1927, p. 1.

Anthony, Elizabeth, *The Compromise of Return: Viennese Jews after the Holocaust* (Princeton, NJ: Princeton University Press, 2021).

Art, David, *The Politics of the Nazi Past in Germany and Austria* (Cambridge: Cambridge University Press, 2010).

Aschheim, Steven E. and Vivian Liska (eds), *The German-Jewish Experience Revisited: Contested Interpretations and Conflicting Perceptions* (Berlin and Jerusalem: Leo Baeck Institute / DeGruyter, 2015).

Ashby, Charlotte, *Austrian and Habsburg Studies 16: The Viennese Café and Fin-de-Siècle Culture* (New York: Berghahn, 2016).

Ashkenazi, Ofer, "The Jewish Places of Weimar Cinema: Reconsidering Karl Grune's *The Street*", in Aschheim and Liska (eds), *The German-Jewish Experience Revisited: Contested Interpretations and Conflicting Perceptions*, pp. 135–54.

Assmann, Jan, *Moses the Egyptian: The Memory of Egypt in Western Monotheism* (Cambridge, MA: Harvard University Press, 1997).

Aubry-Morici, Marine, "The Essayfication of Narrative Forms in the 20th Century: A Comparative Study", in Fusillo, Massimo et al. (eds), *Thinking Narratively – Between Novel-Essay and Narrative Essay*, pp. 101–12.

Augé, Marc, *Non-Places: Introduction to an Anthropology of Supermodernity* (trans. John Howe) (London: Verso, 1995).

Aurelius, Marcus, *The Meditations of the Emperor Marcus Aurelius Antoninus* (ed. James Moore and Michael Silverthorne, trans. Francis Hutchinson and James Moore) (Indianapolis, IN: Liberty Fund, 2008).

Bachmann, Ingeborg, *Werke 1* (ed. Christine Koschel, Inge von Weidenbaum and Clemens Münster) (Munich: Piper, 1978).

Bachmann, Ingeborg, *Wir müssen wahre Sätze finden: Gespräche und Interviews* (ed. Christine Kaschel and Inge von Weidenbaum, trans. Marjorie Perloff) (Munich: Piper, 1991).

Bachmann, Ingeborg, Interview with Joseph-Hermann Sauter, 15 September 1965, in *Wir müssen wahre Sätze finden: Gespräche und Interviews*, pp. 59–63.

Bachmann, Ingeborg, and Paul Celan, *Herzzeit – Briefwechsel* (ed. Bertrand Badiou, Hans Höller, Andrea Stoll, and Barbara Wiedemann) (Berlin: Suhrkamp, 2008).

Bachmann, Ingeborg, and Paul Celan, *Correspondence* (ed. Bertrand Badiou, Hans Höller, Andrea Stoll, and Barbara Wiedemann, trans. Wieland Hoban) (London: Seagull Books, 2019).

Baker, Julia K. and Imelda Rohrbacher, " 'E/motion Pictures': Conversations with Austrian Documentary Filmmakers Mirjam Unger and Ruth Beckermann", *Women in German Yearbook* Vol. 25 (2009), 234–51.

Barthes, Roland, *Image – Music – Text* (trans. Stephen Heath) (London: Fontana 1977).

Barthes, Roland, *A Lover's Discourse: Fragments* (trans. Richard Howard) (New York: Farrar, Straus and Giroux, 1978).

Barthes, Roland, *Camera Lucida* (trans. Richard Howard) (London: Vintage, 2000).

Baudelaire, Charles, *The Painter of Modern Life and Other Essays* (ed. and trans. Jonathan Mayne) (New York: Phaidon, 1964).

Baudrillard, Jean, *America* (trans. Chris Turner) (London: Verso, 1988).

Beckermann, Ruth (ed.), *Die Mazzesinsel: Juden in der Wiener Leopoldstadt 1918–1938* (Vienna and Munich: Löcker, 1984).

Beckermann, Ruth, "Erdbeeren in Czernowitz", in Christoph Ransmayr, ed. *Im blinden Winkel: Nachrichten aus Mitteleuropa* (Frankfurt am Main: Fischer, 1987).

Beckermann, Ruth, "Beyond the Bridges" (trans. Dagmar C. G. Lorenz), in Lorenz and Gabriele Weinberger (eds), *Insiders and Outsiders: Jewish and Gentile Culture in Germany and Austria*, pp. 301–7.

Beckermann, Ruth, "Jean Améry and Austria" (trans. Dagmar C. G. Lorenz), in Lorenz and Gabriele Weinberger (eds), *Insiders and Outsiders: Jewish and Gentile Culture in Germany and Austria*, pp. 73–86.

Beckermann, Ruth, "Elisabeth – Sisi – Romy Schneider", in Beckermann and Blümlinger (eds), *Ohne Untertitel: Fragmente einer Geschichte des österreichischen Kinos*, pp. 305–21.

Beckermann, Ruth, *Jenseits des Krieges: Ehemalige Wehrmachtssoldaten erinnern sich* (Vienna: Döcker, 1998).

Beckermann, Ruth, "We all direct our own memories" (interview with Stefan Grissmemann), in Ruth Beckermann and Stefan Grissemann (eds), *europaMemoria* (Vienna: Czernin, 2003).

Beckermann, Ruth, *Unzugehörig: Österreicher und Juden nach 1945* (Vienna: Löcker, 2005).

Beckermann, Ruth, "Commentary" to *A Fleeting Passage to the Orient*, in Lendl (ed.), *Film Collection: Texte/Texts/Textes*, pp. 104–14.

Beckermann, Ruth, "*East of War*: Shooting Journal, October to November 1995", in Lendl (ed.), *Film Collection: Texte/Texts/Textes*, pp. 93–103.

Beckermann, Ruth, "Interview with Bert Rebhandl", 9 August 2007, *Ruth Beckermann Film Collection* (Vienna: Hoanzl / Ruth Beckermann Film Production, 2007).

Beckermann, Ruth, "Das Leben packen: zum Fotoarchiv der Margit Dobronyi", in Beckermann (ed.), *Leben! Juden in Wien nach 1945* (exh. cat.) (Vienna: Mandelbaum, 2008), pp. 7–16.

Beckermann, Ruth (ed.), *Leben! Juden in Wien nach 1945* (exh. cat.) (Vienna: Mandelbaum, 2008).

Beckermann, Ruth, "Entretien avec Ruth Beckermann, *American Passages*", *Journal du réel* No. 7 (31 March 2011, n.p. 2011), at www.ruthbeckermann.com/files/uploads/44/03-journaldurelno7.pdf (accessed 27 September 2023).

Beckermann, Ruth, "*American Passages*: Auszüge aus dem Arbeitsbuch", in Horwath and Omasta (eds), *Ruth Beckermann*, pp. 96–100.

Beckermann, Ruth, "Growing up Jewish in Austria: A Personal Testimony" (trans. Adrian Sewell) *Jewish Culture and History* Vol. 14 Nos. 2–3 (2013), 165–70.

Beckermann, Ruth, "This Love Has the Character of a Dream" (interview with Karin Schiefer), January 2016 (press release for *Die Geträumten*), n.p.

Beckermann, Ruth, "In Praise of Detours", in Therese Henningsen and Juliet Joffé (eds), *Strangers Within: Documentary as Encounter* (London: Prototype, 2022), pp. 37–42.

Beckermann, Ruth, "Ruth Beckermann introduces her film *Mutzenbacher*", *Notebook*, Column 16, February 2023, at https://mubi.com/en/notebook/posts/ruth-beckermann-introduces-her-film-mutzenbacher (accessed 8 November 2023).

Beckermann, Ruth and Christa Blümlinger (eds), *Ohne Untertitel: Fragmente einer Geschichte des österreichischen Kinos* (Vienna: Sonderzahl, 1996).

Beckermann, Ruth and Stefan Grissemann (eds), *europaMemoria* (Vienna: Czernin, 2003).

Beckermann, Ruth and Stefan Grissemann, "We all Direct Our Own Memories: Interview", in Beckermann and Grissemann (eds), *europaMemoria*, pp. 20–2.

Beckermann, Ruth with Alexander Horwath and Michael Omasta, "Cinema Should also Be about the Before, the After, and Everything in Between", in Kondor and Loebenstein (eds), *Ruth Beckermann*, pp. 15–43.

Bellamy, Will, "*lost clothes* by Elfriede Gerstl, translated from the German with an Introduction and a Translator's Note" (unpublished MA thesis, Wesleyan University, 2019).

Beller, Steven, *A Concise History of Austria* (Cambridge: Cambridge University Press, 2006).

Benjamin, Walter, "Little History of Photography" (1931), in Benjamin, *Selected Writings* Volume 2 Part 2, pp. 507–30.

Benjamin, Walter, *Selected Writings* Volume 2 Part 2 (1931–1934) (ed. Michael W. Jennings, Howard Eiland, and Gary Smith; trans. Rodney Livingstone and others) (Cambridge, MA: Belknap Press of Harvard University Press, 1999).

Benjamin, Walter, *The Arcades Project* (trans. Howard Eiland and Kevin McLaughlin) (Cambridge, MA: Belknap Press of Harvard University Press, 2002).

Benjamin, Walter, *Selected Writings* Volume 4 (1938–1940) (ed. Howard Eiland and Michael Jennings) (Cambridge, MA: Belknap Press of Harvard University Press, 2003).

Bennett, Edna, "Black and White Are the Colours of Robert Frank", *Aperture* Vol. 9 No. 1 (1961), 20–2.

Bergstein, Mary, "Freud's Uncanny Egypt: Prolegomena", *American Imago* Vol. 66 No. 2 (2009), 185–210.

Bernard, Anna, *Rhetorics of Belonging: Nation, Narration, and Israel/Palestine* (Liverpool: Liverpool University Press, 2013).

Bernasconi, Robert, "On Deconstructing Nostalgia for Community within the West: The Debate between Nancy and Blanchot", *Research in Phenomenology* 23 (1993), 3–21.

Bernd, Rudolf, *Ruth Beckermann und das Sichtbarmachen des Verschwindens: Der Beitrag der Autorin und Filmemacherin zur Medien- und Kommunikationsgeschichte in den Jahren 1978–2008* (unpublished MPhil thesis, University of Vienna, 2008).

Bertlmann, Renate, *Discordo Ergo Sum* (Vienna: Verlag für moderne Kunst, 2019).

Bey, Hakim, *TAZ – Temporary Autonomous Zone, Ontological Anarchy, Poetic Terrorism* (New York: Autonomedia, 1991).

Bey, Hakim, "Permanent TAZs", *Talklingmail* Vol. 5 (Winter 1994), at http://dreamtimevillage.org/articles/permanent_taz.html (accessed 26 January 2023).

Biemann, Ursula, "Performing Borders: Transnational Video", in Nora M. Alter and Timothy Corrigan (eds), *Essays on the Essay Film* (New York: Columbia University Press, 2017), pp. 261–8.

Billiani, Francesca, *Fascist Modernism in Italy: Arts and Regimes* (London: Bloomsbury Academic, 2021).

Binder, Otto, *Wien – Retour: Bericht an die Nachkommen Salzburg – Buchenwald – Stockholm* (Köln: Bohlau, 1997).

Birdsall, Carolyn, *Nazi Soundscapes: Sound Technology and Urban Space in Germany, 1933–1945* (Amsterdam: Amsterdam University Press, 2012).

Bischoff, Günter and Anton Pelinka (eds), *Austrian Historical Memory and National Identity* (*Contemporary Austrian Studies* Vol. 5) (New Brunswick: Transaction Publishers, 1997).

Bischoff, Günter, Anton Pelinka, Fritz Plasser and Alexander Smith (eds), *Global Austria – Austria's Place in Europe and the World* (*Contemporary Austrian Studies* Vol. 20) (New Brunswick: Transaction Publishers, 2011).

Bistoen, Gregory, Stijn Vanheule and Stef Craps, "Nachträglichkeit: A Freudian perspective on delayed traumatic reactions", *Theory and Psychology* Vol. 24 No. 5 (2014), 668–87.

Blümlinger, Christa, "Im Gespräch mit Ruth Beckermann", 11 January 1991. Promotional flier, *21 Internationales Forum des jungen Films 26 / 41 Internationale Filmfestspiele Berlin* (Berlin, 1991), n.p.

Blümlinger, Christa, "Meanderings of an Austrian Traveller", in Lendl (ed.), *Film Collection – Texte/Texts/Textes*, pp. 71–6.

Boll, Bernd, Hannes Heer, Walter Manoschek, Hans Safrian, and Christian Reuther (eds), *Vernichtungskrieg: Verbrechen der Wehrmacht 1941 bis 1944* (Hamburg: Hamburger Institut für Sozialforschung, 1996).

Boltanski, Christian, *Reconstitution* (exh. cat.) (London: Whitechapel Gallery, 1990).

Boué, Caroline, "L'identité en marche dans *Route One USA* de Robert Kramer (1989)", *Tumultes* no. 10 (April 1998), 241–57.

Bourdieu, Pierre, *Photography: A Middle-brow Art* (trans. Shaun Whiteside) (Oxford: Polity, 1990).

Boyarin, Daniel and Jonathan Boyarin, *Powers of Diaspora: Two Essays on the Relevance of Jewish Culture* (Minneapolis, MN: University of Minnesota Press, 2002).

Boyarin, Daniel and Jonathan Boyarin, "Diaspora: Generation and the Ground of Jewish Identity", in Braziel and Mannur (eds), *Theorizing Diaspora: A Reader*, pp. 85–118.

Boyer, John W., *Austria 1867–1955* (Oxford: Oxford University Press, 2022).

Brah, Avtar, *Cartographies of Diaspora: Contesting Identities* (London: Routledge, 1996).

Braziel, Jana Evans and Anita Mannur (eds), *Theorizing Diaspora: A Reader* (Oxford: Blackwell, 2003).

Brecht, Bertolt, *Arbeitsjournal 1938–1955* (ed. Werner Hecht) (Berlin: Suhrkamp, 1973).

Brecht, Bertolt, *Journals 1934–1955* (ed. John Willett, trans. Hugh Rorrison) (London: Methuen, 1993).

Brenez, Nicole, "For it is the Critical Faculty that Invents Fresh Forms", in Temple and Witt (eds), *The French Cinema Book*, pp. 230–47.

Brown, Elizabeth H. and Thy Phu (eds), *Feeling Photography* (Durham: Duke University Press, 2014).

Buck-Morss, Susan, *The Dialectics of Seeing: Walter Benjamin and the Arcades Project* (Cambridge, MA: MIT Press, 1989).

Bunzl, Matti, "On the Politics and Semantics of Austrian Memory: Vienna's Monument against War and Fascism", *History and Memory* Vol. 7 No. 2 (1995), 7–40.

Bunzl, Matti, "Political Inscription, Artistic Reflection: A Recontextualisation of Contemporary Viennese-Jewish Literature", *The German Quarterly* (Spring 2000), 163–70.

Bürger, Hans (interviewed), *20 Years on the Stock Exchange*, VoestAlpine Press Release, October 2015, p. 8, at www.ws-akademie.at/group/static/sites/group/.downloads/en/press/2015-voestalpine-ipo-1995-publication-en.pdf (accessed 20 January 2023).

Burri, Michael, "*Prater* (1936)", in von Dassanowsky (ed.), *World Film Locations: Vienna*, p. 26.

Butler, Judith, *Notes Towards a Performative Theory of Assembly* (Cambridge, MA: Harvard University Press, 2018).

Canetti, Elias, *Crowds and Power* (trans. Carol Stewart) (Harmondsworth: Penguin, 1973).

Canetti, Elias, *The Torch in My Ear* (trans. Joachim Neugroschel) (London: Andre Deutsch, 1989).

Cantor, Aviva, "Behind the Headlines – Refusing to Forget the Past", *Jewish Telegraph Agency (New York) Daily News Bulletin* 220 (28 November 1984), p. 4.

Caplan, Debra and Merrill Moss (eds), *The Dybbuk Century: The Jewish Play that Possessed the World* (Ann Arbor, MI: University of Michigan Press, 2023).

Carter, Erica, "Sisi the Terrible: Melodrama, Victimhood, and Imperial Nostalgia in the Sisi Trilogy", in Cooke and Silberman (eds), *Screening War: Perspectives on German Suffering*, pp. 81–101.

Caselli, Daniela, *Beckett's Dantes: Intertextuality in the Fiction and Criticism* (Manchester: Manchester University Press, 2005).

Caws, Mary Ann, *A Metapoetics of the Passage: Architextures in Surrealism and After* (Hanover: University Press of New England, 1981).

Chambers, Iain, *Mediterranean Crossings: The Politics of an Interrupted Modernity* (Durham: Duke University Press, 2008).

Celan, Paul, *Sprachgitter* (Berlin: Fischer, 1959).

Christomanos, Constantin, *Élisabeth de Bavière, Impératrice d'autriche* (trans. Gabriel Siveton) (Paris: Mercure de France, 1986).

Cixous, Hélène, "How to Film Becoming Invisible" (trans. Eric Prenowitz), in Lendl (ed.), *Film Collection: Texte/Texts/Textes*, pp. 85–90.

Cixous, Hélène, *So Close* (trans. Peggy Kamuf) (London: Polity, 2009).

Close Up film festival, London (3–24 September 2017), at www.close upfilmcentre.com/film_programmes/2017/close-up-on-ruth-beckerm ann/ (accessed 21 November 2023).

Coen, Ester, *Boccioni* (New York: Metropolitan Museum of Art, 1988).

Cohen, Josh, *Interrupting Auschwitz* (London: Continuum, 2005).

Cone, Michele C., *Artists under Vichy* (Princeton, NJ: Princeton University Press, 1992).

Cooke, P. and M. Silberman (eds), *Screening War: Perspectives on German Suffering* (Rochester: Camden House, 2010).

Corti, Egon (Count), *Elisabeth: Empress of Austria* (trans. Catherine Alison Phillips) (London: Thornton Butterworth, 1936).

Cuttitta, Paolo, " 'Borderising' the Island: Setting and Narratives of the Lampedusa 'Border Play' ", *ACME: An International E-Journal for Critical Geographies* Vol. 13 No. 2 (2014), 196–219.

D'Agata, John and Deborah Tall, "New Terrain: The Lyric Essay", *Seneca Review* 27 (1997), 7–8.

Dale, Gareth, *Karl Polanyi* (New York: Columbia University Press, 2016).

Daly, Mary, *Gyn/Ecology – The Metaethics of Radical Feminism* (London: The Women's Press, 1979).

Daviau, Donald G. (ed.), *Jura Soyfer and his Time* (Riverside: Ariadne Press, 1995).

Davis, Philip, *Bernard Malamud: A Writer's Life* (Oxford: Oxford University Press, 2007).

Davis, Martha, Dianne Dulicai and Ildiko Viczian, "Hitler's Movement Signature", *TDR* Vol. 36 No. 2 (1992), 152–72.

Day, Jonathan, *Robert Frank's* The Americans: *The Art of Documentary Photography* (Bristol: Intellect, 2011).

De Genova, Nicholas (ed.), *The Borders of Europe: Autonomy of Migration, Tactics of Bordering* (Durham, NC: Duke University Press, 2017).

DeKoven Ezrahi, Sidra, *Booking Passage: Exile and Homecoming in the Modern Jewish Imagination* (Berkeley, CA: University of California Press, 2000).

Dembling, Kerstin Mueller, "Staging the German Family Photo Album: The *Wehrmacht* Exhibit and Thomas Bernhard's *Vor dem Ruhestand*". *Journal of Austrian Studies* Vol. 48 No. 2 (2015), 1–24.

DeRoo, Rebecca, *Agnès Varda between Film, Photography, and Art* (Oakland, CA: University of California Press, 2018).

Derrida, Jacques, *The Other Heading: Reflections on Today's Europe* (trans. Pascale-Anne Braut and Michael B. Naas) (Bloomington, IN: Indiana University Press, 1992).

Derrida, Jacques, "Hospitality" (trans. Barry Stocker with Forbes Morlock), *Angelaki* Vol. 5 No. 3 (2000), 3–18.

Derrida, Jacques, *Sovereignties in Question: The Poetics of Paul Celan* (ed. Thomas Dutoit and Outi Pasanen) (New York: Fordham University Press, 2005).

Dewalt, Christian and Werner Michael Schwarz (eds), *Prater Kino Welt: Der Wiener Prater und die Geschichte des Kinos* (Vienna: Filmarchiv Austria, 2005).

Diana-Colin, Amy and Andrei Corbea-Hoisie, "Paul Celan's Bukovina-Meridians", in Eskin et al. (eds), *Paul Celan Today: A Companion*, pp. 9–15.

Didi-Huberman, Georges, *Images in Spite of All* (trans. Shane B. Lillis) (Chicago, IL: University of Chicago Press, 2008).

Didi-Huberman, Georges, "Opening the Camps, Closing the Eyes: Image, History, Readability", in Pollock and Silverman (eds), *Concentrationary Cinema: Aesthetics as Political Resistance in Alain Resnais's* Night and Fog (1955), pp. 84–125.

Dima, Flavia, "Present Histories: An Interview with Ruth Beckermann", *Kinoscope*, 12 April 2019, at https://read.kinoscope.org/2019/04/12/present-histories-an-interview-with-ruth-beckermann/ (accessed 18 July 2023).

Dolar, Mladen, *A Voice and Nothing More* (Cambridge, MA: MIT Press, 2006).

Drees, Stefan, "Erinnern als Verstehen: Zu einer grundlegenden Konstante von Olga Neuwirths Komponieren", in Ulrich Tadday (ed.), *Musik-Konzepte* 200/201 (IV/2023), 7–33.

Dufourmantelle, Anne and Jacques Derrida, *Of Hospitality* (trans. Rachel Bowlby) (Stanford: Stanford University Press, 2000).

Dworkin, Andrea, *Pornography: Men Possessing Women* (New York: Plume/Penguin, 1989).

Eckstein, Tanja and Julia Kaldori (eds), *Wie wir gelebt haben: Wiener Juden erinnern sich an ihr 20. Jahrhundert* (Vienna: Mandelbaum, 2008).

Eco, Umberto, *A Theory of Semiotics* (Bloomington, IN: Indiana University Press, 1976).

Eliot, T. S., *Collected Poems* (London: Faber and Faber, 1974).

Embacher, Helga, "Controversies over Austria's Nazi Past: Generational Changes and Grassroots Awakenings following the Waldheim Affair and the 'Wehrmacht Exhibitions' ", *Nationalities Papers* Vol. 51 No. 3 (2023), 644–664.

Epstein, Helen, *Children of the Holocaust: Conversations with Sons and Daughters of Survivors* (New York: Penguin/Putnam, 1979).

Ernst, Gustav (ed.), *Wespennest – Zeitschrift für brauchbare Texte und Bilder* 23: *Arenadokumentation* (12 July 1976).

Eskin, Michael, Karen Leeder, and Marko Pajević (eds), *Paul Celan Today: A Companion* (*Companions to Contemporary German Culture* Vol. 10) (Berlin: De Gruyter, 2021).

eva-maria-angela, "ARENA bist du großer Söhne – und wo sind deine Töchter?", *AUF – Eine Frauenzeitschrift*, II:8 (September 1976), 23–5.

Fareld, Victoria, "Ressentiment as Moral Imperative: Jean Améry's Nietzschean Revaluation of Victim Morality", in Roue and Gallagher (eds), *Re-Thinking Ressentiment: On the Limits of Criticism and the Limits of its Critics*, pp. 53–70.

Faschinger, Lilian, *Vienna Passion* (trans. Anthea Bell) (London: Headline, 2001).

Fawcett, Gabriel, "The Wehrmacht Exhibition", *History Today* Vol. 52 No. 4 (2002), 2–3.

Feldman, Gerald D., *Austrian Banks in the Period of National Socialism* (Cambridge: Cambridge University Press, 2015).

'Felicitas', "Frauenhaus = Freudenhaus?", *AUF – Eine Frauenzeitschrift*, II:8 (September 1976), 20–2.

Felstiner, John, *Paul Celan: Poet, Survivor, Jew* (New Haven: Yale University Press, 1995).

Felstiner, John (ed. and trans.), *Selected Poems and Prose of Paul Celan* (New York: W. W. Norton, 2001).

Ferrante, Elena, *Those Who Leave and Those Who Stay* (trans. Ann Goldstein) (London: Europa Editions, 2014).

Feyertag, Karoline, "The Art of Vision and the Ethics of the Gaze: On the Debate on Georges Didi-Huberman's Book *Images in Spite of All*" (trans. Camilla Neilson), at https://transversal.at/transversal/0408/feyertag/en (accessed 5 May 2023), np.

Flapan, Simha, *The Birth of Israel – Myths and Realities* (London: Routledge, 1987).

Florek, Olivia Gruber, *The Celebrity Monarch: Empress Elisabeth and the Modern Female Portrait* (Newark: University of Delaware Press, 2023).

Foltin, Robert, "Squatting and Autonomous Action in Vienna 1967–2012", in van der Steen et al. (eds), *The City is Ours* (Oakland, CA: PM Press, 2014), pp. 255–76.

Fornäs, Johan, "Passages across Thresholds – Into the Borderlands of Mediation", *Convergence* Vol. 8 No. 4 (2002), 89–106.

Foster, David, " 'Thought-Images' and Critical-Lyricisms: The Denkbild and Chris Marker's *Le Tombeau d'Alexandre*." *Image and Narrative* Vol. 10 No. 3 (2009), 3–14.

Foster, Hal, Rosalind Krauss, Yves-Alain Bois and Benjamin Buchloh (eds), *Art Since 1900: Modernism, Antimodernism, Postmodernism* (London: Thames and Hudson, 2004).

Frank, Robert, "A Statement", in Maloney, Tom (ed.), *US Camera* (New York: US Camera Publishing Corporation, 1958), p. 115.

Fresco, Nadine, *On the Death of Jews: Photographs and History* (trans. Sarah Clift) (New York: Berghahn / United States Holocaust Memorial Museum, 2021).

Freud, Ernst L. (ed.), *The Letters of Sigmund Freud and Arnold Zweig* (trans. Elaine and William Robson-Scott) (New York: New York University Press, 1970).

Freud, Sigmund, "The Psychotherapy of Hysteria", in Freud and Breuer, *The Pelican Freud Library* Vol. 3, *Studies on Hysteria*, pp. 337–93.

Freud, Sigmund, *Moses and Monotheism: Three Essays*, in *The Pelican Freud Library* Vol. 13: *The Origins of Religion* (ed. Albert Dickson, trans. James Strachey) (London: Penguin, 1985), pp. 237–386.

Freud, Sigmund, *Civilisation and Its Discontents*, in *The Pelican Freud Library* Vol. 12: *Civilization, Society and Religion* (ed. Albert Dickson, trans. James Strachey) (London: Penguin, 1991), pp. 243–340.

Freud, Sigmund and Joseph Breuer, *The Pelican Freud Library* Vol. 3: *Studies on Hysteria* (ed. Angela Richards, trans. James and Alix Strachey) (Harmondsworth: Penguin, 1983).

Friedberg, Lilian, "'A Time Yet to Come…': Translation and Historical Representation in Ingeborg Bachmann's Poem 'Night Flight / Nachtflug'", *The German Quarterly* Vol. 74 No. 2 (2001), 148–63.

Fritsche, Maria, *Homemade Men in Postwar Austrian Cinema: Nationhood, Genre, and Masculinity* (New York: Berghahn, 2013).

Fuchs, Anne, Mary Cosgrave and Georg Grote (eds), *German Memory Contests: The Quest for Identity in Literature, Film, and Discourse since 1990* (Rochester, NY: Camden House, 2006).

Gay, Peter, *Freud: A Life for Our Time* (Basingstoke: Macmillan, 1988).

Gelbin, Cathy S. and Sander L. Gilman, *Cosmopolitanisms and the Jews* (Ann Arbor, MI: University of Michigan Press, 2017).

Gerstl, Elfriede (ed.), *eine frau ist eine frau ist eine frau … Autorinnen über Autorinnen* (Vienna: Promedia, 1985).

Gerstl, Elfriede, *Kleiderflug – Texte – Textilien – Wohnen* (with photographs by Herbert Wimmer and 'Afterword' by Franz Schuh) (Vienna: Edition Splitter, 1995).

Geva, Dan, *A Philosophical History of Documentary, 1895–1959* (Basingstoke: Palgrave Macmillan, 2021).

Gilroy, Paul, *After Empire: Melancholia or Convivial Culture?* (London: Routledge, 2004).

Ginzburg, Carlo, *Threads and Traces: True False Fictive* (trans. Anne C. Tedeschi and John Tedeschi) (Berkeley, CA: University of California Press, 2012).

Ginsburg, Shia, Martin Land and Jonathan Boyarin, *Jews and the Ends of Theory* (New York: Fordham University Press, 2019).

Giubilaro, Chiara, "(Un)framing Lampedusa: Regimes of Visibility and the Politics of Affect in Italian Media Representations", in Proglio and Odasso (eds), *Border Lampedusa: Subjectivity, Visibility and Memory in Stories of Sea and Land*, pp. 103–17.

Goldhagen, Daniel Jonah, *Hitler's Willing Executioners – Ordinary Germans and the Holocaust* (New York: Alfred A. Knopf, 1996).

Golia, Maria, *Photography and Egypt* (London: Reaktion, 2010).

Gorsen, Peter, "Remaining Serious is Successful Repression" (trans. Larissa Cox), in Bertlmann, *Discordo Ergo Sum*, pp. 140–44.

Fusillo, Massimo, Gianluigi Simonetti and Lorenzo Marchese (eds), *Thinking Narratively – Between Novel-Essay and Narrative Essay* (Berlin: de Gruyter, 2022).

Graml, Gundolf, "We love our Heimat, but we need foreigners! Tourism and the reconstruction of Austria, 1945–55", *Journal of Austrian Studies* Vol. 39 No. 3 (2013), 51–76.

Grissemann, Stefan, "Frame by Frame: Peter Kubelka", *Film Comment* (September–October 2012), at www.filmcomment.com/article/peter-kubelka-frame-by-frame-antiphon-adebar-arnulf-rainer/ (accessed 23 February 2023).

Gruber, Helmut, *Red Vienna: Experiment in Working-Class Culture 1919–1934* (Oxford: Oxford University Press, 1991).

Grünwald, Oskar, "Steel and the State in Austria", *Annals of Public and Cooperative Economics* Vol. 51 No. 4 (1980), 477–91.

Guenther, Christina, "The Politics of Location in Ruth Beckermann's 'Vienna Films'", *Modern Austrian Literature* Vol. 37 No. 3/4 (2004), 33–46.

Guenther, Christina, "Cartographies of Identity: Memory and History in Ruth Beckermann's Documentary Films", in von Dassanowsky and Speck (eds), *New Austrian Film*, pp. 64–78.

Guerin, Frances, "The Ambiguity of Amateur Photography in Modern Warfare", *New Literary History* Vol. 48 No. 1 (2017), 53–7.

Guerin, Frances, *Through Amateur Eyes: Film and Photography in Nazi Germany* (Minneapolis: University of Minnesota Press, 2011).

Hahn, Ulla, *Unscharfe Bilder* (Munich: Deutsche Verlags-Anstalt, 2003).

Halimi, Serge, *Le Monde diplomatique*, 20 March 2007, at www.monde-diplomatique.fr/carnet/2007-03-20-LIP (accessed 23 February 2023).

Hamann, Brigitte, *The Reluctant Empress: A Biography of Empress Elisabeth of Austria* (trans. Ruth Hein) (Berlin: Ullstein, 1986).

Hametz, Maureen E. and Heidi Schlipphacke (eds), *The Empress Elisabeth in Memory and Myth* (London: Bloomsbury, 2018).

Hanegbi, Haim, Moshe Machover, and Akiva Orr, "The Class Nature of Israeli Society", *New Left Review* 1–65 (Jan–Feb 1971), 3–26.

Hartwig, Ina, *Wer war Ingeborg Bachmann? Eine Biographie in Bruchstücken* (Frankfurt am Main: S. Fischer, 2017).

Heer, Hannes and Jane Caplan, "The Difficulty of Ending a War: Reactions to the Exhibition 'War of Extermination: Crimes of the Wehrmacht 1941 to 1944", *History Workshop Journal* 46 (Autumn 1998), 187–203.

Henningsen, Therese, and Juliet Joffé (eds), *Strangers Within: Documentary as Encounter* (London: Prototype, 2022).

Herzog, Hillary Hope, "The Global and the Local in Ruth Beckermann's Films and Writings", in Herzog et al. (eds), *Rebirth of a Culture: Jewish Identity and Jewish Writing in Germany and Austria Today*, pp. 100–109.

Herzog, Hillary Hope, *Vienna is Different: Jewish Writers in Austria from the fin-de-siècle to the Present* (New York: Berghahn, 2011).

Herzog, Hillary Hope, Todd Herzog and Benjamin Lapp (eds), *Rebirth of a Culture: Jewish Identity and Jewish Writing in Germany and Austria Today* (New York: Berghahn, 2008).

Herzog, Todd, "Wonder Wheel: The Cinematic Prater", in von Dassanowsky (ed.), *World Film Locations: Vienna*, pp. 88–9.

Herzstein, Robert Edwin, "The Present State of the Waldheim Affair: Second Thoughts and New Directions", in Bischoff and Pelinka (eds), *Austrian Historical Memory and National Identity* (*Contemporary Austrian Studies Vol. 5*), pp. 116–34.

Hewitt, Andrew, *Fascist Modernism: Aesthetics, Politics, and the Avant-Garde* (Stanford: Stanford University Press, 1993).

Heymann, Florence, *Le Crepuscule des lieux: Identités juives de Czernowitz* (Paris: Stock, 2003).

Hilfrich, Carola, Natasha Gordinsky, and Susanne Zepp (eds), *Passages of Belonging: Interpreting Jewish Literatures* (Berlin: de Gruyter, 2019).

Hirsch, Marianne, *Family Frames: Photography, Narrative, and Postmemory* (Cambridge, MA: Harvard University Press, 1997).

Hirsch, Marianne and Leo Spitzer, *Ghosts of Home – The Afterlife of Jewish Memory in Czernowitz* (Los Angeles: University of California Press, 2010).

Hirsch, Marianne and Leo Spitzer, "School Photos and their Afterlives", in Brown and Phu (eds), *Feeling Photography*, pp. 252–72.

Hoberman, J., "*The Dybbuk*: the movie(s)", in Caplan and Merrill Moss (eds), *The Dybbuk Century*, pp. 128–9.

Hoberman, J., "The Talking Cure: On Ruth Beckerman's *Mutzenbacher*", *LA Review of Books*, 10 January 2023. At https://lareviewofbooks.org/article/the-talking-cure-on-ruth-beckermanns-mutzenbacher (accessed 17 November 2023).

Hödl, Klaus, *Entangled Entertainers: Jews and Popular Culture in Fin-de-Siècle Vienna* (trans. Corey Twitchell) (New York: Berghahn, 2019).

Hoffman, Eva, *After Such Knowledge: A Meditation on the Aftermath of the Holocaust* (London: Vintage, 2005).

Honig, Edwin, "Malraux's Psychology of Art", *New Mexico Quarterly* Vol. 21 No. 4 (1951), 488–94.

Horwath, Alexander and Michael Omasta (eds), *Ruth Beckermann* (Vienna: Synema, 2016).

Hottner, Wolfgang, "Einander-Schreiben verfilmen. 'Die Geträumten' – Überlegungen zu Ruth Beckermanns Verfilmung des Briefwechsels von Ingeborg Bachmann und Paul Celan", *Zeitschrift für Germanistik*, Neue Folge Vol. XXX No. 3 (2020), 662–4.

Hrbeniak, Michael, *Action Writing: Jack Kerouac's Wild Form* (Carbondale: Southern Illinois University Press, 2006).

Hughes, Harold, "The Man Behind *The Fixer*" (interview with Bernard Malamud), *The Oregonian*, 9 October 1966, pp. 8, 21. In Lasher (ed.), *Conversations with Bernard Malamud*, pp. 21–6.

Humbert, Jean-Marcel, "Egyptomania: A Current Concept from the Renaissance to Postmodernism", in Humbert and Ziegler (eds), *Egyptomania: Egypt in Western Art 1730–1930*, pp. 21–6.

Humbert, Jean-Marcel, Michael Pantazzi and Christiane Ziegler (eds), *Egyptomania: Egypt in Western Art 1730–1930* (Paris/Ottawa Vienna: National Gallery of Canada, 1994).

Hurm, Gerd, Anke Reitz and Shamoon Zamir (eds), *The Family of Man Revisited: Photography in a Global Age* (London: Routledge, 2020).

Indiana, Gary, "Valie Export by Gary Indiana", *BOMB* magazine (1 April 1982), at https://bombmagazine.org/articles/valie-export (accessed 22 January 2023).

Ingram, Susan, *Siting Futurity* (London: Punctum Books, 2021).

Insdorf, Annette, *Indelible Shadows: Film and the Holocaust* (Cambridge: Cambridge University Press, 2010).

Jacobus, Mary, *On Belonging and Not Belonging: Translation, Migration, Displacement* (Princeton: Princeton University Press, 2022).

Jakubowska, Agata and Katy Deepwell (eds), *All-women Art Spaces in Europe in the Long 1970s* (Liverpool: Liverpool University Press, 2018).

James, Alice, "Das Briefgeheimnis: Ingeborg Bachmann and Paul Celan's Poetics of Correspondence" (unpublished MA thesis, Durham University, 2013).

Jameson, Fredric, *Brecht and Method* (London: Verso, 1988).

Jelinek, Elfriede, "Elfriede Gerstl", speech delivered 28 November 1999 at the award of the Erich Fried Prize to Gerstl, np, at www.elfriedejelinek. com/fgerstl.html (accessed 3 September 2023).

Kaes, Anton, "29 November 1923: Karl Grune's *Die Straße* inaugurates 'Street Film', Foreshadows Film Noir", in Kapszynski and Richardson (eds), *A New History of German Cinema*, pp. 124–8.

Kamm, Henry, "Waldheim Plans Slander Suit", *New York Times* (8 May 1987), at www.nytimes.com/1987/05/08/world/waldheim-plans-slander-suit-aginst-jewish-group-s-chief.html (accessed 26 May 2023).

Kantor, Débora G., "Ruth Beckermann: Documentarian of the Present", *Jewish Film and New Media* Vol. 8 No. 2 (2020), 226–38.

Kaplan, Caren, *Questions of Travel* (Durham, NC: Duke University Press, 1996).

Kapszynski, Jennifer M. and Michael D. Richardson (eds), *A New History of German Cinema* (Rochester: Camden House, 2012).

Kerouac, Jack, *On the Road* (New York: Viking, 1959).

Klemperer, Victor, *The Language of the Third Reich* (New York: Continuum, 2000).

Kluger, Ruth, *Landscapes of Memory: A Holocaust Girlhood Remembered* (London: Bloomsbury, 2003).

Kondor, Eszter and Michael Loebenstein (eds), *Ruth Beckermann* (Vienna: Synema, 2019).

Kouvelakis, Stathis, "Borderland: Greece and the EU's Southern Question", *New Left Review* 110 (March–April, 2018), 5–33.

Kovach, Elizabeth, Jens Kugele, and Ansgar Nünning (eds), *Passages: Moving Beyond Liminality in the Study of Literature and Culture* (London: UCL Press, 2022).

Kowalke, Kim H., "Singing Brecht vs. Brecht Singing: Performance in Theory and Practice", *Cambridge Opera Journal* Vol. 5 No. 1 (1993), 55–78.

Krasny, Elke, 'For us, art is work': IntAkt – International Action Community of Women Artists", in Jakubowska and Deepwell (eds), *All-women Art Spaces in Europe in the Long 1970s*, pp. 96–118.

Kravis, Nathan, *On the Couch: A Repressed History of the Analytic Couch from Plato to Freud* (Cambridge, MA: MIT Press, 2017).

Krylova, Katya, "Melancholy Journeys in the Films of Ruth Beckermann", *Leo Baeck Institute Yearbook* Vol. 59 (2014), 249–66.

Krylova, Katya, *The Long Shadow of the Past – Contemporary Austrian Literature, Film, and Culture* (Rochester: Camden House, 2017).

Kunfi, Zsigmond, "Lessons of July 15" ("Der 15. Juli und seine Lehren", *Der Kampf* Vol. 20 No. 8 [1927]: 345–52) (trans. Peter Woods), in MacFarland et al. (eds), *The Red Vienna Sourcebook*, pp. 713–17.

Kuttenberg, Eva, "A Postmodern Viennese Narrative: Lilian Faschinger's *Wiener Passion*", *Monatshefte* Vol. 1 No. 1 (2009), 73–87.

Lacan, Jacques, *Seminar Book III, 1955–56: The Psychoses* (ed. Jacques-Alain Miller, trans. Russell Grigg) (New York: Norton, 1997).

Lamb-Faffelberger, Margarete (ed.), *Out from the Shadows: Essays on Contemporary Austrian Women Writers and Filmmakers* (Riverside: Ariadne Press, 1997).

Lasher, Lawrence M. (ed.), *Conversations with Bernard Malamud* (Jackson: University Press of Mississippi, 1991).

Lauterwein, Andréa, *Anselm Kiefer, Paul Celan: Myth, Mourning and Memory* (London: Thames and Hudson, 2007).

Lee, Anthony W. and Tim Cresswell, *Muybridge and Mobility* (Oakland, CA: University of California Press, 2022).

Lendl, Monika (ed.), *Ruth Beckermann Film Collection – Texte/Texts/Textes* (Vienna: Ruth Beckermann Filmproduktion, 2007).

Levinas, Emmanuel, *Difficult Freedom: Writings on Judaism* (ed. and trans. Seán Hand) (Baltimore: Johns Hopkins University Press, 1990).

Lockmann, Zachary and Joel Beinin (eds), *Intifada: The Palestinian Uprising against Israeli Occupation* (London: I. B. Tauris, 1990).

Lorenz, Dagmar C. G. and Gabriele Weinberger (eds), *Insiders and Outsiders: Jewish and Gentile Culture in Germany and Austria* (Detroit: Wayne State University Press, 1994).

Lorenz, Dagmar C. G., "Discovering and Making Memory. Jewish Cultural Expression in Contemporary Europe", *The German Quarterly* Vol. 73. No. 2 (2000), 175–8.

Lorenz, Dagmar C. G., "Post-Shoah Positions of Displacement in the Films of Ruth Beckermann", in " 'Hitler's First Victim'? Memory and Representation in Post-War Austria", *Austrian Studies* Vol. 11 (2003), 154–70.

Lorenz, Dagmar C. G., "The Jewish Topography of Filmic Vienna", in Dassanowsky (ed.), *World Film Locations: Vienna*, pp. 48–9.

Lorenz, Dagmar C. G., "Ruth Beckermann's Journey to Czernowitz: Displacement and Postmemory in *Die papierene Brücke*", *Journal of Austrian Studies* Vol. 53 No. 3 (2020), 71–84.

Lumans, Valdis O., "The Ethnic Germans of the Waffen-SS in Combat: Dregs or Gems?", in Marble, Sanders (ed.), *Scraping the Barrel: The Military Use of Sub-Standard Manpower* (New York: Fordham University Press, 2012), pp. 225–53.

MacKenzie, Scott (ed.), *Film Manifestos and Global Cinema Cultures: A Critical Anthology* (Berkeley, CA: University of California Press, 2014).

McChesney, Anita, "Imagining Austria: Myths of 'Sisi' and National Identity in Lilian Faschinger's *Wiener Passion*", in Hametz and Schlipphacke (eds), *The Empress Elisabeth in Memory and Myth*, pp. 275–300.

McFarland, Rob, Georg Spitaler and Ingo Zechner (eds), *The Red Vienna Sourcebook* (Rochester, NY: Camden House, 2020).

McFarland, Rob, Nicole G. Burgoyne and Gabriel Trop, "Jewish Life and Culture", in McFarland et al., *The Red Vienna Sourcebook*, pp. 191–212.

Madej-Stang, Adriana, *Which Face of Witch: Self-representations of Women as Witches in Works of Contemporary British Women Writers* (Newcastle-upon-Tyne: Cambridge Scholars Publishing, 2015).

Malamud, Bernard, *The Fixer* (Harmondsworth: Penguin, 1968).

Maloney, Tom (ed.), *US Camera 1958* (New York: US Camera Publishing Corporation, 1958).

Malraux, André, *Les Voix du silence* (Paris: La Galerie de la Pléiade, 1951).

Malraux, André, *The Voices of Silence* (trans. Stuart Gilbert) (St Albans: Paladin, 1974).

Mandel, Siegfried, *Group 47: The Reflected Intellect* (Carbondale: Southern Illinois University Press, 1973).

Marble, Sanders (ed.), *Scraping the Barrel: The Military Use of Sub-Standard Manpower* (New York: Fordham University Press, 2012).

Marker, Chris, "Interview", Wolfgang Gersch, "Der schöne Mai", *Filmwissenschaftliche Mitteilungen* I (1964), 194–8; in Alter, *Chris Marker*, pp. 131–5.

Markova, Ina, "Visualizing Waldheim: Mediale Schlüsselbilder der 'Affäre Waldheim'", *Journal of Austrian Studies* Vol. 49 Nos. 1–2 (2016), 71–89.

Marsh, Georgia, "An Interview with Christian Boltanski" (stapled booklet), in Boltanski, Christian, *Reconstitution* (exh. cat.) (London: Whitechapel Gallery, 1990).

Matisse, Henri, *Peintures 1939–46* (with an Introduction by André Lejard) (Pars: Les Éditions du Chene, 1946).

Matthes, Frauke (ed.), *Edinburgh German Yearbook* Volume 14: *Politics and Culture in Germany and Austria Today* (Cambridge: Cambridge University Press, 2021).

Mattl, Siegfried, "Work in Motion" (2007) (trans. Samia Geldner), in Lendl (ed.), *Film Collection: Texte/Texts /Textes*, pp. 82–4.

Maunsell, Jerome Boyd, *Susan Sontag* (London: Reaktion, 2014).

Missac, Pierre, *Walter Benjamin's Passages* (trans. Sherry Weber Nicholson) (Cambridge, MA: MIT Press, 1995).

Mitchell, Timothy, *Colonising Egypt* (Irvine: University of California Press, 1991).

Mitchell, W. J. T., *Picture Theory* (Chicago, IL: University of Chicago Press, 1994).

Mitterbauer, Helga and Carrie Smith-Prei (eds), *Crossing Central Europe: Continuities and Transformations, 1990 and 2000* (Toronto: University of Toronto Press, 2017).

Molodowsky, Kadya, *Paper Bridges: Selected Poems* (ed. and trans. Kathryn Hellerstein) (Detroit: Wayne State University Press, 1999).

Morgenstern, Hana, "A Savage Corpse: Colonialism, Anticolonialism, and the Hebrew Avant-Garde", *Modernism/modernity* Vol. 28 No. 4 (2021), 661–86.

Morris, Benny, *The Birth of the Palestinian Refugee Problem, 1947–1949* (Cambridge: Cambridge University Press, 1988).

Moser, Joseph W., "*Bockerer / Der Bockerer*", in von Dassanowsky, Robert (ed.), *World Film Locations: Vienna*, p. 80.

Moser, Joseph W., "Ruth Beckermann's Reckoning with Kurt Waldheim: *Unzugehörig: Österreicher und Juden nach 1945* (1989) and *Waldheims Waltzer* (2018)", in Matthes et al. (eds), *Edinburgh German Yearbook* Volume 14: *Politics and Culture in Germany and Austria Today*, pp. 207–21.

Mueller, Roswitha, *VALIE EXPORT: Fragments of the Imagination* (Bloomington, IN: Indiana University Press, 1994).

Naficy, Hamid, *An Accented Cinema – Exilic and Diasporic Filmmaking* (Princeton, NJ: Princeton University Press, 2001).

Nancy, Jean-Luc, *The Inoperative Community* (trans. Peter Connor et al.) (Minneapolis: University of Minnesota Press, 1991).

Neuwirth, Olga, *Bählamms Fest: Ein venezianisches Arbeitsjournal* (Vienna: Droschl, 2003).

New Lebow, Richard, Wulf Kansteiner and Claudio Fogu (eds), *The Politics of Memory in Postwar Europe* (Durham: Duke University Press, 2006).

Novotny, Ewald, "The Austrian Social Partnership and Democracy", *Working Paper 93–1* (University of Vienna), at https://conservancy.umn. edu/bitstream/handle/11299/56472/WP931.pdf?sequence=1 (accessed 19 January 2023).

Nugent, Christine R., "The Voice of the Visitor: Popular Reactions to the Exhibition *Vernichtungskrieg: Verbrechen der Wehrmacht 1941–1944*", *Journal of European Studies* Vol. 44 No. 3 (2014), 249–62.

O'Brien, Mary-Elizabeth, *Nazi Cinema as Enchantment: The Politics of Entertainment in the Third Reich* (New York: Camden House, 2004).

O'Donoghue, Diane, "The Magic of the Manifest: Freud's Egyptian Dream Book", *American Imago* Vol. 66 No. 2 (2009), 211–30.

Organisation Arbeiterinnenkampf (ARKA), "Semperit Traiskirchen 1978", at www.arbeiter-innen-kampf.org/publikationen/marxismus-buecher/streiks-der-2-republik/semperit-traiskirchen-1978/ (accessed 18 January 2023).

Oshinsky, David, Edward L. Ayers, Jean R. Soderlund and Lewis Gould, *American Passages: A History of the United States* (New York: Houghton Mifflin, 2006).

Oz, Amos, "Universal Redemption", *TIME*, 15 May 1978, p. 61.

Oz, Amos, *To Know a Woman* (trans. Nicholas de Lange and Amos Oz) (London: Vintage, 1992).

Oz, Amos, *Unto Death* (trans. Nicholas de Lange) (London: Flamingo, 1986).

Pajević, Marco, "Celan's Correspondence and Correspondence with Celan. Transfer Processes of Life", in Eskin, Michael et al. (eds), *Paul Celan Today* (*Companions to Contemporary German Culture* Vol. 10), pp. 299–303.

Papazian, Elizabeth and Caroline Eades (eds), *The Essay Film* (London: Wallflower Press, 2016).

Pauley, Bruce F., *From Prejudice to Persecution: A History of Austrian Anti-Semitism* (Chapel Hill: University of North Carolina Press, 1992).

Paver, Chloe E. M., "Ein Stück langweiliger als die Wehrmachtsausstellung, aber dafür repräsentativer": The Exhibition *Fotofeldpost* as Riposte to the 'Wehrmacht Exhibition'", in Fuchs et al. (eds) *German Memory Contests: The Quest for Identity in Literature, Film, and Discourse since 1990*, pp. 107–25.

Paver, Chloe E. M., *Refractions of the Third Reich in German and Austrian Fiction and Film* (Oxford: Oxford University Press, 2007).

Perec, Georges, *W, or the Memory of Childhood* (trans. David Bellos) (London: Harvill, 1988).

Perec, Georges, *A Void* (trans. Gilbert Adair) (London: Harvill, 1995).

Perec, Georges, *Species of Spaces and Other Pieces* (ed. and trans. John Sturrock) (London: Penguin, 2008).

Perec, Georges, *An Attempt at Exhausting a Place in Paris* (trans. Marc Lowenthal) (Cambridge, MA: Wakefield Press, 2010).

Perloff, Marjorie, *The Vienna Paradox: A Memoir* (New York: New Directions, 2004).

Perrin, David, "Not Reconciled: Ruth Beckermann discusses *The Waldheim Waltz*" (27 March 2018), at https://mubi.com/notebook/posts/not-reconciled-ruth-beckermann-discusses-the-waldheim-waltz (accessed 7 June 2023).

Philipe, Anne, "Medvedkine, tu connais? Interview avec Slon et Chris Marker", *Le Monde* (2 December 1971), 17; in Alter, *Chris Marker*, pp. 139–44.

Pick, Hella, *Guilty Victim: Austria from the Holocaust to Haider* (London: I. B. Tauris, 2000).

Pinkerton, Nick, "The Present Absence", in Kondor and Loebenstein (eds), *Ruth Beckermann*, pp. 2–14.

Pinsker, Sachar M., *A Rich Brew: How Cafés Created Modern Jewish Culture* (New York: New York University Press, 2018).

Pitteloud, Sabine, "'American Management' vs 'Swiss Labour Peace'. The closure of the Swiss Firestone Factory in 1978", *Business History* Vol. 64 No. 9 (2020), 1648–1665.

Pollock, Griselda and Max Silverman (eds), *Concentrationary Cinema: Aesthetics as Political Resistance in Alain Resnais's* Night and Fog *(1955)* (Oxford: Berghahn, 2011).

Pollock, Griselda, in conversation with Nicholas Chare, *RACAR – Canadian Art Review* Vol. 42 No. 1 (2018), 63–80.

Popescu, Gabriel, *Bordering and Ordering the Twenty-First-Century: Understanding Borders* (Washington, DC: Rowman and Littlefield, 2011).

Posthofen, Renata S., "Ruth Beckermann: Re-activating Memory – In Search of Time Lost", in Lamb-Faffelberger (ed.), *Out from the Shadows: Essays on Contemporary Austrian Women Writers and Filmmakers*, pp. 264–76.

Posthofen, Renate. "Erinnerte Geschichte(n): Robert Schindels Roman *Gebürtig*", *Modern Austrian Literature* Vol. 27 Nos. 3–4 (1994), 193–211.

Preece, Julian, *The Rediscovered Writings of Veza Canetti: Out of the Shadow of a Husband* (Rochester: Camden House, 2002).

Proglio, Gabriele and Laura Odasso (eds), *Border Lampedusa: Subjectivity, Visibility and Memory in Stories of Sea and Land* (Cham: Palgrave Macmillan, 2018).

Prosquill, Désirée, "Pepi auf der Couch. *Die Mutzenbacher* und Freuds *Drei Abhandlungen*", in Ruthner, Clemens, Matthias Schmidt and Carolin Schmieding (eds), *Die Mutzenbacher: Lektüren und Kontexte eines Skandalromans* (Vienna: Sonderzahl, 2019), pp. 45–60.

Rancière, Jacques, *The Emancipated Spectator* (trans. Gregory Elliott) (London: Verso, 2009).

Ransmayr, Christoph (ed.), *Im blinden Winkel: Nachrichten aus Mitteleuropa* (Frankfurt am Main: Fischer, 1987).

Rascaroli, Laura, *How the Essay Film Thinks* (Oxford: Oxford University Press, 2017).

Raunig, Gerald, *Art and Revolution* (trans. Aileen Derieg) (New York: Semiotext(e), 2007).

Rebhandl, Bert, "At another place" (trans. Peter Stastny), in Lendl (ed.), *Film Collection: Texte/Texts/Textes*, pp. 66–70.

Rebhandl, Bert, "Das ewige Thema: 'Judenkind, Flüchtlingskind, Wirtschaftswunderkind' – Die Identifikationen von Ruth Beckermann", in Horwath and Omasta (eds), *Ruth Beckermann*, pp. 7–33.

Reiter, Andrea, *Contemporary Jewish Writing: Austria after Waldheim* (London: Routledge, 2013).

Remmler, Karen, "Geographies of Memory: Ruth Beckermann's Film Aesthetics", *Studies in 20th and 21st Century Literature* Vol. 31 No. 1 (2007), 206–35.

Rich, Adrienne, "It is the Lesbian in us", *Sinister Wisdom* Vol. 1 No. 3 (1977), 6–9.

Riedl, Joachim (ed.), *Versunkene Welt* (Vienna: Jewish Welcome Service, 1984).

Robey, David (ed.), *Structuralism: An Introduction* (Oxford: Clarendon Press, 1973).

Rodinson, Maxime, *Israël: fait colonial?* (Paris: Les temps Modernes, 1967).

Rodinson, Maxime, *Israel: A Colonial Settler State?* (New York: Monad Press, 1973).

Rosenberg, Joel, "The Soul of Catastrophe: On the 1937 Film of S. Ansky's *The Dybbuk*", *Jewish Social Studies* Vol. 17 No. 2 (2011), 1–27.

Ross, Alex, *The Rest is Noise: Listening to the Twentieth Century* (London: Fourth Estate, 2008).

Roue, Jeanne and Mary Gallagher (eds), *Re-Thinking Ressentiment: On the Limits of Criticism and the Limits of its Critics* (Bielefeld: Transcript, 2016).

Ruthner, Clemens, "The Back Side of Fin-de-Siècle Vienna: The Infamously Infantile Sexuality of Josefine Mutzenbacher", in Ruthner and Whitinger (eds), *Contested Passions: Sexuality, Eroticism and Gender in Modern Austrian Literature and Culture*, pp. 92–104.

Ruthner, Clemens and Raleigh Whitinger (eds), *Contested Passions: Sexuality, Eroticism and Gender in Modern Austrian Literature and Culture* (New York: Peter Lang, 2011).

Ruthner, Clemens, Matthias Schmidt and Carolin Schmieding (eds), *Die Mutzenbacher: Lektüren und Kontexte eines Skandalromans* (Vienna: Sonderzahl, 2019).

Ryland, Charlotte, *Paul Celan's Encounters with Surrealism: Trauma, Translation, and Shared Poetic Space* (Abingdon: Legenda-MHRA/ Routledge, 2010).

Sagnol, Marc, "Bukovina and its Poets: A Country where Men and Books Lived", *Social Sciences* Vol. 11 No. 5 (2022), 283–90.

Said, Edward W., "Intifada and Independence", in Lockman and Beinin (eds), *Intifada*, pp. 5–22.

Said, Edward W., *The Question of Palestine* (New Edition) (London: Vintage, 1992).

Said, Edward W., *The Politics of Dispossession: The Struggle for Palestinian Self-Determination 1969–1994* (London: Vintage, 1995).

Said, Edward W., *Reflections on Exile and Other Literary and Cultural Essays* (London: Granta, 2008).

Said, Edward W., "The Current Status of Jerusalem", *Jerusalem Quarterly* 45 (2011), 57–72.

Said, Edward W. and Jean Mohr, *After the Last Sky: Palestinian Lives* (London: Vintage, 1993).

Salten, Felix, *Neue Menschen auf alter Erde: Eine Palästinafahrt* (Königstein: Athenäum, 1986) (first published Berlin: Paul Zsolnay, 1925).

Sarfan, Austin, "The Conversion of the Gaze in the Work of Georges Perec", *The Comparative Literature Undergraduate Journal* (Spring 2016), np, at https://ucbcluj.org/the-conversion-of-the-gaze-in-the-work-of-georges-perec/ (accessed 2 September 2023).

Schiefer, Karin, "*American Passages: Interview with Ruth Beckermann*", 24 February 2011, at www.ruthbeckermann.com/en/publications/texts/american-passages/ (accessed 12 January 2023).

Schiefer, Karen, "Ruth Beckermann on Her Essay on Escape and Volatility, *Those Who Go Those Who Stay*" (interview), *Austrian Films* (October 2013), at www.austrianfilms.com/news/en/filmmaking_itself_is_one_theme_of_the_film_ruth_beckermann_talks_about_those_who_go_tho se_who_stay (accessed 12 January 2023).

Schindel, Robert, *Born-Where* (trans. Michael Roloff) (Riverside: Ariadne Press, 1995).

Schlipphacke, Heidi, "Melancholy Empress: Queering Empire in Ernst Marishka's *Sisi* Films", *Screen* Vol. 51 No. 3 (2010), 232–55.

Schmitzberger, Markus, "Semperitwerk – Traiskirchen", at www.geheim projekte.at/firma_semperit_traiskirchen.html (accessed 18 January 2023).

Schoene, Berthold, *The Cosmopolitan Novel* (Edinburgh: Edinburgh University Press, 2009).

Schor, Gabriele (ed.), *Feminist Avant-Garde – Art of the 1970s* (Munich: Prestel, 2016).

Schwarz, Egon, "Austria, Quite a Normal Nation", *New German Critique* No. 93 (Autumn 2004), 175–91.

Schwendter, Rolf, "Das Jahr 1968. War es eine kulturelle Zäsur?", in Sieder et al. (eds), *Österreich 1945–1995*, pp. 166–75.

Scotini, Marco and Elisabetta Galasso (eds), *Politics of Memory: Documentary and Archive* (Berlin: Archive Books, 2014).

Sebald, W. G., *Unheimliche Heimat: Essays zur österreichischen Literatur* (Frankfurt am Main: Fischer, 1995).

Secher, Pierre, "The 'Jewish' Kreisky: Perception or Reality?", *History of European Ideas* Vol. 20 Nos. 4–6 (1995), 865–70.

Segev, Tom, *1949: The First Israelis* (New York: Free Press, 1986).

Seibel, Alexandra, *Visions of Vienna: Narrating the City in 1920s and 1930s Cinema* (Amsterdam: Amsterdam University Press, 2017).

Semprun, Jorge, *Literature or Life* (trans. Linda Coverdale) (New York: Viking, 1997).

Shafik, Viola (ed.), *Documentary Filmmaking in the Middle East and North Africa* (Cairo: The American University in Cairo Press, 2022).

Sheets, Robin Ann, "Pornography, Fairy Tales, and Feminism: Angela Carter's 'The Bloody Chamber'", *Journal of the History of Sexuality* Vol. 1 No. 4 (1991), 633–57.

Sieder, Reinhard, Heinz Steinert and Emmerich Tálos (eds), *Österreich 1945–1995* (Vienna: Verlag für Gesellschaftskritik, 1995).

Silverman, Lisa, *Becoming Austrians: Jews and Culture Between the Wars* (Oxford: Oxford University Press, 2012).

Soule, Jacob, "The End of the City and the Coming of the Urban: Georges Perec's *An Attempt at Exhausting a Place in Paris*", *Novel: A Forum on Fiction* Vol. 55 No. 2 (2022), 324–38.

Solibakke, Karl Ivan, review of Áine McMurtry, *Crisis and Form in the Later Writing of Ingeborg Bachmann*, *Journal of Austrian Studies* Vol. 46. No. 4 (2013), 129–31.

Sperber, Manès, *All Our Yesterdays Volume 1 – God's Water Carriers* (trans. Joachim Neugroschel) (New York: Holmes and Meier, 1987).

Sperber, Manès, *All Our Yesterdays Volume 2 – The Unheeded Warning: 1918–1933* (trans. Harry Zohn) (New York: Holmes and Meier, 1991).

Spiel, Hilde, *Vienna's Golden Autumn – 1866–1938* (London: Weidenfeld and Nicolson, 1987).

Spiel, Hilde, *Rückkehr nach Wien: Ein Tagebuch* (Vienna: Milena, 2009).

Spiel, Hilde, *Return to Vienna – A Journal* (trans. Christine Shuttleworth) (London: Ariadne Press, 2011).

Stackl, Erhard, "Als einen Sommer lang Freiheit war" (22 August 1976), at www.derstandard.at/story/2492068/als-einen-sommer-lang-freiheit-war (accessed 14 October 2023).

Stanton, G. R., "The Cosmopolitan Ideas of Epictetus and Marcus Aurelius", *Phronesis* Vol. 13 No. 2 (1968), 183–95.

Stark, Trevor, "'Cinema in the Hands of the People': Chris Marker, the Medvedkin Group, and the Potential of Militant Film", *October* 139 (Winter 2012), 117–50.

Stevens, Adrian and Fred Wagner (eds), *Elias Canetti: Londoner Symposium* (Stuttgart: Verlag Hans-Dieter Heinz/Akademischer Verlag Stuttgart, 1991).

Stieg, Gerald, "Canetti und die Psychoanalyse: Das Unbehagen in der Kultur und *Die Blendung*", in Stevens and Wagner (eds), *Elias Canetti: Londoner Symposium*, pp. 59–73.

Stift, Linda, *Stierhunger* (Deuticke im Zsolnay, 2007).

Stift, Linda, *The Empress and the Cake* (trans. Jamie Bulloch) (London: Peirene, 2016).

Stompor, Stephan, *Jüdisches Musik- und Theaterleben unter dem NS-Staat* (ed. Andor Iszak) (Hanover: Europäisches Zentrum für Jüdische Musik, 2001).

Suleiman, Susan Rubin, *Crises of Memory and the Second World War* (Cambridge, MA: Harvard University Press, 2006).

Szondi, Peter, " 'Engführung': An Essay on the Poetry of Paul Celan" (trans. David Caldwell and S. Esh), *boundary 2* Vol. 11 No. 3 (1983), 231–64.

Tagliabue, John, "Voest-Alpine Plight Affects All Austria", *New York Times*, 20 January 1986, Section D, p. 6.

Tassin, Étienne, "Philosophie /et/ Politique de la migration", *Raison Publique* 2017/1 (No. 21), 197–215.

Tedeschi, Giuliana, *There Is a Place on Earth: A Woman in Birkenau* (trans. Tim Parks) (London: Lime Tree, 1993).

Temple, Michael and Michael Witt (eds), *The French Cinema Book* (London: Palgrave/BFI, 2007).

Thurnher, Armin, "Andere Zeiten: Zu vier frühen Filmen Ruth Beckermanns", in Horwath and Omasta (eds), *Ruth Beckermann*, pp. 41–6.

Todorov, Tzvetan and Arnold Weinstein, 'The Structural Analysis of Literature: The Tales of Henry James', in Robey (ed.), *Structuralism: An Introduction*, pp. 73–103.

Toukan, Hanan, "Lacan, Sontag, and Israel on Screen", in Shafik (ed.), *Documentary Filmmaking in the Middle East and North Africa*, pp. 279–88.

Tscherkassky, Peter (ed.), *Film Unframed: A History of Austrian Avant-Garde Cinema* (Vienna: Synema, 2012).

Uhl, Heidemarie, "From Victim Myth to Co-Responsibility Thesis: Nazi Rule, World War II, and the Holocaust in Austrian Memory", in New Lebow et al. (eds), *The Politics of Memory in Postwar Europe*, pp. 40–72.

Urquhart, Brian, "Character Sketch: Kurt Waldheim", at https://news.un.org/en/spotlight/character-sketches-kurt-waldheim-brian-urquhart (not dated) (accessed 1 June 2023).

Vagenas, Maria Giovanna, "Rediscovering the Forgotten Gems of a Decade: Austrian Auteurs of the 1970s at the Viennale", *Senses of Cinema* (May 2021), at www.sensesofcinema.com/2021/festival-reports/rediscovering-the-forgotten-gems-of-a-decade-austrian-auteurs-of-the-1970s-at-the-viennale/ (accessed 25 February 2023).

van der Steen, Bart, Ask Katzeff and Leendert van Hoogenhuijze (eds), *The City is Ours* (Oakland, CA: PM Press, 2014).

Varnedoe, Kirk, *Vienna 1900: Art, Architecture, and Design* (New York: Museum of Modern Art, 1986).

von Almstein, August, *Ein flüchtiger Zug nach dem Orient: Reise der allerdurchlauchtigsten Frau Gräfin von Hohenembs im Herbste des Jahres 1885, an Bord der kaiserlichen Yacht 'Miramar'* (Vienna: Alfred Hölder, 1887).

von Dassanowsky, Robert, *Austrian Cinema: A History* (Jefferson, NC: Macfarland, 2005).

von Dassanowsky, Robert, and Oliver C. Speck (eds), *New Austrian Film* (Oxford: Berghahn, 2011).

von Dassanowsky, Robert (ed.), *World Film Locations: Vienna* (London: Intellect, 2012).

von Moltke, Johannes, *No Place Like Home: Locations of Heimat in German Cinema* (Berkeley, CA: University of California Press, 2005).

Wakefield, Thirza, "'A Lovers' Discourse' – Interview with Ruth Beckermann", *Sight and Sound* Vol. 27 No. 1 (January 2017), 9.

Wall, Christine, "Sisterhood and Squatting in the 1970s: Feminism, Housing and Urban Change in Hackney", *History Workshop Journal* 83 (2017), 79–97.

Welzer, Harald, Sabine Moller and Karoline Tschuggnall, *'Opa war kein Nazi': Nationalsozialismus und Holocaust im Familiengedächtnis* (Frankfurt am Main: Fischer, 2002).

West, Franz, "Man war in etwas drinnen, das eine neue Welt schaffen sollte", *Dokumentationsarchiv des österreichischen Widerstandes*, at www.doew.at/erinnern/biographien/erzaehlte-geschichte/erste-republik/franz-west-man-war-in-etwas-drinnen-das-eine-neue-welt-schaffen-sollte (accessed 22 November 2023).

Wettstein, Howard, *The Significance of Religious Experience* (Oxford: Oxford University Press, 2012).

Widdis, Emma, *Alexander Medvedkin* (London: I. B. Tauris, 2005).

Wieber, Sabine, "Vienna's Most Fashionable Neurasthenic: Empress Sisi and the Cult of Size Zero", in Wieber and Blackshaw (eds), *Journeys into Madness: Mapping Mental Illness in the Austro-Hungarian Empire*, pp. 90–108.

Wieber, Sabine, and Gemma Blackshaw (eds), *Journeys into Madness: Mapping Mental Illness in the Austro-Hungarian Empire* (New York: Berghahn, 2012).

Wiedemann, Barbara and Bertrand Badiou, "Commentary: 'Let us find the words' – The Correspondence of Ingeborg Bachmann and Paul Celan", in Bachmann, Ingeborg and Paul Celan, *Correspondence*, pp. 379–87.

Williams, Alastair, "Voices of the Other: Wolfgang Rihm's *Die Eroberung von Mexico*", *Journal of the Royal Musical Association* Vol. 129 No. 2 (2004), 240–71.

Williams, Raymond, and Michael Orrom, *Preface to Film* (London: Film Drama, 1954).

Wistrich, Robert S., *From Ambivalence to Betrayal: The Left, the Jews, and Israel* (Lincoln: University of Nebraska Press, 2012).

Wolfe, Tom, *The Kandy-Kolored Tangerine-Flake Streamline Baby* (London: Picador, 1981).

Yerushalmi, Yosef Hayim, *Freud's Moses: Judaism Terminable and Interminable* (New Haven: Yale University Press, 1991).

Zakim, Eric, "Chris Marker's *Description of a Struggle* and the Limits of the Essay Film", in Papazian and Eades (eds), *The Essay Film*, pp. 145–66.

Zeitlin, Froma L., "Why Did You Go into Jewish Studies?", *Perspectives: The Magazine for the Association of Jewish Studies*, 8 September 2014, at http://perspectives.ajsnet.org/why-did-you-go-into-jewish-studies-zeitlin/ (accessed 9 September 2023).

Zelman, Leon (with Armin Thurnher), *After Survival: One Man's Mission in the Cause of Memory* (trans. Meredith Schneeweiss) (New York: Holmes and Meier, 1998).

Zipes, Jack, "The Critical Embracement of Germany: Hans Mayer and Marcel Reich-Ranicki", in Zipes and Morris (eds), *Unlikely History: The Changing German-Jewish Symbiosis, 1945–2000*, pp. 183–201.

Zipes, Jack and Leslie Morris (eds), *Unlikely History: The Changing German-Jewish Symbiosis, 1945–2000* (Basingstoke: Palgrave Macmillan 2002).

Žižek, Slavoj, *Looking Awry: An Introduction to Jacques Lacan through Popular Culture* (Cambridge, MA: MIT Press, 1991).

Zweig, Stefan, "Heimfahrt nach Österreich", *Neue Freie Presse,* 1 August 1914, p. 1.

Zweig, Stefan, *The World of Yesterday: Memoirs of a European* (trans. Anthea Bell) (London: Pushkin Press, 2009).

Index

www.ingramcontent.com/pod-product-compliance
Ingram Content Group UK Ltd.
Pitfield, Milton Keynes, MK11 3LW, UK
UKHW050154190225
455238UK00004B/27

9 781526 172501